Travelaid

Guide to Egypt

by Michael von Haag, MSc, FRAI

First printing March 1981; second printing, with revisions, January 1982.

Illustrations, cover design and layout by Colin Elgie.

Typeset by North Atlantic Typesetting Company Limited, Connaught House, Warren Street, Tenby, Pembrokeshire.

Printed in Great Britain by litho at The Anchor Press Limited and bound by Wm Brendon & Son Limited, both of Tiptree, Essex.

Published by Travelaid Publishing, Michael Haag Limited, PO Box 369, London NW3 4ER, England.

ISBN 0 902743 14 7

CONTENTS

Practical Information sections follow each chapter, and there are indices at the rear.

ABOUT THIS GUIDE

The monuments of Egypt tell a story. The Pyramids created the Egyptian state; the monasteries of the Wadi Natrun transformed Christianity; the mosques of Cairo recount the struggles of Islam; the High Dam at Aswan is rolling back the deserts of northern Africa. Their stories are as awesome as the monuments themselves. It is not enough for a guide to describe, to list statistics of age and size. It must explain the significance of what is seen.

This Guide, therefore, is in large part a narrative. There are parts, however – for example step by step descriptions of great temples – that may be rewarding only on the spot. But generally the Guide is meant to be read through at any time, or dipped into now and again. The main text of the chapters contain this narrative, and the descriptions. Descriptions of monuments are interwoven with their stories. An outline chronology is provided in the *Background* chapter to get your bearings.

At the end of each chapter is a *Practical Information* section with details on accommodation, eating places, travel, etc., within the area. These sections make it easy for the traveller to plan his journey, get the most for his means, and enjoy his stay. The information is for all price ranges and degrees of adventurousness.

The *Background* chapter provides the information you need before you go; explains in general terms what you can expect when you arrive; and also serves as a reference section on the spot, with an Arabic vocabulary, railway timetables, the Islamic calendar, tables of weights and measures, a glossary of names and terms, etc.

This is a complete Guide to all aspects of Egypt, from boarding a bus in downtown Cairo to unravelling the mystery of the Pyramids. But while the Pyramids can be expected to remain unchanged for some time yet, the price of a hotel or finding a good place to eat can change from year to year. The *Practical Information* sections were up to date when going to press, but inflation and changing circumstances can have their effect.The reader is asked, therefore, to help us keep this Guide up to date by sending us any information that will help with the next edition. Please write to the *General Editor, Travelaid Publishing, PO Box 369, London NW3 4ER, England.* Thank you.

BACKGROUND

In pharaonic times the people of Egypt believed the sun was daily born of the goddess Nut and that it travelled westwards across the heavens until it was swallowed by her at day's end, to be born once more the following dawn. And they believed the waters of the Nile rose from beneath the firmament, flowed through their country and out beyond the Delta where it sank to its source and then rose to run its course again.

The cycle and continuity of natural events was translated into the philosophical basis of ancient Egyptian politics and religion. In hieroglyphs the name of a pharaoh or god always appeared within a cartouche, an oval ring that represented the unbroken, unending, unchanging power of ruler or deity. The order of natural events in Egypt continues to impress a sense of timelessness upon the country.

Herodotus described Egypt as "a gift of the river", and Egypt's gift, like a great river of time, has been to carry within her the presence of the pharaonic, Hellenistic, Christian and Islamic periods, all embraced by the cartouche of the fellahin's millenial toil. Her endurance and stability in a region of conflict, flux and immense creativity has been her outstanding contribution to the world. She herself has not been exceptionally innovative; she did not give mankind mathematics, philosophy, science, medicine, Judaism, Christianity or Islam. But Egypt was essential to each, offering an impetus or a home, sometimes stamping them with the shape by which we know them today.

About 10,000 years ago a dramatic change in climate caused the once fertile lands of northern Africa and the Middle East to turn to dust. Rock drawings in the Sahara depict ancient man hunting gazelle where now there is only sand. The inhabitants of this great belt of arid land migrated towards the few remaining rivers.

The Nile provided water and its annual flood covered the fields with rich alluvial soil. The ancient Egyptians called their country 'The Black Land', and the Nile Valley and Delta is still today the most fertile land in the world. Were it not for the existence of the Nile, no part of Egypt would be capable of agriculture.

Egypt is larger than any European country except Russia. However, about 93 percent of its area is dry and barren desert where only a few oasis-dwellers and nomadic bedouin can survive. Effectively, Egypt is no wider than the Valley and the

Delta. In pharaonic times Egypt was likened to a lotus plant. The river was the stem, the Fayyum the bud, the Delta the flower. Within this figure of fertility today lives 95 percent of the nation's population.

That population is around 50 million, and it is increasing by at least one million every year. The birth rate has been falling, but the death rate has fallen faster, a reflection of improved health services. The strain that rising population puts on Egypt's food supplies, housing and services is the country's greatest problem. Within its narrow cultivable area, Egypt is one of the most densely populated countries in the world, with about half its people now living in cities.

For over 3000 years the body of Ramses II, contemporary of Moses, Pharaoh of Upper and Lower Egypt from 1290 to 1224 BC, lay deep in a secret tomb, bound in a coil of bandages, arms crossed, fists clenched in the Osiris position. When archaeologists unwrapped the left hand it opened, as though still living, in a sign of peace.

Egypt's revolution is expressed in the construction of the High Dam at Aswan; Egypt's hope lies in peace. "In war", I was told by a Luxor doctor, "if you win, you lose something; if you lose, you lose everything. We want peace to build. The Egyptian people are used to living on very little. But we want a future, we want something for our children". The Nile no longer floods. Instead its water flows evenly throughout the year, the harvests have been multiplied, deserts brought to life. And Egypt gains the energy she needs to embark on wholesale industrialisation. Slowly the fellahin are being released from their drudgery, Egypt from her poverty.

Egypt's treasure is her people. They are warm, good humoured and tolerant, yet with extraordinary tenacity and a courage which they express in the ambition and love they feel for their country. It is very common to be greeted warmly by a stranger in the street with "Welcome to my country!" And if you pause, to be asked, as if his life would hang upon your reply, "Do you like my country?".

Tourist Information

Tourist information may be obtained from Egyptian State Tourist Offices abroad. In Britain this is at 62A Piccadilly, London W1 (telephone 493 5282). In the United States, there are offices in New York, 1110 Second Avenue, 10022 (telephone 879-6300); Washington, DC, 2310 Decatur Place, NW, 20008 (telephone 234-3903); and San Francisco, 3001 Pacific Avenue, 94415 (telephone 346-9700).

In Egypt, the headquarters of the Egyptian State Tourist Office is at 5 Sharia Adli, Cairo (telephone 923000). There are

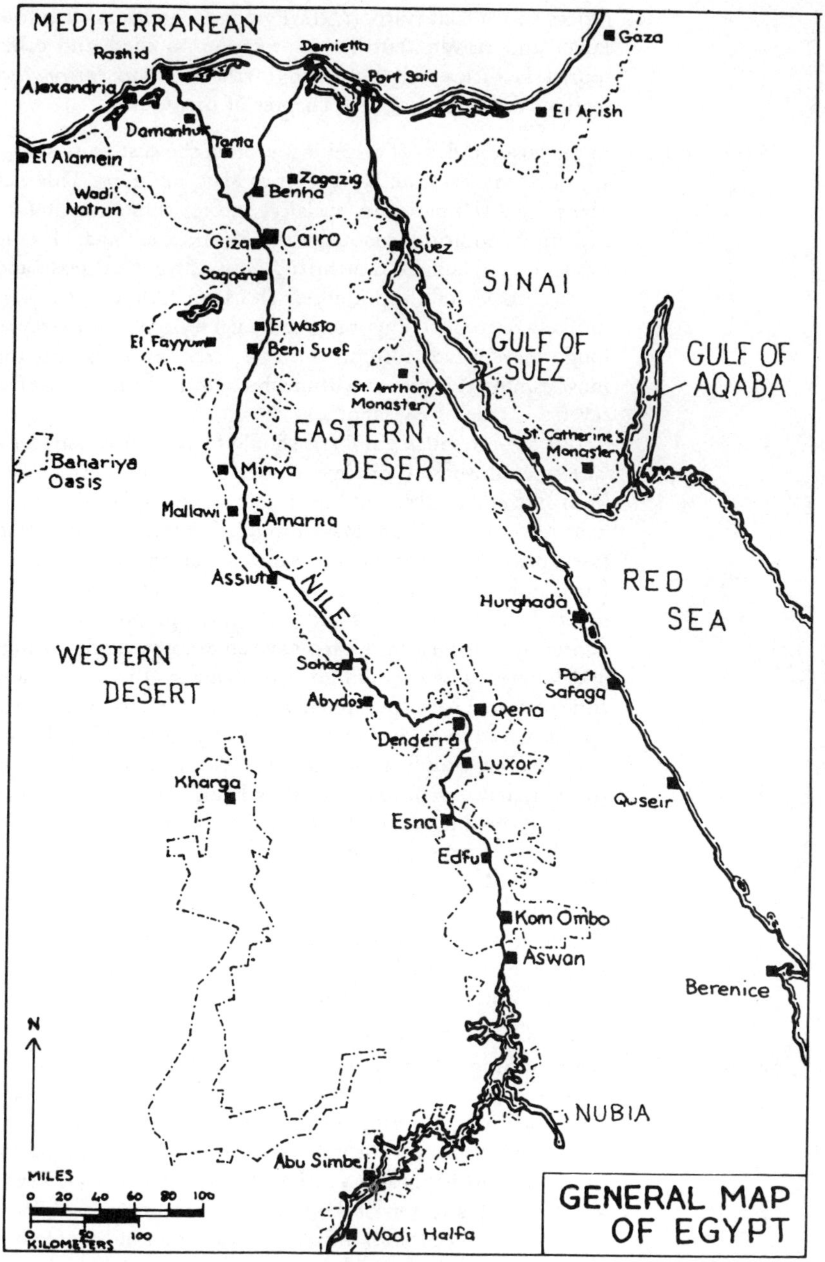
MEDITERRANEAN
Rashid
Damietta
Port Said
Gaza
Alexandria
El Arish
Damanhur
Tanta
El Alamein
Zagazig
Benha
Wadi Natrun
Giza
Cairo
Suez
Saqqara
SINAI
El Wasta
El Fayyum
Beni Suef
GULF OF SUEZ
GULF OF AQABA
St. Anthony's Monastery
EASTERN DESERT
St. Catherine's Monastery
Bahariya Oasis
Minya
Mallawi
Amarna
Assiut
NILE
RED SEA
Hurghada
WESTERN DESERT
Sohag
Port Safaga
Abydos
Qena
Denderra
Luxor
Kharga
Quseir
Esna
Edfu
Kom Ombo
Aswan
Berenice
N
NUBIA
Abu Simbel
MILES
0 20 40 60 80 100
0 50 100
KILOMETERS
Wadi Halfa
GENERAL MAP OF EGYPT

offices also at Cairo airport, the Pyramids, and at Alexandria, Luxor and Aswan. Further information on these and other tourist facilities will be found in the *Practical Information* sections at the end of each chapter of this Guide.

When to go

In the leisured days of travel it was often the custom to spend an entire winter, from November to May, in Egypt. This was 'the season', climatically, socially, and for those in search of dry, mild conditions conducive to relief from asthma, chronic bronchitis, rheumatoid arthritis, gout, Bright's disease and other diseases of the kidneys. The late 20th C. visitor is unlikely to come to Egypt for medicinal reasons, nor to stay so long, though late autumn through early spring is still the most comfortable period within which to visit, except that the reverse is true of Alexandria.

But not too much emphasis should be laid on season, for a variety of reasons. Cairo and Upper Egypt are most visited from November through April and accommodation can be hard to come by. From May through October, the situation eases, prices are lower and hotels now remain open year-round. Air conditioning is general in the newer and better hotels, while the older hotels – some of them the grand relics of the golden age of tourism – often have enormously high ceilings and louvred windows designed to dissipate the heat at any time of year. I have stayed in hotels of the pre-air-conditioned age in Aswan in August and felt perfectly comfortable. In any case, the very people who earlier this century went to Egypt in the winter also went to the South of France in the winter; they were not the sun- and heat-seekers that we are today. It can be very hot in Egypt, especially Upper Egypt, during summer, but a combination of air-conditioning or well-ventilated room, seeing the sights early in the morning and late in the afternoon, and the extraordinary dryness of the air the further south you go, can make your stay entirely agreeable. The proof is that increasingly Egypt is becoming a year-round attraction.

What to take

The clothing you take will depend on the time of year. In winter you will need light woollens and sweaters; in summer light cottons. In spring and autumn, some combination of both is advisable against warm days and cool nights, and the possibility of changeable weather. Even in summer, however, at least one sweater or knit is likely to come in handy, especially against the strong sea breezes of Alexandrian nights.

Clothes should be light in colour to reflect the sun, and should be easily washable and drip-dry. In summer, anywhere in Egypt except Alexandria, you can wash a suit at night and have it bone dry in the morning.

Although far more liberal than most other Arab countries, Egypt is nevertheless conservative by Western standards and your dress should allow for this. Shorts on men and women, revealing blouses and very short skirts are becoming increasingly common in tourist areas, but are not always approved of. One solution, particularly in Upper Egypt, is for visitors, men and women, to wear a long flowing *galabiyya* – it happens to be ideal for the climate, day or night, warm or cool, and is both comfortable and graceful. Egyptians are not conservative on beaches, however, and bikinis are perfectly acceptable – not only on visitors, but on Egyptian women.

Bring sandals and also comfortable walking shoes. Sunglasses and a broad-brimmed hat will keep out the glare of the sun, intense in the desert.

Any items Egypt has to import will be expensive, and while a pharmacy or other stores will have Egyptian shampoos, soaps, toothpastes, razor blades and other toilet items, if you prefer your own brand, bringing it with you will save some money. Batteries are expensive and the range limited; if you are bringing anything that is battery-powered (do not forget camera and flash), bring also a supply of spare batteries. Electrical current in Egypt is 220 volts; bring a converter if need be. Film is very expensive; bring plenty.

A few other items can be useful: insect repellent, especially if you are staying in a non-air-conditioned hotel; a water canteen for excursions (though a plastic bottle of local spring water can serve); salt tablets, not obtainable in Egypt, as an alternative to frequent water drinking; toilet paper, a rare commodity, sometimes even in the best of places; a flashlight, invaluable for exploring pyramids and tombs; binoculars, especially if you are cruising along the Nile, but also for examining details of gargantuan ruins.

Egyptian cotton is famous for its quality; clothes and shoes are inexpensive. Rather than overpack these things, it would be better to buy them once you are in the country.

Climate

Only a thin strip of the northern coastline shares in a Mediterranean climate, giving Alexandria an annual rainfall of 18 centimetres – most of this from December to March, when Alexandria experiences blustery, often stormy weather. This is true inland to Damanhur and Tanta in the Delta. Further south, Egypt is within the arid zone, with rainfall throughout most of the country well under 2.5 centimetres per year.

Temperatures increase as you travel south, though in Cairo during December, January and sometimes even February it can be chilly. Cairo can be very hot from June to September, though the heat is often relieved by a northerly breeze.

Though it is hotter yet in Upper Egypt and summer can be reckoned from May to October, peak temperatures are to a great extent compensated for by extremely low humidity. Also, everywhere in Egypt at any time of year, temperatures can fall off sharply at night.

Leaving aside the summer extremes from Cairo southwards and the winter extremes from Cairo northwards, the climate of Egypt can be described as mild.

Table of Temperature °C	January min./max.	February min./max.	March min./max.	April min./max.	May min./max.	June min./max.
Alexandria	9.3 18.3	9.7 19.2	11.2 21.0	13.5 23.6	16.7 26.5	20.2 28.2
Aswan	8.0 23.8	9.4 26.1	12.6 30.4	17.5 35.0	21.1 38.5	24.2 42.1
Cairo	8.6 19.1	9.3 20.7	11.2 23.7	13.9 28.2	17.4 32.4	17.9 34.5
Dakhla	4.6 21.5	6.1 23.9	9.7 27.9	14.4 33.0	19.6 37.4	22.4 38.8
Hurghada	9.6 20.6	9.9 20.9	12.3 23.0	16.1 26.0	20.7 29.6	23.5 31.4
Izmailia	8.2 204.	9.1 21.7	11.0 23.9	13.6 27.6	17.3 32.1	20.2 34.8
Luxor	5.4 23.0	6.8 25.4	10.7 29.0	15.7 34.8	20.7 39.3	22.6 40.7
Mersa Matruh	8.1 18.1	8.4 18.9	9.7 20.3	11.8 22.7	14.5 25.5	18.2 27.8
Minya	3.9 20.6	5.4 22.5	7.8 25.4	11.7 30.2	16.7 35.4	18.8 36.3
Port Said	11.3 18.0	12.1 18.7	13.5 20.2	16.1 22.6	19.6 25.8	22.4 28.5
Siwa	4.1 19.7	5.7 21.8	8.2 25.0	12.1 39.9	16.8 34.3	19.2 37.1

Table of Temperature °C	July min./max.	August min./max.	September min./max.	October min./max.	November min./max.	December min./max.
Alexandria	22.7 29.6	22.9 30.4	21.3 29.4	17.8 27.7	14.8 24.4	11.2 20.4
Aswan	24.5 41.2	24.7 41.3	22.2 39.6	19.3 36.6	14.5 20.2	9.9 25.5
Cairo	21.5 25.4	21.6 34.8	19.9 32.3	17.8 29.8	19.9 24.1	10.4 20.7
Dakhla	23.0 39.0	22.9 38.9	20.7 36.1	17.4 33.0	12.0 28.0	6.7 23.0
Hurghada	24.8 32.6	25.0 33.0	23.2 30.6	19.7 28.5	15.5 25.7	11.9 22.4
Ismailia	22.2 36.4	22.5 36.5	20.7 33.9	17.8 30.7	13.9 26.6	10.0 21.5
Luxor	23.6 40.8	23.5 41.0	21.5 38.5	17.8 35.1	12.3 29.6	7.7 24.8
Mersa Matruh	20.2 29.2	21.0 29.9	19.7 28.7	16.8 27.0	13.3 23.4	10.0 19.7
Minya	20.2 37.0	20.5 36.6	18.6 33.4	15.9 31.2	11.5 26.6	7.0 21.7
Port Said	24.1 30.4	24.9 30.9	23.9 29.2	21.8 27.4	18.4 24.0	12.7 19.9
Siwa	20.7 38.0	20.7 27.8	18.3 35.1	14.9 31.7	10.1 26.3	6.0 21.3

For conversion to Fahrenheit, see the *Weights and Measures* section below.

Entry regulations

All visitors to Egypt require a visa. To obtain one, your passport must be valid for at least three months following your arrival in the country. Visas can be obtained in person (allow 24 hours) or by post (allow at least two weeks) from an Egyptian Consulate abroad. You will need to present your passport, one passport photograph, and pay the appropriate fee. Immigration officials are empowered to grant visas on arrival, but this method is best avoided if possible, particularly by travellers arriving overland. (Entry to Egypt from Libya is forbidden overland.)

Visitors visas are valid for one month from entry. With the exception of those on pre-paid package holidays, anyone staying in Egypt longer than 72 hours must purchase upon arrival at least 100 Egyptian pounds (LE100). Egyptian currency may not be imported or exported. Visas may be extended by satisfying immigration officials that you are able to transfer sufficient additional funds into Egyptian pounds. Within seven days of your arrival you must register your presence in the country with the police, obtaining a triangular stamp in your passport (hotels will have this done for you automatically).

Other documents required are an International Drivers Licence if you intend to rent a car, and if you are bringing your own car then also a Carnet de Passage en Douane, otherwise you will be required to pay a deposit equivalent to the estimated price of your vehicle, refundable on departure. Cholera and yellow fever vaccination certificates are required if arriving from an infected area.

You may bring into Egypt, exempt from duty and other taxes, all personal effects, used or new, including camera equipment, radios, typewriters, recorders, jewellery, etc., provided these are listed on the customs declaration form. Also exempt are 400 cigarettes, or 250 grams of tobacco or 50 cigars, and one litre of alcohol.

Getting to Egypt: by air

The most common and usually cheapest way of getting to Egypt is by air. All flights arrive at Cairo International Airport.

Regular air fares are extortionate and travellers should look for such deals as the Advance Purchase Excursion (APEX) fare. Conditions may vary with airline and season, but typically an APEX ticket will save you nearly 50 percent on the normal roundtrip economy fare provided you buy your ticket at least 21 days before departure and stay for at least six days and no more than 60. Dates of departure and return must be fixed beforehand. Some airlines permit at least one stopover enroute for an additional charge.

In Britain it is worthwhile consulting the newspapers for those agents (popularly known as bucket shops) offering cheap tickets to various destinations. Most airlines are members of a cartel called IATA which fixes minumum fares, allegedly for the benefit of the air traveller, in reality to exploit the vast majority. But often capacity outstrips demand and the airlines sell off their excess tickets at a great discount through bucket shops. They may be double-dealing their own cartel, but many airlines do it. Fares are cheaper than APEX or even student and youth fares. You can fly direct to Cairo, or to Rome, Athens, Tel Aviv, etc., from where you can continue your journey to Egypt by air or by other means.

Airlines offer student and youth fares between Europe and Egypt which represent a 50 percent reduction on normal one-way or roundtrip economy fares. To qualify for a youth fare you must not yet have reached your 26th birthday. To qualify for a student fare you must be a full-time student at an educational establishment and not yet have reached your 31st (from Britain your 28th) birthday.

Many travellers to Egypt take advantage of package holidays which combine flights with accommodation often at prices less than APEX fares alone. These can be as brief as seven days, though longer ones, especially those including several days of cruising along the Nile between Luxor and Aswan, will be more expensive. Thomas Cook (45 Berkeley Street, London W1), British Airways' Speedbird Holidays (200 Buckingham Palace Road, London SW1) and VIP Travel (42 North Audley Street, London W1) are some of the better operators offering a variety of Egyptian holidays, including Nile and Red Sea cruises. Modernline Travel (Globegate House, Pound Lane, London NW10) offers a two week 'highlights' tour of Israel and Egypt.

Both for flexibility and cost it may suit North American and Australian/New Zealand travellers wishing to include a visit to Egypt in their wider itinerary to buy their package in Britain – though enquiries should be made well in advance.

For those serious about a Nile cruise, seeing everything between Cairo and Aswan in the company of an expert Egyptologist, both Swan Hellenic (237-238 Tottenham Court Road, London W1) and Bales Tours (16 Coventry Street, London W1) are recommended. They are expensive, however, and are sometimes booked up as much as a year in advance.

By sea DFDS Seaways, Adriatica and the Alexandria Navigation Company all operate passenger and car ferry services to Alexandria, variously from Venice, Piraeus and Beirut. For a passenger travelling deck class, though having to pay for food on board, a Mediterranean crossing is marginally cheaper than flying. An entire family with car will work out pretty expensively and to dubious advantage: internal travel is cheap and good and a car can always be rented as necessary.

Overland Entry to Egypt overland from Libya is forbidden. The border between Egypt and Israel, however, is now open and it is possible to fly or take a bus or taxi across via El Arish. From the Sudan there is a scheduled but notoriously unreliable train service between Khartoum and Wadi Halfa on the border, connecting with a twice weekly steamer plying between Wadi Halfa and Aswan. The steamer can also carry cars, minibuses and trucks. In Egypt, information on the steamer and rail service to and from the Sudan can be obtained from the Nile Navigation Company, Ltd., 39 Sharia Qasr el Nil, Cairo; and the Nile Company for River Transport, 7 Atlas Building, Aswan. Also, organised overland journeys through Egypt and the Sudan (air connections from London or Khartoum) are offered by several operators whose brochures are available from Trailfinders, 46 Earls Court Road, London W8; and in Australia, Sundowners, 75 King Street, Sydney 2000.

Travel within Egypt: by air

Egyptair is the sole scheduled airline within Egypt, serving Cairo, Alexandria, Luxor, Aswan, Abu Simbel, Hurghada and the New Valley (Kharga). Aircraft are Boeing 737s. Especially in winter it is advisable to make advance reservations, as flights are often booked up. Even so, it is often worth standing by.

One-way air fares in Egyptian pounds (roundtrip is double):

Cairo to	Abu Simbel	LE48.75
	Alexandria	LE12.00
	Aswan	LE34.40
	Hurghada	LE26.65
	Luxor	LE24.50
	New Valley	LE26.65
Luxor to	Abu Simbel	LE24.50
	Aswan	LE10.10
Aswan to	Abu Simbel	LE14.60
	New Valley	LE10.10

Nile Valley Aviation (NIVA) operates an air taxi and charter aircraft service to all Egyptian airports which, in addition to those served by Egyptair, include Mersa Matruh, Assiut and points along the Red Sea and in Sinai. Aircraft range from single-engined Cessnas through DC3s to executive jets and 117-passenger Convair 880s. NIVA is based at Cairo International Airport.

By rail

Air-conditioned rail travel in Egypt is comfortable and inexpensive, and still more inexpensive for students in possession of an International Student Identity Card (savings are about 50 percent). All first class and combined first and second class trains are air-conditioned; others are not. Local trains serving smaller stations are likely to be slow, crowded and uncomfortable, and they will not be air-conditioned – the experience can be interesting if it does not go on for too long. No matter what class of train you are travelling on, bring toilet paper.

On a non-air-conditioned train between Alexandria and Cairo: like a tenth class Arab hotel, the only difference between second and third class being the number of Egyptians per cubic centimetre. In third class they sit, stand and lie on one another — a few lucky ones stretched out on the luggage racks overhead. Second class under these conditions is quite all right for the comparatively short Alexandria-Cairo run, but third class is to suffer an intimacy one would prefer to do without. I am travelling second class and at every station half a dozen vendors get on with bottles of soft drinks carried in buckets of ice on their shoulders, and with cigarettes, biscuits, cakes and magazines. Each one presses his wares on the passengers, it making no difference that just one pace and five seconds before him another has been selling soft drinks and cigarettes too. Nor does it matter than the odds are very much against me being able to read an Arabic magazine. I shrug and smile and still he presses me to buy one.

A thin, gritty, invisible layer of sand enters the carriage. I feel it between my fingers and filling up the corners of my eyes. I'm sitting in the corridor, stepped on and over by biscuit men and passengers, and I get into conversation with two of them, a business student and a medical student. They say, "Egypt has not the right men in the right positions. When it does, Egypt will be great." And they offer me a cigarette, insisting that I take it, even though I am already raising one to my lips. And they insist I light it from theirs, even though I'm already holding a match in my fingers and am about to strike it. So these are perhaps the right men who may soon assume the right positions. For the moment we are cockroaches endlessly trampled over in the corridor of a second class carriage.

Almost all air-conditioned trains require reservations. You should book at least a day in advance on the Cairo-Alexandria run, and in winter you might have to book as much as a week in advance on the Cairo-Luxor/Aswan run, though in summer you will probably be able to travel on the same or the following day.

Overnight sleepers have compartments for two, with a cabinet for clothes and a pull-down sink. The seat converts into a bed and a second bed pulls down from the wall so that the two beds are one above the other. Sheets, blankets and pillows are provided. It gets dark early in Egypt (in summer by 7pm, in winter still earlier) and the compartment lighting will probably be inadequate for reading. After dinner, therefore, there is nothing to do but turn in. If you are travelling alone, you will be sharing the compartment with another person. Male and female passengers unknown to one another are never put in the same compartment. (The distinction between first and second class sleepers is that first class gives you the compartment to yourself, second class has you sharing it with another.)

The Cairo-Alexandria fare is about LE3 first class, LE2 second class, one way. Sleeper fares to Luxor are LE12 first class, LE7 second class, one way. To Aswan these fares are LE15 and LE9. Dinner aboard the Luxor/Aswan train costs

LE2, and breakfast is available for those continuing on to Aswan. There is also a less expensive day train between Cairo and Luxor/Aswan, a long waking journey, but worth making once for the Valley scenery enroute.

It is nearly impossible in Egypt to get your hands on a complete railway timetable; it is assumed that tourists want only to travel between Alexandria, Cairo, Luxor and Aswan, and then only on certain trains, so these are the only schedules readily available. But for the more adventurous traveller, a complete timetable for the Egyptian railway system follows. It has been the same for several years past and is likely to remain so.

CAIRO – ISMAILIA – PORT SAID

23	23	23	23A	23				23	23A	23	23	23
6 25	1150	1530	1845	2140	dep.	**Cairo**................	arr.	8 40	9 55	1710	2125	2350
7 02	1238	1607	1922	2222	arr.	Benha	dep.	7 56	9 17	1633	2048	2037
7 06	1244	1610	1927	2228	dep.		arr.	7 42	9 07	1623	2039	2254
7 45	1315	1648	2000	2300	arr.	Zagazig	dep.	7 10	8 35	1552	2008	2223
7 56	1324	1700	2015	2113	dep.	....	arr.	6 56	8 25	1546	2003	2218
9 15	1435	1825	2127	0 40	arr.	Ismailia	dep.	5 10	7 00	1430	1838	2105
1205	1715	2205	-	..	arr.	Suez	dep.	..	-	1035	1505	..
1002	..	..	2212	..	arr.	Qantara	dep.	..	6 16	1345	1751	..
1055	..	..	2305	..	arr.	**Port Said**	dep.	..	5 15	1250	1650	..

CAIRO – SUEZ

	23		23					23	23			
..	5 50	..	1535		dep.	Cairo..............	arr.	1225	2200	..	..	..
..	8 35	..	1820	1 00	arr.	Suez	dep.	9 40	1915	..	..	..

ALEXANDRIA – MERSA MATRUH

23	23	23A	23	23	23				23	23	23	23	23	23A
..	..	SUM 7 30	..	D	F	dep.	Cairo	arr.	..	..	..	..	..	SUM 0 25
6 35	7 10	-	1010	1645	1855	dep.	**Alexandria**	**arr.**	7 35	1445	..	1920	2050	-
7 56	8 24	-	1129	1812	2024	dep.	El Amriya	dep.	6 17	1314	1425	1752	1934	-
9 00	9 25	1138	1223	1915	2140	dep.	El Hammam	dep.	5 05	1150	1320	1650	—	2019
9 48	..	-	1318	..	—	dep.	El Alamein	dep.	..	1049	...	1546	..	-
1055	..	1316	1435	..		dep.	El Dabaa............	dep.	..	9 45	..	1445		1843
..	..	-	1713	..	2 3	dep.	Similla	dep.	..	7 13	..	..	2 3	-
..	..	1525	1725	..	Su	arr.	Mersa	dep.	..	7 00	..	..	M	1630
..	..	..	..	..	7 40	dep.	Matruh	arr.	..	..	..	..	1615	..
..	..	..	..	..	8 10	dep.	Similla	dep.	..	..	..	..	1555	..
..	..	..	..	..	1840	arr.	Sallum	dep.	..	..	..	..	7 05	..

CAIRO – UPPER EGYPT

23	12A	23	23A	12A	23A	12A	23	S	2A	23	12A	3				23	12A	3	2	S	12A	23	12A	23A	23	12A	23	23A
3 10	7 30	7 40	1000	1200	1225	1610	1620	1900	2000	2040	2105	2250	dep.	**Cairo**	arr.	5 35	6 00	6 20	9 20	9 45	1130	1330	1635	1730	2010	2055	2335	2400
4 34	-	9 21	-	-	1348	-	1803	-	2123	2226	2251	0 14	dep.	Wasta	dep.	3 39	4 14	4 52	7 52	-	-	1202	-	1602	1843	-	2209	-
5 18	9 24	1005	1154	1355	1426	1804	1846	-	2201	2310	2336	0 54	dep.	Beni Suef	dep.	3 13	3 38	4 21	7 22	-	9 39	1133	1446	1525	1809	1903	2133	2210
6 16	-	1105	1238	-	-	-	1934	-	2247	0 09	0 33	1 43	dep.	Maghaga	dep.	2 11	2 36	3 26	6 30	-	-	1043	-	-	1707	-	2031	2120
7 31	1056	1224	1339	1534	1600	1939	2057	-	2345	1 24	1 46	2 44	dep.	Minya	dep.	0 59	1 25	2 28	5 35	-	8 04	9 50	1311	1348	1558	1728	1921	2022
7 51	-	1245	-	-	-	-	2171	-	-	1 45	2 06	-	dep.	Abu Qerkas	dep.	0 33	0 58	-	-	-	-	9 25	-	-	1534	-	1857-	
9 54	1229	1444	1525	1706	1733	2114	2321	-	1 27	3 49	4 03	4 34	arr.		dep.	2230	2258	0 32	3 42	-	6 24	7 27	1134	1205	1338	1545	1642	1830
1010	1246	1502	..	1720	1745	2129	2337	-	1 44	5 05	4 17	4 50	dep.	**Assiut**	arr.	2215	2243	0 20	3 25	-	6 08	7 12	1127	1145	1326	1529	1628	..
1215	1413	1720	..	1840	1938	2310	2 07	-	3 22	8 05	6 20	7 00	dep.	Sohag	dep.	1943	2050	2229	2 10	-	4 30	5 32	1022	9 37	1147	1424	1440	..
-	1455	1822	-	1925	2024	-	3 05	-	4 08	9 30	7 06	7 51	dep.	Girga	dep.	1823	1930	2131	1 09	-	-	4 31	9 28	8 42	1035	1332	-	-
-	-	1900	-	1947	2047	-	3 27	-	4 31	1000	7 29	8 26	dep.	El Baliana	dep.	1749	1857	2107	0 45	-	-	3 53	9 06	8 20	1003	-	-	-
-	1556	2014	-	2052	2201	-	4 23	-	5 26	1115	8 50	9 45	dep.	Nag Hammadi	dp.	1638	1805	2013	2353	-	-	2 18	8 15	7 29	8 50	1232	-	-
-	1705	2248	-	2203	2341	-	5 36	-	6 37	1309	1004	1059	dep.	Qena	dep.	1433	1638	1856	2238	-	-	1 02	7 04	6 05	6 39	1126	-	-
-	1814	0 50	-	0 20	1 20	-	7 04	5 38	8 10	1457	1135	1235	arr.		dep.	1242	1510	1719	2114	2225	-	2336	5 15	4 15	4 25	1014	-	-
-	1830	..	-	..	..	-	7 35	6 06	8 25	1517	..	1255	dep.	**Luxor**	arr.	1220	..	1655	2054	2200	-	2317	..	..	..	9 54	-	-
-	1954	..	-	..	..	-	8 48	-	9 47	1657	..	1430	dep.	Esna	dep.	1042	..	1526	1951	-	-	2213	..	..	..	8 49-	-	-
-	2110	..	-	..	..	-	9 54	-	1049	1851	..	1600	dep.	Edfu	dep.	8 45	..	1345	1852	-	-	2108	..	..	..	7 31	-	-
-	2223	..	-	..	..	-	1109	-	1202	2112	..	1745	dep.	Kom Ombo	dep.	7 00	..	1203	1738	-	-	1949	..	..	..	1615	-	-
-	2320	..	-	..	..	-	1212	1000	1258	2235	..	1930	arr.		dep.	5 40	...	1015	1638	1810	-	1840	..	..	..	5 15	-	-
-	..	..	-	..	..	-	1232	1037	1327	..	..	..	dep.	**Aswan**	arr.	..	..	..	1623	1743	-	1823	..	..	..	..	-	-
-	..	..	-	..	..	-	1255	1100	1350	..	..	..	arr.	Sadd el Ali	dep.	..	..	..	1600	1720	-	1800	..	..	..	..	-	-

ALEXANDRIA – THE DELTA – CAIRO

		23	3	2A	23	12A	12A	12A	23	12A	3	12A	23	2A	23	12A	12A	23	12A	3	2A	12A	12A	23
Alexandria	dep.	3 35	5 25	6 05	6 45	7 45	8 10	9 20	9 30	1030	1115	1140	1150	1240	1330	1415	1530	1540	1710	1745	1800	1825	1925	2000
Sidi Gabir	dep.	3 45	5 35	6 16	6 55	7 55	8 20	9 30	9 40	1040	1125	1150	1200	1251	1340	1425	1540	1550	1720	1755	1810	1835	1935	2010
Damanhur	dep.	4 41	6 29	7 02	7 55	-	9 03	1013	1037	1122	1209	-	1254	1337	1438	-	1622	1641	1801	1840	1852	-	2017	2106
	arr.	5 35	7 19	7 51	9 00	9 11	9 42	1052	1130	1201	1249	1307	1344	1419	1533	1542	1701	1740	1840	1920	1932	1951	2102	2200
Tanta	dep.	5 42	7 35	7 58	9 25	9 18	9 50	1057	1135	1207	1255	1313	1350	1426	1600	1547	1707	1746	1846	1926	1936	1958	2107	2206
	arr.	6 26	8 17	8 41	1009	-	1020	1127	1216	1242	1326	-	1431	1459	1641	-	1737	1827	1916	1957	2012	-	2137	2248
Benha	dep.	6 35	8 23	8 45	1036	-	1027	1132	1221	1247	1337	-	1436	1504	1647	-	1742	1832	1922	2006	2017	-	2142	2253
Cairo	arr.	7 25	9 00	9 20	1125	1025	1100	1205	1315	1320	1410	1420	1510	1540	1730	1650	1815	1915	1955	2045	2050	2105	2215	2340

		23	3	2A	23	12A	12A	12A	23	12A	3	12A	23	2A	12A	23	12A	23	12A	3	2A	12A	12A	23
Cairo	dep.	3 15	6 05	6 55	7 00	8 00	8 55	9 30	1000	1120	1135	1220	1240	1340	1400	1420	1550	1640	1750	1810	1830	1905	200	2025
	arr.	3 53	6 42	7 28	7 52	-	9 26	1001	1048	1151	1212	-	1312	1343	-	1507	1621	1717	1821	1847	1902	-	2031	2102
Benha	dep.	3 59	6 45	7 33	7 56	-	9 31	1006	1054	1156	1217	-	1317	1349	-	1511	1626	1722	1826	1852	1908	-	2035	2107
	arr.	4 40	7 20	8 10	8 37	9 04	1000	1040	1137	1225	1248	1322	1354	1427	1500	1556	1655	1805	1854	1923	1949	2007	2104	2148
Tanta	dep.	5 09	7 25	8 20	9 17	9 11	1005	1046	1142	1230	1254	13269	1400	1433	1505	1604	1700	1810	1901	1923	1954	2014	2110	2153
Damanhur	dep.	6 17	8 21	9 13	1022	-	1051	1132	1242	1316	1340	-	1459	1522	-	1706	1746	1914	1948	2015	2040	-	2202	2253
Sidi Gabir	dep.	7 18	9 03	9 57	1118	1033	1133	1213	1338	1358	1423	1453	1548	1607	1628	1758	1828	2008	2028	2058	2123	2138	2243	2348
Alexandria	arr.	7 25	9 10	1005	1125	1040	1140	1220	1345	1405	1430	1500	1555	1615	1635	1805	1835	2015	2035	2105	2130	2145	2250	2355

A – Air conditioning in first and second class; or where train has second and third class, air conditioning in second class. Reservations are required on all air-conditioned trains, with the exception of trains without a first class on the Cairo-Upper Egypt line.
S –, Sleeper, first and second class. Air-conditioned. Reservations necessary.
D – Daily except Fridays
F – Fridays only.
Su – Sundays only.
M – Mondays only
SUM – Summer only (July through September).

Other means Other means of travel between towns include buses, taxis, service (or shared) taxis, hired car (you must have an International Drivers Licence unless you hire a driver too), river steamer and felucca. Also, you can hitchhike. Detailed information on each of these methods will be found in the various *Practical Information* sections at the end of each chapter, particularly at the end of the *Cairo 1* chapter.

Fuel Petrol (gas) in Egypt is cheap, about 15PT per litre of super.

Hotels The number of hotel rooms in Egypt has not kept pace with the recent surge in tourism, and getting a room in the hotel of your choice during the winter high season in Upper Egypt, the summer high season in Alexandria, or year-round in Cairo, may not be easy – though this is more true for the more expensive hotels, and a considerable hotel building programme is well on its way to alleviating the problem. If your heart is set on a particular hotel, or if you are travelling at high season, you should try to reserve in advance. An experienced travel agent should be able to help you, or you can try contacting hotels directly – their addresses and phone numbers, and also their telex numbers if they have them, have been included in the *Practical Information* listings. Many of the luxury hotels, eg the Hiltons and Sheratons, will have hotels in your own country through which you can make reservations. Also, several of the hotels included in this Guide's listings belong to the Egyptian Hotels Company, 26 Sharia Sherif, Cairo. Reservations at one can be made through any of the others, or by telexing as follows.

Cairo: Shepheard's, Cleopatra, El Nil – telex Shepheard's (379 SHEPOT UN).
Alexandria: Palestine, Cecil – telex Palestine (94027 PLOTL UN).
Luxor: New and Old Winter Palace, Savoy, Luxor – telex Winter Palace (92160 WINTER UN).
Aswan: New and Old Cataract, Amun, Kalabsha – telex Cataract (92720 ASCAT UN).

Hotels in Egypt are officially rated from 5-star (luxury) to 1-star. The rating system is not always evenly graduated, and you may find that a 3-star hotel is just as good as a 4-star one, or that two 4-star hotels charge markedly different rates. Nevertheless, the official system has been used in this Guide, along with prices and a description which should help you form your own preliminary judgement. There are also hotels that have no star rating; hardly any of these have been included in this Guide as the standard is pretty low. However, in a pinch, they are worth checking out. And there are youth hostels in Cairo, Alexandria, Luxor, Aswan, Suez and Port Said; these are all listed in the *Practical Information* sections, though they are often full and, though they cost less than LE1 per night, it is often possible to find more congenial accommodation at only a slightly higher price.

One of the glories of Egypt is its old hotels, cavernous places with louvred doors and mosquito nets over the beds, and an atmosphere of dying elegance. Not all of them are in the best condition, and for this reason and because they usually lack modern facilities, eg air conditioning, they can be quite inexpensive. Personally, I prefer them to the modern nondescript hotels that are rapidly taking their place and in case you might be of the same mind, I will tell you my favourites. In Cairo there is the Windsor and, more expensive, Shepheard's and the old part of the Mena House; in Alexandria there is the Cecil; in Luxor the Savoy and, more expensive, the Old Winter Palace; and in Aswan the inexpensive Grand and the more expensive Old Cataract.

Another pleasant thing about Egyptian hotels, old or new, is having – for a small surchage – your breakfast brought to you in bed, often by robed and turbaned Nubians.

Food Most Egyptian hotels, particularly the larger ones, cater to the tastes of foreign visitors by serving an international cuisine. In Cairo, as befitting a large cosmopolitan city, there are also many restaurants specialising in one or other national cuisines, eg French, Italian, Lebanese, Greek, Chinese, Indian. Alexandrian cuisine is Levantine.

Though the classic Arab-Turkish cuisine of Egypt is best encountered in private houses, you should venture forth to Egyptian eating places, spanning the gamut in price and sophistication, for a taste of Egyptian cooking. Except in the simplest eating places frequented exclusively by Egyptians, restaurant menus will be available in English and French as well as in Arabic, and the maitre d'hotel will speak English. In the simple Egyptian places, as at a Greek taverna, you can go into the kitchen, have a look, a taste, and then point to what you want. Here you can have a meal for well under an Egyptian pound.

Typically, an Egyptian will have an early light breakfast, often only a mint tea or coffee, Turkish-style. A mid-morning snack may follow, perhaps consisting of fool with a fried egg on top, unleavened bread and Turkish coffee. Lunch, in the mid-afternoon, is the major meal. It could be stuffed pigeons, rice, salad, fruit and beer. An early evening snack might consist of tamiya, tomato salad, olives, bread and lemon juice. Supper is eaten very late, after 10pm. Taheena, falafel and stuffed aubergines would be typical.

Snacks at a low-priced eating place will often cost no more than the average bus ride. Also, drinking water, mango juice, slices of coconut and other tidbits are sold in the streets. Street vendors are often landless fellahin who have left the countryside and have no other way of earning a living. The preparation of mint tea and coffee is a ritual. Thick and black, Turkish-style, it is ordered according to the amount of sugar: sweet *(ziyada)*, medium *(mazboota)*, bitter *(saada)*.

There follows a list of some typical Egyptian foods.

Hors d'oeuvres and snacks:

Babaghanoug – a mix of taheena with mashed eggplant, flavoured with lemon, garlic and olive oil; it is served as a dip, or with salad, or as a first course vegetable dish.

Batarikh – Egyptian caviar; it is pressed, dried and preserved in salt and oil, and is served in thin slices with bread or biscuits.

Feteer – served at an eating place called a *fataran*, it is made of filo dough wrapped round a variety of fillings, eg onion, egg, meat, or, in its sweet variety, raisins with sugar and spices.

Gibna beida – a white cheese, equivalent to Greek feta.

Gibna rumi – literally 'Roman' cheese, a hard light-yellow cheese with a sharp flavour.

Leban zabadi – plain white yogurt to which honey, jam or mint can be added. It is recommended for stomach upsets.

Makarona – baked macaroni and white sauce, often served with gravy and ground meat.

Mashi – a cold mixed vegetable dish, usually of peppers, tomatoes, courgettes, eggplants. A light meal in itself.

Mish – a paste made from dry cheese and spices.

Shakshouka – of North African origin, chopped lamb and tomato sauce with an egg on top.

Taamiya – also known as *falafel*, these are patties of mashed *fool* with parsley, highly seasoned and fried in oil.

Taheena – an oil paste from sesame seed, combined with lemon, garlic and spices; sometimes an ingredient in other foods, but also served on its own as a dip.

Turshi – spicy mixed pickled vegetables.

Wara einab – grape leaves stuffed with rice, sometimes with meat or lentils, and flavoured with lemon juice; the equivalent of Greek dolmades.

Main courses:

Firakh – chicken, usually pretty scrawny, though the quality is being improved. Grilled chicken is best.

Fool mudhammas – the national dish of Egypt, *fool* is fava bean cooked with spices, sometimes tomatoes, into a thick sauce; at breakfast it is served with an egg on top.

Gamoosa – water buffalo, though cattle have now been introduced on a large scale from abroad and beef is increasingly available.

Hamam – pigeon, a great favourite with Egyptians, though often even scrawnier than chicken. It is usually grilled.

Kebab – either grilled marinaded chunks of lamb or ground lamb (*kufta*) made into long patties, skewered and broiled.

Mouluqiya – a steamed green vegetable, often served with rice or as a viscous soup. Although common throughout the Middle East, Egyptian mouluqiya sets the standard. It is a heavy dish, not usually eaten late.

Roz bel khalta – fried rice with currants, nuts, liver and meat.

Samak – the generic term for fish; the particular type will usually be identified in English on the menu. Other seafoods include *gambari* (shrimp), *calamari* (squid) and *gandofli* (scallops).

Desserts:

Aish el saraya – custard topped with cake.

Ata'if – a special sweet dessert during Ramadan.

Baklava – the well-known Levantine pastry of filo with honey and nuts.

Dondurma – a sherbet of sweet white milk ice.

Kanafa – as *baklava*, but made with shredded wheat instead of filo.

Mohallabiya – a thick cream (often creamed rice) confection with fruit, nuts (often pistachios) and a fruit syrup.

Om ali – corn flakes with milk, sugar, coconut, raisins and cinnamon, served hot.

Drinks

Beer long antedates wine as the regional drink of the Mediterranean, so it is not so strange to find it reintroduced and very popular in Egypt. The commonest brand is *Stella*, in green litre bottles, unpredictable but fairly good. *Stella Export* is sweeter, of more consistent quality, but is harder to come by and more expensive. It is in smaller brown bottles. Both are lagers. *Aswali* is an excellent dark beer from Aswan, sometimes found elsewhere. Bock beer is available briefly in the spring and is referred to as *Marzen* (ie *Marzenbier*, March beer).

Egyptian wines are from ex-Greek vineyards around Alexandria and Lake Mareotis, 'mobilised' by the government. Red, white and rosé are available and pleasant enough. *Omar Khayyam* is a dry red, *Cru des Ptolemes* a dry white, and *Rubis d'Egypte* a decent rosé. All years are equally vintage years. In shops, these wines sell for about LE1.50; at a hotel or restaurant the markup will be at least 200 percent.

Imported liquors are extremely expensive even in shops and the same order of markup makes them nearly prohibitive at clubs and restaurants. Egypt does make its own: the gin is undrinkable; the brandy compares with the Spanish variety and is satisfactory for punches and brandy sours; while *arak*, the Arab equivalent of Greek ouzo, Turkish raki, French anisette, and referred to in Egypt as *zibib*, is excellent, whether neat, on the rocks, or diluted with water, which turns it a characteristic milky colour.

Soft drinks, Egyptian-made or imported, are widely available, including a local variety of Coca-Cola and imported 7-Up. Egypt scores well on fruit drinks and cane juice, delicious, cheap and variously available with season. Finally, it is said that if you drink water from the Nile, you will be sure to return to Egypt. You might think you would drop dead instead. But in fact it is fresh, if somewhat organic in taste, and many people extol it (see *Health,* below). Tap water is heavily chlorinated and entirely safe. Bottled spring water is available.

Health The World Health Organisation has declared smallpox eradicated worldwide, and it is not necessary therefore to have a smallpox vaccination certificate to enter Egypt. Cholera and yellow fever vaccination certificates are required, however, if arriving from an infected area.

There are two diseases associated with Egypt, trachoma and bilharzia, though neither need unduly worry the visitor. Trachoma is a contagious infection of the eye, specifically the conjunctiva and cornea, and causes a cloudy scar and hence blindness. Unfortunately, many Egyptians have suffered from it. If you notice any inflammation of the eyes, you should at once consult an ophthalmologist. Bilharzia (or schistosmiasis) is caused by a worm which enters the body, causing disorders to the liver, bladder, lungs and nervous system. The worm lives only in stagnant water, eg some irrigation channels and slow-moving parts of the Nile. The Nile is entirely safe for swimming and drinking between the Aswan High Dam and Esna where, apart possibly from along its banks, it runs swiftly. To repeat, there is little risk of the visitor contracting either disease. Both can be successfully treated.

If you are unwell, you should first seek advice from your hotel. They will be able to refer you to a doctor, dentist or hospital, and may even have a doctor on call. Your embassy will also be able to recommend medical assistance. Particularly in the major centres, the standards of medical care are high. Many doctors will have trained in Europe or the United States and will speak English. More detailed information on medical care, and on pharmacists, will be found in the *Practical Information* sections.

Most likely the worst you will suffer will be a brief upset stomach. This is an entirely normal reaction to a change of diet and passes after a few days. There is no need suddenly to stop eating Egyptian food; on the contrary, after a pause, you should continue. During the upset you might benefit from plain unsweetened lemon juice, or a standard preparation can be obtained from any pharmacist. The one rule you should observe when eating in Egypt is to be sure your food has been washed; provided even the simplest eating place has running water, there should be no problem. Drinking water is heavily chlorinated and safe, though you can always have bottled water if you prefer.

The sun can be hot at any time of year, and the temperature can fall off sharply at night. At both times it is wise to be appropriately covered. During the day you should wear a head covering and sunglasses. It is not advisable to drink spirits before sundown, nor to consume iced drinks during the heat of the day. Unless you do not mind drinking lots of water, it would be helpful to bring along a supply of salt tablets. These are not available in Egypt. Also insect repellent would be helpful.

And of course it can pay to be medically insured.

Money The unit of currency is the Egyptian pound (LE) which is divided into 100 piastres (PT). There are coins for ½, 1, 5 and 10PT, and notes for 5, 10, 25 and 50PT, as well as for LE1, 5, 10 and 20. Also, notionally, piastres are divided into 10 milliemes, so that there are 1000 milliemes to the pound. Apart from the ½PT coin which is really 5 milliemes, there is no millieme currency. However, prices may be expressed in pounds, piastres or milliemes, so that four pounds might be written LE4 or 400PT or LE4.000. This can get a bit confusing, as when a restaurant bill states, say, 843.7, meaning 843PT and 7 milliemes, or LE8.437. What is more, instead of using a decimal point, Egyptians follow the continental European practice of using a comma instead, so the bill would appear as 843,7. Usually, your own common sense will tell you what is meant.

At the time of going to press (and currency fluctuations can change these figures up or down), £1 = LE1.64 and US$1 = 70PT. Or, the other way round: LE1 = £0.61 or US$1.43.

There are exchange banks at the airport and at major hotels throughout Egypt for converting to Egyptian currency. American Express and Thomas Cook also exchange money. You should hold onto your receipts in the event you need to change money back out of Egyptian pounds (see the *Practical Information* section at the end of the *Cairo 1* chapter).

Credit cards are just making an entry on the Egyptian scene. All the major hotels take them, as do some restaurants and shops. Some shops will impose a surcharge on credit card purchases to counter the percentage they have to pay the credit card company. The most commonly accepted cards are

American Express, Diner's Club, Carte Blanche, Visa and Master Charge (Access).

Baksheesh Tipping is expected for all services, and often for no service at all. 10-25PT is reasonable, though do not be surprised if sometimes you are grumbled at – too often tourists are absurdly ignorant or generous, which has led some Egyptians to believe, often rightly, that if they pull a sour face, even vociferously complain, they can milk you for more. The Egyptian term for a tip is *baksheesh* which means literally 'share the wealth' and helps explain why sometimes an Egyptian is not at all abashed at wanting something for nothing: you have it, he does not but feels you should pass it round. Baksheesh can be a plague, and you may find yourself pestered for it in the streets. The rule is obvious: offer baksheesh only in return for a service, do not pay until the service has been performed, and do not pay too much. Never be reluctant, when appropriate, to tell someone to get lost (*Imshee!*).

Electricity Electrical current throughout Egypt is 220 volts. Sockets take the standard continental European round-pronged plug. Plug adaptors and current converters, as well as dual voltage appliances, can be bought at home.

Communications Detailed information on mail, telephones, telegrams and telexes will be found in the *Practical Information* chapters, particularly at the end of the *Cairo 1* chapter.

Language The language of the country is Arabic, but English is taught to every schoolchild and, with French a close second, is the foreign language most spoken by Egyptians. In particular, most staff at hotels, restaurants and travel companies catering to foreigners will speak English, probably French, and perhaps also German and Italian. So along the well-beaten tourist paths, language is unlikely to prove a great problem.

However, even the least adventurous will sometimes encounter incomprehension – Cairo taxi drivers, for instance, may prove to be multilingually loquacious or, just as likely, may know only Arabic. It is useful, therefore, to know a few Arabic words and phrases, and it is always appreciated.

Arabic vocabulary A basic Arabic vocabulary, expressed phonetically, follows. The consonantal sounds are all approximately as in English, though in Arabic a distinction is made between 'hard' and 'soft' consonants, not indicated here. Vowels and diphthongs are pronounced thus:

ay as in *fate*	*ii* as in *machine*
ee as in *feet*	*o* as in *social*
i as in *it*	*u* as in *put*

There is also the *ain,* a gutteral vowel sound, indicated here by the raised *c* as in *mat* ^{c}*am* (restaurant), which is pronounced more or less like *aw,* but as far back in the throat as possible.

General Words and phrases

Hello/goodbye	*sa* ^{c}*eeda*
Please	*minfadlak*
Thank you	*shukran*
No thank you	*la shukran*
Yes	*aywa*
No	*la*
I want	^{c}*aayiz* (m)/ ^{c}*ayza* (f)
Do you have?	^{c}*andak?* (m)/ ^{c}*andik?* (f)
What is this?	*ayda?*
There is/Is there?	*fee/fee?*
There is no	*mafeesh*
Give me/us	*id dee nee/id dee na*
This	*di*
That	*da*
Much/many	*ki teer*
Little	*a leel*
Very	*aa wee*
Good	*kuwayyis*
Bad	*mish kuwayyis*
Hot	*sukhn*
Cold	*baarid*
And	*wa*
Or	*walla*
Not	*mish*
Possible	*mumkin*
Impossible	*mish mumkin*
Never mind	*ma* ^{c}*alish*
Enough/stop	*bass*
Go away	*imshee*

People

I	*ana*
You (m,f, sing., pl.)	*enta*
He	*howwa*
She	*heyya*
We	*ehna*
They	*homma*
Man	*ragil*
Woman	*sitt*
Boy	*walad*
Girl	*bint*

Medical

Doctor	*doktor*
Dentist	*doktor is si naan*
Hospital	*mustashfa*
Headache	*sooda*^{c}
It hurts	*byu ga*^{c}
My stomach hurts	*ba ta nee buy ga*^{c} *nee*

Accident	*hadsa*
Pharmacy	*say da lya*
Medicine	*da wa*

Official

Post Office	*bosta*
Embassy	*sefara*
Ministry	*wizaara*
Ministry of Culture	*Wizaaret el Sekafa*
Ministry of the Interior	*Wizaaret el Dakhleyya*
Ministry of Tourism	*Wizaaret el Seyaha*

Hotel

Hotel	*lookanda*
Room	*oda*
Bed	*sireer*
Bathroom	*hamaam*
Toilet	*twalit*
Restaurant/dining room	*mat^{c}am*
How much?	*bekaam?*
Cheap	*rikhees*
Expensive	*ghaali*

Restaurant and food

Restaurant	*mat^{c}am*
Breakfast	*fetaar*
Lunch	*ghada*
Dinner	*^{c}asha*
How much?	*bekaam?*
The bill	*el hesaab*
Bread	*^{c}aysh*
Butter	*zebdah*
Cheese	*gebnah*
Eggs	*bayd*
Olives	*zatoon*
Rice	*roz*
Tomatoes	*tamatem*
Potatoes	*batatis*
Onions	*baasal*
Lettuce	*khass*
Garlic	*tome*
Carrots	*gazzar*
Fish	*samak*
Chicken	*ferrakh*
Meat	*lahma*
Beef	*kandoos*
Lamb	*daani*
Oil	*sayt*
Vinegar	*khal*
Salt	*malh*
Pepper	*fifil*
Herbs	*a^{c}shaab*
Spices	*buharat*
Sugar	*sokkar*
Milk	*laban*
Tea	*shaay*
Coffee	*bon*

Travel

Station/stop	*mahatta*
Train	*atr*
Airport	*mataar*
Plane	*tayyara*
Car	*otomobeel*
Bus	*otobees*
Taxi	*tax*
Map	*khareeta*
Street	*shari*^{c}
Square	*midaan*
Bridge	*kubri*
Timetable	*gadwal*
Ticket	*tazkara*
First class	*daraga oola*
Second class	*daraga tanya*
Sleeping car	^{c}*arabee yit nom*
Dining car/restaurant	*mat*^{c}*am*
Reserved	*mafooz*
What time does it arrive?	*yoosal is saa* ^{c}*a kam?*
What time does it leave?	*yisaafir is saa* ^{c}*a kam?*
(Two) o'clock	*is saa* ^{c}*a (etnayn)*
... a.m.	*... bin na harr*
... p.m.	*... bil layl*
Hour/s	*saa* ^{c}*a/sa* ^{c}*aat*
I want a taxi	^{c}*aayiz tax (m)/*^{c}*ayza tax (f)*
Take me to (Ramses Station)	*waddiyni (Mahattat Ramses)*
Wait a little	*estanna shiwayya*
Where is?	*fayn?*
Straight ahead	^{c}*ala tool*
Right	*yemeen*
Left	*shemal*
Stop	*waaf*
Here	*hina*
There	*hinaak*
Far	*bi*^{c}*eed*
Near	*urayyib*
Now	*dilwaatee*
Later	*ba*^{c}*dayn*
Morning	*el sobh*
Noon	*el dohr*
Afternoon	*ba*^{c}*d el dohr*
At night	*bellayl*
Today	*enneharda*
Yesterday	*embareh*
Tomorrow	*bokrah*
Next week	*el esbou*^{c} *iggay*

Money and numbers

Money	*feloos*
Bank	*bank*
The bill	*el hesaab*
One	*wahed*
Two	*etnayn*
Three	*talatah*
Four	*arba*^{c}*a*
Five	*khamsah*
Six	*settah*

Seven	*sab^{c}aa*
Eight	*tamannya*
Nine	*tes^{c}aa*
Ten	*^{c}ashrah*
Eleven	*hedashar*
Twelve	*etnashar*
Thirteen	*talattashar*
Fourteen	*arbaa^{c}tashar*
Fifteen	*khamastashar*
Sixteen	*settashar*
Seventeen	*sabaa^{c}tashar*
Eighteen	*tamantashar*
Nineteen	*tessa^{c}tashar*
Twenty	*^{c}eshrin*
Twenty-one	*wahed we ^{c}eshrin*
Twenty-two	*etnayn we^{c} eshrin*
Thirty	*talatiin*
Forty	*arbe^{c}iin*
Fifty	*khamsiin*
Sixty	*settiin*
Seventy	*sab^{c}iin*
Eighty	*tamaniin*
Ninety	*tes^{c}iin*
Hundred	*meiyah*
Thousand	*alff*
Million	*milyon*
Pound	*genayh*
Half pound	*nus genayh*
Piastre	*ersh*
Two piastres	*ershayn saagh*
Three piastres (to ten)	*talatah saagh (etc.)*
Eleven piastres (etc.)	*hedashar ersh (etc.)*

The calendar

Day	*yom*
Night	*layl*
Week	*esbou^{c}*
Month	*shahr*
Year	*sana*
Sunday	*el had*
Monday	*el etnayn*
Tuesday	*el talaat*
Wednesday	*el arba^{c}*
Thursday	*el khamiis*
Friday	*el gom^{c}aa*
Saturday	*el sabt*
January	*yanayer*
February	*febrayer*
March	*maris*
April	*abriil*
May	*mayo*
June	*yonyo*
July	*yolyo*
August	*aghostos*
September	*sebtember*
October	*octobar*
November	*november*
December	*disember*

Arabic, of course, has its own alphabet (read from right to left), so the above list can help you only in verbal communication. However, it is important that you learn to recognise the

Numerals

Arabic numerals (read from left to right) – this will prove a great help when shopping or catching numbered buses.

ARABIC NUMERALS

١	٢	٣	٤	٥	٦	٧	٨	٩	١٠
1	2	3	4	5	6	7	8	9	10

Transliteration

Note that there are several methods of transliterating Arabic into English. For example, the town of Minya can also be written as Minia, or as Minieh. Also, Sultan Qaytbay can be written as Kait Bay, Qaitbai, Qait Bey, etc. So first, I apologise for any inconsistencies; and second, in consulting the index, or looking for places on maps, bear in mind possible variant spellings.

Religion

The principal belief of Islam is the existence of one God, the same God worshipped by Christians and Jews, whom the Moslems call Allah. Islam means submission. Moslem means one who submits to monotheism as interpreted by the religion's founder, Mohammed (AD 570-632).

To be a Moslem, it is only necessary to say once in one's life, "There is no god but Allah. Mohammed is the Prophet of Allah". In fact, the devout repeat this submission five times a day, while prostrate and facing Mecca. They hope that these might be the last words they have on their lips when they die.

Mohammed was a merchant in Arabia. He often contemplated in the desert and at the age of 40 had a vision of the Angel Gabriel who commanded him to proclaim monotheism to the pagan Arabian tribes. In Arabic, 'to proclaim' is *Qur'an,* and so the Koran is the word of Allah as given to Mohammed. The merchants of Mecca, concerned by the unsettling effects of this new religion, drove Mohammed out of the city in 622. His flight (the *hegira,* though literally this means 'withdrawal of affection') from Mecca to Medina, where Islam first took root, is the event from which the Islamic calendar begins.

Though Islam spread throughout the Middle East and across North Africa by conquest, it usually treated other religions with tolerance, and this has been particularly true in

Egypt. The population is 80 to 90 percent Moslem, adherents of the Sunni sect (for discussion of the Sunni and Shi'a sects, see the *Cairo 4* chapter, under the Mosque of Sayyidna al-Hussein).

The remainder of the population includes resident foreigners of various Christian denominations, Egyptian Jews and, primarily, Christians of the Egyptian Church, called Copts, who represent anything from five to 17 percent of the population (sources vary remarkably; some Copts have told me they constitute 20 percent of the population). Copts are particularly numerous in Upper Egypt and in the larger Delta towns.

For an outline of the Coptic Church, see under the history of Alexandria in the *Alexandria and the Delta* chapter. Suffice to say that until the Arab invasion, Egypt was a Coptic country and it remains today the only Moslem country in which Christianity has survived. It is not unusual when walking around Cairo, or elsewhere in Egypt, to come upon Christian celebrations, the streets festooned with decorations and lights, pictures and ikons of Christ and Mary and the various saints. Because the Copts have intermarried least with the Arab invaders, they are most truly the descendants of the ancient Egyptians, their language, now confined to liturgical use, the repository of the demotic tongue of pharaonic times.

Copts may have a small cross tatooed on their wrist, but otherwise it is impossible for an Egyptian to say whether a person is a Moslem or a Copt. Copts enjoy all civil, political and religious rights and occupy high posts in government, the military and in business. Where there is discontent amongst Copts, it derives most often from their achievement and ambition being frustrated by state inefficiency and restrictions, side-effects of Nasserist reforms. But then Copts are not the only ones to complain.

Time and Egyptian calendars

Egypt is two hours ahead of Greenwich Mean Time. Noon GMT is 2pm in Egypt.

Egypt uses three calendars: the Islamic, the Coptic and the Western. Both the Western and Coptic calendars are solar; the Islamic calendar is based on 12 lunar months and therefore rotates in relation to the other two, each Islamic year beginning 11 days sooner than the last. The Western calendar of course dates from the birth of Christ; the Coptic dates from the persecutions under Diocletian (see the *Alexandria and the Delta* chapter); while the Islamic calendar dates from the flight of Mohammed from Mecca in AD 622. (Because the Islamic year is shorter than the Western, you cannot simply subtract 622 from our year to determine the current AH year. In fact, 8 November 1980 saw the beginning of AH 1401.)

Another point worth noting is that a day in the Islamic calendar begins at sundown (so that technically AH 1401 began at sundown on 7 November 1980). A consequence of this is that Islamic festivals start on the evening before you would expect if going by the Western calendar, that evening assuming as sacred a character as the following waking daylight period (compare Christmas Eve and Christmas Day in Western usage).

You will be relieved to learn, however, that in all official transactions in Egypt the Western calendar and method of reckoning the day are used. The Islamic and Coptic calendars only really come into their own at festivals.

The Islamic months are as follows.

First month:	*Moharram* (30 days)
Second month:	*Safar* (29 days)
Third month:	*Rabei el Awal* (30 days)
Fourth month:	*Rabei el Tani* (29 days)
Fifth month:	*Gamad el Awal* (30 days)
Sixth month:	*Gamad el Tani* (29 days)
Seventh month:	*Ragab* (30 days)
Eighth month:	*Shaaban* (29 days)
Ninth month:	*Ramadan* (30 days)
Tenth month:	*Shawal* (29 days)
Eleventh month:	*Zoul Qidah* (30 days)
Twelfth month:	*Zoul Hagga* (29 days, or 30 in leap years)

Important Moslem festivals include:

Ras el Sana el Hegira, the Islamic New Year, beginning on the first day of Moharram.

Moulid el Beni, the Prophet's birthday, on the twelfth day of Rabei el Awal, marked in Cairo by a spectacular procession.

Ramadan, a month of fasting from dawn to sunset. As the last full meal is taken just before dawn, working hours are usually cut short to reduce afternoon effort to a minimum. Nothing is permitted to pass the lips during fasting hours, and so while visitors are permitted to eat, drink and smoke, you should not do so in the presence of fasting Moslems out of common courtesy. Interestingly, more food is consumed during Ramadan than at any other time of year, everyone making up at night for what they gave up during the day. Every Ramadan night, therefore, has the character of a festival.

Ramadan Bairam, a short period of fasting after Ramadan, on the first, second and third days of Shawal.

Qurban Bairam, a period lasting four days and beginning approximately 70 days after Ramadan, consecrated to the Pilgrimage.

Coptic festivals centring around Easter do not follow the Western (Gregorian) calendar. Other festivals fall on fixed dates: Christmas, 7 January; Epiphany, 19 January; the Annunciation, 21 March. A national holiday that is an important Coptic-pharaonic inheritance is *Sham el Nessim,* which falls on the first Monday after the Coptic Easter and during which the entire population of whatever religion takes a day off. This is a celebration of the advent of spring; families go out into their fields or gardens, or into the country, early in the morning and eat salted fish, onions and coloured eggs. The fish and onions are said to prevent disease, while the eggs symbolise life.

Weights and Measures Egypt officially employs the metric system, though sometimes traditional weights and measures will be encountered.

Temperature

Fahrenheit =	Centigrade/Celsius
122	50
113	45
110	43.3
107.6	42
104	40
102.2	39
100	37.8
98.6	37
96.8	36
95	35
93.2	34
91.4	33
90	32
87.8	31
86	30
84.2	29
80	26.7
75	23.9
70	21
65	18.3
60	15.6
55	12.8
50	10
45	7.2
40	4
32	0
23	-5
14	-10
0	-17.8

Fahrenheit into Centigrade/Celsius: subtract 32 from Fahrenheit temperature, then multiply by 5, then divide by 9. *Centigrade/Celsius into Fahrenheit:* multiply Centigrade/Celsius by 9, then divide by 5 then add 32.

Linear Measure	
0.39 inches	1 centimetre
1 inch	2.54 centimetres
1 foot (12 in.)	0.30 metres
1 yard (3 ft.)	0.91 metres
39.37 inches	1 metre
0.62 miles	1 kilometre
1 mile (5280 ft.)	1.61 kilometres
3 miles	4.8 kilometres
10 miles	16 kilometres
60 miles	98.6 kilometres
100 miles	160.9 kilometres
Square Measure	
1 sq. foot	0.09 sq. metres
1 sq. yard	0.84 sq. metres
1.20 sq. yards	1 sq. metre
1 acre	0.96 feddans
1.04 acres	1 feddan
4201 sq. metres	1 feddan
Weight	
0.04 ounces	1 gram
1 ounce	28.35 grams
1 pound	453.59 grams
2.20 pounds	1 kilogram
1 ton (2000 lbs.)	907.18 kilograms
0.99 pounds	1 rotel
0.45 kilograms	1 rotel
100 rotels	1 qantar
Liquid Measure	
0.22 imperial gallons	1 litre
0.26 US gallons	1 litre
1 US gallon	3.79 litres
1 imperial gallon	4.55 litres

Pharaonic dynasties The following is a list of the royal dynasties ruling Egypt successively or, where dates overlap, simultaneously and so indicating periods of disunity. The priests drew up long lists of monarchs, attaching to the years of a pharaoh's reign the events they wished to record. An example is the list of Seti I's

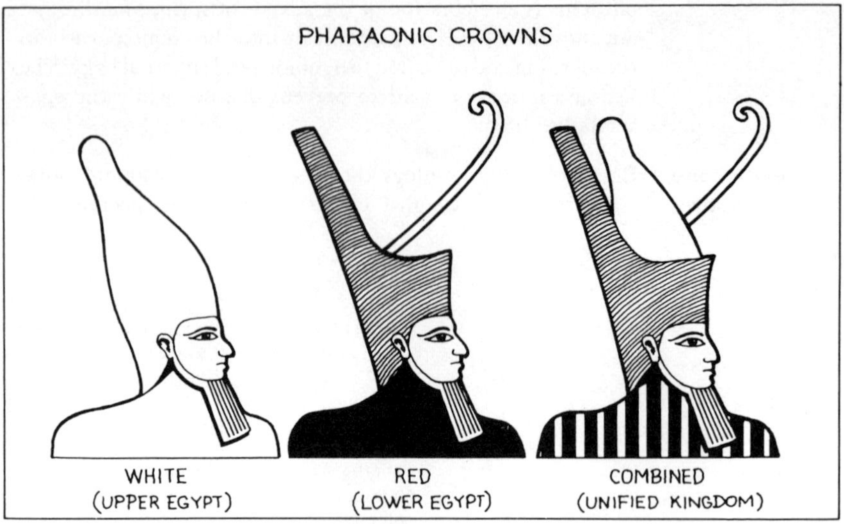

predecessors in his mortuary temple at Abydos. Working from such lists, Manetho, an Egyptian priest under the early Ptolemies, arranged all the rulers of Egypt from Menes to Alexander into 31 dynasties. Egyptologists have relied on Manetho's list, and have been able to confirm its essential correctness while sometimes improving upon it. The dates, however, are approximate, those around 3000 BC having a margin of error of 100 years, those around 2500 BC of 75 years, those following 2000 BC of 10 years, those around 1500-1000 BC of 10-15 years, while fairly precise dates are possible around 500 BC. This dynastic arrangement has historical validity, for Egypt's fortunes were closely linked to the rise and fall of the various royal houses. Throughout this Guide the dynasty of each Pharaoh is mentioned after his name so that his place in the scheme of things can readily be ascertained. Only the most important Pharaohs have been mentioned below within their dynasties; where their reigns overlap, this indicates joint rule.

Early Dynastic Period (3100-2700 BC)
First Dynasty
Menes (Narmer) – unification of Egypt; capital at Memphis
Second Dynasty
Old Kingdom (2700-2200 BC) – period of stability
Third Dynasty (2700-2650 BC)
Zoser (2700 BC) – start of the Pyramid Age
Fourth Dynasty (2650-2500 BC)
Snofru (2650 BC)
Cheops (2600 BC)
Chephren (2560 BC)

Mycerinus (2525 BC) – end of the Pyramid Age
Fifth Dynasty (2500-2350 BC)
Unas (2375 BC) – Pyramid Texts
Sixth Dynasty (2350-2200 BC) – period of decline
Pepi I (2325 BC)
First Intermediate Period (2200-2050 BC) – collapse of central authority
Seventh and Eighth Dynasties (2180-2155)
Ninth and Tenth Dynasties (2155-2055 BC)
Eleventh Dynasty (2135-2000 BC)
Mentuhotep II (2060-2010 BC) – reunites Egypt; capital at Thebes.
Middle Kingdom (2050-1800 BC) – conquest of Nubia
Twelfth Dynasty (1990-1780 BC) – royal residence moved to Memphis
Sesostris I (1972-1927 BC)
Second Intermediate Period (1800-1550 BC) – collapse of central authority
Thirteenth through Seventeenth Dynasties (1780-1570 BC)
Hyksos rule in Lower Egypt (1730-1570 BC) – introduction of the chariot
New Kingdom (1570-1090 BC) – period of power, luxury and cosmopolitanism
Eighteenth Dynasty (1570-1305 BC) – period of greatest contribution to the splendour of Thebes and Karnak.
Ahmosis I (1570-1545 BC) – expels Hyksos; establishes royal residence, and religious and political capital at Thebes.
Amenophis I (1545-1525 BC)
Tuthmosis I (1525-1495 BC) – burials begin at Valley of the Kings.
Tuthmosis II (1495-1490 BC)
Tuthmosis III (1490-1436 BC) – struggle with Hatshepsut; after her passing, he lays foundation of Asian and African empire.
Hatshepsut (1486-1468 BC)
Amenophis II (1439-1406 BC)
Tuthmosis IV (1406-1398 BC)
Amenophis III (1398-1361 BC) – apogee of New Kingdom opulence.
Amenophis IV (Akhenaton) (1369-1353 BC) – assault on priesthood of Amun; establishes worship of the Aton.
Smenkhkere (1355-1352 BC)
Tutankhaton (Tutankhamun) (1352-1344 BC) – return to orthodoxy.
Ay (1344-1342 BC)
Horemheb (1342-1303 BC) – military dictatorship.
Nineteenth Dynasty (1303-1200 BC) – restoration of royal power.
Ramses I (1303-1302 BC)
Seti I (1302-1290 BC) – new building work in Old Kingdom style.
Ramses II (1290-1224 BC) – prodigious builder, eg Rammesseum and Abu Simbel.
Merneptah (1224-1214 BC) – Pharaoh of the Exodus.
Syrian interregnum (1202-1197 BC)
Twentieth Dynasty (1200-1090 BC) – dislocations as Egypt enters Iron Age.
Ramses III (1195-1164 BC) – defeats Sea Peoples; succeeded by incompetent rulers.
Ramses VI (1153-1149 BC)
Herihor (1098-1090 BC) – Priest-Pharaoh at Thebes; rival ruler at Tanis.
Late Dynastic Period (1090-332 BC) – period of decline; often foreign rule.
Twenty-first Dynasty (1090-945 BC)
Twenty-second Dynasty (945-745 BC) – warriors of Libyan origin.
Sheshonk 1 (945 BC) – loots Jerusalem (I *Kings* 14, 25-26).
Twenty-third Dynasty (745-718 BC) – Ethiopian kings control Upper Egypt.
Twenty-fourth Dynasty (718-712 BC) – Ethiopian kings control all Egypt.

ROYAL CARTOUCHES

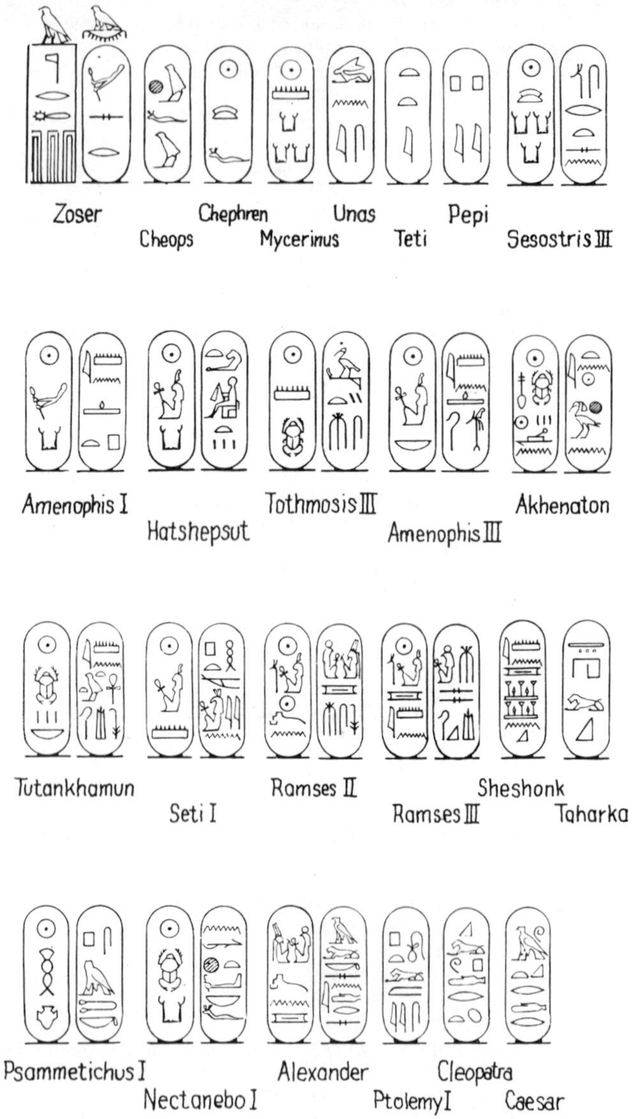

Twenty-fifth Dynasty (712-663 BC)
Taharka (695-671 BC) – Ethiopian king defeated by Assyrians who sack Thebes.
Twenty-sixth Dynasty (663-525 BC) – Delta rulers; Assyrians ejected with Greek help.
Psammetichus I (663-610 BC)
Necho (610-595 BC) – attempts to link Red Sea and Mediterranean by a canal; circumnavigation of Africa.
Twenty-seventh Dynasty (525-404 BC)
Cambyses (525-522 BC)
Darius I (522-486 BC)
Xerxes the Great (486-466 BC) – Persian rule.
Twenty-eighth Dynasty (404-399 BC) – Persians ejected with Greek help.
Twenty-ninth Dynasty (399-380 BC) – Delta remains the vital centre of power.
Thirtieth Dynasty (380-343 BC)
Nectanebos I (380-343 BC) – great builder, eg at Philae.
Thirty-first Dynasty (343-332 BC) – Persian rule.
Alexander enters Egypt in 332 BC

The Ptolemies

When Alexander died, his empire was divided between three of his Macedonian generals, Ptolemy taking Egypt. He established a dynasty which ruled the country for 300 years in the guise of pharaohs, albeit Greek-speaking ones, respecting the customs and religion of the Egyptians. The first three Ptolemies ruled ably, their greatest achievement Alexandria, which they adorned with Greek architecture and scholarship. In Upper Egypt the Ptolemies built archaic temples to please the priests, but otherwise they tied Egypt to the Mediterranean. Inevitably they encountered Rome, and through incompetence abroad and strife at home the later Ptolemies relied on the Romans for their very thrones. The last in the line was the great Cleopatra, who with Mark Antony attempted to create a new Hellenistic empire in the east.

323 BC: The death of *Alexander*.
323-282 BC: *Ptolemy I Soter* (Saviour). He added Cyrene, Palestine, Cyprus and parts of the Asia Minor coast to his realm, and at Alexandria, its geographical centre, he founded the Mouseion and Library.
282-46 BC: *Ptolemy II Philadelphus* (Lover of his Sister). To the shock of the Greeks, though with Egyptian precedent, he married his sister. He was a patron of poets, first invited the Jews to settle in Alexandria, and constructed the Pharos.
246-21 BC: *Ptolemy III Euergetes* (Benefactor). A soldier with a taste for science, during his rule Alexandria reached its height of splendour. In Upper Egypt he began the temple at Edfu. Abroad, he nearly reached India, and earned the title Conqueror of the World.
221-05 BC: *Ptolemy IV Philopator* (Lover of his Father). Setback in Syria, revolt at Thebes; he began construction of the temples at Esna and Kom Ombo.
205-181 BC: *Ptolemy V Epiphanes* (God Manifest). Child-king. Revolt at Alexandria, the interior in a state of anarchy. Epiphanes was placed under the protection of the Roman Senate, but by the time he came of age, Egypt had lost most of her overseas possessions.
181-45 BC: *Ptolemy VI Philometor* (Lover of his Mother). Seleucid invasion, Memphis captured, Egypt saved by Roman intervention.

145-4 BC: *Ptolemy VII Neos Philopator.*

145-16 BC: *Ptolemy VIII Euergetes II.* Also known as Physcon (Fatty): when he came puffing along the quay to greet Scipio Africanus the younger, the Roman sniggered, "At least the Alexandrians have seen their King walk". This Roman contempt applied to Egypt's sovereignty as well.

116-07, 88-80 BC: *Ptolemy IX Soter II.* Competed with his brother, Ptolemy X Alexander I, for the throne, both borrowing money from the Romans to raise arms.

107-88 BC: *Ptolemy X Alexander I.* To cover his debts he bequeathed Egypt to the Roman people, but as he had by then lost the throne, his offer could not easily be accepted. But it was remembered.

80 BC: *Ptolemy XI Alexander II.* Forced by Sulla to marry his (Ptolemy's) elderly stepmother, he then killed her and was killed in turn by an Alexandrian mob.

80-58, 55-51 BC: *Ptolemy XII Neos Dionysos.* Also known as Nothos (Bastard), he rushed back from Syria so that the vacant throne should not attract Roman annexation, and bolstered his pedigree by adding Philopator to his official names. He was the son of Ptolemy IX and father of Cleopatra VII. He built at Dendera, completed the temple at Edfu and left his mark on Philae. His reign was briefly interrupted by internal disruption.

51-49, 48-30 BC: *Cleopatra VII.* Ruled jointly with her younger brother Ptolemy XIII who banished her (**48 BC**), but in the same year she received the support of Julius Caesar and Ptolemy was drowned in the Nile. Another brother, Ptolemy XIV, succeeded to the co-regency (**47 BC**), but was assassinated (**45 BC**) at Cleopatra's instigation. Bore Caesar a son (**47 BC**), named Caesarion. He never ruled. Caesar assassinated (**44 BC**). Met Antony (**41 BC**). The battle of Actium (**31 BC**). Suicide of Antony and Cleopatra; Octavian (Augustus) makes Egypt a province of the Roman Empire (**30 BC**).

Roman and Byzantine periods

30 BC: *Octavian* (Augustus) incorporates Egypt into the Roman Empire. The Roman Emperors followed the example of the Ptolemies in representing themselves to the Egyptian people as successors of the Pharaohs and in maintaining the appearance of a national Egyptian state.

c. AD 30: Crucifixion of *Jesus Christ* at Jerusalem.

AD 45: *St Mark* makes his first convert to Christianity in Egypt, a Jewish shoemaker of Alexandria.

AD 98-117: Reign of *Trajan.* The canal connecting the Nile with the Red Sea reopened (**AD 115**).

AD 117-38: Reign of *Hadrian.* Visits Egypt.

AD 204: Edict prohibiting Roman subjects from embracing Christianity. The Delta is studded with Christian communities.

c. AD 251-356: *St Antony;* becomes the first hermit.

AD 284-305: Reign of *Diocletian.* His accession marks the beginning of the 'Era of Martyrs' from which the Copts date their calendar. Persecution of the Christians (**AD 303**).

AD 324-37: Reign of *Constantine the Great.* Converts to Christianity. Founds Constantinople (**AD 330**).

c. AD 330: Founding of the first monasteries at Wadi Natrun.

AD 379-95: Reign of *Theodosius I.* Declares Christianity to be the religion of the Roman Empire.

AD 395: Partition of the Roman Empire into East (Constantinople) and West (Rome). Notional date for the beginning of the Byzantine Empire.

AD 451: Council of Chalcedon declares monophysism a heresy, effectively expelling the Egyptian (Coptic) Church from the main body of Christianity.

AD 476: Fall of the Roman Empire in the West.

AD 622: *Mohammed's* flight from Mecca, the *hegira,* from which the Moslem calendar is reckoned. His death (AD 632).
AD 636: Arabs defeat Byzantine army and take Damascus.
AD 637: Arabs destroy the Sassanian (Persian) Empire.
AD 638: Arabs take Jerusalem.
AD 640: An Arab force under *Amr* enters Egypt. Fortress of Babylon taken (AD 641). Fustat founded; Alexandria surrenders and welcomes Arabs as liberators from Byzantine persecution (AD 642).

Arab and Turkish periods

All dates are according to the Western calendar (AD).
661: Murder of *Ali,* son-in-law of the Prophet; the Caliphate passes to the Umayyads.
661-750: The *Umayyad Caliphate,* with its capital at Damascus, rules over a united Arab empire stretching from the borders of China to the shores of the Atlantic, and up into France.
750-935: *Abbassids and Tulunids.* The Abbassids put a bloody end to the Umayyads in Syria and succeed to the Caliphate, ruling the Arab world from Baghdad. *Ibn Tulun,* an Abbassid governor of Egypt, makes himself independent of Baghdad and establishes a dynasty (870-935).
c. 820: The Copts, resentful of their Arab conquerors, rise in revolt several times during the 8th and 9th C. After their defeat, the majority of Copts convert to Islam.
909: Establishment of Fatimid Caliphate in North Africa.
935-69: A Turkish dynasty, the *Ikhshidids,* seizes power through the governorship.
969:1171: The *Fatimid Caliphate* in Egypt, which now follows Shi'a rather than Sunni Islam. Cairo, its capital, founded (969). Al-Azhar founded (971). The Fatimid empire reaches its peak under *Caliph Abu Mansur al-Aziz* (975-96). He introduces the practice of importing slave troops, the forerunners of the Mamelukes. His successor, *al-Hakim* (996-1021), is an all-powerful psychotic; the decline of the Fatimid empire begins with his death.
1055: The Seljuq Turks take Baghdad, leading to a resurgence of Sunni Islam in Iraq, Syria and Iran.
1099: The Crusaders take Jerusalem.
1171-1250: The *Ayyubids;* the dynasty of *Saladin,* a Kurd from Syria. He converts Egypt back to Sunni Islam. Drives the crusaders from Jerusalem (1187). The Mamelukes rise to power during the rule of *Shagarat al-Durr* (1249-50).
1250-1382: The *Bahri Mamelukes.* The most celebrated of these Mameluke Sultans are *Baybars* (1260-77); *Qalaun* (1279-90); *al-Nasr* (1309-40) – the beautiful mausolea of these last two are on Sharia Muizz in Cairo; and *al-Hassan* (1347-51, 1354-61), builder of the great madrasa bearing his name.
1382-1517: The *Burgi Mamelukes.* The most celebrated of these Mameluke Sultans are *Barquq* (1382-89, 1390-98), whose mosque is on Sharia Muizz, his mausoleum in the City of the Dead in Cairo; *Baybars* (1422-38), whose mausoleum is in the City of the Dead; *Qaytbay* (1468-95), known for his fortress on the site of the Pharos in Alexandria, and his mausoleum in the City of the Dead; and *al-Ghuri* (1500-16) whose monuments stand near Al-Azhar. *Tumanbay* (1516-17) was the last of the Burgi Sultans; he was hanged three times by the Turks outside Bab Zuwayla in Cairo.
1517: The Rule of the *Ottoman Turks* begins in Egypt and continues, if only nominally, until 1914.

The modern period

1798-1801: *French occupation* of Egypt. *Napoleon* lands at Alexandria; Battle of the Pyramids; Battle of the Nile (1798). *Napoleon* departs from Egypt (1799). A British army compels the French to evacuate the country (1801).
1805: *Mohammed Ali* becomes Viceroy of Egypt and after massacring the Mamelukes (1811) becomes, effectively, the independent ruler of Egypt, establishing a dynasty that was to end with *Farouk*.
1869: Opening of the Suez Canal during the reign of *Ismail*.
1882: Nationalist uprising led by *Arabi*. *British occupation* of Egypt begins.
1883-1907: *Evelyn Baring (Lord Cromer)* is British Consul in Egypt and effective ruler of the country.
1902: British complete construction of dam at Aswan.
1914: Britain declares Egypt to be a *British Protectorate.*
1918: *Saad Zaghloul,* nationalist leader, demands British withdrawal.
1922: British recognise Egypt as a sovereign state, but maintain an army in Egypt.
1936: Anglo-Egyptian Treaty, formally ending British occupation. British army withdraws, except from the Canal Zone.
1939-45: Egypt nominally neutral during the Second World War, but British Army invited to return to fight the encroaching Germans. Battle of el Alamein (1942); *Rommel* repulsed.
1948: End of British Mandate for Palestine. Establishment of the state of Israel. Arab-Israeli war; Arab debacle. Resentful of political corruption, *Gamal Abdel Nasser* (1918-70) gathers round him a group of dissident army officers.
1952: 25 January, British soldiers kill several Egyptian police in the Canal Zone. 26 January, rioting in Cairo at British action and Egyptian government's inaction. 23 July, *Nasser's* group stages a coup. 26 July, *King Farouk* abdicates and leaves the country.
1953: Egypt declared a *republic.*
1954: *Nasser* becomes head of state.
1954-56: British evacuate the Canal Zone.
1956: United States cancels loan to Egypt for construction of the High Dam at Aswan. *Nasser* nationalises the Suez Canal to use its revenues to pay for High Dam's construction. Israel invades Sinai in collusion with a British and French troop landing in the Canal Zone. Britain, France and Israel withdraw after international protest.
1958-61: Egypt and Syria combine to form the short-lived United Arab Republic (name retained until 1971).
1961: *Nasser* introduces sweeping socialist measures, limiting incomes, nationalising banks and the cotton industry, further redistributing land.
1967: The June 'Six Day War'. Israel attacks and defeats Egypt, occupies all of Sinai. The Suez Canal is blocked.
1970: *Nasser* dies. *Anwar Sadat* becomes President.
1971: Egypt's official name becomes the Arab Republic of Egypt (ARE).
1973: October, Egyptian forces cross the Canal and drive back the Israeli army. Israeli forces continue to occupy the Gaza Strip and most of Sinai.
1975: Suez Canal reopened.
1977: *Sadat* visits Jerusalem in a dramatic peace bid.
1980: Egypt and Israel exchange ambassadors.
1981: 6 October, *Sadat* assassinated. *Hosni Mubarak* becomes President later that month.

PHARAONIC ARCHITECTURAL FEATURES

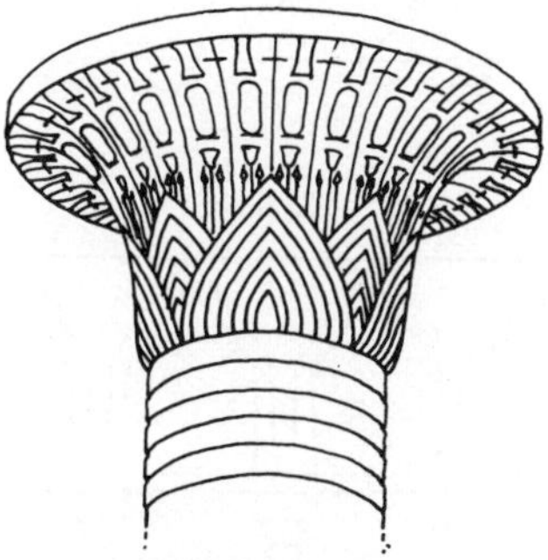

OPEN PAPYRUS CAPITAL

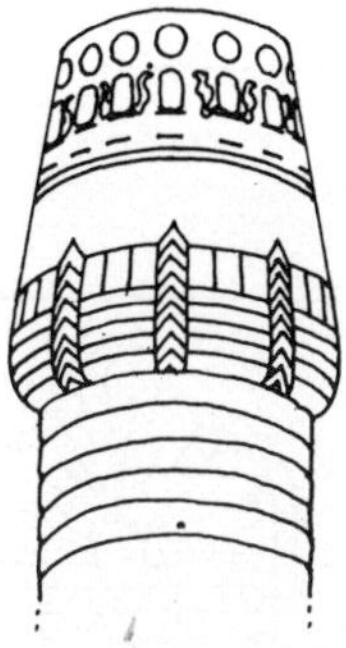

CLOSED PAPYRUS CAPITAL

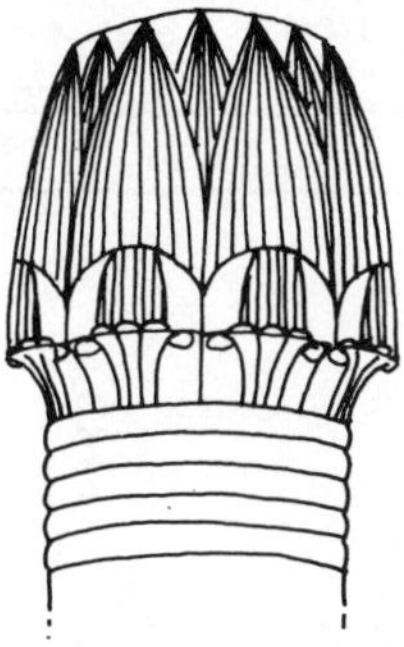

CLOSED LOTUS CAPITAL

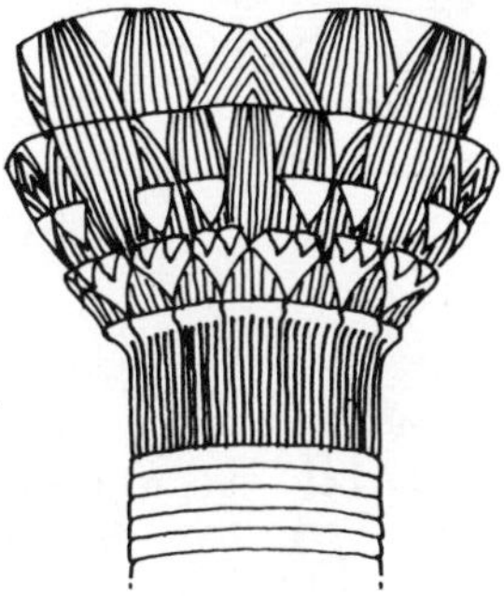

OPEN LOTUS CAPITAL

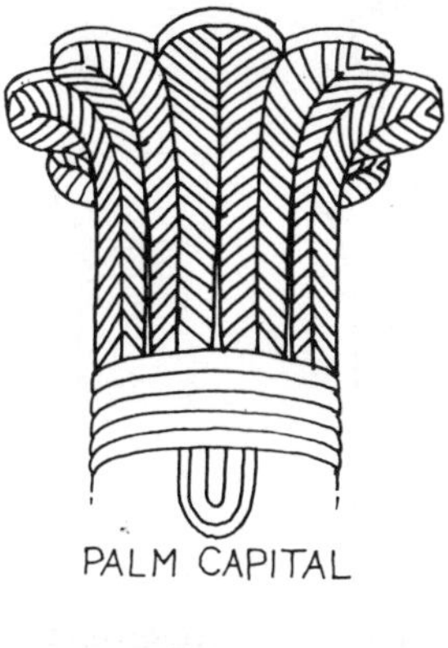

PALM CAPITAL

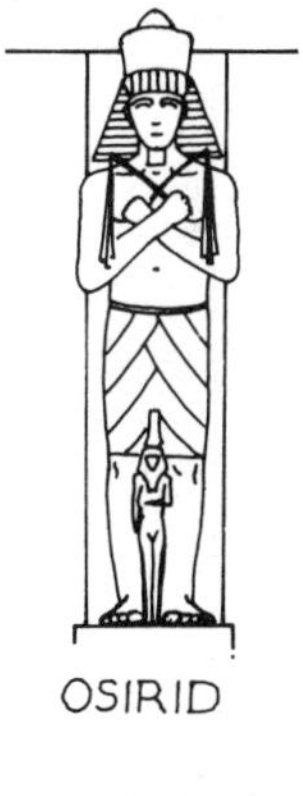

OSIRID

ISLAMIC ARCHITECTURAL FEATURES
ARCHES
KEEL ARCH DOORWAY
FATIMID KEEL ARCH WITH WOODEN TIE BEAM
MINARETS
FATIMID AYYUBID
EARLY MAMELUKE
LATE MAMELUKE
TURKISH

Glossary of religious, architectural and other names and terms

Abu: The Arabic for saint, whether Moslem or Christian. Holy man.
Amun: God of Thebes; he was made a sun god under the name *Amun-Re* and became the national god during the New Kingdom. His sacred animal was the ram. Along with his wife, *Mut,* and their son, *Khonsu,* Amun was one of the Theban triad.
Ankh: The hieroglyphic sign for 'life', resembling a cross with a loop in place of the upper arm.
Anubis: God of the dead, associated with interment. His sacred animal was the dog or jackal.
Apis: The sacred bull of Memphis, buried in the Serapeum at Saqqara.
Apse: A semi-circular domed recess, most frequently at the east end of a church.
Aton: The sun's disc; the life force. Worshipped by Akhenaton, who attacked the priesthood of Amun.
Azan: The Moslem call to prayer (see *muezzin).*
Ba: A spirit that inhabits the body during life but is not attached to it; at death it leaves the body and joins the divine spirit. (See *ka*).
Bab: A gate, as Bab Zuwayla.
Basilica: A church in the form of a long colonnaded hall, usually with one or more apses at the east end, and a narthex at the west end.
Bastet: The goddess of Bubastis, a goddess of joy. Her sacred animal was the lioness or cat.
Bayt: A house, or the self-contained apartments into which Ummayad mansions and Abbasid palaces were divided.
Canopic jars: Containers placed within ancient tombs to preserve those organs and viscera thought essential for the dead man's continued existence in the afterlife.
Capitals: Pharaonic and Ptolemaic temples employed capitals decorated either with plant forms *(palmiform, papyriform, lotiform)* or other motifs *(Hathoric,* ie with the human face and cow's ears of Hathor; forms deriving from timber construction eg *tent poles).* (See illustration.)
Cartouche: In hieroglyphs, the oval band enclosing the god's or Pharaoh's name and symbolising unchanging continuity.
Cavetto cornice: One of the most characteristic decorative features in ancient Egyptian architecture, a concave moulding decorated with palmettes. It was used along the tops of walls and *pylons,* projecting at front and sides. Below it would be a *torus* moulding.
Colours: Primary colours usually had particular applications and significance in ancient Egyptian painting. *Black* represented death: mummies, also Osiris as king of the dead, were commonly depicted in black. *Blue* was for sky and water, the sky gods painted this colour. *Green* was the colour of rebirth: Osiris, who overcame death and was reborn, often had his face and limbs painted green; also the solar disc was commonly painted light green on sarcophagi, instead of its usual red. *Red* was for blood and fire; men's bodies were depicted as reddish brown or brown; it also had a maleficent connotation: Seth was painted reddish brown. *White* represented silver and was the colour of the moon; it was also the colour of the garments of the gods and the crown of Upper Egypt. *Yellow* represented gold and was also used at the colour for women's bodies until the mid-XVIII Dynasty; thereafter the only women painted this colour were goddesses.
Columns: Like capitals, ancient columns followed certain decorative motifs, eg papyrus columns modelled after either a single stem and therefore smooth, or after a bundle of stems and therefore ribbed.
Crowns: The red crown of Lower Egypt was joined with the white crown of Upper Egypt to represent unification of the country (see *colours).* No matter what headdress the Pharaoh wore, he was always shown with the *uraeus* on his forehead.

Evil eye: The superstition that the envious glance of any passer-by, attracted by an immodest show of wealth, achievement or beauty, can harm or bewitch. Reciting certain verses of the Koran is one way of warding it off. *Uzait Horun,* the Eye of Horus, is meant to ensure safety and happiness and wards off the evil eye; it may be painted on cars, trucks and fishing boats, or worn as an amulet, particularly by children, who are especially vulnerable. Children also leave their handprints on walls to avert the evil eye. The probable value of the belief is as a social control, minimising at least the appearance of disparity in people's fortunes and so promoting solidarity.
Exonarthex: The outer vestibule of a church.
Fellahin: Egyptian peasants. The singular is *fellah.*
Flagellum: A flail or rattle to drive away evil spirits; it could be used only by a pharaoh and so represented the royal authority in carvings and statues. In the other hand was the *crook,* another royal symbol.
Hajj: The pilgrimage to Mecca that all Moslems should make at least once in their lifetime. When they have done so, they will often paint a scene of the event on their houses.
Hamam: A bath, public or private.
Harem: The private family (or specifically the women's) quarter in a house.
Hathor: The goddess of heaven, joy and love; the Greeks identified her with *Aphrodite.* She was the deity of Dendera and protector of the Theban necropolis. Her sacred animal was the cow.
Hegira: Mohammed's flight, or more properly his 'withdrawal of affection'. from Mecca in AD 622. The Moslem calendar starts from this date.
Herakhte: A form of *Horus,* 'Horus of the horizon', often combined with the sun god as *Re-Herakhte* and so worshipped at Heliopolis. The falcon was sacred to him.
Horus: The son of *Isis* and *Osiris,* and revered as the sun god. He was represented as the sun disc or a falcon, his sacred animal.
Hypostyle: A hypostyle hall is any chamber whose ceiling is supported by columns or pillars.
Ikonostasis: The screen carrying ikons between the main part of a church and the sanctuary or choir.
Isis: Sister and wife to *Osiris,* mother of *Horus,* the patron goddess of Philae. She was highly revered at a late period. Her sacred animal was the vulture.
Ithyphallic: Denoting the erect phallus of a depicted god or pharaoh, most commonly the god *Min.* It was a sign of fertility.
Ka: A spirit that inhabits the body during life and may leave it in death, but requires the continued existence of the body (hence mummification or, by substitution, ka statues) for its survival. The ka was personal and individual, in a sense the ideal image of a man's own life. (See *ba.*)
Khan: See *wakala.*
Khnum: The patron god of Elephantine Island and the Cataracts. He fashioned man on his potter's wheel. His sacred animal was the ram.
Khonsu: Son of *Amun* and *Mut;* god of the moon. The falcon was sacred to him.
Kufic: An early style of Arabic calligraphy with angular letters.
Lily: The plant identified with Upper Eygpt.
Liwan: A vaulted hall (see *mosque).*
Maat: The goddess of truth, whose symbol was the ostrich feather. Maat is actually the deification of a concept which Egyptians strove for, both personally and for the state. As well as truth, one can attempt to define it as justice, correctness, balance. The best definition is the now rare English word meet.
Madrasa: See *mosque.*
Mashrabiyya: Interlaced wooden screenwork, used for example to cover street-facing windows in a house.

Mausoleum: A domed chamber with one or more tombs inside; though simple in form, these structures, characteristic of the City of the Dead, are sometimes of considerable beauty.
Mihrab: The niche in the *qibla wall* of a mosque, indicating the direction of Mecca.
Min: The god of the harvest, frequently amalgamated with *Amun.* He was *ithyphallically* represented. The Greeks identified him with *Pan.*
Minbar: The pulpit in a mosque from which the Friday prayer is spoken.
Mont: A Theban god of war, represented with a falcon's head.
Mosque: The first mosque was the courtyard of Mohammed's house at Medina, with no architectural refinements except a shaded area at one end. Indeed, the only requirement for a mosque is that it should demarcate a space in which people may gather for saying prayers, eg an open quadrangle marked off by a ditch. From this notion developed the *congregational mosque,* of which the Ibn Tulun is the most outstanding example. Among non-congregational mosques are two special types which are of Cairene inspiration and development, the *cruciform madrasa* and the *sabil kuttab.* The *madrasa* served as a theological college, introduced by Saladin to combat Fatimid Shi'ism. Later it became more complex, a tomb appended and the madrasa formed of four *liwans,* each opening into a central court, hence *cruciform.* The outstanding example of this type is the Hassan. This pattern was subsequently modified, the court covered over, the east and west liwans reduced to vestigial proportions, a Koranic school for boys *(kuttab)* added as a floor above, a public fountain *(sabil)* below.
Muezzin: A crier who, as from a minaret, calls the faithful to prayer (see *azan).*
Mut: The wife of *Amun* and mother of *Khonsu.* Her sacred animal was the vulture.
Naos: The enclosed inner 'house of the god' (also *cella),* the central room of a temple, though sometimes referring to the entire temple. The sanctuary.
Narthex: The entrance vestibule at the west end of a church.
Naskhi: A cursive form of Arabic writing, subsequent to *Kufic.*
Nut: Goddess of the sky, often shown supported by *Shu.*
Okel: See *wakala.*
Osiris: Originally a vegetation god, later the god of the underworld. Murdered and dismembered by *Seth,* he was the husband of *Isis* and father of *Horus.*
Papyrus: The plant identified with Lower Egypt.
Pronaos: A columned porch, leading to the *naos.*
Ptah: The patron god of Memphis and father of the gods. His sacred animal was the bull *(Apis).*
Pylon: Arranged in pairs, forming a monumental gateway to a temple. Where there are several sets of pylons, each preceeding a court, they descend in size as the sanctuary of the god is approached, while the floor level rises, creating a focussing or tunnelling effect.
Qibla wall: The wall of a mosque facing Mecca.
Re: The sun god, usually combined with another god, eg *Amun-Re* or *Re-Herakhte.* His priesthood was at Heliopolis.
Riwaq: The arcade around a *sahn,* or a student apartment within the arcade.
Sabil kuttab: See *mosque.*
Sahn: An interior court, usually in a mosque.
Sakiya: An irrigation device consisting of buckets attached to a wheel which lifts water to the fields and is driven by circling oxen.
Sekhmet: The lion goddess of war.
Serapis: A god invented by the Ptolemies, looking like *Zeus* but identified with *Osiris-Apis.*
Seth: Brother and slayer of *Osiris,* adversary of *Horus,* he became a god of war,

though after the XXII Dynasty he was reduced to the god of the impure. His sacred animal was possibly the aardvark.

Shaduf: A simple lever device for lifting water to irrigate the fields. It is operated by hand.

Shu: The god of the air. He is often shown supporting Nut.

Sobek: God of the waters, patron of the Fayyum, the crocodile was sacred to him.

Squinches: Small arches or supports across the corners of a square, enabling the carriage of a dome.

Stele: An upright stone slab or pillar with an inscription or design, used as a monument or grave marker.

Thoth: A moon deity and the god of science. The ibis and baboon were sacred to him.

Torus: A convex moulding (see *cavetto cornice).*

Türbe: The Turkish term for a *mausoleum.*

Uraeus: The cobra worn on the forehead of a pharaoh as both an emblem and an instrument of protection, breathing flames and destroying enemies.

Ushabti: A mummiform figurine, serving in the tomb as deputy for the dead man, carrying out his labour obligations.

Wakala: An inn for travelling merchants built around a courtyard, with stables and warehouses at ground level and living accommodation above. Other names are *khan* and *okel.*

Waqf: An endowment for the upkeep of a mosque, eg a nearby apartment house, or shops built into the street level of the mosque, earning rents.

Ziyadah: The outer court of a mosque.

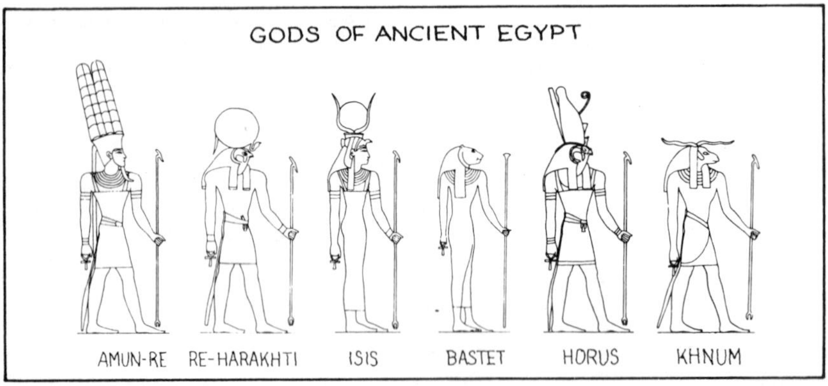

Some books about Egypt

Although there is a vast selection of books about all aspects of Egypt, disappointingly few are available in Egypt and the reader is advised to pursue his interest at home. The following titles are offered as a start. All quotations in the text are from among the books listed here, and acknowledgement is hereby given. I have mentioned the publisher and date and place of publication for the editions I am acquainted with. There are likely to be other editions published elsewhere. There may also be paperback editions of those I have cited as hardcover.

Aboudi, Mohammed *Aboudi's Guide Book* M Aboudi, Luxor 1963. Useless as a guide book, but entertaining for its doggerel. Pick up a copy as a souvenir. Paperback.

Aldred, Cyril *Akhenaten, Pharaoh of Egypt* Abacus, London 1972. Aldred is an authority on Egyptian art and offers his interpretation of the events and style of the Amarna revolution. Paperback.

Baedeker, Karl *Baedeker's Egypt 1929* David and Charles, Newton Abbot 1974. The most complete travel guide to Egypt ever written, this facsimile edition is still very useful, and on such subjects an 'Intercourse with Orientals' it grows more amusing with time. Hardcover.

Breasted, James Henry *A History of Egypt* Hodder and Stoughton, London 1959. First published before the discovery of Tutankhamun's tomb, this once definitive history of ancient Egypt has been superseded by later research. But it remains useful, and Breasted could write with panache. Hardcover.

Budge, E A Wallis, translation and introduction *The Book of the Dead* University Books, New Hyde Park, NY 1960. For the most part, of interest only to dead Egyptians with time on their hands. The hieroglyphs are reproduced and keyed line for line to the translation, and this can be interesting. The adamancy is sometimes startling: "I shall live, I shall live; I shall flourish, I shall flourish, I shall flourish, I shall wake up in peace, I shall not putrefy, my intestines shall not perish, I shall not suffer injury". And sometimes it is triumphantly beautiful: "I have seen Osiris, my father, and I have gazed upon my mother, and I have made love. I am led into celestial regions, and I make the things of the earth to flourish; and there is joy of heart. I have tied up my boat in the celestial lakes. I have recited the prescribed words with my voice, and I have ascribed praises unto the gods". Hardcover.

Cavafy, C P: the great Alexandrian poet, his work appears in several editions, eg *Collected Poems,* translated by Edmund Keeley and Philip Sherrard, Chatto and Windus, London 1975. Paperback

Cocteau, Jean *Maalesh, A Theatrical Tour of the Middle East* Peter Owen, London 1956. Written as a journal, it is full of delightful and often penetrating observations. Hardcover.

Durrell, Lawrence *Justine, Balthazar, Mountolive* and *Clea (The Alexandria Quartet)* Faber, London 1963. Powerfully evocative novels set in Alexandria before the Second World War. Paperback.

Fedden, Robin *Egypt, Land of the Valley* John Murray, London 1977. The best general introduction to the country. Hardcover.

Fowles, John *Daniel Martin* Triad/Panther, London 1978. A big fat novel to read along the Nile, where much of it is set. Some good travel writing on Egypt.

Flaubert, Gustave: a romantic until he visited Egypt, which sharpened his eye. His travel journal has been translated and edited by Francis Steegmuller, *Flaubert in Egypt* The Bodley Head, London 1972. A marvellous antidote to a surfeit of temples. Hardback.

Forster, E M *Alexandria: A History and a Guide* Annotated edition, with a preface by Lawrence Durrell. Michael Haag, London 1982. First published in 1922, this has been called the greatest guide book every written. "The whole historical perspective of the city, in all its variety, has been captured and fixed in a series of short essays brightly starred with all the virtues of this fine artist. With a marvellous economy he brings the place to life – and gives life to the great personages who inhabited it: philosophers, poets, mathematicians, courtesans. It is a work of deep affection and a noble monument raised to this most haunting of cities" – Lawrence Durrell. Paperback and hardcover.

Forster, E M *Pharos and Pharillon* The Hogarth Press, London 1967. Sketches of Alexandria past and (sometimes first person) present, first published in 1923. Hardcover.

Fox, Robin Lane *Alexander the Great* Futura, London 1975. The definitive life; erudition enlivened with an imaginative insight into Alexander's mind and times. Paperback.

Frankfort, Henri and others *Before Philosphy, The Intellectual Adventure of Ancient Man* Penguin, Baltimore 1949. A stimulating analysis of Mesopotamian and Egyptian cosmogony, etc. Paperback.
Fuller, J F C *The Decisive Battles of the Western World* Abridged in two volumes. Paladin, London 1970. A highly readable and incisive view of history. The first volume touches on the Battle of Megiddo (1479 BC), the second on Alamein (AD 1942). I mention these because I have drawn on or quoted from them, but anyone interested in the detail of these battles should consult the unabridged hardcover edition or a specialised work. Also useful and authoritative, if again general, is the *History of the Second World War* by Liddell Hart. The abridged Fuller is in paperback.
Gardiner, Sir Alan *Egypt of the Pharaohs* Oxford University Press, London 1961. A scholarly introduction to Egyptology presented through a history of Egypt by an outstanding Egyptologist. Hardcover.
Giedion, S *The Eternal Present: The Beginnings of Architecture* Oxford University Press, London 1964. A conceptual history of Mesopotamian and Egyptian architecture. Hardcover.
Grant, Michael *Cleopatra* Panther, London 1974. A lively reconsideration of the life and policies of the last Ptolemy. Paperback.
Harris, James E and Weeks, Kent R *X-Raying the Pharaohs* Macdonald and Company, London 1973. A fascinating illustrated study of pharaonic mummies, full of revelations. Hardcover.
Herodotus *The Histories* Penguin, Harmondsworth 1972. By way of setting the scene for the great conflict between Greece and Persia, Herodotus included a lengthy digression on Egypt full of information and some misinformation acquired during his visit. The first great prose work in European literature. Paperback.
Hoag, John D *Western Islamic Architecture* Studio Vista, London 1968. Photographs, plans and text show the development of and relationship between Islamic secular and religious architecture. Hardcover.
Johnson-Davies, Denys, translator *Egyptian Short Stores* Heinemann, London 1978. A must for getting into the atmosphere and mind of modern Egypt. Paperback.
Keating, Rex *Nubian Rescue* Robert Hale and Company, London 1975. As Nubia was flooded beneath the waters of Lake Nasser, its major monuments were saved and a last series of excavations of its uncertain history attempted. This relates the results. Hardcover.
Lane, E W *Manners and Customs of the Modern Egyptians* Facsimile of the 1895 edition. First published in 1836. East-West Publications, London 1978. A classic account of Egyptian, principally Cairene, life in the early 19th C. Paperback.
Lauer, Jean-Philippe *Saqqara* Thames and Hudson, London 1976. A description of Saqqara and an account of its discovery and excavation by the most recent great Egyptologist on the spot. Hardcover.
Liddell, Robert *Cavafy, A Critical Biography* Duckworth, London 1974. Important to Cavafy and Alexandria buffs. Hardcover.
Mabro, Robert *The Egyptian Economy 1952-1972* Clarendon Press, Oxford 1974. Though now in need of an update, this is the best general review of the enormous economic problems Egypt is struggling with. Paperback.
MacQuitty, William *Island of Isis: Philae, Temple of the Nile* Macdonald and Jane's, London 1976. A well-illustrated look, not only at Philae, but at the monuments of Upper Egypt generally and their salvaging, and a review of Ptolemaic history. Hardcover.
Mahfouz, Naguib *Midaq Alley* Heinemann, London 1975. Egypt's greatest novelist and his most popular book, set in the backstreets of the Azhar district of Cairo. Paperback.

Mahfouz, Naguib *Miramar* Heinemann, London 1978. An Egyptian response to Durrell's *Alexandria Quartet,* with an introduction by John Fowles. Paperback.

Mansfield, Peter *The Arabs* Penguin, Harmondsworth 1978. A readable history of the Arabs, followed by an examination of each Arab country. Paperback.

Mansfield, Peter *The British in Egypt* Weidenfeld and Nicholson, London 1971. An account of the British occupation of Egypt. Hardcover.

Mendelssohn, Kurt *The Riddle of the Pyramids* Sphere Books, London 1977. A fascinating account of the pyramid phenomenon and a radical but convincing solution to the riddle by an Oxford physicist. Paperback.

Nerval, Gerard de *Journey to the Orient* (Abridged) Panther, London 1973. An early surrealist (19th C.) finds stimulation in Egypt. Written in the style of a travel journal, he soon soars on hashish wings. Paperback.

Parker, Richard B and Sabin, Robin *A Practical Guide to Islamic Monuments in Cairo* American University in Cairo Press, Cairo 1974. If you want to explore Islamic Cairo in greater detail, this is the guide you should have. Paperback.

Schwaller de Lubicz, R A *The Temple in Man, The Secrets of Ancient Egypt* Autumn Press, Brookline, Mass. 1977. A silly book and largely unreadable, but as Cocteau thought so highly of his theories, I mention it. Paperback.

Stewart, Desmond *Great Cairo, Mother of the World* Rupert Hart-Davies, London 1969. An excellent history of Cairo since its founding. Hardcover.

Twain, Mark *The Innocents Abroad* The New English Library, London 1966. Twain led a party of American tourists through Europe and the Middle East and wrote this absurdly funny and iconoclastic account. The part on Egypt is fairly brief. Paperback.

von Haag, Michael *Egypt, The Land and its People* Macdonald Educational, London 1975. An illustrated survey of the country, its history and its way of life for younger readers. Hardcover.

Wellard, James *Desert Pilgrimage, A Journey into Christian Egypt* Hutchinson, London 1970. A personal exploration of this important but neglected aspect of Egypt. Hardcover.

Wilson, John A *The Culture of Ancient Egypt* (originally titled *The Burden of Egypt*) The University of Chicago Press, Chicago 1956. An excellent and readable cultural history of dynastic and pre-dynastic Egypt. Paperback.

CAIRO 1: MOTHER OF THE WORLD

From the air Cairo is a city of circles and radiating avenues at the head of the Nile Delta, its houses and buildings dull brown as though camouflaged to blend with the impinging desert. The colour is of the local stone, but also the residue of sandstorms which sometimes dust the city. At sundown you can see a thin layer of sand clinging to the polished dome of the Mohammed Ali Mosque atop the Citadel, and as you walk along the cracked pavements the desert wells up from below. Apart from the broad slow-flowing river and minarets like blades of tall grass against the sky, there is a heavy, airless feeling, an architectural jumble of fake pharaonic, blocklike modern, oppressive Victorian.

But in spirit Cairo remains as it began, an Arab encampment on the edge of the desert: hot, dry, the smell of dung, glowing coals and musk, lively with throngs of people. To this sprawling carvanserai come visitors from all over the Arab, African and Asian world, fantastically varied in colour, dress, characteristics, yet easily talking, mingling, bargaining like distant villagers meeting again in their market town.

For Cairo is the largest city in Africa and the political and cultural fulcrum of the Arab world. Its population has been officially estimated at eight million, and that itself represents a doubling over the past decade or so, but as many as 14 million people could be living here. It has always attracted people from the villages of the Valley and the Delta, but owes its recent staggering growth to the damage inflicted on the Suez Canal towns during the wars with Israel. At rush hours the buses threaten to burst or collapse with the pressure of Cairenes scrambling through doors and windows or clinging on outside for the long ride to or from the suburbs of Heliopolis, Maadi and Helwan. But as the sun sets over the Nile the present slips away into timelessness, and from a high window over the river you can see the Pyramids at Giza glow gold against the Western Desert as they have done for one million, seven hundred thousand evenings past.

History of the city

Your orientation about the city is aided by a knowledge of its history, and its history, as with so much else in Egypt, is linked to the Nile. In the Old Kingdom the capital of Egypt was at Memphis, 20 kms to the south of Cairo – but at that time the Delta had not pushed as far north as it has today and Memphis stood closer then to the conjunction of the Delta and the Valley, controlling Egypt to north and south. In this strategic sense Cairo is heir to Memphis, for the Nile divides just to the north of the city.

Ancient Heliopolis, its scant ruins near a modern suburb bearing the same name at the northeast of the city enroute to the airport, was once the religious centre of Egypt; and in pharaonic times there was a settlement, perhaps even a town, on the east bank of the Nile opposite the island of Roda, but Cairo cannot be said to have developed out of these, and even its connection with what is now called Old Cairo is tenuous. In Roman and Byzantine times when there was a fortress here, Old Cairo was called Babylon in Egypt, probably a Greek corruption of the ancient name of Roda, *Per-Hapi-en-Yun,* House of the Nile of Heliopolis. Fortress rather than administrative centre was sufficient role for the settlement, and Babylon never amounted to much. In the last centuries before Christ, Egypt was ruled by Alexander's successors, the Ptolemies, from their Mediterranean capital, Alexandria.

Babylon in Egypt

It was the Arabs, for whom the deserts and not the sea provided familiar lines of communication, who developed the logic of the site. In AD 641, Amr arrived in Egypt at the head of a small army and both Alexandria and Babylon opened their gates to him. Amr was enchanted with Alexandria and wrote back to the Caliph at Medina that this should be the Moslem capital of the conquered country, but Omar replied, "Will there be water between me and the Moslem army?" Amr returned to Babylon where only sand separated him from Arabia; the tent *(fustat)* he had pitched there before marching on Alexandria was still standing and a dove had nested in it with her young. On this spot Amr built his mosque, the first in Egypt, and Fustat, the City of the Tent, grew up around.

Arab foundations: Fustat

Fustat was the first of several planned developments which over the centuries contributed to the growth of the medieval city. The Nile in those days lay further to the east along what is now Sharia el Gumhuriya which runs up into Midan Ramses where the railway station is. All of what is now modern Cairo lay then on the west bank of the river, if not beneath it. And an ancient canal, once joining the Nile with the Red Sea, lay still further to the east, along the line of Sharia Port Said, built when the canal, called the Khalig by the Arabs, was filled in during the 19th C. So the city developed along the narrow corridor of land between the canal to the west and the Moqattam Hills to the east, and extended northwards as successive rulers were intent on catching the cool summer breezes blowing in from the Mediterranean.

When Ibn Tulun, Abbasid Governor of Egypt, made

The Tulunid city

himself virtually independent of the Baghdad Caliph in 870, he built his palace, government buildings, a hippodrome and the famous mosque bearing his name to the north of Fustat. His mosque apart, little survives of the Tulunid city, and still less of Fustat. The heart of what grew into the Cairo of today was established by the Fatimids.

The Fatimids

On 5 August 969, with Mars in the ascendant, the first stone of the Fatimid capital was laid to the north of the Tulunid city. The city took its name, *al-Qahira,* The Triumphant, from the warrior plant. The Fatimids, of the persistent though minority Shi'ite sect of Islam, invaded Egypt from Tunisia where their Caliphate declared its legitimacy through descent from Ali, husband of the Prophet's daughter Fatima. They imposed their Shi'ite doctrines (those same followed today in Iran) on Egypt which, apart from the Fatimid interlude, has kept within the orthodox Sunni fold. The al-Azhar Mosque dates from this period and is still the centre of Koranic studies for the whole Moslem world.

(Our name for the city, Cairo, derives from this al-Qahira found on maps, though as often as not Egyptians call it *Misr.* Of vague and haunting meaning, far antedating Islam, Misr is emotionally the more important name of the two and refers to both city and the country as a whole. An Egyptian abroad who says, "I am going to Misr", means he is returning to Egypt. If he says the same thing in Luxor, he means he is returning to Cairo. In either case, "going to Misr" carries the sense of going home. For the fellahin, Cairo is *Misr um al-dunya:* Misr, Mother of the World.)

Saladin

This walled city, centred on the popular market area known as Khan el Khalili and extending from the gate known as Bab Zuwayla in the south to Bab al-Futuh in the north, remains astonishingly intact both in structure and in atmosphere, the medieval city nonpareil in all the world. Its walls and area were extended by Saladin, a Kurdish general in the service of the Abbasid Caliph in Baghdad. Foreign failures and the failure of the Nile itself led to the weakening of the Fatimid dynasty which trembled in confusion before the onslaught of the First Crusade. In triumphing over the armies of the West, Saladin established his own empire in Egypt and Syria and his own Ayyubid dynasty which ruled from 1171 to 1250. Orthodoxy was re-established and the Citadel begun, the redoubt of power and the centre of government throughout the troubled centuries of Mameluke and Ottoman rule.

The Mamelukes

Saladin's Ayyubid successors, however, relied increasingly on their slave militia, the Bahri Mamelukes. (*Mameluke* means white slave, while *bahri* means riverine and refers to their barracks on the island of Roda; these were mostly Turks and Mongols. The later Burgi Mamelukes, mostly Circassian, were quartered in the Citadel, hence *burg).* The Mamelukes soon became an indispensable elite and successive sultans rose from their number, legitimising their authority more by the blood on their hands than the blood in their veins. The Mamelukes ruled Egypt until the Ottoman domination in 1517. In spite of the violent and repressive character of Mameluke rule, they enriched the city with their architecture, their most outstanding monuments the Mosque of Sultan Hassan and the Mausoleum of Qaytbay.

The Ottomans

Around 1300 the island of Gezira was formed as the Nile shifted westwards but the city remained largely within its old boundaries right through the Ottoman period, its architecture following traditional styles with only a few baroque exceptions inspired by the mosques of Istanbul. As a province of the Ottoman Empire, Egypt was ruled by a Turkish governor housed in the Citadel who delegated most of his authority. Though no longer providing sultans, the Mamelukes perpetuated their slave aristocracy by levees of Christian youths from the Caucasus. But their power now was chaotic and rapacious. What the Turks did not take, the Mamelukes did, and Egypt suffered from famine and disease, its population falling to two million compared to eight million in Roman times.

Napoleon

The brief French occupation of Egypt, from 1798 to 1801, was to have a profound effect on Cairo. Napoleon stayed in what was still then a country district, on the site where the old Shepheard's Hotel was later built, overlooking the Ezbekieh lake, subsequently the Ezbekieh Gardens, only recently turned into nearly a dustbowl by having a main street cut

Key to Cairo Map

Principal squares

A. Midan el Tahrir
B. Midan Talaat Harb
C. Midan Orabi
D. Midan Ramses (main railway station)
E. Ezbekieh Gardens
F. Midan Ataba

Some hotels

a. Nile Hilton
b. Shepheards
c. Meridien
d. Sheraton
e. Continental Savoy
f. Windsor

Places of interest

1. Egyptian Museum
2. American University in Cairo
3. Bab el Luq station (for Old Cairo, Maadi and Helwan)
4. Cairo Tower
5. Zoological Gardens
6. Cairo University
7. Manyal Palace
8. To Old Cairo and Fustat
9. Abdin Palace
10. Ibn Tulun Mosque and the Gayer-Anderson House
11. The Citadel
12. Southern Cemetery
13. Sultan Hassan Mosque
14. Saladin's walls
15. Bab Zuwayla
16. Islamic Museum and Egyptian Library
17. Al-Azhar Mosque
18. Muski and Khan el Khalili bazaars
19. Mosque of Qalaun
20. Bab al-Futuh and Bab al-Nasr
21. To Northern Cemetery (City of the Dead)

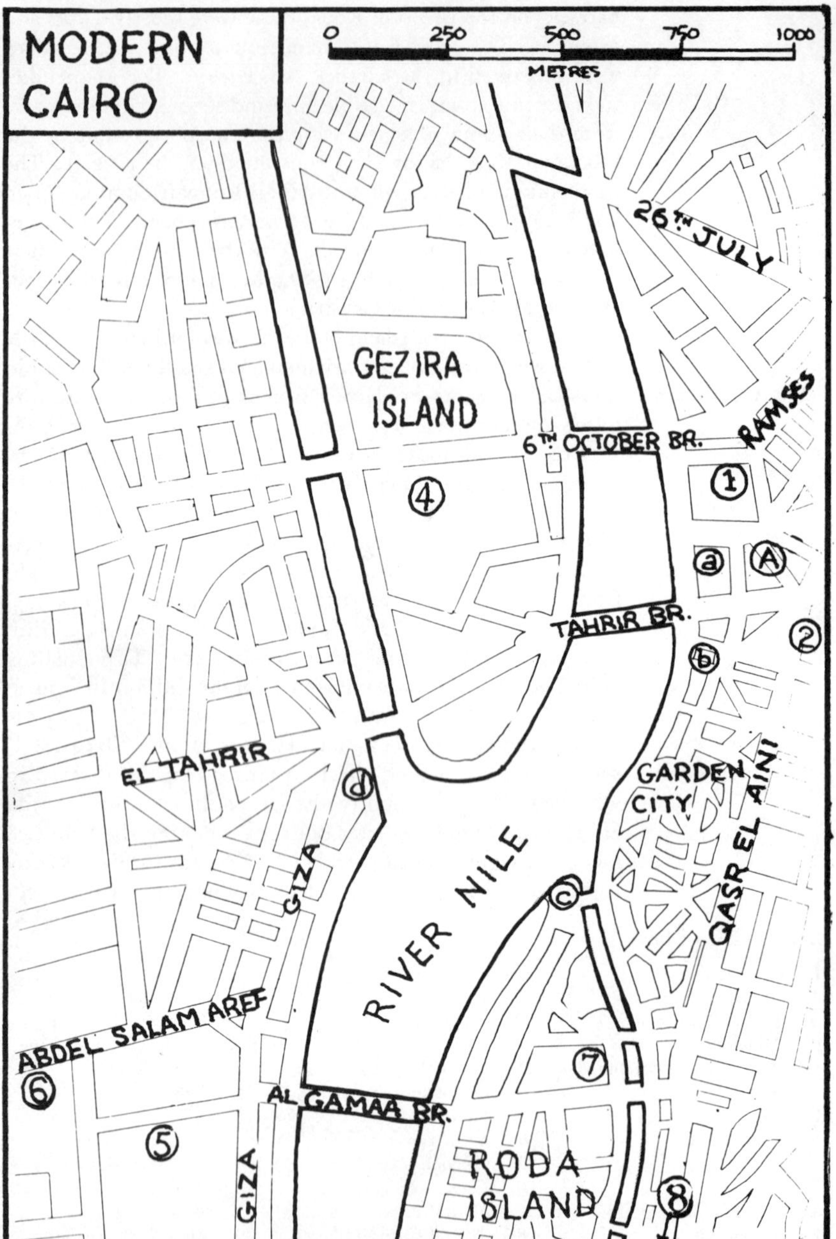
MODERN
CAIRO
0
250
500
750
1000
METRES
26TH JULY
GEZIRA
ISLAND
RAMSES
6TH OCTOBER BR.
1
4
a
A
TAHRIR BR.
2
b
EL TAHRIR
d
GARDEN
CITY
QASR EL AINI
RIVER NILE
c
GIZA
ABDEL SALAM AREF
7
6
AL GAMAA BR.
5
RODA
ISLAND
8
GIZA

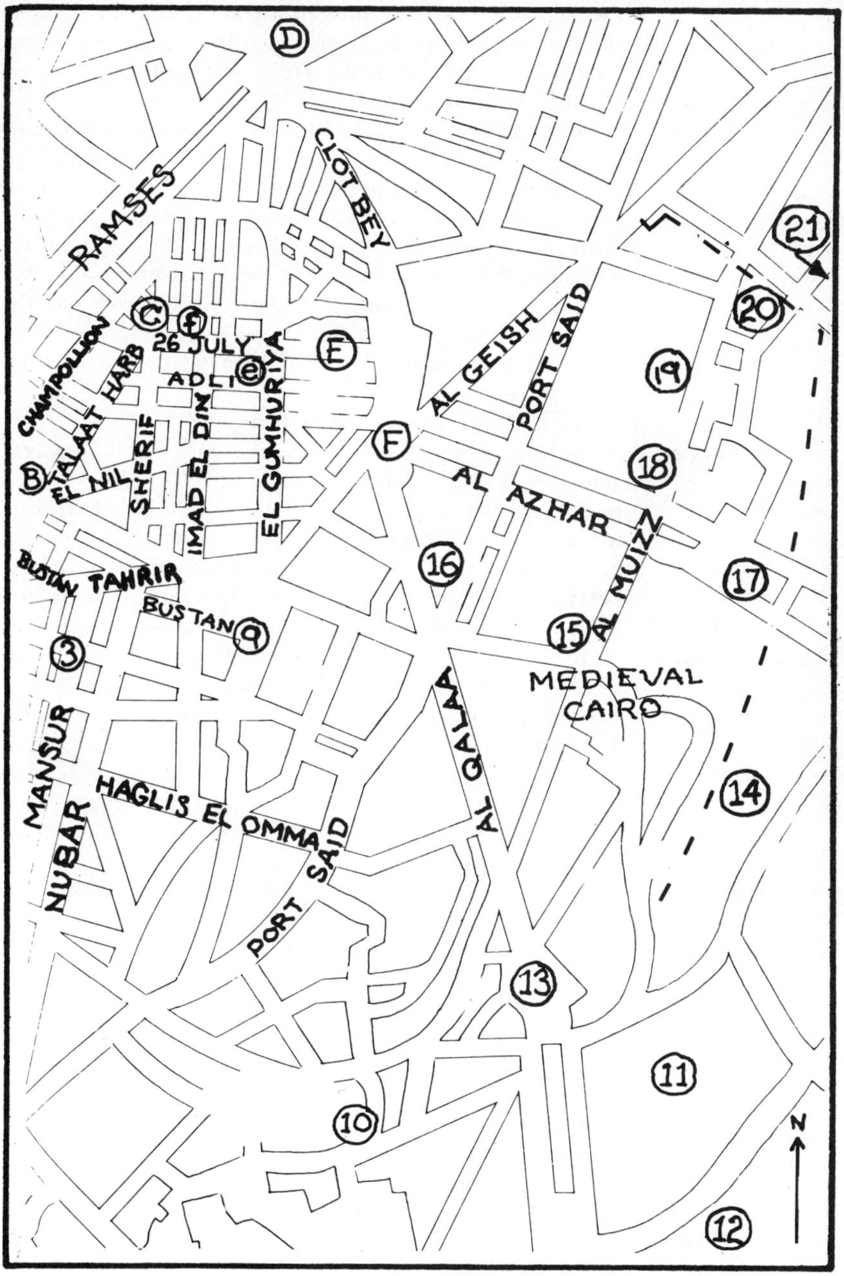
RAMSES
CLOT BEY
CHAMPOLLION
TALAAT HARB
26 JULY
ADLI
SHERIF
IMAD EL DIN
EL GUMHURIYA
EL NIL
AL GEISH
PORT SAID
AL AZHAR
AL MUIZZ
BUSTAN
TAHRIR
BUSTAN
MEDIEVAL
CAIRO
AL QALAA
MANSUR
NUBAR
HAGLIS EL OMMA
PORT SAID
D
C
f
E
e
F
B
3
9
10
11
12
13
14
15
16
17
18
19
20
21
N

through it. While reorganising the government, introducing the first printing press, launching a balloon and installing windmills on the Moqattam Hills, Napoleon also planned Parisian boulevards.

The 19th century

When Mohammed Ali finally massacred the Mamelukes in 1811, founding a dynasty which ended only with the abdication of Farouk in 1952, he proceeded with the Westernisation of Cairo which saw the canal filled in and the great swaths of Sharia el Muski and Sharia el Qalaa (formerly Sharia Mohammed Ali) mow down long rows of the medieval city. Fortunately, however, most of the modernising of Cairo – those circles and radiating avenues you see from the air – took place on the virgin land that the Nile provided when it settled in its present bed.

We can start our orientation here.

Orientation

Midan el Tahrir

What now passes for the centre of town – for foreigners, anyway – is Midan el Tahrir, or Liberation Square, bounded by the Egyptian Museum to the north and the Nile Hilton to the west, with a madhouse of a bus terminus slap in the middle. The square is encircled by an elevated walkway for the safety of pedestrians – or perhaps for the safety of the traffic, for in Cairo the struggle between people and machines is still in the balance. Hot, noisy, characterless and thick with exhaust fumes, Midan el Tahrir is among the more recent schemes to bring Cairo up to date. It was created after the 1952 revolution on the site of a British barracks, the Qasr el Nil, and at the same time powers of compulsory purchase were used to cut the Corniche el Nil through the many embassy and villa gardens to the south, the new roadway extending clear down to Maadi and Helwan.

South along the corniche to Garden City

A short walk along the corniche are the Semiramis Intercontinental and Shepheards – though the famous Shepheards Hotel of the past, whose guest list included General Gordon and Sir Richard Burton and where anyone who was anyone was seen on the terrace drinking four o'clock tea, was located near the Ezbekieh Gardens and was burnt down by demonstrators in 1952. Further south along the river is the convoluted pattern of Garden City, a pleasant residential district of tree-lined streets.

East to the presidential palace

Immediately to the south of Midan el Tahrir is the Mugamaa, the suitably massive headquarters of the state administration, and next to it are the American University in Cairo and the National Assembly. Behind the American University, in Sharia Mansur, is the small Bab el Luq station for commuter trains to Maadi and Helwan, and convenient too for visiting Old Cairo. Going east beyond the campus and the station you come to Abdin Palace, formerly a residence of King Farouk, now partly a museum and partly the offices of the President of the Republic.

To the north of Midan el Tahrir, beyond the overpass leading to the new 6 October Bridge (named for the 1973 war), is the Ramses Hilton and past that the poorer districts of Bulaq and Shubra. On the corniche here is the Television Tower Building, housing radio and television studios and the press office. Sharia Ramses runs out from the top of Midan el Tahrir and turns northeast, leading to Midan Ramses with more elevated walkways and a colossal statue of Ramses II brought from Memphis in 1955. Here you will find the Mahattat Ramses or Bab el Hadeed, the main Cairo railway station for trains north to Alexandria and south to Luxor and Aswan.

North to Midan Ramses

Downtown

Around Midan el Tahrir and along the streets radiating out from it are numerous airline offices and travel agencies, and extending into the downtown area to the northeast several less expensive hotels. This downtown area is bordered by Sharia Ramses to the northwest, Sharia Tahrir to the south and Sharia el Gumhuriya to the west. Parallel to Sharia Ramses is Sharia Champollion with the office of Thomas Cook on the left-hand side just after you leave Midan el Tahrir. Sharia Qasr el Nil heads more eastwards in the direction of the Ezbekieh Gardens, though not quite reaching that far; soon after leaving Midan el Tahrir you will find American Express on the right-hand side. Further on, this street intersects with several others at Midan Talaat Harb. Along Sharia Talaat Harb, beginning at Midan el Tahrir and ending at Midan Orabi, are numerous shops, cinemas and eating places – also along Sharias Adli and 26 July running east-west. This is the liveliest area of modern Cairo, particularly on a Thursday night, that is preceding Friday's day of rest.

Ezbekieh Gardens

Until the creation of Midan el Tahrir, the Ezbekieh Gardens were the focal point for foreign visitors. The old Shepheards Hotel stood on the corner of Sharias el Gumhuriya and Alfi at the northwest corner of the gardens; the Continental Savoy on el Gumhuriya overlooking Opera Square, which is immediately to the south of the gardens, is now a dishevelled reminder of those grand days of tourism. The Opera House mysteriously burnt down in 1971; it had been built in 1869, and the Khedive Ismail commissioned Verdi to write *Aida* to celebrate here the opening of the Suez Canal and Egypt's return to the crossroads of the world. In the event, *Aida* was late and *Rigoletto* was performed instead before a glittering international audience which included the Empress

Eugénie, wife of Napoleon III. This area around Ezbekieh, though not what it used to be, is – along with the downtown area most adjacent to it – one of the best places to stay for anyone who is serious about exploring the city on foot. It enjoys the ambivalence of being on the edge of modern Cairo and within easy walking distance of the Fatimid city to the east.

The development and layout of the medieval city has already been outlined, and the details of its sights will be provided later. Suffice to say for the purpose of orientation that if you walk along the southern flank of the Ezbekieh Gardens, past the bookstalls you will come to Midan Ataba with its central post office, open 24 hours a day. From here you can press on into the heart of the bazaar area along Sharias el Muski or al-Azhar; or if instead you leave the square along Sharia al Qalaa (formerly Sharia Mohammed Ali) running south you come to the Islamic Museum at the intersection with Sharia Port Said, and still further down you reach the Sultan Hassan Mosque and the Citadel. West of the Citadel is the Mosque of Ibn Tulun.

The Islamic City

Returning again to Midan el Tahrir for bearings, there is the Tahrir Bridge which crosses the Nile to the island of Gezira (*Gezira* is in fact Arabic for island), the El Borg Hotel on your right as you come to the island, and carrying on across its southern tip past gardens and cafés another bridge leads to the west bank of the Nile, the Sheraton on your left. (You will have guessed by now that hotels are among the principal landmarks of modern Cairo, and not only for visitors: they play an important role in the social lives of better off Egyptians, especially when throwing wedding celebrations.) The central part of Gezira is taken up with the Sporting and Racing Club, next to it rising in lotus motif the 180-metre Cairo Tower, completed in 1962. There is an open observation deck up top, and below it an enclosed coffee lounge and a restaurant of the revolving kind, said by wags to have achieved a full revolution before breaking down. There are sweeping views of the city and beyond, and this is a good place (easy too on the feet) to establish the topography of Cairo's outlying areas in your mind.

Gezira

The view from the Cairo Tower

The north part of the island is called Zamalek, a residential area with the occasional fine old home amidst leafy streets, though more often expensive apartments. This part of Gezira can be reached directly from Midan Orabi along Sharia 26 July and across an old metal bridge. Following 26 July across to the west bank of the Nile you see the suburb of Embaba, the site where Napoleon fought the so-called Battle of the Pyramids.

The Delta and Heliopolis Far to the north you can see the dark fan of the Delta. The suburb of Heliopolis is nearer, to the northeast, though the ancient site of Heliopolis is a bit to the north of it.

Below you, barges, feluccas and small motor craft pass up and down stream, the prevailing north wind giving the impression by the ripples it causes on the surface of the river that the Nile flows south – you get the same impression from the corniche – though of course it is flowing north, one of the very few rivers in the world to do so. The island to the **Roda** south is Roda with the Meridien Hotel magnificently perched like a figurehead upon its northern prow – the finest location of any hotel in Cairo. At its southern tip is a nilometer constructed by the Ummayads in 716. About as far down but **Old Cairo** on the east bank of the Nile is Old Cairo with its Coptic Museum, Coptic churches and a synagogue. Much further south is the beautiful town of Maadi, the favoured home of a large part of Cairo's foreign community, and further on still **Maadi and Helwan** the industrial town of Helwan, both on the east bank, the indiscernible remains of Egypt's ancient capital, Memphis, on the west bank opposite Helwan.

Sweeping your gaze around to east and west you see how **The Moqattam Hills** Cairo is bounded on either side by desert. The Moqattam Hills are to the east and beyond them the Arabian Plateau. On a spur of the hills is the Citadel, distinguished by the dome of the Mohammed Ali Mosque, and spread before it in dark sand-brown confusion is the old quarter of the city, as though lurking in past centuries behind the higher, more lightly dusted buildings of the new. The windows of the Nile Hilton cast a silvery cubistic pattern of setting sunlight on the river. Away to the west is the plateau of the Western Desert. Along the west bank of the Nile, opposite Gezira and south of Embaba, are the new suburbs of Agouza, Medinat el Mohandiseen (Engineer's City) and, around the Sheraton, Dokki. President Sadat had his Cairo residence in an old villa here overlooking the Nile just south of the hotel (as in the days of the monarchy, the President's summer residence is at Alexandria). Sharia el Giza runs southwards from the Sheraton **Giza** to the Zoological Gardens and Cairo University. This is Giza, here long before the suburbs began their sprawl along the west bank to the north and out towards the desert escarpment, obliterating the once extensive fields of the fellahin. From the Cairo Tower you can still make out some arable land but it is fast disappearing beneath the furious antlike progress all around you. It is best to be up in the tower at early evening as the sun sets over the Western Desert, the sharp outline of the **The Pyramids** Pyramids as ever marking the great divide between the distant haze of the void and the nearer ephemeral activity of the hive.

Itineraries

Each of the following Cairo chapters offers an itinerary, each representing a day's activity more or less, though you might prefer breaking them down into half days and perhaps combining parts of one with another for greater variety. The first is a visit to the Egyptian Museum; the second and third are walks through Islamic Cairo; and a final itinerary covers Roda, Old Cairo, Fustat and Heliopolis. No matter how you slice them, these itineraries taken all together deserve at least four full days of your time. The Pyramids at Giza, though easily visited from central Cairo (and some travellers might actually be staying near the Pyramids), begin a new sequence because of their significance as part of a long line of pyramids stretching from the Fayyum to Abu Roash at the beginning of the Desert Road to Alexandria, a journey back nearly 4000 years to the Old Kingdom.

PRACTICAL INFORMATION

ACCOMMODATION

See the *Background* chapter for general information on Egyptian hotels.

Hotel rates in Cairo are higher than elsewhere in Egypt and constant year round. The rates shown below do not include taxes or other standard charges which will add 15% to your bill, nor do they include breakfast which is obligatory. Usually, double room rates are given; in the 5- and 4-star hotels, almost all rooms are double rooms and if taken as singles will cost about 10% less than the doubles rate. In 3- to 1-star hotels doubles taken as singles may be as much as 33% cheaper than the doubles rate.

In the past there has been a shortage of hotel space in Cairo, now relieved somewhat by a massive building programme. All the same, it's best to reserve in advance if possible (see *Background* chapter). Otherwise, at Cairo Airport you should go to the Tourist Information Office or, better yet, Misr Travel, both outside the customs hall, and see if they can help (see *Information*). A useful and free publication is *Cairo by Night and Day*, containing an extensive list of hotels, their amenities and prices. You can pick up a copy at most hotels or at the Tourist Information Offices at the airport or downtown. With this you can do your own room hunting, probably running no greater risk than having to visit 2 or 3 hotels before finding something suitable. Often a hotel will volunteer, or can be prevailed upon, to phone around on your behalf, saving legwork and taxi fares.

The following is a selective list of hotels in the Cairo/Giza/Heliopolis area:

Nile Hilton (5-star), Midan el Tahrir. Tel: 740777. Telex: 92222 UN. Unless you can get a Nile-side room here you should go elsewhere; the other side overlooks a new wing of the hotel (which may still be abuilding) or the bus depot in Midan el Tahrir. The Hilton's lobby has the atmosphere of a well-equipped airport waiting lounge. Ground floor arcades have numerous tourist shops and travel offices (eg American Express and Egyptair), and a 24-hour bank. The Ibis Café is open 24 hours; the Hilton Pizzeria is excellent; there is a tavern imported stick by stick from Belgium, a first floor restaurant and a rooftop nightclub in winter which moves to the poolside in summer. Also there are tennis courts, a sauna, disco and casino. Rooms are air-conditioned and have T.V. Doubles are LE39.

Shepheard's Hotel (5-star), Corniche el Nil. Tel: 33800. Telex: 379 SHEPOT UN. Built to recapture the glory of the old Shepheard's, the new does not succeed, though it has some architectural charm and the rooms are spacious and well furnished. Those on the preferred Nile side have ceiling to floor picture windows and balconies. The 24-hour café is very comfortable; the restaurant is on the rooftop; and there's a bar, shops, and a 24-hour bank. No swimming pool. Rooms are air-conditioned. Doubles are LE30; a bit less if facing the Moqattam Hills rather than the Nile.

Meridien Hotel (5-star), Roda Island. Tel: 845444. Telex: 325 HOMER UN. The most beautifully sited of Cairo's hotels, its curved shape at the north tip of Roda permits all rooms a splendid view of the Nile (the corridors are kept to the rear). Expensively French atmosphere. Boutiques, rotisserie, 24-hour Fontana Café, Middle Eastern and European restaurants, bars, nightclubs, casino, swimming pool and 2 films a day on closed-circuit TV. In addition to the usual travel offices and 24-hour bank, there's a non-stop Reuter telex with up to the minute international news and financial reports. All rooms air-conditioned. Doubles are LE39.

Sheraton Hotel (5-star), Midan el Galaa, Dokki. Tel: 983000. Telex: 92041 SHERA UN. A 20-storey tower on the west bank of the Nile, across the Tahrir Bridge, the Sheraton compensates for its greater distance from the main sights in Cairo by its relative peacefulness, its good views and its rejection of Hiltonesque monumentality in favour of comfort and intimacy. As well as having all the luxury class features mentioned for the others (including a swimming pool), the Sheraton also offers broad panoramas from any of its well-appointed rooms: those on the east face the Nile and Cairo; on the west they look towards the distant Pyramids; on the south they take in both the Citadel and the Pyramids; on the north they look down the Nile and avoid the glare of the summer sun. The 24-hour café is excellent, and the bookshop is the best of any hotel. Egyptair has an office here, operating at a marginally lower key of pandemonium than those elsewhere in town. Rooms have TV and air conditioning. Doubles are LE39.

When wealthy or at least aspiring Egyptians get married they hold a reception at one of the big hotels. I've been to weddings at several. Everyone comes dressed to kill. Men smoking priapic Havanas, ponderous wives rolling in pink taffeta, bride and groom on flowered podium, a band playing weaving music and an unmarried guest tying a scarf round her hips and doing a votive belly dance. At the Hilton, when this phase of the reception ended, a procession wound around the ground floor lounge led by two guys in Arab headgear, long red and gold jackets, playing bagpipes. Three fat women, their enormous breasts straining against diaphanous costumes, thumping tambourines, twirling, smiling toothily at bridal couple. The groom dressed in ordinary black suit, overwhelmed and insignificant. The bride in white, a tall, large-boned but as yet unfat woman. Beaming well-wishers trail behind. They all disappear to the swimming pool.

Sheraton Heliopolis Hotel (5-star), Sharia el Orouba, Heliopolis. Tel: 861116. Telex: 93300 HELSH UN. This is newly opened, with the usual luxury facilites (though no pool). But Heliopolis is a long way from central Cairo, with poor transportation services, leaving you dependent on taxis. Doubles are LE39.

Mena House Oberoi (5-star), Sharia al-Ahram, Giza. Tel: 853789. Telex: 92316 OB UN. 11 kms from town, though linked by a regular free hotel bus service, the Mena House is convenient rather for the Pyramids (across the road) and as an edge of desert resort with golf course, riding stables and swimming pool – and with ready access to the nightlife along the Pyramids Road. Along with the old Shepheard's, this was one of the great hotels of Cairo, and the older section, decorated in Arab style and with superb views of the Pyramids, is the place to stay. A new section, Mena Gardens, has been added – with all the atmosphere of motel bungalows and less favoured views of the Pyramids. All have air conditioning, a small refrigerator, piped music and closed-circuit TV. Old wing doubles are LE39; bungalow doubles are LE31.

Jolie Ville (4-star), Alexandria Desert Road, Giza. Tel: 855510. Telex: 92567 UN. The road to Alexandria via the desert turns off just before reaching the Mena House and is rapidly turning into a hotel strip. The Jolie Ville is 12 kms from central Cairo, and you must rely on fare-charging limos, taxis or public buses. Modern bungalows are set in beautiful gardens around a pool; there are views of the Pyramids. Also there are tennis courts, a children's pool, a bar, café and good restaurant. All rooms are air-conditioned. Doubles are LE26.

El Nil Hotel (4-star), Sharia Ahmed Ragab, Garden City. Tel: 22805/9. Along the corniche, near the British Embassy. The roof restaurant and café offer fine views of the Nile. Service is poor. All rooms are air-conditioned and with bath. Doubles are LE16.

Cleopatra Palace (4-star), Midan el Tahrir. Tel: 759945. As central as you can get, and so suffering somewhat from the noise. The higher the room, the better. You enter on Sharia Bustan, on the same block and around the corner from TWA; the lobby is on the ground floor but the rooms are on the 8th through 14th floors with good day and night views of the city. All rooms are air-conditioned and have baths, though standards vary, so check your room first. Doubles are LE21.

Atlas Hotel (4-star), 2 Sharia el Gumhuriya, near Opera Midan. Tel: 918311. Telex: 92564 UN. Located in the former centre of town, before Midan el Tahrir came into being, and convenient for downtown and Islamic Cairo. There's a rooftop restaurant and nightclub; the service is good, the rooms clean and, in winter, better heated than in most older hotels. All rooms have air conditioning and TV. Doubles without bath are LE13.60; with bath, LE17.70 and up.

Continental Savoy (3-star), Opera Midan, near Ezbekieh Gardens. Tel: 911322. Like the old Shepheard's, once nearby, this was a favourite with fashionable British travellers. It has now fallen on shabby times, though once through the lobby and up to the 3 sprawling floors of rooms some of the old atmosphere is with you: cavernous corridors, large high-ceilinged rooms, wooden floors and ornate furniture. The bathrooms are being modernised. Many rooms have air conditioning. Doubles are LE11.25.

Horris (3-star), 5 Sharia 26 July. Tel: 910855. A recently renovated downtown hotel with 14th floor restaurant and clean, bright rooms, bath or shower, some with air conditioning. Doubles are LE12.20

Khan el Khalili (3-star), 7 Sharia Bosta, Midan el Ataba. Tel: 900230. Near the west end of Sharia el Muski, though still a kilometre from the heart of the Khan el Khalili bazaar, this hotel is between the old European centre and Islamic Cairo. Room standards can vary and should be checked beforehand, but generally the hotel offers good value. Doubles are LE14.75.

Windsor Hotel (3-star), 19 Sharia Alfi. Tel: 915810. Well situated in downtown Cairo, an old-style hotel in a good state of preservation with high-ceilinged rooms for ventilation, much old wooden furnishing, good atmosphere. Rooms with either shower or bath. Doubles with shower are LE13.50; with bath, LE14.70.

National Hotel (2-star), 30 Sharia Talaat Harb. Tel: 46081. An old and somewhat worn hotel, you should check out your room first, particularly the bathroom – these can sometimes be grotty. Conveniently located between Midans Talaat Harb and Tahrir. Doubles are LE3.50; with shower, LE3.85; with bath, LE4.15 and up. Rooms with a view over the back alley cost less.

New Hotel (2-star), 21 Sharia Adli. Tel: 978013. Not far from the downtown Tourist Information Office, this hotel is a cut above the National, with large, simply furnished and clean rooms – and clean bathrooms. Doubles without bath are LE5.30; with bath, LE6.

El Hussein (2-star), Midan el Hussein. Tel: 818164. In the Azhar district, the best located hotel for those wanting to be amidst the sights and atmosphere of Islamic Cairo. Café and restaurant. Double are LE6; with bath, LE8.25.

Garden City House (1-star), 23 Sharia Kamal el Din Salah. Tel: 28126. Near the new Semiramis Intercontinental, this is the best value in Cairo, and is one of the most popular and difficult places to get a room. It is best to write to Mme Georgette Scarzella, who runs this family-style hotel, a month in advance, stating precisely your requirements and date of arrival, and specifically requesting confirmation if desired. From outside there's a small sign 3 storeys up; the rooms are there and on the floor above; you take the lift. The place is well-run, clean and friendly, and the food is excellent. Some rooms face the river, most have balconies. There aren't many single rooms. Doubles are LE9.35 without bath, LE11.70 with.

Golden Hotel (1-star), 13 Sharia Talaat Harb. Tel: 41159. Well located between Midan el Tahrir and Midan Talaat Harb, the Golden Hotel has a good reputation amongst young travellers. Mr Fares Sarufim is a friendly and well-informed man, a great help in advising how to get everywhere cheaply. There's a storage room for leaving gear while travelling. Singles start at LE2, doubles at LE4, doubles with bath at LE5. Rather than turn anyone away, 'Mr. Fares' will sometimes cope with overflows by offering dorm-style accommodation at LE1 or so per person.

There are 2 **youth hostels** is the Cairo area: **El Manyal Youth Hostel,** Sharia Abdel Aziz, on Roda Island near Kobri el Gamaa (University Bridge). Tel: 840729.

Kohinoor Youth Hostel, 8 Sharia Shoukri, off Sharia al-Ahram, Giza. Tel: 852480. Hostels charge around 75PT per night but are often full.

EATING PLACES

You can spend a fortune or a few piastres on a meal in Cairo, and choose between the world's cuisines. For notes on Egyptian food, see the *Background* chapter. Not only restaurants, but coffee shops, tea rooms and snack bars are included here; though places which also provide entertainment will be found under the *Entertainment* heading further on.

Western-style food is served at all the hotels, regardless of category. Only the restaurants at a few major hotels, however, are worth going out of your way to dine at. The Sheraton's *Aladin* (Tel: 983000) and the Meridien's *La Palme d'Or* (French cuisine) (Tel: 845444) are the best, meals starting at LE12. The *Swissair Restaurant* (Tel: 981487), a short walk south of the Sheraton along Sharia el Nil, has an expensive formal restaurant upstairs, a less expensive informal restaurant downstairs where a good meal (French cuisine, some Swiss specialities) will cost from LE8. Reservations are recommended at each of these restaurants. More moderately-priced Western-style food is found at the following:

Caroll, 12 Sharia Qasr el Nil, off Midan Talaat Harb. Reckoned by foreign residents in Cairo to be the best Western-style restaurant, Caroll's is small and congenial, with consistently good service and food, and generous portions. Entrées start at around LE3.50.

Estoril, 12 Sharia Talaat Harb, in a passageway running to Sharia Qasr el Nil, near American Express. An older restaurant, a bit threadworn in its gentility, with an interesting clientele. Entrées start at LE3, with less expensive daily specials.

Groppi, Midan Talaat Harb. An interwar Cairo institution, now refurbished and recapturing its reputation for quiet gentility. There is also a café here where you can spend hours reading the papers, writing letters, enjoying Viennese coffee and delicious pastries. At either, you are served impeccably and unobstrusively. The food is good, the prices too, with entrées starting at LE2.50..

Specialty restaurants offer one fare, with variations, though alternatives may be available:

Kasr el Rachid, Meridien Hotel, Roda. Extremely expensive but delicious Middle Eastern dishes. In the evenings there is an oriental buffet, costing around LE11 per person. Reservations recommended. Tel: 845444.

The Farm, 23 Sharia Maryutia, off Sharia al-Ahram (Pyramids Road) – signposted. Rustic setting, though fashionable and moderately expensive. The speciality is roast lamb. Food and service are excellent. Reservations recommended, Tel: 851870.

Vue des Pyramides, at the southeast corner of the Pyramids Road/Alexandria Desert Road junction. Casual outdoor dining, with Cheops' Pyramid close by. The speciality is grilled and fried fish, though there are meat and non-meat dishes too. Entrées from LE1.75. Very pleasant garden atmosphere, especially recommended towards sundown.

Pizzeria, Hilton Hotel, Midan el Tahrir. The atmosphere is pleasant, the food good and not too expensive. Pastas and pizzas start at LE2, entrées at LE2.50. Wine, beer, dessert and coffee will be extra.

Taverna, 3 Sharia Alfi, near Midan Orabi. Principally Cypriot, though other dishes too. A complete meal from about LE2.50. Their speciality is shrimp.

Indian Tea Centre, off the passageway at 23 Sharia Talaat Harb. Primarily a place to come for tea and an afternoon snack, but also serving light meals in the early evening. A curry with rice, soup and fried bread will cost about LE1.50.

Sofar, 21 Sharia Adli. Syrian and Lebanese specialities, though short on atmosphere. Entrées from about LE1.75.

Egyptian-style restaurants do not usually impress from the outside, and may not be very atmospheric inside; they are to be judged by their fare, which is a mixture of native tradition and Egyptian versions of Turkish, Levantine, Greek, Italian and French cuisine. Some of the better places follow:

Abu Shakra, 69 Sharia Qasr el Aini, at the south end, about 3 kms from Midan el Tahrir, near the bridge crossing over to Roda at the Manyal Palace. The epitome of its type, in marble and alabaster – also a strict Moslem establishment, serving no alcoholic beverages and closed Fridays and during Ramadan. The specialities are kofta and kebab, costing around LE2, though sometimes pigeon and grilled chicken are also available. Usually (though not always) the food is excellent.

El Dahan, in Khan el Khalili, next door to the El Hussein Hotel. Also specialising in kofta and kebab. Not so much to be searched out, as to dine at if you are already wandering about the bazaar.

El Shimy, 45 Midan Orabi. Friendly atmosphere and varied Egyptian menu. Meals from LE2.50.

El Hatti, 8 Midan Halim, behind the Cicurel department store on Sharia 26 July, and virtually next door to the Horris Hotel. Unusually for an Egyptian restaurant, El Hatti sparkles –

mirrors cover the walls and brilliant chandeliers hang from the high ceiling. The service, food and atmosphere all make this a worthwhile place to search for. Kebab costs around LE2, but the speciality here is roast lamb at around LE2.50.

Fatarane el Tahrir, 166 Sharia el Tahrir, 2 blocks from Midan el Tahrir and on the right. The sole meal is *feteer,* a kind of pancake filled with your choice of meat, cheese, eggs, nuts, etc. Cost depends on size and filling, with LE1 the maximum.

Filfila, 15 Sharia Hoda Sharawi, off Midan el Tahrir. You pass through the kitchen at the front and into the garden, taking your seat around a slice of tree trunk serving as a table. The specialty is fool, in all its varieties of preparation. This will cost no more than 50PT, though meat dishes are more, and a pair of quail running to LE3. Alas, the place is very popular with tourist groups and is sometimes overwhelmed by the busload.

Coffee shops, tea rooms and drink and snack bars abound, convenient for resting, cooling off and perhaps a light meal during the day:

The cafés in the major hotels have the advantage of being open 24 hours; also, they are air-conditioned. There is a minimum: LE1.50 to LE2. The **Fontana Café** at the Meridien is marvellous for its Nile views, while the **Arous el Nil** in the Sheraton does the best hamburgers and shakes. The Hilton's **Isis Coffee Shop,** though conveniently situated, will disappoint the connoisseur. On the other hand, the Hilton does get credit for its **Taverne du Champ de Mars,** a fin de siècle Brussels tavern, dismantelled and reconstructed on the ground floor of the hotel. Beer, spirits and snacks are served from noon to 2am.

Numerous **cafés line the banks of the Nile** on Roda and Gezira islands. These are garden affairs, where beer, tea, sandwiches and snacks are served. Otherwise:

Cairo Tower, Gezira island. Coffee, tea, beer, a snack are all available up top, at a slight surcharge for having got it up there, but the atmosphere it pleasant, the views wonderful.

Brazilian Coffee Shop, 38 Sharia Talaat Harb and 12 Sharia 26 July. Open from 7am to midnight, this is where to come if you care about coffee. The beans are freshly ground (unground beans can be taken away), the espresso, cappucino, café au lait – or almost any other way of drinking coffee – are excellent.

L'Americaine, corner of Sharias Talaat Harb and 26 July. A large stand-up restaurant, serving coffee, juices, pastries and ice cream.

The Indian Tea Centre, already mentioned under specialty restaurants – this is principally a tea room, with imported Indian teas and Indian-style pastries.

Groppi, already mentioned under Western-style restaurants, the café is excellent in taste, price and atmosphere. A patisserie and confisserie, for taking your sweets away with you, adjoins (though Egyptian chocolate is not very good). There is another Groppi, usually called **Garden Groppi** to distinguish it from the original, opening onto Sharia Adli at the Midan el Opera end. In addition to the café, there's a delicatessen here too, selling cold cuts, pastas, jams and bottles of wine.

Lappas, 17 Sharia Qasr el Nil, is a Groppi-like place of Groppi-like vintage, popular amongst those who don't want to be disturbed.

Café Riche, on Sharia Talaat Harb near the midan and next to the Brazilian Coffee Shop at No. 38, with a nondescript indoor restaurant (very cheap) and an outdoor café, frequented by Cairo's literati and where Nasser, Sadat and other officers met while planning the 1952 coup.

In wandering around the streets, either in modern or Islamic Cairo, you will encounter numerous simple establishments for having a snack, even a meal, and certainly a refreshing mint tea (5PT maximum). There are also peripatetic street-vendors, good for drinks though perhaps less so for food which may not be particularly clean. In buying anything to eat, always be sure the place has running water – if so, a modicum of hygiene can be counted upon. Cokes and, even moreso, 7-Ups are expensive; instead pause for guava, mango, orange, sugar cane or strawberry juice (after you've drunk it you scoop the strawberries from the glass with a spoon). Or have a *koshary,* a mixed dish of rice, beans, macaroni, with various spices and sauces, usually hot (you can say no), sprinkled on. One koshary place, mentioned here by way of introduction to the dish and because its appearance is reassuringly clean and modern (before you get accustomed to sampling the fare in more uncompromising places) is the **Lux,** Sharia 26 July near the intersection with Sharia Sherif. You can have a meal here for 20PT. Finally, the café to go to when wandering round Khan el Khalili is the famous **Fishawi's** in a small alley near the Sayyidna Hussein Mosque.

ENTERTAINMENT

Nightclubs catering to a preponderantly Arab clientele will keep to an oriental show, ie one or more belly dancers, an Egyptian singer and several variety acts. But at places which cater also, even mainly, to Western tourists (the major hotels and the nightclubs along the Pyramids Road and in the desert), a belly dancer will share the bill with Western acts. The Sheraton, Meridien, Hilton and Mena House Oberoi all have combined oriental/Western shows, with the Sheraton's **Aladin** nightclub usually presenting the best belly dancer in town. Shows start at around 11pm, but dinner may be served as early as 9.30. Reservations are recommended. The night will prove expensive, with cover charge, drinks and obligatory dinner probably coming to LE15-LE20 per person. The Hilton's **Belvedere** offers a buffet twice a week, costing around LE8 per person, drinks and service probably adding on another LE4-LE5. So what do you get for your money?

Went to the Belvedere *on roof of Hilton to check out the topflight entertainment and decor. They say it's designed to look as Cairo was when Napoleon conquered. Looked like Pasadena to me. First and last a French ya-ya group, competent enough to have been the losers of the Eurovision Song Contest. Then the belly dancer, long hennaed hair and technically superb, but something missing — that sensual response to the music and the audience, though maybe she had it and didn't show it, for what was really lacking was response in the audience, all Westerners or Uncle Tom Arabs.*

For more of this, in different surroundings, go to the Omar Khayyam – not the nightclub in the hotel of that name, but the **Bateau Omar Khayyam,** a fine old houseboat tied up by the Sporting Club at Gezira. Cosy, with agreeable oriental decor, perfect for dining quietly on the Nile – except that a rock band shatters all tranquility between belly dancing sets. Of course, if you came for the rock band, that's fine.

And still more, but now in overblown Las Vegas style: **Auberge des Pyramides** on the Pyramids Road, and **Sahara City** in a desert tent beyond the Pyramids. There are many others out this way, all neon signposted and advertised (see under *Information* below), and also several in town, eg **Salt and Pepper,** at the end of Sharia Abul Feda, at the northern tip of Gezira island – dark and loud, with a band, a dance floor and a belly dancer.

I prefer the strictly Arab places, though the performances can be uneven, or downright bad. There is, for example, the **New Arizona** in Sharia Alfi, with millionth-rate belly dancers, fat and ugly, though often a good Egyptian singer and on one occasion a marvellously laid back and funny finger-cymbal player. Dinner (not obligatory) costs around LE4; otherwise it will cost about LE2 to get in and LE2 for a drink. Quite a few notches up is the **Scheherazade,** also in Sharia Alfi, near Midan Orabi. It's a bit more expensive than the New Arizona, and a half bottle of whiskey or similar expenditure will get you a front seat.

The audience is predominantly Arab, and these are almost all men, though a few women and even children may be present. A few Europeans are there and bring their women: a great mistake since these now sit prune-faced throughout the performance. First a series of singers and bands from all over the Islamic world, oriental and African rhythms, wailing and plaintive drone of male singers, marvellous squeaky violins, tinkling harpsichords, also flutes, bass, tambourines. Belly dancer comes on, dead ringer for Rita Hayworth. Less squeaks and tinkles; now there are deep strokes of violins, pulsation of drums, the low hum of the saxaphone. No bumps and grinds to detract from a performance of incredible sensuality, a slow motion of sea waves and sand dunes, the slightest flick on orgasm.

The Arab audience takes it generally with a warm, contained appreciation. The odd whistle, applause, a shout at some particular movement of the hips — or a shout sometimes when there is no movement: when almost nothing happens and she is at her most erotic. The perfectly still position: arms arabesqued, one leg extended, the hips at an angle, a continuous ripple running up and down her body and then one flank is gyrated ever so slightly, like the minimal, most controlled movement of a toreador before the horns of the bull. The music stops, the band claps in a flamenco rhythm, Arab after Arab comes up on the stage with gifts of flowers, flower necklaces, glasses of whiskey (which she knocks back in mid-movement), cigarettes and money, every one of them a desert king, but she is master of their fantasies.

Fire-breathers, circuses, puppet shows, belly dancers: this Arab patronage of the popular mysteries. And so, after this dance, with as much attention as it had accorded to the former, the audience watches a dull Lebanese riding a bicycle across a wire 5 feet above the stage.

At **discos** you skip live entertainment, Western or oriental, and twitch instead to the vibrating recorded music. The two best places for this are the **Saddle Room** at the Mena

House Oberoi, and **After Eight,** 6 Sharia Qasr el Nil, a popular place where reservations are recommended. (Tel: 43455), closed July and August.

Casinos (admission only to non-Egyptians) are found at the Meridien, the Sheraton and the Hilton. Play is in US dollars, free drinks for punters, doors close at dawn.

Concerts and theatrical events with Western content are often sponsored by the Egyptian Ministry of Culture in cooperation with the cultural sections of one or other of the foreign embassies. The **Oum Khalsoum Theatre,** Sharia el Nil, at Agouza, just south of the Zamalek bridge, has nightly performances (October-March) in Arabic by local music and dance companies, mostly folkloric.

Cinemas are mostly located around Midans Talaat Harb and Orabi, and several are likely to be showing English-language films, subtitled in Arabic. The *Egyptian Gazette* carries listings. The problem is that the Egyptians, being able to read the subtitles, don't have to listen to the dialogue. Instead the audience chatters throughout the film, which often has its sound turned down anyway, so that you'll be lucky to hear much of it – perhaps not so important when considering the entertainment potential of the audience. Tickets are cheap, well under LE1, and all seats are reserved. You should buy your tickets several hours in advance of the performance you intend seeing, as seats go very quickly.

It is the **popular mysteries** – the man staging a backstreet show with a snake and a guinea pig or a marriage procession of loud cries and ribald song strolling down the middle of a road – that are most entertaining in Cairo. Two fixtures appealing at this level are the **Egyptian National Circus,** a good one-ring affair usually found at Agouza, south of the Zamalek bridge; and the **Cairo Puppet Theatre** in Ezbekieh Gardens, its season from October to May, with nightly performances at 6.30 as well as Friday and Sunday shows at 11am. The puppet shows are in Arabic, which hardly matters as it's easy to follow the action, and which anyway adds to the enchantment of the productions, appealing to adults and children alike.

It's probably best to approach the son et lumiere at the Pyramids on this level too, therefore so much the better if you go to the Arabic programme, not an English-language one. The **Sound and Light** show (say this to a taxi driver and you'll be taken straight there) starts at 7.30pm; there is no performance on Friday. Usually, English-language programmes are on Mondays, Wednesdays and Saturdays. The Arabic programme is on Thursday. There are also programmes in French and German. Tickets are LE2. Seating for the Sound and Light is facing the Sphinx; if you don't go by taxi, you can take the 800 or 900 bus from Midan el Tahrir, terminating at the Mena House Oberoi, and then backtrack on foot through the village at the edge of the escarpment, a 15 minutes walk – though you can shorten the hike by getting off the bus along the Pyramids Road when you see (on your left) the sign for the Sound and Light, about 1000 metres before the Mena House Hotel.

After all that high- and low-lifing, you might like some recreation. You can have a game of **tennis** at the Gezira Sporting Club: the courts (clay) are hired out to non-members. **Swimming pools** are open to non-residents at the Mena House and the Meridien for a fee, and to non-members at the Gezira Sporting Club.

SHOPPING

While shopping at the bazaar stalls is a matter of haggling over prices, shops and department stores in the modern part of Cairo sell at **fixed prices.** Except in shops found in the arcades of major hotels, prices are usually marked in Arabic numerals (see *Background* chapter), and are often stated in piastres (100PT = LE1). So an item priced at 1000 is likely to be 1000PT or LE10. Usually, common sense will tell whether piastres or pounds is intended.

Opening hours for most shops are from 9.30 or 10am to 1 or 1.30pm, and from 4.30 or 5pm to 7.30 or 8pm, though some may remain open continuously throughout the day, particularly in Khan el Khalili. Most are closed Saturday evenings and Sundays, while some may close on Fridays. During Ramadan, shops hours are likely to be from 9.30am to 3.30pm and from 8 to 10pm or even later.

In the bazaars, price is usually what you agree on after a bout of **bargaining.** A stallkeeper will always ask more than he expects to get; the traditional response is to offer half as much. After several minutes, perhaps half an hour, a price midway between the extremes is agreed. That is the traditional way, but the visitor's impatience or foolishness can spoil the market, traders asking for and getting far more than their goods are worth. This is particularly true of hawkers at places like the Pyramids, and every now and again it's worth making a ridiculous counter-offer, perhaps only one-tenth of the asking price...and finding it immediately accepted.

Hawkers at tourist sights are taking advantage of their isolation and yours in demanding exhorbitant amounts. The virtue of a bazaar is that there is plenty of competition. In Khan el Khalili you'll find all the copperware, all the spices, all the wood and ivory inlay, etc., in the same area, and you should browse around, examining the goods, asking the prices, getting a feel for the market. Try to be dispassionate; the more you want something the more you are likely to pay for it. A good technique is to bargain first over something you *don't* want and then casually to start bargaining over what you do want – almost as though you didn't want anything and just bargained for the sport. It *is* a sport, and there are rules as well as tricks of the game. Your first extreme counter-offer will be laughed at and you may feel silly; don't worry, that's part of the game. After a few offers and counter-offers, walk out. If the shop or stall owner stops you, it means he thinks there's still a deal to be made; if he doesn't, you may have learnt you're aiming at too low a price – go back later, or go to another shop, with an adjusted view of the item's worth. The essence of a bargain, of course, is not to arrive at some formula fraction of the original asking price, but to feel that you have paid the right price, a price you could not have bettered elsewhere, a price that makes the item worth it to you.

Clothing will be found in the hotel shops, shops in the downtown area (Sharias Talaat Harb and 26 July, for example), boutiques in Zamelek, Heliopolis and downtown, and in the big department stores: **Chemla,** 11 Sharia 26 July, where low prices are more important than quality; **Cicurel,** 3 Sharia 26 July, for quality and higher prices; **Omar Effendi,** a good department store with several branches – on Sharia Talaat Harb just off Midan el Tahrir, on Sharia Adli near Sharia Talaat Harb, and also at Heliopolis and Dokki. Sizes are continental.

Shoes are found in the plethora of shoeshops along Sharias Qasr el Nil, Talaat Harb and 26 July.

The **galabiyya,** the full-length traditional garment of Egyptian men, is popular with both male and female visitors as comfortable casual wear. Fancier versions can also serve as evening wear for women. There are three basic styles: the *baladi* or peasant style, with wide sleeves and a low rounded neckline; the *saudi* style, more form-fitting, with a high-buttoned neck and cuffed sleeves; and the *efrangi* or foreign style, looking like a shirt with collar and cuffs but reaching all the way down to the floor. Several shops sell galabiyyas along Sharia Talaat Harb between Midan Talaat Harb and Sharia 26 July, and also the department stores. Fancier ones are at **Ammar,** 26 Sharia Qasr el Nil, and at **Atlas** in Khan el Khalili. Both are fixed price. Atlas is on Sharia Badestan which is reached by walking north along the main Fatimid street (Sharia Muizz which goes from Bab Zuwayla to Bab al-Futuh), passing across Sharia al-Azhar and across Sharia el Muski (properly known here as Sharia Gohar el Qaid), until you see a narrow alley on your right, marked by two upright metal poles rising about a metre out of the ground: turn into it, and when it ends turn right and then left. You are now on Sharia Badestan, a main street of the bazaar, but dark and so narrow it's closed to cars. Along the left is Atlas. Mrs Sadat is known to buy her evening wear here; for all the difficulty of reaching it deep in the bazaar, the place has an international reputation.

Fabric, either for galabiyyas (Atlas and other good stores will tailor-make them for you, either from their own or your fabric) or to take home, is found in variety and quality at **Omar Effendi** (see *Clothing* above); **Salon Vert,** Sharia Qasr el Nil; or **Ouf** in el Mashhad el Hussein – heading south along Sharia Muizz and approaching Sharia al-Azhar, take the first right after Sharia el Muski/Sharia Gohar el Qaid and the first left; Ouf is on the right down this alley. Each of these stores also sell off-the-peg galabiyyas.

Weavings, carpets, tents and tapestries require further adventures if you want the best. In fact, Egypt is not particularly well-known for carpets, and if you are going to Aswan you should look around there first for small rugs and weavings. Old rugs are from time to time auctioned off, and you should look in the *Egyptian Gazette* for announcements. Carpets and rugs are found in Khan el Khalili and al **El Fatarani** and **Kazarouni,** both on Sharia Qasr el Nil.

Tent-making, on the other hand, is a Cairene Speciality, and you should go to the **Street of the Tentmakers** immediately south of Bab Zuwayla. There are 6 or 7 workshops along this covered section of medieval Cairo's major north-south street, creating beautiful applique tents used at mosques or street festivals (and funerals). Some are decorated with scenes of pharaonic or Islamic themes, but the best have abstract arabesque designs or intricate calligraphy. Not that you have to buy a tent; they are made in sections and you can buy a piece about big enough to serve as a pillow cover.

Two village outside Cairo are centres of the best tapestry-weaving in Egypt. **Harraniyya,** about 3 kms along the canal road from Giza to Saqqara, was developed by the late Ramses Wissa Wassef; he taught the children how to card, dye and spin their own wool, and weave it into tapestries of their own design, usually village scenes, primitive and boldly coloured. Harraniyya's tapestries are now world-famous, and the workshop, on the right of the road, continues to be run by Wassef's wife. Tapestries cannot actually be bought here, however; for that you must go to **Senouhi,** 54 Sharia Abdel Khalek Sarwat, 5th floor, in downtown Cairo. This is also one of the best places to buy jewellery and (genuine) antiques. The other village is **Kardassa,** about 3 kms off Sharia al-Ahram (turn right several hundred metres before the Mena House at the Pyramids, at the sign for Andrea's Restaurant). Here you can buy tapestries, and also bedspreads, rugs, shirts, dresses and (imported from Sinai) black Bedouin dresses with bright cross-stitching – usually old, with a patchwork look after repairs, and becoming quite expensive and rare.

There are numerous **jewellery** shops is Sharia Abdel Khalek Sarwat (near Groppi) and in the small street leading off it, Sikket el Manakh. And of course, there are numerous jewellers in Mouski and Khan el Khalili. By and large, Egyptian jewellery is disappointing, much of it mimicking the more obvious pharaonic motifs (cartouche, ankh, Eye of Horus), and those of Islamic motif showing little popular imagination – hands and eyes for warding off evil, or pieces inscribed with 'Allah'. It may seem at first exotic but is limited and grows tiresome, while anything outside these two motifs is usually conceived in bad taste. **Senouhi,** 54 Sharia Abdel Khalek Sarwat, 5th floor, will have the finest selection.

Brass and copper work has long been a Cairo tradition, the standards still high today. The best place for it is in Khan el Khalili along or just off Sharia Muizz, south of the Madrasa of Qalaun. Small plates intended as ornaments and candlesticks, gongs, lamps, mugs and pitchers are the easiest to carry off – though be sure that anything you intend to drink out of it coated on the inside with another metal, like silver, as brass or copper in contact with some substances can be highly poisonous. The finest items, however, are the big brass trays which can serve as table tops (wooden stands are available).

Inlay of **wood and ivory,** and also **leatherwork,** are also plentiful in the bazaar. Egyptian leather is not the best, however. The most common items are handbags, suitcases and hassocks. Also, more interesting than useful or comfortable, are camel saddles (for buying a camel, see below). Wooden trays, boards (including backgammon and chess boards) and boxes inlaid with ivory, mother of pearl and coloured bits of wood are not quite as good as those made in Syria, but are intricate and beautiful enough. Mashrabiyyas, those intricate screens found in old Cairene houses, made from bits of wood fitted together without nails or glue, occasionally come on sale in the bazaars; you'll almost certainly find it at the **Wakala (or Okel) of el Ghouri** near al-Azhar which is also a craft centre.

Muski **glass,** usually turquoise or dark brown and recognisable by its numerous air bubbles, has been hand-blown in Cairo since the Middle Ages, and is now turned out as ash trays, candlesticks and glasses. It's inexepnsive, but also very fragile. The best **nargilehs** (hubbly-bubblies) will have glass, rather than brass, bottoms. For these, try around the Street of the Coppersmiths, south of the Madrasa of Qalaun, and for glass visit the Wakala of el Ghouri.

Alabaster statuettes, also vases and scarabs, are produced and are cheapest in Luxor; **baskets** made of palm fronds are best bought in the Fayyum, though platter-shaped basketry, woven in brilliant colours, should be sought in Luxor or Aswan. **Aswan** also is excellent for woven fabrics, for ivory, ebony and spices, and indeed it has the best bazaar outside of Cairo.

Antiquities offered to you on the street are bound to be fake. Which is not to say there aren't any genuine pharaonic, Coptic and Islamic artefacts around, but they will cost a lot of money and your only guarantee of their authenticity is to buy them from a shop displaying a **licence from the Department of Antiquities.** The shop will also give you a certificate of authenticity. There are several such shops in modern Cairo and in Khan el Khalili; the best is the already-mentioned **Senouhi,** 54 Sharia Abdel Khalek Sarwat, downtown. There are more shops in **Luxor,** with prices lower than in Cairo.

One of the most enjoyable excusions, whether you intend to buy or not, is to wander through the **spice market** which lies off Sharia Muizz between Sharia el Muski (Sharia Gohar el Qaid) and Sharia al-Azhar. There are bottles of perfume essences, boxes of incense and bags of herbs and spices. Also there is kohl, a black eye cosmetic. The fragrances, and the quality of the light in awninged alleyways, awaken sensation.

A similarly enjoyable excursion (though the fragrance is not the same) is to the **camel bazaar,** northwest of the city just beyond Embaba. In Arabic it is the *Souk el Gimaal,* where camel herders from the Sudan bring their animals for sale, and farmers bring their horses, donkeys, goats and other livestock. The market is every Friday and starts very early: get there by 7 or 8am. You cross over to the west bank of the Nile and head north along the corniche (Sharia el Nil), going past the 26 July Bridge until you come to a square. Here you turn left, away from the river, following Sharia Sudan for several kilometres. After a housing estate on your left (built for felaheen pouring into Cairo), a road goes off to the right across railway tracks. Take this, and immediately after crossing the tracks turn left. You'll parallel a walled-in area on your right and soon meet up with people and animals heading for the market. Eventually, a road to your left crosses railway tracks again; take this and then immediately turn right. The market entrance will be on your left.

Books on Egypt and Egyptology, but also light holiday reading in paperback, are found in the major hotel bookshops, which also sell magazines and newspapers. The best hotel for this is the **Sheraton.** There is also the shop in the **Egyptian Museum.** Other bookshops around town are: **Lehnert and Landrock,** 44 Sharia Sherif, near Sharia Adli – English though principally German books on Egypt, while magazines and paperbacks are almost all German. They also sell (under their own imprint) the excellent Kuemmerly + Frey map of Egypt. And they do a map of Cairo, no better than the one issued free by the Tourist Office, except that it does have the virtue of a street index. **Librairie Mengozzi,** 19 Sharia 26 July, near the intersection of Sharia Talaat Harb. A good selection of English, French and Italian paperbacks. **Reader's Corner,** 33 Sharia Abdel Khalek Sarwat, downtown, with English, French and some German books. **Madbouly,** Midan Talaat Harb, with English, French and some German books downstairs. Also in Midan Talaat Harb is **Hachette** for French books. Between Shepheard's Hotel and the British Embassy along the corniche is the **Garden City Bookstore.** In Zamalek is the **Shady Bookstore,** Sharia 26 July near Sharia Hassan Sabri. Bookstalls line the south side of the **Ezbekieh Gardens,** selling mostly Arabic books but sometimes second-hand foreign language books, with the possibility of an occasional 'find'. Bargaining is necessary.

OF INTEREST

Places of major interest are described in the main chapter texts throughout this Guide. However, in the *Practical Information* sections following each chapter, the *Of Interest* listings will carry further details on major sights as well as mention other sights of interest not covered in the main text. Also, a helpful feature in the *Of Interest* column following each chapter will be **abbreviated itineraries** for those with limited time.

INFORMATION

There are **Tourist Information Offices** at the airport (Tel: 966475), downtown (head office) at 5 Shari Adli (Tel: 923000) and at the Pyramids on Sharia al-Ahram (Tel: 850259). They can provide brochures, a good free map of Cairo (with practical information on the reverse) and copies of *Cairo by Night and Day,* filled with listings of hotels, restaurants, entertainments, travel agents, embassies, etc.

The people working at their offices are charming and helpful (most helpful is the head office), but they are used to tourists going to the obvious places by the slickest means, and so have to be pressed for alternative information. If you don't want a tour, don't want to take taxis everywhere, then make it clear that you don't mind taking the local bus or train to Amarna, Meidum, Saqqara, Wadi Natrun, etc., and they'll come up with the information you require.

It would be nice if the Tourist Information Office at the **airport** could pick up the phone and check with hotels in town for room availability. Alas, the Cairo telephone system is hopelessly antiquated and overburdened (though Siemens has now won a contract to modernise it), and only rarely can telephone contact be established between airport and town. You might have more luck with Misr Travel. Both have desks outside the airport customs hall.

The **Tourist Police** are found browsing about ports of entry, in the bazaars and at tourist sights, and are recognised by a small blue strip on their left chest and a green armband with 'Tourist Police' written in Arabic and English. Otherwise they wear the normal police uniform, which is black in winter and white in summer. They usually speak at least 2 foreign languages and are helpful with information while doing their best to ensure that tourists are not fleeced (see taxis under the *Travel* listings). They are based at the airport

(Tel: 965239), at the Midan Ramses railway station (Tel: 753555), at the Pyramids (Tel: 58458), in Khan el Khalili (Tel: 904827) and on Sharia Adli (Tel: 912644).

A useful source of information, as well as a brief up to date review of the news, is the *Egyptian Gazette* (published as the *Egyptian Mail* on Saturdays), Cairo's daily English-language **newspaper.** (In French there are 2 dailies, *Le Progres Egyptien* and *Journal d'Egypte.*). The *Gazette's* 'What's On' columns will tell you of current and forthcoming concerts, gallery shows, films, etc., both in Cairo and in Alexandria, while its 'Round and About' columns list opening times at museums and tourist sights in Cairo, Alexandria and Luxor, and may also tell you that barbers are normally closed on Mondays, while butchers don't sell meat on Mondays, Tuesdays and Wednesdays. There are also cinema, restaurant, nightclub and travel advertisements; television and radio listings; temperatures up and down the country; foreign community church services; and horoscopes – "A romantic interlude adds interest and excitement to an otherwise mundane day. Be ready with answers at evening" (Aquarius).

Your own **hotel desk** or those at the major hotels, as well as such **travel agents** as Thomas Cook and American Express, and your own **embassy** can all be useful sources of varied information.

TRAVEL

The general information here on Cairo travel is supplemented by further details in subsequent chapters.

There are 3 ways of getting from the **airport into Cairo.** The first is to take the **public bus** (No. 400 – in Arabic numerals); the stop about 70 metres directly across from the arrivals building and the fare is 15PT to Midan Ramses or Midan el Tahrir, with a few stops along the way. From 7am to midnight departures are every half hour on the hour and half hour; from midnight to 7am it departs only on the hour. When travelling *to* the airport, catch the bus in Midan el Tahrir (same departure times and frequencies) at the furthest bus shelter from the Hilton. You should allow 1½ hours for the journey to be on the safe side. At rush hours (morning, evening and from 2 to 4pm) you may not get a seat. The second way is to take an airport **limousine** from immediately outside the arrivals building; to central Cairo the fare will be about LE4 and a bit more if to Dokki or Giza. These limos are comfortable Mercedes. The third way is to take a **taxi.** The driver will almost certainly try to avoid using his meter, and though the fare should be no greater than for the limo, he will probably demand more. Don't give it to him. (For how to deal with taxi drivers, see below.)

The cheapest way of getting about **within and around Cairo** is by **public bus.** Fares are rarely more than 4PT, usually less. They are usually very crowded, and Cairenes are adept at boarding and exiting through the windows as often as through the doors. They are fun to watch at Midan el Tahrir (where nearly all buses originate and terminate), and quite an experience to ride. From near the Hilton you can catch the No.66 to Khan el Khalili and the No.72 to Midan Salah al-Din (for the Sultan Hassan Mosque and the Citadel). From the far south end of Midan el Tahrir by the Mugamaa you can catch the No.800 or 900 to the Pyramids, departing every 10 minutes. The numbers are on the front of the buses in Arabic.

Also there is the **metro** from Bab el Luk station, a short walk from Midan el Tahrir east along Sharia Mohammed Mahmud. This will take you south to Old Cairo (Mari Girgis stop) and on to Maadi and Helwan. First class to Old Cairo is about 4PT at the station, a couple of piastres more on the train.

In theory, **taxis** are a very cheap way of getting around Cairo. Unfortunately, Cairo taxi drivers hold to an opposite theory when giving rides to tourists. There are 2 types of taxi: metered and unmetered. Unmetered taxis are government-licenced and the driver is free to set his own fare. If you get into one of these (recognisable by a medallion on each side of the taxi), agree the fare first. Occasionally you will get into a metered taxi and the driver will actually turn the meter on, in which case you pay accordingly. For example, I have gone from Old Cairo to downtown Cairo (5 kms) for 40PT. But more often than not the driver will 'forget' to turn his meter on, or say it is broken, or simply refuse to do so. There is no point in arguing about this as you start off, or even drawing it to the driver's attention. Take your ride and then pay him according to the following scale: from Midan el Tahrir to Zamalek, Khan el Khalili or Midan Ramses (2 to 2.5 kms), 50PT; from Midan el Tahrir to Old Cairo (4 to 4.5 kms), LE1; from Midan el Tahrir to the Pyramids (11 kms), LE2. You can feel generous in knowing you are paying about double the proper fare. Your driver, of course, will have a fit. You then make noises about calling the police. Your driver will then calm down, but even if he doesn't, ignore him. There is another rule of thumb, a costlier one, but which might reduce the ructions, and that is to pay a flat LE1 for any ride within Cairo. LE1 is the magic sum that taxi drivers expect from tourists, and sometimes, as when the taxi has queued at Ramses Station and taken you with all your baggage to your hotel (however near), it seems fair enough.

A word about **taxis and the Tourist Police:** when leaving the airport, and sometimes when leaving hotels and major tourist sights, the Tourist Police will check the taxi's number, your identity and your destination, virtually ensuring that you will arrive in good order. The taxi driver may still try to hustle you on principle, but you know that your position has been reinforced.

If travelling extensively in and around Cairo and further afield, it could be worthwhile **hiring a car.** Remember that you will need an International Driver's Licence and a sense of adventure: Cairenes especially have little road-sense, meandering from side to side as the fancy takes them. and the only way to survive is to meander with them. For a few pounds more you can hire a car with driver.

Avis is the internationally-known company most in evidence, while **Bita** is a reliable and less expensive local outfit. They both rent Fiats as economy models, Peugeots in the medium range and Mercedes at the top. Rates are around LE8 per day and 8PT per km for a Fiat 128, LE12 per day and 12PT per km for a Peugeot 504, and LE16 per day and 16PT per km for a Mercedes 230. Insurance and waiver charges plus a 10% tax are on top of that; a chauffeur will cost about LE4 per 10-hour day extra. You will probably have to reserve at least a day in advance. **Avis** has offices at the Hilton, Meridien, Sheraton and Sheraton Heliopolis hotels and at Cairo Airport, while **Bita's** office is at 15 Sharia Mahmoud Bassiouni, off Midan Talaat Harb, with also an airport branch.

The alternative to public transport or car hire are **tours by car or bus with guide.** There are morning, afternoon and evening tours to the Antiquities Museum, the Pyramids and Sphinx, Memphis and Saqqara, Islamic Cairo, Old Cairo, Cairo by night with nightclub, etc. **Thomas Cook,** 4 Sharia Champollion, just off Midan el Tahrir (Tel: 743698), has a comprehensive list of tours by car with driver/guide. The more passengers, the less expensive per person. **American Express,** 15 Sharia Qasr el Nil, a short walk from Midan el Tahrir (Tel: 753142), and with branches at the Nile Hilton, Meridien and Sheraton hotels, does coach tours which for 1 or 2 people will work out about 40% cheaper than Cook's tours.

These companies also offer **tours throughout Egypt by rail or air.** American Express, for example, offer tours by rail to Alexandria, and by rail or air to Luxor, or to Luxor and Aswan combined, with an optional excursion to Abu Simbel. And by request, tours by car can be arranged to the Suez Canal towns and to the Fayyum. You may find lower prices and some additional destinations, eg Hurghada on the Red Sea, with other tour companies like **Royal Tours** (United Tour Services), 14 Sharia Mahmoud Bassiouni, off Midan Talaat Harb (Tel: 40610), with a branch at the Continental Savoy Hotel; or **Green Valley Tours,** 26 Sharia Adli, downtown (Tel: 975739), with a branch at Cairo Airport. You will usually find a selection of tour brochures at your hotel.

Fuller information on **long-distance travel** will be found in the *Practical Information* sections of the relevant chapters and also in the *Background* chapter. But here is some general information on where and how to get out of Cairo.

Long-distance **bus** travel in Egypt is not recommended, except between Cairo and Alexandria over the Desert Road. These buses are fast, comfortable and air-conditioned – also cheap at about LE1.25. They depart hourly (from 7am to 5pm) from Midan el Tahrir by the Hilton. Their destination is inscribed in Arabic and English. They also stop at the Rest House halfway where you can get off for Wadi Natrun.

Also there are **service** or **shared taxis,** ie several people going more or less in the same direction. These are usually comfortable Peugeots. In Cairo they can be found at the south side of Midan el Tahrir; as you face the Mugamaa, they are across the street in a parking lot on your right. A service taxi to the Pyramids will cost you around 30PT; but you can find some going a lot further: I caught one to the Desert Road Rest House (for Wadi Natrun) and paid only LE1. For about LE2 you can get to Alexandria in 2 hours.

The main Cairo **train station,** Mahattat Ramses, is at Midan Ramses, northeast of Midan el Tahrir. From here there are trains north into the Delta and to Alexandria, east to the Canal towns and south into Upper Egypt –

Minya, Assiut, Luxor and Aswan. A full schedule of services will be found in the *Background* chapter. Remember that almost all air-conditioned first and second class trains require reservations, so book as far ahead as possible (which is not to say you won't be able to board a same-day train for Alexandria, Luxor or Aswan, but you can't count on it). Never accept an initial answer that the train is full. They might be turning everyone away, but if you wait, prod, suggest half a dozen ways in which they might have made a mistake, odds are you'll get a seat. In Egypt one bargains not only over prices but over facts.

As you enter the station, the sleeping-car reservations counter (for Luxor and Aswan) is in a room on your near left; otherwise tickets are purchased on the windows at the far left of the station.

Students in possession of an ISIC should go to the sleeping-car reservations counter (whether travelling by sleeper or not) to obtain their 50% fare discount.

Overland travel between Egypt and Israel has only just begun and the **bus** service is still in its teething stage. You should ask around Midan el Tahrir (buses for Israel have been departing from outside the Egyptian Museum around 6am). This is also where you would find a service (or shared) **taxi.** Neither buses nor taxis are as yet permitted beyond the Canal or border, so first you take one to Ismailia, cross the Canal and continue on to El Arish on the frontier, covering the third leg through southern Israel in another bus or taxi. You can make the entire trip by **car,** but getting insurance is a tedious process and requires crossing the Canal by a floating bridge at Qantara, in place only as shipping traffic allows. The wait can be 1 hour or 6. With luck, the entire journey from Cairo to Tel Aviv – by private car, taxi or bus – can be accomplished in 7 hours, but it can take much longer. (As this Guide went to press, a tunnel was opened beneath the canal. Traffic flow may now be faster.)

Overland travel between Egypt and Libya is not permitted; you must fly.

To travel **overland to the Sudan,** you take the train to Aswan (High Dam: *Sadd el Ali)* and continue by steamer. Third class (deck) tickets can be bought in Aswan, but first and second class tickets must be bought in Cairo: the **Sudan Nile Navigation Co.,** 8 Sharia Qasr el Nil (Tel: 48883). For more information, see the *Practical Information* section at the end of the *Upper Egypt 3* chapter.

Most **airline offices** are in the vicinity of Midan el Tahrir, eg:

Air France, Midan Talaat Harb (Tel: 743494).
British Airways, 1 Sharia Abdel Salam Aref, on the corner of Midan el Tahrir (Tel: 759914).
Egyptair, 12 Sharia Qasr el Nil (Tel: 59915); also at 6 Sharia Adli.
KLM, 11 Sharia Qasr el Nil (Tel: 740717).
Lufthansa, 9 Sharia Talaat Harb (Tel: 750366).
MEA, 12 Sharia Qasr el Nil (Tel: 743151).
Olympic, 23 Sharia Qasr El Nil (Tel: 751277).
Pan American, 2 Sharia Talaat Harb (Tel: 747399).
PIA, 22 Sharia Qasr el Nil (Tel: 744213).
SAS, 2 Sharia Champollion (Tel: 753546).
Sudan Airways, 1 Sharia el Boustan (Tel: 979198).
Swissair, 22 Sharia Qasr el Nil (Tel: 744299).
TWA, 1 Sharia Qasr el Nil, on the corner of Midan el Tahrir (Tel: 749900).

Additionally, **Air France** has a branch at the Meridien; **Egyptair** has branches at the Nile Hilton and the Sheraton; while the main offices of **Alitalia, Ethiopian** and **Japan Airlines** are at the Nile Hilton.

It is now possible to fly between Egypt and **Israel.** There are at least 6 flights a week to Tel Aviv on El Al and Nefertiti Airlines, though these are often booked up in advance. The fare is around $90. **El Al's** handling agents in Cairo are Salah Nabhan and Co., 5 Sharia El Makrizi, Zamalek (Tel: 807795 or 807912). Egyptair does not fly to Israel for fear of being banned in other Arab countries. Therefore a new company, **Nefertiti Airlines,** makes the run under the Ghanese flag with a British crew. Its agents are Nile Valley Aviation at Cairo Airport (Tel: 963270), who also charter aircraft.

Egyptair's flights to Luxor, Aswan and Abu Simbel will often be booked up several days in advance – or so you will be told. In truth, there is often a seat and to get it you should imagine you are asking for baksheesh, running the gamut of insistence, contrition and desperation – as at the train station, never accept an unpromising response as final. It can also pay to go out to the airport and stand by. Even less should you accept the word of anyone in Cairo that the flight, say, from Aswan to Abu Simbel is booked up. When you get to Aswan, enquire on the spot.

The time-honoured way of making a progress through Egypt is to **cruise along the Nile** (see also Luxor and Aswan). This is the most leisurely way to see the country and remains very popular, with sailings booked up sometimes months in advance. For those interested in seeing all the major and many of the lesser archaeological sites in the company of an international expert, the best cruises are those of **Swan Hellenic** and **Bales Tours** (see *Background* chapter). These are 21-day cruises between Cairo and Aswan and are part of an inclusive package which includes air fare from London. Prices start at around £1000 per person.

Otherwise there are a number of shorter cruises you can build into your visit to Egypt:

The **Hilton** operates the *Isis* and *Osiris*, floating equivalents of the Nile Hilton Hotel. They sail year-round between Luxor and Aswan (you can travel in either direction). Two nights are spent tied up at Luxor, 1 at Edfu, 1 at Aswan; altogether you spend 5 days and 4 nights with the ship and call also at Esna and Kom Ombo. The high season (September-May) cost per person in a double cabin is about LE200 and includes meals and sightseeing. Singles and triples are also possible.

The **Sheraton** has 4 ships in service, the *Tut*, *Aton*, *Htop* and *Any*. Like the Hilton's, these are luxurious floating hotels. They also make the Luxor-Aswan run, but have cruises, too, which include Dendera and Abydos, lasting 7 days. Prices are proportional to the Hilton cruises. Reservations can be made through any Sheraton Hotel.

Eastmar, 13 Sharia Qasr el Nil, Cairo (Tel: 970445, telex 93743 ESMAR UN), sails the *Nefertari*, *Memphis* and *Lotus* between Luxor and Aswan at a variety of cabin prices which can be much cheaper than Hilton or Sheraton fares.

More companies are offering cruises each year, building new ships or fitting up older ones. Nor do all cruises confine themselves to Aswan, Luxor, Dendera and Abydos. Some will come as far down from Aswan as Minya, others will start at Cairo. For information on new offerings, contact your nearest Egyptian Tourist Office, a competent travel agent at home or in Egypt, or look through the *Cairo by Night and Day* booklet.

A selective list of reputable **travel agents** in Cairo follows. All of them can assist you with accommodation and travel reservations, cruises, tours, guides, etc. Where they offer a special service, this is mentioned.

American Express, 15 Sharia Qasr El Nil (Tel: 753142). Offers its own range of daily tours around Cairo and throughout Egypt, and can arrange for Nile cruises and car hire. Has a foreign exchange desk and will serve as a mail drop for anyone with American Express travellers cheques or card.

Gabry Travel, 1 Midan Talaat Harb (Tel: 40268). Operates a Nile cruise ship, smaller, less luxurious than the Hilton/Sheraton ones, but also cheaper, with good food and service.

International Wagons-lits Company, Shepheard's Hotel, Corniche el Nil (Tel: 31538). Rumour has it that Wagons-lits may soon be introducing its own sleeping-cars on the Cairo-Luxor/Aswan run.

Memnon Tours, 18 Sharia Hoda Sharawi, between Sharia Talaat Harb and Sharia el Tahrir (Tel: 750195). If you have trouble getting a railway ticket, particularly making a return reservation, some travel agencies can help – and Memnon is one of them.

Misr Travel, 1 Sharia Talaat Harb (tel: 752537). The Egyptian state travel agency. Particularly useful in finding hotel accommodation in Cairo and throughout Egypt. For example, Misr block books hotel rooms in Luxor and Aswan during the winter high season for the benefit of its clients.

OTHER THINGS

There was a time when the Ezbekieh Gardens were cut with trenches and anti-mine barrages were strung across the Nile upriver from the bridges – precautions against Israeli air attacks. Now you will notice police and soldiers stationed at key intersections and buildings on the lookout for PLO attacks. **Security** is tight, at the airport, at hotels, at public places such as post offices and telephone exchanges, where you are likely to have your person and belongings searched. The precautions are effective, and Egyptian intelligence appears to be extremely good.

Communications, on the other hand, are not so good. Foreign mail is slow, the local telephone system operates in epileptic bursts, and foreign calls can require long waits.

The **Central Post Office** is at Midan el Ataba, near the Ezbekieh Gardens, and is open 24 hours daily. Other post offices are open from 8.30am to 3pm daily except Fridays. Most hotels can supply you with stamps for cards and letters. There's a good chance that post cards sent home will arrive after you do: air mail *can* take 10 days to Europe, more to the US. Mail is faster if posted at the Hilton or one of the other luxe hotels.

To send a parcel out of Egypt requires an export licence. You must obtain this at the Central Post Office, Midan el Ataba. Go there with your parcel unwrapped; go to the third building on the left in the rear of the complex; here it will be inspected and for a small fee sewn into a cloth cover; for a further small fee you will be guided through the remaining formalities and paperwork. Your parcel must not weigh more than 20 kilos nor exceed 1.5 metres in any direction. If sending home fabrics or souvenirs you've bought, ask first at the shop whether they will do it for you. Most shops catering to tourists have export licences and are reliable.

You can **receive mail** at your hotel or care of American Express (if you have their travellers cheques or card) or care of your Embassy (the envelope should be marked "Visitors' Mail"). American Express will forward any mail arriving for your after your departure for LE3.

Telegrams in foreign languages (English or French) can be sent from the PTT offices on the north side of Midan el Tahrir (open 24 hours daily), or in Sharia Alfi or Sharia Adli – or from major hotels. Night letters (no service to London) cost about half as much as full rate telegrams.

Most 3- to 5-star hotels have **telex** services available to guests.

Local telephone calls can be made from some cigarette kiosks or from shops and restaurants – or from your hotel. Don't expect too much: "Telephones of Cairo are not well". **Long-distance calls** can be made (at any rate attempted) from major hotels or from the Midan el Tahrir (north side), Sharia Alfi or Sharia Adli PTT offices. The one at Midan el Tahrir is open 24 hours daily. You must usually reserve your call some hours in advance. If reserving at a PTT office, you will also have to pay in advance for 3 minutes minimum (if you think you'll speak longer, pay for more time in advance, otherwise you'll be cut off). You will be given a slip of paper with your reservation number on it; this is also your receipt. Hold onto it for when you return to complete your call, or for when you want a refund. Sometimes the PTT can refer your reserved call to your hotel.

To exchange money, go to Thomas Cook, American Express, or to the banks in the major hotels – the Sheraton, Meridien, Hilton and Shepheard's, for example, all have 24-hour banks. You can sometimes change money at your embassy; the American Embassy gives a preferred rate to US citizens. For a full-scale commerical banking service, there's Barclays International Bank, 12 Midan el Sheikh Youssef (PO Box 2335), Garden City, Cairo (Tel: 22195, 27950, 29415. Telex: 2343 CABAR UN).

If you have Egyptian pounds which you want to convert back into foreign currency before your departure, you can go to any bank (eg the one at the airport) and show them a receipt indicating that you had previously converted at least such an amount from foreign currency into Egyptian pounds. You should, therefore, always hold onto your receipts (the American Embassy does not give receipts when changing money at the preferential rate).

For **medical care,** ask at your hotel. Most will be able to refer you to a doctor or dentist, while some of the major hotels will have a doctor on call. Most Egyptian doctors have been trained in Europe or the US and speak English. Your embassy can also recommend doctors and dentists. In an emergency, the following private hospitals are recommended: the **Anglo-American Hospital,** Gezira (Tel: 806165) and the **Italian Hospoital,** Abbasiyya, in northeast Cairo (Tel: 821497). A recommended government hospital is **Dar el Shifa,** 373 Sharia Ramses, just past the Coptic Patriarchate to the northeast of Midan Ramses (Tel: 829910). For **first aid** service, you can trying ringing 743499.

There are several **pharmacists** around Midan el Tahrir and downtown with a wide range of medications not requiring prescriptions – describe your symptoms and, if the ailment is minor, the pharmacist will prescribe on the spot. Cosmetics, perfumes and toilet articles are also stocked.

Your **embassy** can assist you by acting as a mail drop, advising on emergency financial and medical problems, effecting emergency communications home, etc. Embassies also encourage visitors, especially those not travelling in large groups, to register with them. It should be noted, however, that embassies cannot lend money to **stranded travellers** – though they can find ways of helping you. If stranded, you can go to Thomas Cook, American Express, Barclays International or the Nile Hiltón Hotel and have them send a telegram or telex requesting your bank or persons at home to arrange the transfer of money to you in Egypt. This can be accomplished in 2-3 days. Or you can go to an airline office and ask for a pre-paid ticket, the airline cabling whomever you suggest to pay for the ticket home. Authorisation to issue you with a ticket can be received back in Cairo within 2 days.

A full list of embassies can be found in *Cairo Night and Day;* a few are listed below.
Austrialia, 1097 Corniche el Nil, Garden City (Tel: 28197).
Canada, 6 Sharia Mohammed Fahmi el Sayed, Garden City (Tel: 23110).
Ireland, Sheraton Hotel (Tel: 983000).
Israel, 23 Sharia Mohi el Din Abu el Ez, Dokki (Tel: 700198).
Sudan, 1 Sharia Mohammed Fahmi el Sayed, Garden City (Tel: 25043).
United Kingdom, 2 Sharia Ahmed Raghab, Garden City (Tel: 28850).
United States, 5 Sharia Latin America, Garden City (Tel: 28219).

When **leaving Egypt** from Cairo Airport, remember that there is an LE3 **departure tax.** Once that is paid, the rest of your money should be converted back to foreign currency. The **duty-free shop** sells cigarettes, tobacco, liquor, perfume, etc., but will not accept Egyptian money.

If you want a **view of the Pyramids,** sit on the right-hand side of the plane.

CAIRO 2: THE EGYPTIAN MUSEUM

The Museum of Egyptian Antiquities, to give it its proper name, is on the north side of the Midan el Tahrir, near the Nile Hilton. It was founded at Bulaq in 1858 by Auguste Mariette, the great pioneer archaeologist who first excavated the Serapeum at Saqqara, the Temple of Amun at Karnak, Hatshepsut's mortuary temple at Deir el Bahri, and the temples at Dendera and Edfu. The collection has occupied the present classical-style building since 1902 and has long since outgrown it. There are over 100,000 exhibits which could easily fill half a dozen museums this size, a unique storehouse of one of the oldest and grandest civilisations on earth.

The museum has suffered from the several Middle East wars – not damaged, but denied necessary development. When I was here immediately before the 1973 war, the museum was like a grand but dilapidated hotel, badly lit and darkened still further with its windows blacked over to permit no show of light in the event of Israeli bombing raids. The guards had flashlights and would shine them at ancient faces when you showed a close interest. And at closing time a man softly trod amongst the chariots, sarcophagi, amulets and mummies, striking a gong with a hammer. But the gong had worn thin, a hole had been beaten through it so that it sounded like an old garbage can lid. There are still charming moments, as when the cleaning women beat scribes, queens and pharaohs with their dusting cloths, but the gong has been supplanted by an urgent and impersonal electric bell. The lighting system has been improved, though half the neon strips are burnt out at any one time. Vague plans have been aired to set up separate museums for mummies and treasures.

Allowing one minute for each exhibit, you could see everything in the museum in about nine months. The average guided tour lasts two hours. (Once a year in Paris, certain resident Americans put on their track shorts and sneakers for a race through the Louvre, having to pass check points at the Wingless Victory and the Mona Lisa. Appropriate check points for an Egyptian Museum sprint would be the Akhenaton Room, King Tut's burial treasure and the body of Seti I in the Mummy Room.) A less furious progression, though still glimpsing only the highlights, will take at least three long visits, though the selection below can be covered in a day. The exhibits are numbered (though no comprehensive guide is available) and some carry background notes in English, French and Arabic. The rooms are also numbered, as shown on the plans. The collection is arranged more or less chronologically, so that starting at the entrance and walking clockwise round the ground floor you pass from Old Kingdom through Middle and New Kingdom exhibits, concluding with Ptolemaic and Roman exhibits. The first floor contains prehistoric and early dynastic exhibits and the contents of several tombs, including Tutankhamun's. *Not every room is mentioned in the tour below.*

The ground floor Immediately upon entering, you walk into a rotunda that is *Room 48.* Apart from the monumental Sphinx, the colossal head at the rear (6051) of Userkaf (V Dyn) is the only large

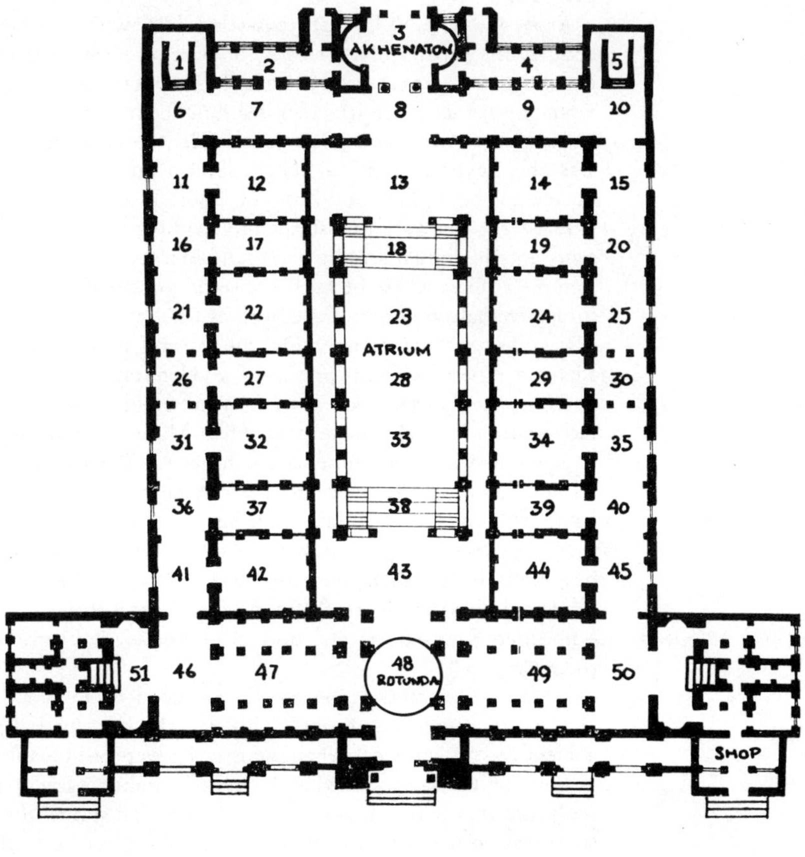

EGYPTIAN MUSEUM- GROUND FLOOR

sculpture surviving from the Old Kingdom. The rotunda contains other giant works (out of chronological order), including three colossi (1, 2, 4) of Ramses II (XIX Dyn) and a statue of Amenhotep son of Hapu (3), architect to Amenophis III (XVIII Dyn). There is an aerial photograph on the rear wall showing clearly the mud brick remains of Amenophis III's palace near Medinet Habu, and the lake he claimed to have dug in 15 days for Queen Tiy.

The Old Kingdom

Room 47: Contains IV, V and VI Dynasty items. The walls are lined with sarcophagi. Most interesting are the figures in the central aisle cases, including statuettes of the dwarf (160), the man with a deformed head (6310) and the hunchback (6311), but also those of people grinding corn, kneading dough, preparing food (a goose about to be gutted and plucked).

Room 41: The V Dynasty bas-relief (79) with scenes of country life is particularly worthy of close observation. Farm tasks and crafts are carried on through a series of registers. The women wear ankle-length chemises, but the men wear only a cloth or are sometimes entirely naked. They are circumcised as was the Egyptian custom. There is also one episode of a malefactor being held and brought before a court.

Room 42: The very fine statue of Chephren (138) in black diorite with white marbling was found in a shaft at his Valley Temple at Giza where he built the second of the Great Pyramids. The falcon god Horus embraces Chephren's head with his wings, at once transferring the ka and protecting the Pharaoh. The remarkably preserved wooden statue of Ka-aper (140) is vividly executed. You feel you would recognise the face in the original, and indeed when Mariette found it at Saqqara his workmen immediately dubbed it Sheikh el Beled because of its resemblance to their village headman. The living eyes are copper inlaid with quartz. It is said of some paintings that the eyes follow you; in this case it is uncanny how they fix you with their sure and level gaze when faced head on, but as soon as you shift even a centimetre they gaze off – not inert, but reflectively, into an internal dream world of their past.

Room 31: Outstanding here are the six wooden panels of the II Dynasty priest Hesire (88). This was the brief period in ancient Egyptian history when moustaches were fashionable.

Room 32: One gets so used to the rigid frontality of Egyptian sculpture that it is a surprise to see the wooden statue in the southeast corner with its slight twist. At the centre of the room are the IV Dynasty statues (223, 195) of Prince Rahotep and Princess Nafrit, her skin painted yellow, his ruddy brown. He has short back and sides and sports a natty moustache. In his white waist cloth he looks all the world like an advertising executive taking a sauna. The III/IV Dynasty 'Geese of Meidum' (136) are vividly coloured. The copper statues (230, 231) of Pepi I and his son are the first metal statues known, and that of Pepi the largest of its kind. He is a great striding figure, reminiscent of an archaic Greek kouros.

The Middle Kingdom

With *Room 26* you pass into the Middle Kingdom.

Room 22: Generally sculpture and stone monuments of the Middle Kingdom. At the centre is the burial chamber of Horhotep (300). It illustrates an aspect of a primitive vestige in Egyptian thinking: that representation and reality are one. The walls are painted with oil jars and offerings are closely listed. The decorated doors, like patchwork curtains, were for the ka to flit in and out at will. Around the chamber are ten statues of Sesostris I (301). On the sides of each throne are reliefs of the gods of Upper and Lower Egypt entwining the lotus and papyrus, symbolising the unity of the country.

The New Kingdom

With *Room 11* you pass into the New Kingdom. 400: a fine statue of Tuthmosis III (XVII Dynasty) in grey schist.

Room 12: XVIII Dynasty sculpture. The chapel built for Amenophis II once contained Hathor as cow (445, 446) – she now stands before it in a glass case. On either side are granite statues (6013, 6014) of Hatshepsut. To the left is a small statuette (6257), delicately carved out of Sudanese ebony, of Thay, a royal equerry.

Room 8: It is unusual for mud brick houses, even palaces, to survive, and so our impression of ancient Egypt is largely determined, often distorted, by rock tombs and stone mortuary temples. But the Egyptians did concern themselves with this world and remains of their houses can be visited at Tell el Amarna. At the centre of this room is a model of one. There is also a wooden gilt coffin lid (3873), probably belonging to Smenkhkere, Akhenaton's son-in-law and successor, beautifully inlaid with carnelian and coloured glass.

The Akhenaton Room

Room 3 contains perhaps the most astonishing works in the museum, from the reign of Akhenaton. Some find the Amarna style – particularly when applied in its most exaggerated form to Akhenaton himself – grotesque. I think it powerful and often beautiful. Staring down at you are four colossi of the Pharaoh: the glare of revolution. Elongated face, narrow eyes, long thin nose with flaring nostrils and full, perhaps sardonic lips. The belly and thighs protrude like some primitive female fertility figure. These are from the temple he built at Karnak, later destroyed, its blocks serving as foundations and pylon filler for others' works. There is a magnificent head (6026), probably of Nefertiti, and this is not distorted at all – though examples of Amarnan distortion applied to Nefertiti are seen on the stele in Case F, and the centre stele in Case H. A sculptor's study (6211), supposedly of two royal heads (in which case probably Akhenaton and his successor Smenkhkere), is like two frames in an animation sequence, as though to demonstrate how, by elongating and rotating the subject, you can achieve the extreme Amarna style. This is in Case F, as also are several small male and female figures, interesting because they reverse the Egyptian (and the later archaic Greek) convention of having the male with one foot forward, the female with feet together. Note also the cuneiform tablets, the famous 'Amarna Letters', in Case A, and the representational masks, either models or perhaps death masks, eg 478 in Case D. There is a theory, argued principally by Cyril Aldred, that Akhenaton was indeed deformed and that the Amarna style was a mass acquiesence to this misfortune. It is a theory I do not accept: too often, not only in facial features but for example in the reversed positioning of feet in Case F, referred to above, the style seems deliberately experimental, calculated for effect, intended to illustrate opposition, and as readily dispensed with (as with 6206, the bust of Nefertiti) when sheer beauty rather than shock value is desired.

Coins

Room 4 contains a poorly displayed collection of Greek, Roman, Byzantine and Arab coins. Quite a few bear the head of Alexander, and on the left side of the first case on the right are several coins bearing the head of Cleopatra VII.

Room 10: The falcon god protects a roly-poly Ramses II (6245), while 6183 could be either Tutankhamun or Horemheb, but is too dull and obliterated to be interesting.

The Ramessids

Room 15: Items from the reign of Ramses II, including 741, a painted limestone statue of a XIX Dynasty queen from the Ramesseum (Case A).

Room 14: On the right is a statue (743) of Ramses VI (XX Dyn), unusual for its attempt at movement, dragging a doubled up Libyan by the hair. A painted sunk relief (769) in the left near corner shows Ramses II similarly apprehending three prisoners, one black, one red, one brown. At the centre (unnumbered, but catalogued as 765) is a unique free-standing coronation group sculpture, Ramses III at the centre, Horus on the left, Seth on the right. Though greatly restored, enough was found to determine that the figures stood on their own legs without supports.

The Late Period

The New Kingdom, in any case tottering since the end of the XX Dynasty, ended with the XXI Dynasty. Objects from the Late Period begin with *Room 25.* One ruler of the

XXV Dynasty, Taharka, left his mark at several sites in Upper Egypt, eg the remains of his kiosk in the Great Court at Karnak. In *Room 24* is his sculpted head (1185, to the right) with curled hair – he was from Ethiopia. He enjoys the distinction of being mentioned in the Bible (*Kings* 19, 9). Otherwise, the most interesting items are the Osiris, Isis and Hathor group (855, 856, 857) at the centre, and to the left 1184, an attempt at portraiture of the Mayor of Thebes.

Room 30: At Medinet Habu are the mortuary chapels of the Divine Adorers of Amun. Amenardis, in white stone (930), was one of these princesses, of the XXV Dynasty.

The Graeco-Roman Period

Room 34: The Graeco-Roman period begins here. Note the colossal bust (1003) of Serapis. This god was an invention of Ptolemy Soter and combined Osiris with Apis, the bull god of Memphis, but with Greek features and dress.

Room 49: An exceptional piece is the coffin of Petosiris (6036), a high priest of Thoth at Hermopolis (c. 300 BC). The hieroglyphs are beautifully inlaid with stone and enamel. From Saqqara during the Persian Period is the stone sarcophagus (1294) of a dwarf dancer at the Serapeum Apis ceremony. He has been well rewarded: his true to life figure is cut on the outside of the adjacent lid, while on the inside of the lid and at the bottom of the sarcophagus is carved a sex-bomb Nut for him to lie on and stare up at for eternity.

The Atrium: large objects of various periods

On the ground floor there now remains only the atrium to visit. The area is in process of slow rearrangement. You could once pass through it directly from the entrance and rotunda but temporarily there is a railing between Rooms 43 and 38, making a detour through Room 8 necessary. Nevertheless, we will pretend this railing does not exist (as it may not by the time you get here).

At the centre of *Room 43* is a wooden frame found near Chephren's pyramid and possibly used in wrapping mummies. On either side of the room are two large wooden boats for solar sailing from the pyramid of Sesostris III at Dahshur.

Room 38 is really a stairway leading down into the well of the atrium and contains the rectangular stone sarcophagus of Ay, at first an advisor to Akhenaton and later his successor. Four goddesses at each corner extend their wings protectively: Isis, Nephthys, Neith and Selket. The sarcophagus was found intact in 1884 but smashed in 1896 by a Moroccan searching for treasure.

Room 33 displays various pyramidions from Dahshur, the capstones to pyramids. Under 6175 you can see the stone peg which slotted into the pyramid top. The sarcophagus (6337A) of Psusennes I, a XXI Dynasty pharaoh ruling from Tanis in the Delta after Egypt had split in two, has its lid (6337B) raised over a mirror so that you can see the lovely raised relief of Nut suspended from its underside. From the XIX Dynasty are two stone sacred boats (590, 591), while to the left, from the XVIII Dynasty, are the stone sarcophagi of Tuthmosis I (619), that of his daughter Hatshepsut made before she came to the throne (6024) and her final sarcophagus (620).

At the centre of the atrium *(Room 28)* is a painted floor with a river scene (627) from the palace of Akhenaton at Tell el Amarna. It is covered with dirty and barely transparent plastic sheets.

Glass cases in *Room 23* once held the bodies of Nedjemet, wife of Herihor (XXI Dyn), and Ramses II (XIX Dyn). Nedjemet's full head of long dark hair and inset eyeballs gave a fullness to her face. Ramses was magnificent: a long fine nose (slightly flattened by the bandages), delicate facial bone structure, broad shoulders and a surprisingly long body. Both had been removed when I was last here, Ramses flown off to Paris for "cure by doctor" (as an attendant told me) where he was received with the full honours due a head to state. He is now back, but may not yet be on display – and in any case, the Egyptian government is no longer sure that it is seemly for tourists to gawk at such illustrious dead. * So otherwise, there are two interesting lintels, the one on the left (6189) showing the Heb-Set of Senusret III (XII Dyn) very finely cut in sunk relief, while the one on the right is a tenth-rate copy by a later pharaoh.

Room 18 (the stairway leading out of the atrium well) has the colossal group (610) of Amenophis III and his wife Tiy with three of their daughters (XVII Dyn). They are serene, almost a portrait of Victorian contentment but for the play of a smile on their lips and the physicalness of their bodies. Despite the formality of the work and its size, there is a great sensuality to it. The reign of Amenophis was marked by luxury and a sudden eruption (or at least recording) of fashion consciousness: note particularly Tiy's full wig, the hair falling down to her breasts, a style associated almost exclusively with this reign.

Room 13: On the right is a fascinating document, a stele (599) inscribed on the reverse during the reign of Amenophis III with all that the Pharaoh had done for Amun, but later inscribed on the obverse by Merneptah, Pharaoh of the Exodus, with the sole known reference in Egyptian texts to the Israelites: "Israel is crushed, it has no more seed"!

The *corridors* on either side of the atrium (allowing com-

---

* See *Practical Information* section.

munication between Rooms 43 and 8 but not with the atrium itself) are lined with pottery, wall paintings and inscription fragments.

The first floor

To see the first floor rooms in approximate chronological order you should start at Room 43 overlooking the atrium from the south and follow the corridors in a clockwise direction.

Old and Middle Kingdom tomb contents

Outside *Room 42* is a panel (6278) inlaid with blue faience, from Zoser's Step Pyramid at Saqqara. Inside the room you should spend time with the alabaster vase (3054) on the left, beautifully round and smooth and yet criss-crossed in raised stone with ropes from which it would have been suspended. Here also is the Palette of Narmer (3055), possibly the oldest

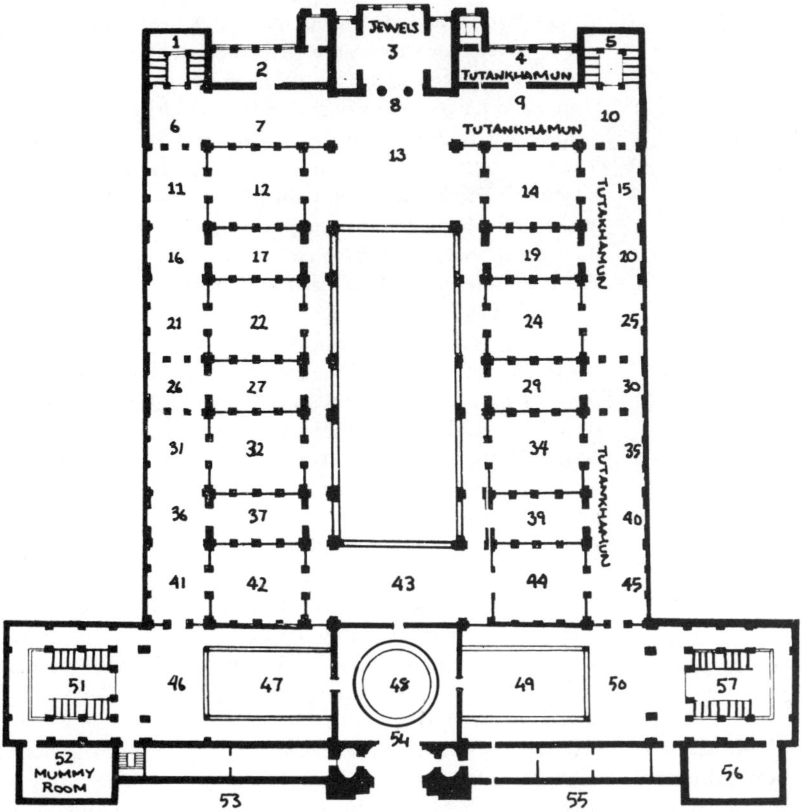

EGYPTIAN MUSEUM- FIRST FLOOR

record of a political event, the unification of Egypt, c.3100 BC. Narmer was probably one of the names of Menes, the founder of the I Dynasty, from which Egypt's historical period is dated. Writing was not yet able to convey complex sentences and this slate palette tells its story by means of pictures which are easily translated into words. On the obverse, Narmer is shown braining an enemy, and to the right is a complex symbol relating the significance of this action. The falcon is Narmer, holding a rope attached to the head of a bearded man. The head protrudes from a bed of papyri, representing Lower Egypt. Therefore the symbol reads, "The falcon god Horus (Narmer) leads captive the inhabitants of the papyrus country". Narmer came from Upper Egypt, as the crown he wears on this side shows. On the reverse, Narmer wears the crown of Lower Egypt as he reviews the spoils of his victory, which include the decapitated bodies of his foes. The centre panel shows two fantastic beasts, their necks entwined but restrained from fighting by bearded men on either side: Upper and Lower Egypt joined, if not yet altogether at ease.

Room 37 is full of wooden coffins and sarcophagi of the Middle Kingdom. The coffin of Sepa (301), a XII Dynasty general, is particularly well-painted. Artefacts from the tomb of General Mesah at Assiut are displayed in several cases and include his sandals, mirror and neck pillow, and models of Egyptian soldiers (3345), black soldiers (3346) and a pleasure barge (3347).

In the corridor facing *Room 32* is a rare and astonishing wooden ka statue of the Pharaoh Hor (XII Dyn) stepping out from its naos. It actually stands on a sliding base to demonstrate the wanderings of Hor's double – and that it is his ka is clear from the ka hieroglyph of upraised arms on his head, and his nakedness. Inside the room are models (Case E: 3246, 3247) of solar boats.

Room 27 contains marvellous models (6077-86) from the XI Dynasty tomb of Meketre at Thebes, including a plantation owner reviewing a parade of his cattle and workers (6080); a carpenters' workshop (6083); a pleasure garden with pool, lined with sycamore-figs, at one end a columned verandah (6084); and two boats dragging a net between them, taking fish from the Nile (6085).

Middle and New Kingdom ushabtis

Room 22 contains many interesting small figures, including XII-XXX Dynasty ushabtis (Cases I and J: 6062-72), and women, perhaps concubines of the dead man, lying on beds (Case C: 3367A-E).

Room 17 is particularly interesting for the papyri on its walls from the Book of the Dead.

New Kingdom tomb contents

Room 12 contains artefacts from royal tombs: a chariot of Tuthmosis IV (3000); the mummies of a child and a gazelle (Case I: 3776, 3780); a collection of priestly wigs and wig boxes (Case L: 3779).

Room 13 at the north end of the atrium displays furnishings from the intact Theban tomb of Yuya and Tuyu, parents-in-law of Amenophis III, with beds, chairs, whippet-like chariots, mummified food and time-serving ushabtis.

The north end of the first floor and all the outer rooms along its east side are devoted to Tutankhamun's treasures, but it is not easy to include their profusion in the middle of this tour. Come back to it later. In any case, more affecting are the

Roman burials

exhibits in *Room 14* from Roman burials. These people, mostly from the Fayyum, continued the Egyptian practice of mummification, yet from their portraits, so lifelike and modern, you cannot imagine they would have accepted the ancient belief. The encaustic portraits (colours mixed into molten wax) were bound onto the mummies – there are shelves of these. A collection of panels is against the south wall (4310): the technique is superb, with shading, highlighting and perspective, two or three of them qualifying as masterpieces in their own right. Those garbage bodies, yet these living faces in which you can read whole lives. All are marked by a seriousness, rarely pompous, occasionally sad, a faint smile on one man's lips. They have faced the passing millenia with Roman steadfastness, they look at you as you look at them as though suddenly we might recognise one another.

In *Room 19* are the gods of the Egyptian pantheon.

Sketches, papyri and decorations

Room 24 is full of painted ostraka, limestone fragments. Case 18 contains interesting representations of animals: a monkey eating, a man leading a bull, a lion devouring a prisoner, etc. People too: to the upper right an intriguing picture of a woman relaxing and playing a stringed instrument. There is also a plan of a Theban tomb (4371), with what appear to be doorways shown in elevation.

In *Room 29* are further ostraka, but written on, and papyri – 6335 especially worthwhile: a Ptolemaic Book of the Dead in finest detail, showing the 'Weighing of the Heart' ceremony.

In the corridor outside *Room 34* is an Amarna toilet seat. Is this the loo on which Akhenaton sat?

Room 44 displays decorative details, most interesting the faience from palaces of Ramses II and III.

Room 57 is around the southeast staircase. The square red and green leather tent (32848) belonged to a XXI Dynasty queen and was used at her funeral.

At the centre of the south wings is *Room 48* with a model of a funerary complex, showing how a river temple linked with the pyramid on the desert's edge. There is also a cross-sectioned pyramid showing the internal buttressing. A case to the west contains beautifully worked statuettes from various periods.

Prehistoric and predynastic periods

Rooms 54, 55 and 53 are devoted to prehistoric and predynastic artefacts, eg pottery and tools, and are generally dull, except that in *Room 53* are mummified baboons, a dog, a crocodile and the skeleton of a mare – and these are disgusting. You can understand that the Egyptians, having convinced themselves of the efficacy of preservation, would wrap each other up. But to impose it on animals (look at their little linen-wrapped legs) seems perverse. This is perhaps an unfair view, for human beings are at the centre of our cosmology, animals only soulless lookers-on, while Egyptian religion grew out of animal worship, totemism, or at least an admiration for the qualities of animals – their strength, swiftness, beauty (though what they saw in baboons I cannot imagine) – and so piety towards them at death would be a priority. Nevertheless, it is here, more than in a Theban tomb, that you sense the gulf between the ancient Egyptians and ourselves.

The Mummy Room

Room 52 is the Mummy Room* where many of the mightiest men in ancient history lie naked and bird-boned in glass cases. Many are in a bad or poor state of preservation, not so much from the failure of the embalming process but because of early exposure by grave robbers. The heads and feet are laid bare, but the rest of their bodies are shrouded out of respect for pharaonic modesty. It is worth looking closely at the preserved detail of the bodies, the toes for instance, and the varying features, even the expressions, on the better-preserved faces. Also notice the strikingly strong family resemblances within dynasties. Some of the more interesting pharaohs and queens are:

Amenophis III, whose colossal statue with wife and daughters is downstairs, has been reduced to a horrifying skeleton. Amenophis II (XVIII Dyn), with his head flung back, looks almost sad, while Seti I (XIX Dyn), father of Ramses II, is serene and looks as though he is asleep. Nefertari, wife of Ahmose I (XVIII Dyn), could still convince you that she had once been a lovely woman. Sekenenre (XVII Dyn) died of an axe wound in the forehead (clearly visible) received in the heat of battle and was probably mummified on the spot. His lips scream with agony, his legs are contracted with pain.

"The more I walk along, the more I listen, the more I move around the columns, the more do I experience the feeling of a dark world which fastens on to ours and which will not loosen the suckers through which it takes its life. Whatever it may

* See *Practical Information* section.

cost, they find it necessary to confirm their existence, to perpetuate themselves, to incarnate, to reincarnate, to hypnotise nothingness and to vanquish it . . . They did not hide themselves in order to disappear, but in order to await the cue for their entry on the stage. They have not been dragged from the tomb. They have been brought from the limbo of the wings with masks and gloves of gold . . . Seti the First! How beautiful he is, with his little nose, his pointed teeth showing, his little face which belongs to death, reduced to one requirement alone – not to die. 'I! I! I!' This is the word which the rafters throw back" (Cocteau).

Returning to the New Kingdom

You can now walk back to the north end of the first floor for the Tutankhamun exhibition which begins at *Room 7.* You pass through *Room 6* with a collection of scarabs. The black dung beetle, running everywhere about the desert sands, pushing a ball of dung before it, symbolised the self-creator, the morning sun. Amenophis III placed a giant granite scarab by the Sacred Lake at Karnak, and also used it to commemorate events like his marriage to Tiy (6274).

Rooms 2 and 3, though leading off from the Tutankhamun exhibition area, are not properly a part of it. In *Room 2,* to the right, is a falcon-style coffin, very impressive in black with gold leaf design and gold bird's face (Case 4).

The Jewellery Room

Room 3 closes a quarter of an hour before the rest of the museum and is specially guarded: it contains jewellery from the I Dynasty through to the Byzantine period: necklaces, pectorals, diadems, daggers and much else in gold, silver and precious stones. If I could walk out with any of it, you would find the VI Dynasty gold falcon head (Case 3: 4010) missing, and Mary Astor, Peter Lorre and Sidney Greenstreet hot on my trail.

The Tutankhamun Exhibition

Walking round the Tutankhamun exhibition, you occasionally notice a dust-free silhouette where a piece has been removed to join one of the Tut Tours around America, Britain, France, etc., and yet these absences hardly relieve the overwhelming impression of the whole. There is just so much, yet Tutankhamun was a minor figure who died young and was stuffed into a small tomb: imagine the impedimenta that Seti I tried taking with him. I have seen three Tutankhamun roadshows and have in each case preferred their careful choice and presentation to the jumble sale effect at the Cairo Museum. *Rooms 7, 8, 9, 10, 15, 25, 30, 35, 40 and 45,* and also *Room 4* (off Room 9) and part of *Room 13,* contain 1700 items in all. The eyes jadedly search for the highlights of the highlights, or otherwise fix on curiosities.

Tutankhamun's mummy, his outermost coffin of gilded

wood and his granite sarcophagus are all in his tomb in the Valley of the Kings, but the second coffin of gilded wood and the third of solid gold are in *Room 4,* along with the gold mask. Each of these, placed one within the other like Russian dolls, in turn were placed within a gilded wood shrine – which again fitted within three more *(Rooms 7 and 8)*. These shrines remind me of Wilhelm Reich's orgone boxes, a crackpot device for concentrating orgone energy around the human body: "Quite unexpectedly the knowledge of the biological function of tension and charge led me to the discovery of hitherto unknown energy processes in bions, in the human organism and in the radiation of the sun . . . This energy, which is capable of charging non-conducting substances, I termed *orgone* . . . The orgone energy has a parasympatheticotonic effect and charges living tissues . . . The human organism is surrounded by an orgonotic field which varies according to the individual's vegetative motility" (Reich, *The Function of the Orgasm).* The ancient Egyptians, however, were born and died too soon to benefit from Reich's teachings, and employed these gold casings in part because gold was thought to be the flesh of the gods, and also because it warded off all outside contamination, presumably including, alas, orgone.

The gold mask

In *Room 9* is a curiosity other examples of which you may have noticed elsewhere in the museum: a vegetating Osiris. It is a wooden silhouette of the god, his image again carved out within this and the depression once filled with earth from which grass would sprout with symbolic effect.

A vegetating Osiris

Among the finer or more curious items in the east gallery (Rooms 15 to 45) are a jewellery casket of gilded wood (447) in the form of a naos with the figure of Anubis on top; a chest (324) for the Pharaoh's clothes decorated on the lid with a desert hunt, on the large panels with Tutankhamun waging war, and on the small panels with the royal sphinx trampling on his enemies; a lock of Queen Tiy's hair (444) – all that is known to remain of her; two life-size statues of Tutankhamun (96, 181) which guarded the entrance to the burial chamber; and the famous small throne (1), its back richly decorated with a scene of Tutankhamun's Queen placing her right hand on his left shoulder, often interpreted as a relaxed domestic scene, through probably a gesture confirming his position, as she was after all the daughter – and possibly a widow – of Akhenaton, and there was an early tradition of matrilineal succession (explaining the frequent sister and daughter marriages of pharaohs). The armrests too are beautiful, the lovely shape of falcons' wings extending in protection, the birds' heads wearing the crown of Upper and Lower Egypt. Finally, there is an

The throne

object (435) which is meant to be an emblem of Anubis, an animal skin attached to a rod. Except it looks more particularly like a fertility symbol: from an alabaster bucket base rises a gold stem with a bud at the top. Around the stem is entwined a tendril which leads down to a kind of sack on two legs (or two distended testicles) with a short broad penis pendant. Maybe that is not what it is, but that is what it looks like.

PRACTICAL INFORMATION

The Museum of Egyptian Antiquities is **open in winter** from 9am to 4pm daily except Fridays when it closes between 11.15am and 1.30pm. **In summer** (May to October) it's open from 8.30am to 1pm daily except Fridays when it closes at 11.15am. **Admission** is 75PT plus 5PT tax. (An additional 25PT was charged for the Mummy Room, but see below.)

No **bags or cameras** may be taken into the museum. These may be checked free of charge (which does not stop the attendant, *sotto voce*, asking for 50PT – ignore him) and to my knowledge will be entirely secure, but I can imagine a mistake, eg someone else being given your expensive camera, so perhaps such items should not be brought along at all.

The main entrance and the entrance to its right have several **shops** selling books, cards, reproductions and junk. There is also a **post office** branch, a **bank** and a **cafeteria**. They keep the same hours as the museum.

There's a luxe **guidebook** for sale, *Museum Aegiptium, Egyptian Museum Guide,* by Dr Edouard Lambelet, published by Lehnart and Landrock, Cairo 1978, in French, German and English, printed on artpaper with black and white and colour photographs, hardcover, LE12. Otherwise there's only a slim picture book available, not really a guide.

Shortly before this Guide went to press it was announced that visitors would be banned from the **Mummy Room,** the royal bodies to be reburied either in their original tombs or in a chamber built for the purpose. This is meant as a gesture to Islam, though only the most orthodox Moslems can have been offended by the display. I'm inclined to go along with Cocteau, that the Pharaohs "did not hide themselves in order to disappear, but in order to await the cue for their entry on the stage". The description of the Mummy Room has been left in the text so that you know what you are missing.

CAIRO 3: THE ISLAMIC CITY (THE SOUTHERN QUARTERS)

The route This chapter tours the southern quarters of the old city, beginning with the oldest and finest mosque in Cairo, the Ibn Tulun, and proceeds northwards to the Sultan Hassan Mosque, the Citadel, and along Sharia Bab el Wazir past several other monuments to end outside Bab Zuwayla, the southern gateway into the Fatimid city. There is also a visit to the Southern Cemetery which is most easily reached from the Citadel. (See map in following chapter.)

The method The Islamic monuments of Cairo, and there are hundreds of them, are each marked with a small green enamelled plaque bearing an Arabic number. These numbers are given after the name of each monument covered in the tours of this and the following chapter to ensure identification. Although these are historical monuments, they are often places of current worship and when touring this most conservative part of the city you should dress and act with decorum. Women should not wear short dresses or too-revealing blouses. Inside mosques you must remove your shoes, or shoe coverings will be provided. For this, and for entry to some of the monuments, there is a small fee, while if you accept the services of a guide, or sometimes if you ask to be shown the way up a minaret, baksheesh will be expected. In short, it is a good idea to carry around a lot of small change.

Comfortable walking shoes are recommended. Though you might rely on a taxi or other transport to get you to the beginning of the itinerary or to some of the major monuments along the route, walking is otherwise preferable for a sense of leisure and atmosphere, and also because some places are difficult to get at or to discover even once you are in the vicinity. There are numerous *kahwehs* along the way, that is places to sit – often just a few chairs beneath the shade of a tree or awning, or a *mastaba,* a brick or stone bench outside a shopfront – for a coffee or more likely a refreshing cup of mint tea. Then there is immediate tranquillity; you give your feet a rest and let the city parade by before you.

The grandeur of Islam In the 14th C. the great Arab historian Ibn Khaldun wrote that "he who has not seen Cairo cannot know the grandeur of Islam. It is the metropolis of the universe, the garden of the world, the nest of the human species, the gateway to Islam, the throne of royalty: it is a city embellished with castles and palaces and adorned with monasteries of dervishes and with colleges lit by the moons and the stars of erudition". Along with Cordoba and Baghdad, it was one of the great centres of the Arab world, but while Cordoba fell to the *Reconquista* and Baghdad was destroyed by the Mongols, medieval Cairo survives. The erudition Ibn Khaldun refers to was more the Moslem version of how many angels could dance upon the head of a pin, but otherwise many of the marvels he describes still wait for you, often so unobtrusively that you could pass a facade a hundred times and never guess at the grandeur within. Some of the monuments remain neglected, others have been restored over the past century or are only being restored now. The streets may be ancient, narrow and dusty, full of strange colour and smell. People may be curious, children occasionally a nuisance and merchants in the tourist bazaars importunate, but generally the inhabitants of these quarters, like Egyptians throughout the country, will be friendly and helpful. This is the heart of Cairo, a heart that anyone with the least sense of adventure will come to love.

Mosque of Sayyida Zeinab

If you are heading for the Mosque of Ibn Tulun from Midan el Tahrir, you will probably come into the square before the Mosque of Sayyida Zeinab at the bottom of Sharia Port Said. Dating in its present form only from the 19th C., it is not an Islamic monument, but this mosque and that of Hussein near the al-Azhar are of special importance to Moslems, and non-Moslems are not admitted except by special permission. At the Sayyida Zeinab is the tomb of the Prophet's granddaughter, while the Hussein is said to contain the head of the Prophet's grandson, the son, that is, of Ali from whom the Shi'ites claim spiritual descent. Both these mosques, and the al-Azhar, are today the principal congregational mosques of Cairo.

Despite the prohibition against infidels, while hanging around outside the Sayyida Zeinab at evening prayers I was invited in by a group of men. Whether any of them had the authority to make an exception of me, or whether I was mistaken for a prodigal son, I do not know. When prayers began, I was the only one left standing – in case a mistake had been made, I thought it best then to leave, and to leave anyway out of respect as there is something unseemly about being a sightseer at other people's devotions. You may sometimes find yourself in a mosque at prayer time, and then, though visitors are otherwise welcome, you might be asked to retreat into an alcove or out onto the street. Normally, though, the atmosphere is relaxed, even to the point where many of Mohammed's precepts on mosque conduct are ignored. Egypt in this as in many other ways is more liberal than most Moslem countries.

Mosque of Ibn Tulun

If you have time to visit only one Islamic monument, the Mosque of Ibn Tulun (220) should be your choice. The mosque can be reached by going east from Midan al-Sayyida Zeinab at the bottom of Sharia Port Said or west from Midan Salah al-Din below the Citadel. The area, though not ancient, is poor and rundown, but behind its outer courtyard or *ziyadah* the mosque achieves an isolation which heightens the dramatic effect of the inner courtyard's bold simplicity.

Ibn Tulun was sent to govern Cairo by the Abbassid Caliph at Baghdad and the mosque, built in 876-9, displays strong Mesopotamian influences.

Congregational plan

A congregational mosque with an inner courtyard or *sahn* of parade ground proportions, it strives to fulfill the ideal of accommodating all the troops and subjects of the fortress capital for Friday prayers. Arcades run round the sahn on four sides, deeper along the qibla wall facing Mecca. Brick piers support the pointed horseshoe arches which have a slight return, that is they continue their curve inwards at the bottom, and the arches are decorated with carved stucco (restored on the outer arches but original on the others within the arcades), a technique Ibn Tulun introduced to Cairo. The windows along the qibla wall (to your left as you enter the mosque) have stucco grilles (the fifth and sixth from the left are original), permitting a faint light into this deeper arcade with its prayer niche or *mihrab* and beautifully carved pulpit or *minbar,* 13th C. restorations. The roof, like the repaired stucco work, is owed to the efforts of 20th C. restorers. Original, however, is the Koranic inscription carved in sycamore running at a height round the interior of the four arcades.

The effect as you enter the sahn is of severe simplicity, yet these details of carved stucco and sycamore and returning arches offer subtle relief. You should walk round the sahn under the arcades to appreciate the play that is made with light and shadow, the rhythm of the arches, the harmony of the ensemble.

At the centre of the sahn is a 13th C. fountain. All these 13th C. restorations and additions were undertaken by Sultan Lajin who had assassinated the incumbent Sultan and hid in the then decrepit mosque. He vowed that if he survived to be raised to the Sultanate he would restore his hideaway, and to him belongs an explanation also for the striking minaret opposite the qibla wall. The original was Tulun's, in the form of a spiral, and there is a story of Tulun, normally of grave demeanor, absentmindedly twiddling a strip of paper round his finger to the consternation of his audience, excusing himself with the explanation that it was the model for his new minaret. In fact its prototype, still standing, was the minaret of the Great Mosque of Samarra in Iraq. But Lajin had to rebuild it and out of taste or for stability gave it a squared base. It succeeds in being extraordinary and along with the merlons along the parapets of the arcades, like a paperchain of cut-out men, it has the alertness of the surreal. You can climb the minaret right to the top, though as you round the spiral there is nothing to steady you and a high breeze adds to the vertigo. There is nothing much close by but tenements with views into

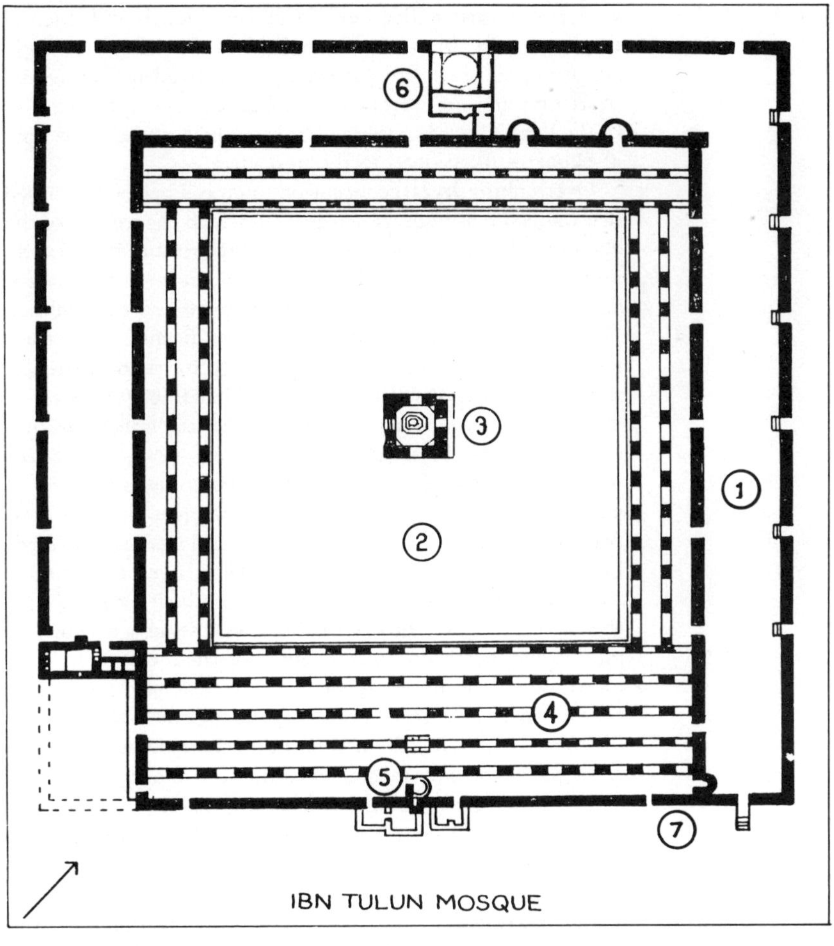

IBN TULUN MOSQUE
1. Entry
2. Sahn
3. Fountain
4. Sanctuary liwan
5. *Mihrab*
6. Minaret
7. Gayer-Anderson House

bedroom windows, though to the west you can see the Pyramids, to the north pick out the major landmarks of the Fatimid city, and below you again the forthright plan of the mosque.

The Gayer-Anderson House

At the northeast corner of the Ibn Tulun Mosque is the Bayt al-Kritliyya, the House of the Cretan Woman, though in fact it is two 17th C. houses knocked together. It is better known as the Gayer-Anderson House, named for the British major who restored and occupied it earlier this century, filling it with his eclectic collection of English, French and oriental furniture and bric-a-brac which can be disconcertingly anachronistic, but does give the place a lived-in feeling. Its tourist reputation must be founded on this, and its proximity to the Ibn Tulun, for otherwise it is not half as fine as the Bayt al-Suhaymi mentioned in the next chapter.

Overlooking its large reception room is a balcony enclosed in a wooden mashrabiyya screen from which the women of the harem could discreetly observe male visitors and their entertainments. Lane in his *Manners and Customs of the Modern Egyptians,* which describes Cairo in the 1830s, says the women "have the character of being the most licentious in their feelings of all females who lay any claim to be considered as members of a civilised nation . . . What liberty they have, many of them, it is said, abuse; and most of them are not considered safe unless under lock and key, to which restraint few are subjected. It is believed that they possess a degree of cunning in the management of their intrigues that the most prudent and careful husband cannot guard against". Indeed, Lane believed that Egyptian women were under less restraint than those in any other country of the Turkish Empire, with those "of the lower orders flirting and jesting with men in public, and men laying their hands upon them very freely". As for those of the upper classes: "They generally look upon restraint with a degree of pride, as evincing the husband's care for them, and value themselves upon their being hidden as treasures". The only man allowed into the harem, that is the female domestic quarters, was the husband – and so the strictures worked against men, too, the only unveiled women they could see being their wives or female slaves.

Tomb of Shagarat al-Durr: the only Moslem Queen

Those interested in making a romantic pilgrimage to the Tomb of Shagarat al-Durr should walk southwards along the medieval city's main street which passes just to the east of Ibn Tulun's mosque. The tomb (169) is at the edge of the Southern Cemetery in one of Cairo's poorest areas. Built in 1250, it is small and simple, with fine glass mosaics in the prayer niche, an original Kufic frieze and fragments of Naskhi inscription round the cenotaph – not entirely empty, for some of her body was saved from the dogs. The only female Moslem sovereign in history, indeed the only woman to have ruled over Moslems until Queen Victoria, she played fast and loose and came to a sticky end. Her story is told in the next chapter.

Rifa'i Mosque

Walk to Midan Salah al-Din; to your left (north) are two large mosques pressed against each other like the walls of a canyon, Sharia El Qalaa cutting between them. The mosque on the right is the Rifa'i, a modern imitation of Bahri Mameluke style, where members of the late royal family, including King Farouk, are buried – and now also the ex-Shah of Iran. The best thing about the Rifa'i is its near-abutment with the Mosque of Sultan Hassan on the left, the canyon enhancing the massiveness of the latter. Both mosques are lit by orange lights at night, as though the light itself was old, not bright and white, and had been lingering on the facades for some long time until it darkened with age. But then in the darkness is the booming call to evening prayer, not mysterious but electrically amplified, saving the muezzin not only his voice but the long trudge up to the top of the minaret. This is one liberalisation in Islamic practice, prevalent now throughout the Middle East, which is to be regretted.

Mosque of Sultan Hassan

The Mosque-madrasa of Sultan Hassan (133) is genuinely of the Bahri Mameluke period and was built – of stone (reputedly from the Great Pyramid), unlike the brick of Tulunid and some Fatimid mosques – in 1356-63. Its short distance from the Mosque of Ibn Tulun allows a ready comparison between these exemplars of the two principal forms of Cairo mosque. The purpose of the congregational is to gather in and architecturally the emphasis is on the rectangular and the horizontal. But the Sultan Hassan served as a theological school, a *madrasa*. The madrasa was first introduced to Egypt by Saladin as part of his effort to combat and suppress the Fatimid Shi'ites. Class and dormitory space required a vertical structure, most functionally a cube. The central courtyard remains a feature, but opening onto each of its sides are four

Cruciform plan

enormous vaulted halls or *liwans,* creating a cruciform plan. The doctrinal justification for four liwans was that each served as a place for teaching one of the four Sunni, that is orthodox, Moslem rites (Shafite, Malikite, Hanefite and Hanbalite), though the origins of the liwan are found at Hatra in Iraq, an Arab city flourishing at least 400 years before Mohammed. But it was the Mamelukes who arranged them with magnificent effect in cruciform plan and who also added to their mosque-madrasas domed mausolea. Hassan's mausoleum is appended to the south end of his mosque but his tomb is empty; he was executed two years before its completion and his body disappeared.

There are many who regard the Sultan Hassan as the outstanding Islamic monument in Egypt, and certainly it vies with the Ibn Tulun. Though entirely different in type, the two mosques share a boldness of conception and clarity of execution, gathering still more strength in restraining decoration to the minimum necessary solely to underline architectural form. There is self-confidence, and at the Sultan Hassan even architectural insolence, but rarely indulgence.

Exterior The Sultan Hassan already impresses from the outside. Though it stands beneath the glare of the Citadel it holds its own, its great cornice and the strong verticals of its facade rising to the challenge. Notice how the broad surfaces along the east and west sides are relieved by blind recesses into which the paired arched windows of the dormitories are set. Height is especially emphasised as you enter on Sharia el Qalaa the towering portal with its stalactite decorations – a favourite Mameluke motif. The portal is at an angle to the main east flank of the mosque and the west flank too is bent, though at first sight the building had seemed more regular. Earlier periods had enjoyed more space, but as Cairo grew and became more dense the Mamelukes had to squeeze their buildings in where they could, though they had a fetish for achieving a cubistic effect no matter how irregular the plot. The liwans had also to be cruciform regardless of the exterior and in the Sultan Hassan this has been neatly done, all hint inside of the irregularity of the outer walls suppressed except for the slight angle of the door in the west liwan.

Interior The portal leads to a domed cruciform vestibule and you turn left into a dark angled passage. It empties suddenly into the north end of the brilliantly sun-filled sahn, certainly a deliberate effect and a preparation for the play of light and shadow, concrete and void, intended for the courtyard and its liwans. It is important that you do not come too late in the day, indeed it is best that you visit the Sultan Hassan in the morning when the sun lights up the mausoleum and west liwan and begins its long and rarely accomplished reach into the full depth of the sahn. Its depth is considerable, for the liwans lift about as high as the sahn is long. The sun soon passes, illuminating hardly more than the merlons by late afternoon, and much of the architectural effect of direct sunlight and strong shadows is lost so that the mosque can then

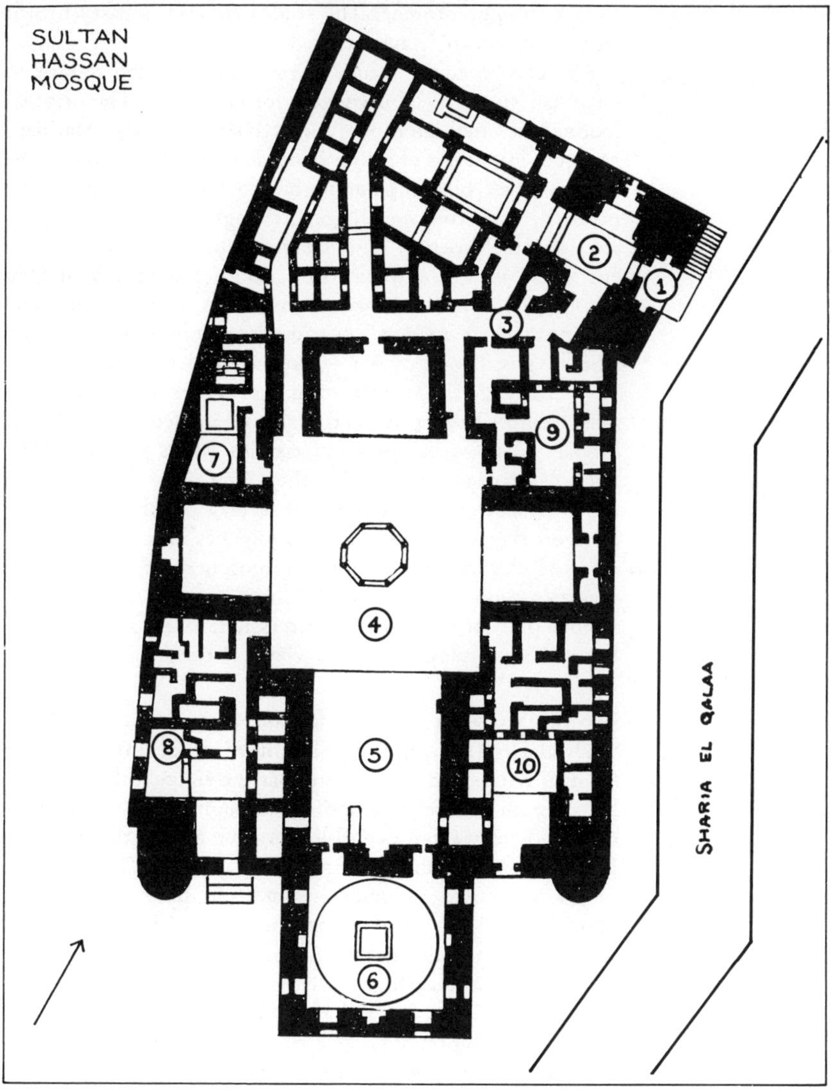

SULTAN HASSAN MOSQUE

1. Entrance
2. Vestibule
3. Corridor
4. Sahn
5. Sanctuary liwan
6. Mausoleum
7. Hanbalite school
8. Hanefite school
9. Malikite school
10. Shafite school

seem a disappointment. The stucco anyway is pasty brown with sand and dirt, and other details need cleaning.

The gazebo at the centre of the sahn has been rebuilt in Ottoman style and is used now for ablutions. The original fountain is met later on in this chapter at the Maridani Mosque. Hundreds of chains hang down from the liwans, the glow of their oil lamps at night a delight reserved for the imagination as they are all gone, though some can be seen in the Islamic Museum. The sanctuary liwan is opposite the entrance passage, a Kufic band running within it and an unfortunately fussy marble decoration on its qibla wall. The columns on either side of the mihrab are from some Christian edifice, possibly Crusader – they do not seem Byzantine. Further to either side of the mihrab are doors leading into the mausoleum. The right-hand door is panelled with original bronze inlaid with gold and dazzles when polished. The mausoleum dome collapsed in the 17th C. and was rebuilt in the 18th C. in the lofty imperial style of Istanbul, though it rests on the original stalactite squinches. Rich though the restored decorations are, the atmosphere is sombre and Hassan's cenotaph, surrounded by a wooden screen where women pray for the Sultan's intercession, is very simple. From the grilled windows there are views of the Citadel.

Returning towards the Citadel you once more enter Midan Salah al-Din, extended by clearances at the instruction of General Kitchener. It was here that the annual pilgrimage to Mecca gathered before winding through streets lined with thousands of spectators and leaving the city at the northern Fatimid gates of Bab al-Futuh and Bab al-Nasr. The long park to its south was a parade ground and polo field for the Mamelukes. Up a ramp at the front of the Citadel is a gate, closed to the public, Bab al-Azab. The crooked lane hehind the gate, enclosed by high walls, was the scene of the massacre of the Mamelukes by Mohammed Ali in 1811. Only one escaped, leaping on horseback through a gap in the wall into a moat. During the Ottoman occupation and even under Napoleon the Mamelukes had survived and were a power to be reckoned with. Mohammed Ali invited them to dinner at the Citadel, bidding them homewards via this cul-de-sac and cutting them down with their bellies full.

Massacre of the Mamelukes

The Citadel

The entry to the Citadel is round to the left, that is clockwise round its base. There is another entrance round the rear, off the Heliopolis and airport road. Much of the Citadel is off-limits, reserved for the military, an echo of its role as stronghold of the city from the time Saladin in 1176 built his fortress here to the reign of Mohammed Ali. For nearly 700 years nearly all Egypt's rulers lived in the Citadel, held court, dispensed justice and received ambassadors. A succession of palaces and elaborate buildings thrown up during the Mameluke period were mostly levelled by Mohammed Ali when he built his mosque and Bijou Palace in their place. The palace, to the south of the mosque, is now a museum housing objects of its era and makes a pleasant visit if you have the time.

Mosque of Mohammed Ali

The Mosque of Mohammed Ali, a Turkish delight on the Cairo skyline, proves disappointing close up – though perhaps not for those who have never visited an imperial Ottoman mosque in Turkey. Half domes rise as buttresses for the high central dome and the two thin minarets add an ethereal touch, more in tune perhaps with our oriental dreams than the robust Arab minarets of Cairo. But the alabaster cladding, a gesture of baroque luxe, has cheapened with time, while the pretty courtyard with its gingerbread clock (given by Louis Philippe in exchange for the obelisk in the Place de la Concorde), suggests a folly rigged up for fashion and amusement. That could explain why the mosque is so popular with tourists, for also the interior is vast and agreeably cool, the dome huge and the decorations in opulent bad taste. Principally, though, the architecture is routine; there is no feeling of lift or weightlessness to the dome that you find in the better Istanbul mosques, nor an appeal to spiritual contemplation. Mohammed Ali, whose tomb is on the right as you enter, meant this more as a symbol of the Ottoman power he had snatched.

Panorama

From the parapet to the southwest there is a good view of the mosques of Hassan and Tulun and a panorama of the city which will be more or less impressive depending on the cinerous haze that heat and Helwan together smother Cairo with.

Mosque of al-Nasr Mohammed

Across from the entrance to the courtyard of the Mohammed Ali Mosque is the Mosque of al-Nasr Mohammed (143), not much visited, dating from 1318-35. Once the principal mosque of the Citadel, it was built in the congregational style with an arcaded courtyard, many of the columns re-used from pharaonic, Roman and Byzantine buildings. Plain though it is outside, it is beautiful inside, all the moreso as Turkish vandals stripped it of its marble panels, revealing its simple elegance. The two minarets are unique for the pincushion shape of their tops and their Mongol-inspired faience decoration, of which only traces remain.

Joseph's Well

On leaving the Mosque of al-Nasr, turn right and go round it, then take the first road to the right on the east side of the mosque. This bring you to a tower which stands over Yusuf's (or Joseph's) Well (305), also known as Salah al-Din's Well or Dir al-Halazun, the Well of the Snail for the spiral staircase leading 88 metres down the great central shaft to the level of the Nile. Yusuf was one of Saladin's names and the well was dug during his time by Crusader prisoners, providing a secure source of water in case of siege. The water reaches the well by natural rather than artificial channels, and was brought up by donkeys, the rock steps covered with earth to provide them with a foothold.

Mausoleum of Imam al-Shaf'i in the Southern Cemetery

At this point you can interrupt your progress north with a visit to the Southern Cemetery, a vast, confusing and often dilapidated Moslem necropolis stretching as far as Maadi. The Northern Cemetery offers the more impressive monuments and will be covered at the end of the following chapter. But if you avail yourself of transport (it would be a long walk, there and back), the Mausoleum of Imam al-Shaf'i (281) in the Southern Cemetery would repay an excursion.

The mausoleum is most easily reached by heading south from the Citadel along the street bearing the Imam's name, a distance of about 2 kms from Midan Salah al-Din. A descendant of an uncle to the Prophet, al-Shaf'i was the founder of one of the four rites of Sunni Islam and died in 820. The cenotaph was put here by Saladin and the mausoleum built by his brother-successor's wife who is also buried here. The mausoleum is covered by a large wooden dome sheathed in lead and is the largest Islamic mortuary chamber in Egypt. The interior is colourful and the original lighting system of lamps suspended from carved beams is intact – the only such in Cairo. The spot itself is of significance: it was here that Saladin founded the first madrasa in Egypt to counter the Fatimid heresy, and it became a centre of Shafite missionary work, the rite predominant even today in southern Arabia, Bahrain, Malaysia and East Africa. The majority of Cairenes, too, are Shafites, and as the Imam is revered as one of the great Moslem saints (achieved by popular acclamation, as there is no formal notion of sainthood in Islam), the mausoleum is annually – in the eighth month of the Moslem calendar, lasting for a week from, usually, the first Wednesday – the site of a great *moulid,* an anniversary birthday festival, in honour of Shaf'i. Atop the dome, like a weathervane, is a metal boat in which there used to be placed, on the occasion of the moulid, about 150 kilos of wheat and a camel-load of water for the birds. The boat is said to turn sometimes when there is no wind to move it, and, according to the position it takes, to foretoken various events, good or evil, such as plenty or scarcity, or the death of some great man.

But to continue our journey northwards, let us assume we are back at the Citadel. You should leave the Citadel by the northeast entrance (the one you entered if you came up from Midan Salah al-Din), turning left as soon as you pass through the gate. Down the hill you cross over the road which issues east out of the midan and you enter Sharia el Mahga. The road plunges downhill and soon becomes Sharia Bab el Wazir, the Street of the Gate of the Vizier, and later becomes Darb el Ahmar, the Red Road, as it runs up to Bab Zuwayla. This entire district is known as Darb el Ahmar, a name which nowadays epitomises a poorer, broken-down section of the city. At the Citadel end which is entirely residential the street is fairly quiet and fairly filthy; it becomes livelier, and you do not notice the filth so much, as you enter the bazaar area further north. Apart from the ruins of many old houses and some fine intact monuments, you may also encounter the gaiety of a marriage procession, a great noise of motor scooters, car horns, tambourines, ululations, whistling, chanting and cries, an amazing public racket by no more than two dozen people escorting the bride and groom through the streets.

Along Sharia Bab el Wazir

Aqsunqur, the Blue Mosque

Soon on your right you come to the Mosque of Aqsunqur (123), better known as the Blue Mosque and much beloved for the wrong reasons by tour guides. It was built in 1347 but usurped in 1652 by the Turkish Governor Ibrahim Agha who slapped up the tiles that give the mosque its popular name. The best Turkish tiles were from Iznik; these were made in Ottoman factories at Damascus and are poorly decorated and often marred as well in the glazing. They are along the qibla wall and around the walls of Agha's tomb which you enter through a door on the right side of the courtyard. The worst thing about the tiles is their inappropriateness, for the mosque is otherwise charmingly simple. A stand of palms and other trees makes the courtyard an agreeable place to linger after the hot desolate sahns of other mosques. The pillars round the courtyard, and especially the octagonal ones of the sanctuary, are crude, but contribute to the rustic pleasantness of the whole. The finest work is the carved stone minbar, which is original. On the left before entering the courtyard is the tomb of Sultan Kuchuk, The Little One, a brother of Hassan who ruled for five months at the age of six, but was then deposed, imprisoned in the Citadel, and three years later strangled by another of his brothers.

From the street you can see behind the Aqsunqur a section of Saladin's walls which extended from the Fatimid city in the north to Fustat in the south, the Mamelukes using a part of its southern section to carry their aqueduct. Across the street from the mosque is a Turkish apartment building from 1625.

Maridani Mosque

Continuing north, Sharia Bab el Wazir becomes Darb el Ahmar and set at an angle to this street, on the left-hand side, is the Maridani Mosque (120). Built in 1339-40 in the early Mameluke period, it is one of the oldest buildings in the quarter which until the 14th C. had been Fatimid and Ayyubid cemeteries.

Removing Shoes

Entering from the hurly-burly of the street you are soon absorbed into the restfulness of the Maridani, a monument, yes, but no museum, no entry fee, no one to ask baksheesh for shoe covers for there are none, and you leave your shoes inside the door and walk about in your socks. Not that you need worry about form, but as a matter of interest a Moslem will carry his shoes in his left hand, sole to sole (the left hand being for unclean uses), and he will put his right foot first over the threshold. If he has not already performed the ablution outside, he will at once go to the inner fountain. Before praying, he will place his shoes on the matting, a little before the spot where his head will touch the ground, and again, to avoid contaminating the mosque, he will put his shoes one upon the other, sole to sole.

Isolation from the outside world is as much a matter of tranquil ambience as it is of ritual cleanliness. The atmosphere attracts many who come not only for prayer: here I have seen men sleeping, boys doing their homework leaning up against the qibla screen, a dozen women talking and their children playing at the fountain (the one removed from the Sultan Hassan). Yet all of these things are against the precepts of Mohammed, and even though Lane reported, 150 years ago, eating, sewing and spinning as well, these activities ceased during prayers, though here, too, I have seen the hum of irreligion continue while men were on their palms and knees, submitting themselves to Allah.

Prayers

Prayers are performed five times a day, though mostly at home, with better off people rarely visiting a mosque except for Friday prayers. But wherever they are performed, prayers follow the same procedure, which is quite involved. First the worshipper will stand, facing Mecca, and inaudibly propose a prayer of so many *rek'ahs,* or inclinations of the head. He then says "Allahu Akbar", God is great, and recites the opening chapter of the Koran, followed by three or more other verses, again says "Allahu Akbar" and makes an inclination of the head and body. Next he drops gently to his knees, places his palms upon the ground, his nose and forehead touching the ground between them, and during this prostration says "I extol the perfection of my Lord, the Great", three times. Though still kneeling, he raises his head and body, again says "God is great", and bends his head a second time to the ground and repeats what he has said before. This – and it is a simplification of the full litany – completes one rek'ah and will take about a minute, though several rek'ahs will be preformed and there must be no wandering of the mind, no irregular movement and no interruptions, otherwise the procedure must be gone over from the beginning. Islam literally means submission and that is what the procedure achieves. The concentration required explains why mosques are often so austere: architecturally they should be conducive to prayer, but should not distract with decorations. That does not explain why, nowadays, and in some mosques, women should be chattering in the corner and children splashing in the fountain, yet it does all fit together most agreeably, and if you stand here in the open courtyard of the Maridani at evening, you may see a crescent moon hanging from the approving sky.

An easy rhythm of arches on slender columns runs round the courtyard, an inner and an outer series, a third and partial fourth (on either side of the mihrab) added to the qibla arcade. A wooden screen separates the qibla from the courtyard, a unique feature in Cairo, and, inside, the arcade is pleasantly dark. The mihrab and the minbar wall have had their mosaic decorations well restored. The dome above the mihrab is supported by two pink granite pharaonic columns. The merlons along the parapet of the courtyard are at intervals topped by curious pots. Try, if you can, to climb up the minaret for a more immediate view of the medieval city than you can get from the Citadel.

Mosque of Qijmas al-Ishaqi

Another 150 metres up the street is the Mosque of Qijmas al-Ishaqi (114), built in 1480-1 during the Burgi Mameluke period. It has been squeezed into a triangular plot where a street joins Darb el Ahmar from the right, yet despite this the Mameluke fashion for rectangular illusion succeeds, at least at first glance. Inside, however, a sacrifice has been made in the cruciform plan: the north and south liwans are merely vestigial. So restricted was the space that the *kuttab,* the Koranic school usually part of the mosque, had to be sited across the street joining from the right; it is now derelict.

But the mosque itself has been very well restored and

though around this period – only a few decades before the Turkish domination – Mameluke architecture began to deteriorate, there was a last bravado of decorative artistry with fine marble inlays and beautifully carved stone and stucco. Within this covered mosque is a feast of detail, yet all of it harmonious and restful; nothing jitters, jumps or jars. The east and west liwans are supported by arches with a slight return, the stonework in alternating red and white, the vaults very fine and the stucco windows excellent. The inlaid marble floor is covered with mats (the mosque is in daily use), but the keeper will lift these if you ask, the best section being the mosaic flooring of the east liwan. You can also ask to go up the minaret from which there is a clear view of Bab Zuwayla.

The tomb chamber by the entrance is plain and dignified beneath a lofty dome. But Qijmas, Master of the Sultan's Horse and officer in charge of the yearly pilgrimage to Mecca, died in Syria and is buried at Damascus; the chamber contains the more recent tomb of a 19th C. holy man. Mamelukes and Turks of Qijmas' rank built not only for Allah or themselves, but also for the community, and a *sabil* or public watering fountain was often provided. This was in keeping with Mohammed's reply when asked what was the most meritorious act: "To give people water to drink". You can see its grille outside at what was a convenient height for drawing water 500 years ago, though now well below street level.

To Bab Zuwayla

Darb el Ahmar now bends to the west, a surviving section of Fatimid wall concealed by the buildings on your right, and opens into a square dominated by Bab Zuwayla (see following chapter), the massive southern gate into the Fatimid city. The place has long had a reputation for being unlucky, perhaps because it led out to the cemeteries now built over by the Darb el Ahmar quarter, though also it was the site of public executions. Tumanbay, the last independent Mameluke Sultan, was hanged here by the Turks. Twice the rope broke, the third time his neck.

The street running directly south from Bab Zuwayla is the continuation of the principal Fatimid street to the north and extends all the way down, past the Mosque of Ibn Tulun and through Saladin's walls to the vicinity of the Mausoleum of Imam al-Shaf'i. This was the longest thoroughfare of the medieval city and along here amidst great festivity the Mecca pilgrims would begin their arduous journey. It changes its name several times and can be worth following for its own sake a little to the south where it is first the Street of the Tentmakers, becoming less colourful as the Street of the Saddlemakers before crossing Sharia el Qalaa.

Mosque of Salih Talai

On the corner of this street and Darb el Ahmar, facing the square, is the Mosque of Salih Talai (116), built in 1160 towards the close of the Fatimid period. A congregational mosque, perfectly rectangular in the Fatimid pattern, it is one of the most handsome in Cairo. A lower level of shops, again once at street level, was part of Salih Talai's *waqf* or endowment, as other mosques might have had fields or adjacent apartment buildings, the rents contributing to the mosque's upkeep. The facade, therefore, would have been higher, its effect still more imposing. Its five keel-arches, supported by classical columns linked by wooden tie-beams, are flanked by sunken false arches or panels topped by stylised shell niches – the whole a perfect expression of the Fatimid style. The arches, however, form a narthex or porch unique in Cairo. Along its interior wall another set of panels, each one immediately behind an open keel-arch, runs in muted harmony. In its proportion and reserve the narthex is a fine composition in classical measure. The mosque interior is spacious, an agreeable rhythm of keel-arches and tie-beams running round the arcades.

PRACTICAL INFORMATION

To reach the starting point of this tour you can take a **taxi** or you can ride to Midan Salah al-Din (for the Sultan Hassan Mosque and the Citadel) on the **No. 72 bus** from Midan el Tahrir.

Mosques that are still places of worship are usually open throughout the day and into the evening. There is no entrance fee, though baksheesh should be paid for services, eg shoe coverings, being taken up a minaret. The mosques of Mohammed Ali, Hassan and Ibn Tulun, however, all charge an **entrance fee** of 10PT to 25PT. You should not assume that these will be open after 4pm. The Gayer-Anderson House is a museum and charges 25PT entry (a ticket to the Islamic Museum – see next chapter – gains you entry here on the same day); its hours are 8.30am to 4pm daily except on Fridays when they are 9am to noon.

For those with limited time, an **abbreviated itinerary** for the southern quarters of Islamic Cairo should concentrate on the Citadel, the mosques of Hassan and Ibn Tulun and the Gayer-Anderson House.

CAIRO 4: THE ISLAMIC CITY (THE NORTHERN QUARTERS)

The route This chapter starts with a visit to the Islamic Museum and then picks up where the last chapter left off, at Bab Zuwayla, for a walk northwards through the Fatimid city, still more richly adorned with monuments – Mameluke and Ottoman as well as Fatimid – than the southern quarters. The distance covered is not as great but the places visited are more numerous. Along the way you pass through the Muski and Khan el Khalili bazaars and eventually arrive at the northern gates, Bab al-Futuh and Bab al-Nasr. To the west of the Fatimid city is the Northern Cemetery or City of the Dead.

Remember that along this route the Islamic monuments are identified by little numbered green and white plaques, corresponding to the numbers given here in parentheses.

The Islamic Museum The Islamic Museum is at the intersection of Sharias el Qalaa and Port Said, its entrance on the latter. Of course the museum could be visited before you explore any part of Islamic Cairo, but for the neophyte, anyway, a visit at this point, halfway through the tour, might be best: you will already have seen enough to make you conversant with form and curious about detail, and you will explore the Fatimid city with greater appreciation.

A revelation, met especially here, is how much you miss human and animal representation in Islamic art and architecture. This is a museum without statues or paintings, where nearly every object is beautifully worked design. A different sort of attention is required, and perhaps you wish sometimes, more here than at other museums, that the exhibits could have remained *in situ,* admired as parts of a whole. But then the collection began, in 1880, precisely because the monuments from which they mostly came had suffered a long period of neglect – it was only then, in part at European instigation, that the Egyptian government first seriously undertook preservation of Cairo's Islamic treasures.

The exhibits are well presented and lit and are arranged in 23 rooms which proceed chronologically for the most part, though some rooms specialise in examples of a single subject, eg textiles, from several periods. Though no guide book is available, the exhibits are numbered and labelled, often in English and French as well as in Arabic. A satisfying tour can be accomplished in an hour and a half. The rooms are on one floor and a brief outline follows, but note that some rooms may be closed and their contents either inaccessible or to be found in another nearby room.

Room 1 contains recent acquisitions, though also some permanent exhibits, including a 14th C. bronze lantern and a collection of Islamic coins.

Ummayad

Room 2 deals with the Ummayad period (7th-8th C.) whose art was representational and drew on Hellenistic and Sassanian (Persian) sources.

Abbasid and Tulunid

Room 3 is Abbasid (8th-10th C.) and includes Tulunid (9th-10th C.) works. Here there is greater stylisation, with the emphasis on decoration rather than representation, with great use of stucco, characterised by its slant cut. There are stucco panels from Samarra in Iraq, and tombstones, of which 3904, dating from 858, has fine Kufic inscriptions.

Fatimid

Room 4 displays works of the Fatimid period (10th-12th C)., with examples of very fine woodwork, carved with human and animal figures and foliage. The Fatimids, who were Shi'ites, did not observe the Sunni prohibition on representation of high living forms, and were much influenced by the Persians, whose craftsmen they imported. Note especially the carved wooden panels from the Maristan of Qalaun. Also there are frescoes from an 11th C. *hamam* or baths.

Ayyubid

Room 4B, off Room 4, has fine wood, marble and stucco carving of the Ayyubid period (12th-13th C.).

Before entering *Room 5,* note above the dividing arch the windows of openwork plaster filled with coloured glass (16th-18th C., Ottoman period). (The museum, incidentally, is not visited nearly as much as it deserves to be, so that you often receive personal attention. In this case, the attendant will turn off the main lights and illuminate the coloured windows for effect.)

Mameluke

The room contains works of the Mameluke period (13th-16th C.). There is a beautiful 14th C. fountain sunk into the floor (the attendant will turn it on). Despite the bloody succession of Mameluke sultans, Egypt during much of this period enjoyed peace and the decorative arts flourished. A Chinese influence was felt in Mameluke ceramics and pottery. Soft woods were inlaid with ivory, bone, tin and ebony, usually in star-polygons, the Naskhi cursive supplanted the squat Kufic style of decorative inscription, and arabesque floral designs found favour. A 13th C. wooden door (602) at the far end of the room shows both square Kufic and cursive Naskhi calligraphy. It is from the Mosque of al-Salih Ayyub.

Woodwork *Rooms 6-10* are devoted to woodwork, illustrating the development of the art. In *Room 6* on the far wall is a carved frieze from the Maristan of Qalaun, showing scenes of hunting, music and other personal activities rarely found in Islamic art. In *Room 7* are *mashrabiyyas,* wooden screens which preserved the privacy of the house from the gaze of the street while still admitting refreshing breezes. They were also used to screen off interior harem rooms from courtyards and reception halls. The projecting niches were for placing porous water jars for cooling. *Room 8* has examples of inlaid wood, while *Room 9* displays wood and bronze work.

In *Room 10,* off Room 9, you will be asked to sit down on a lattice-backed seat round a column fountain which will be turned on for you and illuminated. This is a restful and eye-filling place to linger: gaze up at the exquisite woodwork ceiling, carved and coffered, with three dome recesses, the centre one with windows round it for ladies of the harem to see below. The period is 17th-18th C.

Metalwork *Room 11* is hung with 14th C. bronze chandeliers, and in the cases are various metal objects, eg a perfume brazier (15111, Case 7).

Room 12 contains armour and weapons, many of them chased and inlaid. In Case 7 are swords belonging to Mehmet II, who conquered Constantinople (4264), and Suleiman the Magnificent (4263). And another in the same case, opposite the windows on the right, which has had a remarkable history: the sword of Muradbey, commander of the Mamelukes, was taken by the French general Murat after he had chased the Mamelukes up the Nile, and was presented to Napoleon who in turn wore it when calling on the Directory shortly before seizing power on 18 Brumaire 1799. He had it with him also at Waterloo, and leaving it in his carriage which he abandoned in haste after the battle, it was presented to Wellington.

Pottery *Rooms 13-16* contain pottery of various periods from Egypt and as far west as Spain, as far east as China.

Tapestries *Room 17* displays tapestries of various periods from Egypt, Iraq and Persia, and an assortment of damaged pottery (though this room may still be closed and its contents found in Room 16).

Stonework Leading off Room 19 is an outdoor court which is *Room 18* and is principally of Turkish headstones and tombs, but also other stone objects, including a sundial and water level measures.

Books and manuscripts *Room 19* is devoted to the art of the book with many illuminated manuscripts and, in the centre case, manuscripts of Avicenna on anatomy and botany. While Europe slept through its Dark Ages, Islam sparkled with genius. Avicenna, as he was known in Europe, Ibn Sina (980-1037) in the Moslem world, was one of the greatest physicians of his time. He is mentioned by Chaucer in *The Canterbury Tales*. The Arabs did not alter the basic medical theory of the Greeks, but they enriched it by practical observation and clinical experience, recorded in manuscripts such as these, and passed on their learning to the world.

Turkish

Room 20 exhibits Turkish art since the 15th C., including tapestries, china and jewellery.

Lamps

Between Rooms 20 and 21 are enamelled glass lamps which the attendant will illuminate, while there are more glass lamps in cases round the walls of *Room 21* and in the centre a fine Isfahan carpet that once belonged to King Farouk. The lamps are from mosques (and include some of those now entirely missing from the liwans of the Sultan Hassan) and are arranged chronologically from left to right from the 12th through the 15th C.

Persian

Room 22 contains Persian objects, mostly pottery, some of which (Cases 1 and 2) has been copied from Chinese models.

Room 23 is for temporary exhibitions.

The Egyptian Library

In the same building but on the upper floor is the Egyptian Library with its entrance on Sharia el Qalaa. Containing over 750,000 volumes and a vast collection of manuscripts of the Koran dating back to the 8th C. and, most outstanding visually, a collection of Persian manuscripts adorned with miniatures of imaginative conception and frequently employing living forms as distinct from the purely ornamental art of the Korans.

Entering the Fatimid city by Bab Zuwayla

We now turn to Bab Zuwayla, built at the same time (11th C.) and in a plan similar to Bab al-Futuh and Bab al-Nasr to the north. These three are the last surviving of the 60 gates that once encircled medieval Cairo and which, well into the 19th C., were shut at night, enclosing the city's then 240,000 population. Except that Bab Zuwayla had long since found itself outflanked by the growth of the city to the south (where it was delimited by Saladin's walls), and in fact marked the city centre. The architects of all three were probably Christian, from Syria or Anatolia, and the projecting round towers connected by a walkway and an arch repeating the curve of the gateway below show Byzantine rather than Arab inspiration. Springing from the massive towers are the elegant minarets of the Mosque of Muayyad, its serrated dome further back seeming to rise between them.

The gate was named for the al-Zawila, a Berber tribe whose Fatimid soldiery were quartered nearby. But most inhabitants know it as the al-Mitwalli after El Kutb al-Mitwalli, the holiest man alive at any one time, who would assume a humble demeanour and simple dress, and station himself inconspicuously, even invisibly, at certain favourite places. Bab Zuwayla was the most famous of these in Egypt, though he could flit to Tanta in the Delta, or to Mecca and back, in an instant. His service was to reprove the impious, expose the sanctimonious, and to distribute evils and blessings, the awards of destiny. Into the earlier part of this century, passers-by would recite the opening verse of the Koran, while those with headache would drive a nail into the door, or sufferers from a recent toothache would fix their tooth to it as a charm against recurrence. Locks of hair, bits of clothing, would also be attached by the sick in search of a miracle, and, it is said, even without these entreaties, the saint still makes his presence known by a gleam of light mysteriously appearing behind the west door.

Mosque of Muayyad

Passing through the gate, you should enter the Mosque of Muayyad (190) on your left, less for any intrinsic interest, though it is restful and has a garden, than for access to the top of Bab Zuwayla or even up one of the minarets. This is a view of medieval Cairo from its heart and it is splendid. The last of the great open courtyard congregational mosques, the Muayyad was built in 1416-20 by the Burgi Mameluke Muayyad Shaykh who had been imprisoned on the spot before becoming Sultan.

Souks

This street running north from Bab Zuwayla is Sharia Muizz (named for the Caliph of the Fatimid conquest), though over its distance between Bab Zuwayla and Bab al-Futuh it enjoys successive traditional names, each one demarcating a souk reserved to a particular trade or the sale of a particular type of merchandise – ensuring, subject to proper bargaining, price control by competition between neighbours. Alongside Muayyad's mosque, for example, the street is Shari'es-Sukkariya, the sugar bazaar. Competition, however, was not the only control on market prices: the Mohtesib, an officer on horseback, would regularly ride through the souks, preceded by a man carrying a pair of scales and followed by the executioner. If spot checks revealed short weights, a butcher for example, or a baker, would have his nose pierced with a hook, a piece of meat, a loaf of bread, suspended from it as the poor man was himself tied to the grilled window of a mosque and left to endure the heat of the sun, the indifference of passers-

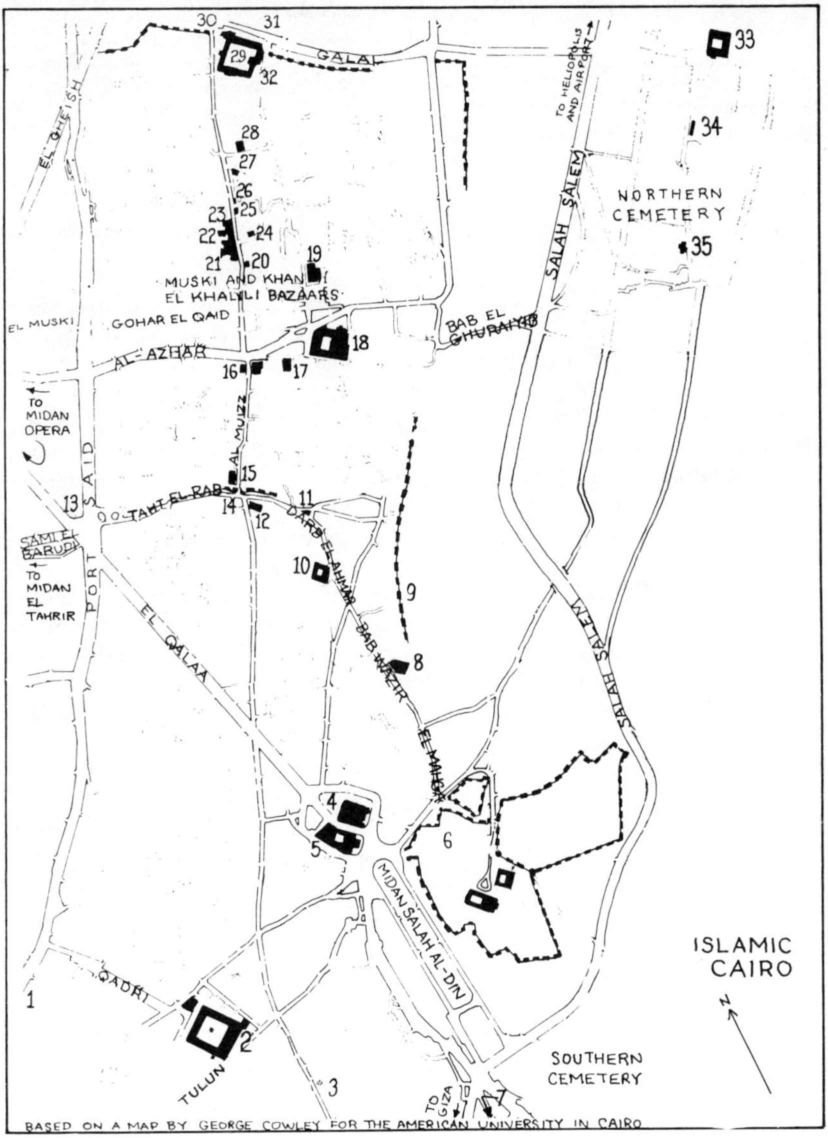

1. Mosque of Sayyida Zeinab
2. Mosque of Ibn Tulun and the Gayer-Anderson House
3. Tomb of Shagarat al-Durr
4. Rifa'i Mosque
5. Mosque of Sultan Hassan
6. The Citadel
7. Mausoleum of Imam al-Shaf'i
8. Aqsunqur (Blue) Mosque
9. Saladin's walls
10. Maridani Mosque
11. Qijmas al-Ishaqi Mosque
12. Mosque of Salih Talai
13. Islamic Museum and Egyptian Library
14. Bab Zuwayla

15. Mosque of Muayyad
16. Madrasa and Mausoleum of al-Ghuri
17. Okel of al-Ghuri
18. Mosque of al-Azhar
19. Mosque of Sayyidna al-Hussein
20. Mausoleum and Madrasa of al-Salih Ayyub
21. Madrasa, Mausoleum and Maristan of Sultan Qalaun
22. Mausoleum of al-Nasr
23. Mosque of Barquq
24 .House of Uthman Katkhuda
25. Qasr Beshtak
26. Sabil Kuttab of Abdul Rahman Katkhuda
27. Mosque of al-Aqmar
28. Bayt al-Suhaymi
29. Mosque of al-Hakim
30. Bab al-Futuh
31. Bab al-Nasr
32. Wakala of Qaytbay
33. Mausoleum of Barquq
34. Mausoleum of Ashraf Baybars
35. Mausoleum of Qaytbay

by. One butcher who sold short was deprived of that much flesh from his own body, while a seller of *kunefeh,* that vermicelli pasta you still see prepared along the streets at night, was fried on his own copper tray for overcharging.

Madrasa and Mausoleum of al-Ghuri

Continuing up to the intersection with the modern Sharia al-Azhar, you find yourself between two Mameluke buildings, the Madrasa of Sultan al-Ghuri (189) on the left and his Mausoleum (67) on the right. Al-Ghuri was the penultimate Mameluke Sultan and the last to reign for any duration (1500-16). A keen polo player into his seventies, a grandiose builder, an arbitrary despot, a torturer, murderer and thief, in short no less than what you would expect a Mameluke sultan to be, he inaugurated his madrasa in May 1503 with a great banquet attended by the Abbasid Caliph and all the principal civil, military and religious officials, the souks down to Bab Zuwayla magnificently illuminated and decorated. A contemporary chronicler, Ibn Iyas, wrote that "the new building was richly decorated and garnished with a profusion of marble. It was a splendid construction of sumptuous elegance, to which one could compare no contemporary monument. Nevertheless, the Sultan was generally reproached for having built it with the aid of illicit confiscations, not to mention the fact that most of the marble had been taken from other buildings, extorted at ridiculous prices".

Perhaps that bit of gossip at the end was meant to balance the saccharine appreciation of al-Ghuri's confection, for though agreeably exotic at first impression, with strong lines and bold *ablaq,* that red and white pattern of the minaret with its curious topping of five small bulbous domes, on closer inspection there is a lack of elegance in the details, and in climbing up to the roof you see that the ablaq is not contrasting stone but crudely painted on.

Across the street, the mausoleum dome, now collapsed, had to be rebuilt three times during al-Ghuri's reign, and as though shrewdly realising that this might be an unsafe place to be buried, he got himself killed outside Aleppo in a losing battle against the Turks. His luckless successor, that same Tumanbay who was hanged three times at Bab Zuwayla, is buried here instead.

The spice bazaar

If you thread your way through the narrow passages behind the madrasa you arrive at the heart of the bazaar area, especially when you find your way to the Suq el Attarin, the spice bazaar, with its appeal to all the senses. Sacks of saffron, cinnamon and ginger pile on either side, fruits and flowers are dried and powdered, and precious attar of roses is caught in bottles, the unadulterated essence of perfume. Awnings submerge alleyways in watery twilight, colour blurs, texture turns to dust and hangs in shafts of sunlight, past centuries return on caravans of imagination.

Okel of al-Ghuri

Heading east instead, along Sharia al-Azhar, you come after about 100 metres to the Okel of al-Ghuri (64) on your right, unmistakably Mameluke with its ablaq masonry and strong, square lines. Built in 1504-5, this is Cairo's best preserved example of a merchants' hotel, the animals quartered on the ground floor and their masters above. The courtyard would be the scene of unloading aromatic cargoes, with buyers and sellers sitting round and bargaining. This okel was built just at the time that the Portuguese were dealing a blow to Egypt's overland trade with the East by their discovery of new routes round the Cape to India. Even so, as late as 1835 there were still 200 okels serving Cairo's bazaars.

Midaq Alley

Egyptian novelist Naguib Mahfouz' *Zuqaq al-Midaq* or *Midaq Alley* is set in the Azhar quarter of the medieval city: "Many things combine to show that Midaq Alley is one of the gems of times gone by and that it once shone forth like a flashing star in the history of Cairo. Which Cairo do I mean? That of the Fatimids, the Mamelukes or the Sultans? Only God and the archaeologists known the answer to that, but in any case, the alley is certainly an ancient relic and a precious one. How could it be otherwise with its stone-paved surface leading directly to historic Sharia Sanadiqiya. And then there is its coffeeshop known as 'Kirsha's'. Its walls decorated with multicoloured arabesques, now crumbling, give off strong odours from the medicines of olden times, smells which have now become the spices and folk-cures of today and tomorrow. Although Midaq Alley lives in almost complete isolation from all surrounding activity, it clamours with a distinctive and personal life of its own. Fundamentally and basically, its roots connect with life as a whole and yet, at the same time, it retains a number of the secrets of a world now past". Though the new Sharia al-Azhar has obliterated Sanadiqiya itself, Midaq Alley survives – in any of the side streets hereabouts.

Mosque of al-Azhar

The famous Mosque of al-Azhar (97), 'the most blooming', is 100 metres east of al-Ghuri's caravanserai, the first mosque of the Fatimid city (completed in 971), the oldest university in the world and the foremost centre of Islamic theology. Its age and importance have caused it to be rebuilt and added to many times, the result confusing and unremarkable. The court and arcades are basically Fatimid, but their interest lies in the people gathered here, students and teachers at lessons, some pacing back and forth, mumbling to themselves, memorising religious texts, others dozing.

Throughout the millenium of its existence, al-Azhar has offered free instruction and board to students from all over the Islamic world, form West Africa to the East Indies, its courses sometimes lasting 15 years. *Riwaqs* or apartments are set aside around three sides of the court for specific nationalities or provinces of Egypt, and here students have traditionally studied religious, moral, civil and criminal law, grammar, rhetoric, theology, logic, algebra and calculations on the Moslem calendar which is based on the moon, its festivals changeable but always advancing against the secular solar calendar. The Chapel of the Blind at the eastern angle of al-Azhar accommodates blind students, once notorious for their outrageous behaviour. Fanatical in their belief and easily thinking themselves persecuted, they would rush out into the streets, snatching at turbans, beating people with their staves and groping about for infidels to kill.

Al-Azhar's religious curriculum has remained unchanged since the days of Saladin, who turned al-Azhar from a hotbed of Shi'ism to the home of orthodoxy, though Nasser obliged the university to include, too, schools of medicine, science and foreign languages, so that now in many ways it is competitive with other institutions of higher education in Egypt. The more conventional buildings of the modern university are behind the mosque proper.

You enter the mosque through the double-arched Gate of the Barbers (the only one open to visitors) where formerly students had their heads shaved, and for a bit of baksheesh can ascend the minaret of Qaytbay. Passing into the courtyard, on the left is the library, worth a visit, and to the right a 14th C. madrasa with a fine mihrab. The sanctuary hall directly opposite the entry gate is very deep, though in Fatimid times it did not extend beyond the fifth row of columns (that is five rows beyond the two of the east arcade), and the original mihrab remains. These columns were taken mostly from early churches. The sanctuary was extended to eight rows in the 18th C. and a new mihrab placed at its furthest, qibla, wall.

Mosque of Sayyidna al-Hussein

Leaving al-Azhar and walking north, you cross the busy Sharia Gohar el Qaid and enter a large square, used as a parking lot, before the Mosque of Sayyidna al-Hussein, a modern structure with slender Turkish-style minarets. A Fatimid mosque stood here originally but very little if any of it remains. This is now the main congregational mosque of Cairo and the President of the Republic comes here on feast days for prayers, while the open square is the centre for popular nightly celebrations throughout the month of Ramadan – well worth seeing.

Like the Sayyida Zeinab, the Hussein, named for a grandson of the Prophet, is not open to non-Moslems. Hussein's head brought to Cairo in 1153 in a green silk bag, is in the mausoleum, a relic of one of the most critical events in Islamic history, the schism between the Sunni majority and the Shi'ites.

The Sunni-Shi'ite schism

Mohammed was more than a prophet, he organised the Arab tribes into an enduring political and military force that within a hundred years or so of his death in 632 advanced as far west as Morocco and Spain, as far north as Poitiers and as far east as the Indus. But Mohammed died without naming a successor. His son-in-law Ali, husband of the Prophet's daughter Fatima, advanced his claim but after some argument Abu Bakr, one of Mohammed's companions, won acceptance as *Khalifat rasul-Allah* or successor to the Apostle of God. Abu Bakr was succeeded by Omar who was succeeded on his death by Othman, an old, weak and vacillating man, but a member of the powerful Umayyad family of Mecca. Tribal tensions within the ever-expanding Arab Empire led to revolt and his murder in 656. Again Ali put himself forward as the natural inheritor of the Caliphate, for not only was he related to Mohammed through Fatima, but he was a man of considerable religious learning and sincerity, while his supporters claimed the Umayyads were no more than power-seeking opportunists. The reality is that both sides cloaked political and economic aspirations in religious arguments. Ali however was opposed by Aisha, who had been Mohammed's favourite wife, along with her Umayyad family and many of Mohammed's surviving companions. He took to arms and won his first battle, but later saw his authority dissolve when rebels advanced on his army with copies of the Koran fixed to the points of their spears and his troops refused to fight. Ali was assassinated and the Umayyads were installed once again in the Caliphate.

The real wound to Islam occurred, however, when Ali's son – no mere in-law of the Prophet but of his blood – led a revolt against the by now overwhelming forces of the Umayyads and after a fanatical struggle was slain with all his men. In a sense, the Prophet's own blood had been shed – excusable, said the Ummayads, for Hussein was no more than an outlaw; martyrdom, replied those who had supported Ali and Hussein. It was on this matter of succession – divine right versus might – that Islam was riven, for the partisans or *Shia* of Ali refused to accept as caliph any but Ali's descendants, while the *Sunni,* followers of the *sunna,* The Way, barred the Caliphate to the Prophet's descendants for all time.

In fact, the Shi'ites went on to win some notable victories as when the Fatimids took Egypt, and to this day one-tenth of all Moslems (Iranians, most Iraqis and significant numbers in Yemen, Syria, Lebanon and eastern Arabia) still hold to the Shi'ite conviction that with the deaths of Ali and Hussein the greater part of Islam was stained with betrayal. All the same, this division within Islam is much less important than the doctrinal rifts within Christianity, and it is remarkable that it is here in the old Fatimid city, by the mausoleum containing the very head of the Shi'ite martyr, that the President of thoroughly Sunni Egypt should come to pray.

Muski

Muski and Khan el Khalili are used interchangeably by both foreigners and Egyptians alike to describe what are historically two different bazaars. Muski lies astride Sharia el Muski, a street of Mohammed Ali's period running east from Midan Ataba, pots, pans, plastic bowls and other prosaic wares sold at its western end but blending with the oriental atmosphere of Khan el Khalili which it joins to the east.

Khan el Khalili

Khan el Khalili is the larger and older of the two, and grew round a khan or caravanserai built in 1382 by Sultan Barquq's Master of Horse, Garkas el Khalili. It became known as the Turkish bazaar during the Ottoman period and has always attracted foreign merchants – Jews, Armenians, Persians and non-Egyptian Arabs – and so it is not surprising that today, along with the Muski, it is Cairo's tourist bazaar, selling souvenirs, perfume oils, jewellery, leather goods and fabrics. Of course the sight of so many tourists invites relentless importuning, but there is adventure all the same. Escape down back alleyways where an artisan sitting in his hole in the wall may patiently be making beads one by one from rough bits of stone, turning them on a spindle by means of a bow. Or start in bargaining and then break off – an accepted, indeed the expert pattern – and instead sip a proffered glass of tea, idling for hours if you like upon a pile of carpets without there being any sense of the need for business. Or go into Fishawi's, the famous café just off Midan Sayyidna Hussein. Here you can have the chance of easy conversation and a gentle smoke of a water pipe ("Don't inhale, it is not hashish.") On one occasion I sat here with a tourist brochure to Khalili and some of the habitués noticed it was of the area. They had not seen it before and looked through it, recognising in the photos friends of theirs: "Oh! He's down the street; and that is Gamal" they laughed, and "Ah, the old man there, he is dead now", etc.

You will probably want to spend more time here than our continuing tour of the Fatimid city allows. Return again, and meanwhile note that Khan el Khalili extends in part over the site of the now vanished Fatimid palaces which covered an area of 400,000 square metres and housed 12,000 domestics. The palaces, al-Muizz on the east side of Sharia Muizz and al-Aziz on the west, loomed like mountains when seen from afar; near to, they could not be seen at all, so high were the walls. Awe had returned to Egypt.

The Fatimid palaces

Street of the Coppersmiths

Sharia Muizz, as you leave the awning-covered alleyways of Khan el Khalili and walk north along it, is the Street of the Coppersmiths, some bashing of metal, much flashing of sunlight. Some reminders of the Fatimid period survive, though mostly the monuments are Mameluke. There should be a mosque on every street, it is said. Here mosques fight for every corner, their domes and minarets bunched like palms in an oasis grove. The scene is still that of the *Thousand and One Nights,* ostensibly set in Baghdad, though Baghdad by then had been razed by Tamerlane and it was the Cairo of the Mamelukes that was described. Sweet juices, cool water is sold in the street, the waterseller with a large flask slung under one arm like a bagpipe, round his waist the cups. He leans forward to pour, and for a moment you imagine this an obeisance to a passing sultan, and in the sweep of robes, the clattering of donkey carts, the bursts of reflected light from the coppersmiths' stalls, you easily imagine a triumphal entry, a parade of state, singers and poets preceding the royal appearance, celebrating the achievements of his reign. You see fluttering banners of silk and gold thread, then carried before the Sultan himself the jewelled saddlecloth, symbol of his sovereignty, and above his head a parasol of yellow silk surmounted with a golden cupola on which perches a golden bird, this held aloft by a prince of the blood, a band of flutes, of kettledrums, trumpets and hautboys passing now, their music mingling in the clamour of the street and then lost.

There is spectacle enough in Sharia Muizz, and behind its facades, to remind you that this was a city of beauty and mystery. Ruthless for power, cunning in government, brutal and barbarous often, the Mamelukes at their best were resourceful and vital, with an incomparable flair for architecture. Their grandiose designs, bold, vigorous and voluminous, were gracefully decorated with the play of arabesques, the embroidery of light through stained-glass windows.

Mausoleum and Madrasa of al-Salih Ayyub

You come first, on the right, to the Mausoleum and Madrasa of al-Salih Ayyub, diagonally opposite the Maristan of Qalaun. Where the street now presses its way was once, in Fatimid times, a broad avenue, so broad it served as a parade ground, the great palaces looking down upon it from either side. Throughout the Fatimid and Mameluke periods, this was the very centre of Cairo.

The Mausoleum and Madrasa of al-Salih Ayyub (38) need to be searched for. You turn right off Muizz into a lane – there is a tiny teashop on the corner with some round brass tables outside (an agreeable place to sit for a while). A short distance along the lane is an arch set into a facade with a Fatimid-style minaret rising from it. This is the madrasa, and you enter what remains of it by turning left into what is now used by neighbourhood youths as a playing field, liwans to east and west. The mausoleum is reached by returning to the Street of the Coppersmiths and turning right. You will see the dome on your right, and the door will be locked, but ask (or gesture to) anyone nearby for the key: they will find the keeper.

The interest of this place is historical, for it marks a political and architectural transition. Al-Salih Ayyub was the last ruler of Saladin's dynasty. His wife, who completed his madrasa and mausoleum after he died in 1249, was Shagarat al-Durr, a beautiful Turkish slave girl who ushered in Mameluke rule. While it has Fatimid elements, the madrasa was also the first to provide for all four schools of Sunni Islam, and was the first also to link madrasa and mausoleum – in short, it was the prototype for the Mameluke mosque-madrasa-mausolea to follow. Throughout the Mameluke period it was used as Cairo's central court (the schools teaching, amongst other things, law as at al-Azhar), and the street outside, Sharia Muizz, served as the place of execution.

Shagarat al-Durr

Shagarat al-Durr, whose name means Tree of Pearls, shares with Hatshepsut and Cleopatra that rare distinction of having been a female ruler of Egypt. She rose to power at a critical moment, when St Louis at the head of the Seventh Crusade seized Damietta in the Delta. Ayyub, dying from cancer, was too weak to dislodge him, and St Louis was content to await the Sultan's death and what he imagined would be the collapse of government and all resistance to Christian occupation of the country.

But Shagarat al-Durr was of independent nomadic stock, a society in which women went unveiled and were the equals of their men. She hid her husband's corpse in the Mameluke barracks on Roda while pretending he was merely ailing, and for three months ruled Egypt by appearing to transmit orders from Ayyub to his generals.

Egypt played for time and offered the Crusaders Jerusalem if they would abandon Damietta. St Louis refused. But meanwhile in the heat, and fed bad fish by the Delta people, the Crusaders became sick with scurvy and plague. St Louis then accepted the offer of Jerusalem, but it was the Egyptians now who refused, and the Mameluke general Baybars fell upon the Crusaders, capturing St. Louis, who had to buy his freedom with a vast indemnity and the renunciation of all claim to Egypt.

Shagarat al-Durr now openly proclaimed herself Sultana of Egypt and ruled for 80 days as the only female Moslem sovereign in history, but the Abbasid Caliph refused to recognise her, quoting the Prophet who had said, "The people that make a woman their ruler are past saving". So she married the leader of her Mameluke slave-warriors, Aybak, ruling through him, but when she heard he was considering another marriage she hired assassins to murder him in his bath. Hearing his screams, seeing his body hacked at with swords, at the last moment she tried to save his life, but the assassins went on: "If we stop halfway through, he will kill both you and us".

When the murder was discovered, Shagarat al-Durr offered to marry the new Mameluke chief, but she was imprisoned instead and is said to have spent her last days grinding up all her jewels so that no other woman should wear them. The Mamelukes had discovered their power to make and unmake rulers; in future they ruled themselves. Shagarat al-Durr was turned over to the wife she had made Aybak divorce who instructed her female slaves to beat her to death with bath clogs. They tossed her naked body over the Citadel wall to be devoured by dogs. Her few remains were deposited in her tomb on the edge of the Southern Cemetery not too far from the Mosque of Ibn Tulun.

Sultan Mansur Qalaun's complex

Looking up and across Sharia Muizz you see on its west side the splendid cluster of domes and minarets that are the Madrasa and Mausoleum of Qalaun, the Mausoleum of al-Nasr, his son and successor, and the Mosque of Barquq. Qalaun – the name means duck and has an absurd ring in Arabic – was one of the ablest, most successful and long-lived (1220-90) of the notoriously short-lived Mameluke Sultans, who moreover founded a dynasty lasting nearly 100 years years. His name suggests Mongol origins, and he is known to have been brought from the lower Volga region, ruled at the time by the Golden Horde. It was al-Salih Ayyub, buried across the street, who first began importing slaves from there, employing them as bodyguards. Qalaun served the country of his purchase well: Damascus and Baghdad had fallen to the Mongols, Egypt and Arabia the sole remaining bulwarks of Islam; Baybars checked the threat, Qalaun eliminated it, and then marched against the Crusaders at Acre, their last stronghold in the Holy Land, but died enroute. An outstanding builder, his tribute to his Christian enemies was the adoption of Romanesque elements in his complex here.

The maristan

First you go through a gate and down a wide tree-shaded walk, the heat and noise of the Street of the Coppersmiths falling away behind you. At the end is a modern hospital, built within the vaster limits of Qalaun's *maristan* or hospital and insane asylum – a hospital has stood on this spot for 700 years. Three great liwans of the original remain, the windows of the east liwan still displaying their carved stucco surrounds. The north liwan, it seems, is now used as a dump for surgical dressings.

Islam was a wonder of enlightened medical care at a time when the ill, especially the mad, were pariahs in Christian Europe. From Spain to Persia, hospitals flourished, were divided into clinics, surgery was perfected, such delicate operations as the removal of cataracts were performed, musicians and singers entertained the sick, and upon their discharge patients were given a sum of money to enable them to live until they could again find employment.

The madrasa

Returning now to the street and turning left, the wall on your left-hand side is that of Qalaun's madrasa. At the far corner the line of the building then retreats and you come to what was the original entrance to the maristan. The entrance opens onto a corridor, blocked at the far end, which runs between the mausoleum on the right and the madrasa on the left. The madrasa is damaged and recently the opportunity was taken to excavate for clues to the Fatimid's western palace which stood here. The plan is a courtyard with a liwan at either end, the sanctuary or eastern liwan suggesting a north Syrian basilical church, with three aisles and classical columns. The stucco work further in from the arch is original. The last time I was here, however, the excavators had gone and instead the courtyard was lined with squatters' tents, most of the eastern liwan filled with them. At least one had an aerial rigged up outside, a television audible within. The tents were held up by string and ropes tied to columns and to the beautiful carved wooden minbar. One appreciates the problems of restoring monuments in Cairo. All the same, I was greeted by some people emerging from a tent: they were well-dressed, well-spoken; and I saw several presentable young fellows enter from the corridor – students home from school.

The Mausoleum

Qalaun's mausoleum is off the other side of the corridor. The plan has been influenced by the Dome of the Rock at Jerusalem, well known to the Sultan: an octagon approaching the circular within a square, the arches supported by square piers and classical columns. The dome has been restored. The structure perhaps does not seem light enough, the decorations too rich, and the mashrabiyya screen obstructs a total view (the best is from the entrance) – though it also has the effect of making the relatively small interior seem endless. But there is splendour all the same, in carved stucco, the stone inlay, the wood ornamentation, slowly revealed as your eyes get used to the filtered coloured light from the stained-glass windows – those high, double round-arched windows with oculi above, framed (from both inside and out on the street) by deeply recessed pointed arches, Qalaun's borrowing of the Romanesque.

On your way out through the corridor, have a look at its beamed and coffered ceiling, which is marvellous. The street is just before you, yet in this complex all has been private, cool and quiet, birds chirping, trees and shade and shafts of sunlight. The buildings and their purpose reveal a dignity and humanity; they provide the peace by which you recognise an unexpected civilisation.

Mausoleum of al-Nasr

The next building along, that is continuing north on Sharia Muizz and on the left, is the Mausoleum of al-Nasr Mohammed (44), now ruinous except for the facade with its Gothic doorway, removed from the Crusader Church of St John when al-Nasr completed his father's work and took Acre. Al-Nasr's reign marked the zenith of Mameluke civilisation; his principal monuments are the mosque on the Citadel and the aqueduct bringing water there from the Nile. He is in fact buried next door in Qalaun's mausoleum.

Mosque of Barquq

The third of this group is the Mosque of Barquq (187), the first Burgi Mameluke Sultan. It dates from 1386, about a century later than Qalaun's buildings, and the change in style is evident; the minaret, for example, is octagonal and, compared to the square blocks of Qalaun's, slender, while here is the high monumental entrance topped with stalactite decorations, seen also at the Sultan Hassan, which became typical of Mameluke architecture. This mosque-madrasa, in çruciform plan, was in use until this century and has been well maintained and restored. The portal is of black and white marble, the doors of bronze inlaid with silver. The sanctuary liwan is flat-ceilinged, not vaulted like the others, and receives support from four pharaonic columns of porphyry quarried in the Eastern Desert. The exquisite domed tomb chamber with marbled floors and walls of varying colours, painted ceiling, latticed and stained-glass windows and ornate wooden stalactites in the corners, contains the grave of one of Barquq's daughters – he was removed to his mausoleum in the Northern Cemetery.

House of Uthman Katkhuda

Nearby are two houses of the Bahri Mameluke period. The House of Katkhuda (50) is in the street running east off Sharia Muizz, opposite Qalaun's mausoleum. It is about halfway down on the left-hand side. The doorway is entirely ordinary, but knock, or go to the apartment up the stairs, and someone will appear to show you round. (When soliciting local assistance, baksheesh is expected – usually demanded; but you should avoid paying until you have seen everything you want to, otherwise the demand for baksheesh will be made again and again, at each stage.)

Katkhuda was an 18th C. lieutenant governor of the city who made what in fact was a mid-14th C. palace into his home. Only a part of the whole remains, but it is an impressive example of Mameluke domestic architecture. Suddenly you are in a narrow hall of enormous height, its bare stone walls rising to the support of a wooden dome, distant sunlight streaming through the windows of its octagonal drum. This was the reception room, and guests sat in the raised area at the south end. The walls were once wainscotted with marble; the woodwork remains, though the consoles within the arches date from the 16th C. Ask to go up to the roof for a view of the quarter, and look at the *malqaf* or ventilator, a rectangular scoop common to old Cairene houses and always facing north to catch the Mediterranean breeze. One of the best things about this place is that you will almost certainly be the only visitor, and its fresh bareness invites pleasing, undisturbed thoughts of moving in and where to put the furniture.

Qasr Beshtak

The other house, even moreso a palace, is the Qasr Beshtak (34). This is back on Sharia Muizz, just to the north of Barquq's mosque and on the right-hand side. The entrance is the second door along the little street of the north facade – and again you will have to find someone, with some difficulty this time, who has the key.

The Emir Beshtak was married to the daughter of al-Nasr and was a man of great wealth. He built his palace on part of the foundations of the eastern Fatimid palace and it once rose to five storeys, with running water on all floors. You pass through a courtyard, up some stairs, and enter the harem reception room, vaster yet than Katkhuda's, with mashrabiyya screens along the galleries. From these there is a perfectly medieval view of the streets below.

Sabil Kuttab of Abdul Rahman Katkhuda

The Sabil Kuttab (21) of Abdul Katkhuda (Uthman's son) was built in 1744 and is one of the most charming structures in Cairo. It stands on a triangular plot, causing a fork in the street, the kuttab's porches overhanging the roadways on either side, the great grille of what was the fountain at its base facing south towards you as you approach. The kuttab is still used as the neighbourhood Koranic school, while the rest of the block is taken up with a renovated 14th C. apartment building.

Mosque of al-Aqmar

You continue along the left-hand fork and at last, on the next block, on the right-hand side, discover a rare surviving Fatimid structure in this Mameluke-dominated part of the city. The Mosque of al-Aqmar (33) dates from 1125 and displays a typically Fatimid keel arch portal. The niche ribbing, used here for the first time, was to become a favourite Cairene motif. The medallion set into the niche ribbing is very finely executed. The recesses on either side of the portal have stalactite decorations, also appearing here for the first time and later taken up by the Mamelukes. The interior is original, but the slapdash minaret is modern. Aqmar means moonlit, so named for the pale stone – the Fatimids, who meant to stay, building in stone rather than the earlier brick and stucco.

Bayt al-Suhaymi

The Bayt al-Suhaymi (339) is not a palace and not a refuge for an English major's bric-a-brac. It is a merchant's house of the Ottoman period, built in the 16th and 17th C., and completely furnished to the age. It is the finest house in Cairo and wonderfully achieves the ambition of Islamic secular architecture – the anticipation of paradise. You reach it by taking the first right a block after the Mosque of al-Aqmar. The street is called Haret ed-Darb el Asfar and the house is at No. 19 (in case you do not notice the little green and white plaque) on the left-hand side. There is a broad wooden door. Knock.

There is nothing at the facade that prepares you for what lies within. The house consists of numerous rooms on irregular levels, mashrabbiya screen windows looking out onto the streets at one side, screened and latticed windows and arched galleries giving onto a garden courtyard on the other. You will want to wander, to enjoy the perspectives across the court from every possible angle and elevation, though you will probably be guided – by well-informed students. They will take you, for example, to the women's bedroom which faces the street but is closely latticed, to the women's chapel outside it, a malqaf 'air conditioner' above your head. You will then be deposited in the harem reception room overlooking the garden, its floors of marble, its walls covered with the most delicate green and blue plant-patterned enamel tiles, and with carved and painted wood decorations. Here you can rest and perhaps send out for tea, and begin taking it all in. For it is not the plan, not the details, but the ambience of the place that seduces you and you want time.

Though this house was built in later centuries, in ambience it cannot be different from Cairene houses of earlier times, and it becomes obvious why Crusaders crusaded – the East offered such a luxuriantly pleasurable life for those with the means, far exceeding anything back in Europe. Medieval Western architecture and certainly domestic living (with the possible exception of Provence) was crude in comparison and worst of all uncomfortable. In Europe there were the seasons of cold and wet to contend with; in Egypt the heat. But here in this house they so easily defeated heat and burning sun, creating shadows and breezes, bringing plants and birds into their home, embracing a nature they had made kinder.

Return once again to Sharia Muizz and turn right. It becomes wonderful walking along this seemingly humble street, learning its secrets, its treasures offered in this Guide still only a sampling of the many more that would require a far longer exploration. You are heading north towards Bab al-Futuh and the walls which limit the Fatimid city. But first, on your left, is the clean, pencil-like minaret of the Silahdar mosque, a Turkish-style structure of Mohammed Ali's time. Though centuries out of place for this quarter, the minaret is a graceful landmark that never fails to draw your attention as you pass by.

Minaret of the Silahdar mosque

After about two blocks, the street broadens into a market area where garlic and onions are transported into the city and sold. The trucks which rumble in and out of Bab al-Futuh are painted with eyes as talismans against the evil eye. It is an appropriate place for superstition: on your right and leading to

Mosque of al-Hakim

the Fatimid wall is the facade of al-Hakim's mosque (15), completed in 1010, forbidding, and inside mostly ruinous. The entrance is by the domed square Tomb of Qurqumas (17), a late Mameluke structure of 1511.

Al-Hakim was the third of the Fatimid Caliphs who ruled with absolute political, military and religious authority. He was a paranoic who declared himself God and answered objections by inciting mobs to burn half the city while he lopped off the heads of the well-to-do, claiming the assistance of Adam and Solomon in angel guise. Jews he made walk about Cairo wearing clogs round their necks and Christians to carry heavy crosses. He would spend his wary nights riding a donkey, in the company of only a mute slave, into the Moqattam to observe the stars for portents. Then exchanging clothes with his slave he would secretly descend into the city and mix with the people to learn their complaints, though assuming the role of a cadi to punish infractions with summary decapitations. One night, returning from the hills, he was assassinated – at the instigation, it is thought, of his sister Setalmulq, whom he had intended to marry.

Some say he survived the attack and retreated to the desert. The Copts claim that Christ appeared to him, and that he begged for and was granted pardon. Others say he withdrew to the sanctuary of Ammon at Siwa, where more than a thousand years before Alexander had heard himself declared the son of Zeus, and there formulated his doctrine of a tolerant religion, similar to Islam, which was carried by Darazi, his disciple, to Lebanon where the Druze view the life of al-Hakim as a kind of Passion, giving him his due as their messiah. Gérard de Nerval in *Journey to the Orient,* one of the seminal works of surrealism, recounts a Druze sheikh's tale of al-Hakim's life.

So this mosque has some mystery to it, an aura avoided by Cairenes who have rarely used it for worship and have let it crumble, though happily restoration has begun to the fine wood and stucco carving of the sanctuary liwan. It has been used as a prison for Crusader captives, as a stable by Saladin and as a warehouse by Napoleon. Today it incorporates a school and the courtyard is used as a football field. It is similar in size and plan to the Mosque of Ibn Tulun and is built of brick, though faced in stone. Its roofless arcades are haunting, its minarets massive and in keeping with the Fatimid wall. These minarets soon needed buttressing by great trapezoid bases that project out into the street, so that they seem like ziggurats (especially when viewed from outside the walls), with pepperpot domes, placed there by Baybars II at the beginning of the 14th C.

The return of the Mecca pilgrimage

It was at Bab al-Futuh, the Gate of Conquests, that the great caravan of pilgrims returned each year from Mecca and then made its way along Sharia Muizz and Sharia Bab el Wazir to the Citadel. Nowadays the journey is made by jet, but in 1844 Nerval witnessed it like this: "As many as 30,000 people were about to swell the population of Cairo. I managed to make my way to Bab al-Futuh; the whole of the main street which leads there was crammed with bystanders who were kept in orderly lines by government troops. The sound of trumpets, cymbals and drums directed the advancing procession; the various nations and sects were distinguished by their trophies and flags. The long files of harnessed dromedaries, which were mounted by Bedouins armed with long rifles, followed one another, but it was only when I reached the countryside that I was able to appreciate the full impact of a spectacle which is unique in all the world.

"A whole nation on the march was merging into the huge population which adorned the knolls of the Moqattam on the right, and, on the left, the thousands of usually deserted edifices of the City of the Dead; streaked with red and yellow bands, the turreted copings of the walls and towers of Saladin were also swarming with onlookers. I had the impression that I was present at a scene during the Crusades. Further ahead, in the plain where the Qalish meanders, stood thousands of chequered tents where the pilgrims halted to refresh themselves; there was no lack of dancers and singers; all the musicians of Cairo, in fact, competed with the hornblowers and kettledrummers of the procession, an enormous orchestra whose members were perched on top of camels.

"Late in the afternoon, the booming of the Citadel cannons and a sudden blast of trumpets proclaimed that the Mahmal, a holy ark which contains Mohammed's robe of golden cloth, had arrived within sight of the city . . . From time to time the Mahmal came to a halt, and the entire population prostrated themselves in the dust, cupping their heads in their hands. An escort of guards struggled to drive back the Negroes who were more fanatical than the other Moslems; they aspired, in fact, to the honour of being trampled to death beneath the camels, but the only share of martyrdom bestowed upon them was a volley of baton blows. As for the Santons, who are an even more ecstatic species of saints than the Dervishes and whose orthodoxy is more questionable, several of them pierced their cheeks with long, pointed nails and walked on, showered in blood; others devoured live serpents, while a third group stuffed their mouths with burning coals."

I have said that Nerval was a precursor of surrealism; he enjoyed going over the top. But in this case that sober chronicler Edward William Lane, who observed the arrival of the caravan ten years before, is hardly less fantastic in his description, though he says the swallowing of serpents went out with the Mamelukes. The journey from Mecca took 37 days across rocky desert, the caravan moving at night. Not everyone survived: "Many of the women who go forth to meet their husbands or sons receive the melancholy tidings of their having fallen victim to privation and fatigue. The piercing shrieks with which they rend the air, as they retrace their steps to the city, are often heard predominant over the noise of the drum and the shrill notes of the hautboy which proclaim the joy of others".

Lane also mentions that the Mahmal was empty; its purpose was entirely symbolic, dating back to the reign of Shagarat al-Durr. She went on the pilgrimage one year, travelling in a magnificent *hodag* or covered litter borne by a camel, and for several successive years her empty hodag was sent with the caravan merely for the sake of state. The practice was continued by Egypt's rulers till 1927, when the puritanical Saudi King, on the pretext of objecting to the soldiers accompanying it, forbade passage of this "object of vain pomp". These days, alas, you wait in vain for pomp at Bab al-Futuh.

Bab al-Futuh, Bab al-Nasr and the Fatimid wall

The gate is similar to Bab Zuwayla, with projecting oval towers, though the masonry is finer and the impression greater for the space outside it has been cleared and there is a magnificent view of the ensemble of Bab al-Futuh, Bab al-Nasr – the Gate of Victory – (to the east), the linking Fatimid wall and al-Hakim's minarets. The Fatimid wall extends to the west; beyond that, where it retreats, and also to the east of Bab al-Nasr, the wall dates from Saladin. You can walk both within and along the top of the wall between the gates, and to do this you should walk along the outside to Bab al-Nasr and try to find someone with the key.

Re-entering the medieval city through Bab al-Nasr, the immediate area is noisy with metal workshops. On the right

Wakala of Qaytbay

(west) against the east facade of al-Hakim's mosque is a wakala (11) or caravansarai built by Sultan Qaytbay in 1481. It is now inhabited by tinsmiths and their families; women scrubbing, washing strung across the courtyard, children beating a kitten and throwing it into the air. I had asked in Upper Egypt why I saw so few cats; I was told they stayed indoors out of the sun, while dogs, being unclean to Moslems, remained outside. The sport to which this kitten was put suggested another reason (though I rescued it, temporarily).

The City of the Dead

The Northern Cemetery or City of the Dead lies to the east of the Fatimid city. The Mausoleum of Barquq is one and a half kilometres from Bab al-Nasr, for example, and Qaytbay's mausoleum is a kilometre from al-Azhar. So a walk from Bab al-Nasr, visiting these two mausolea as well as that of Ashraf Baybars' – the three most outstanding buildings – and then back to al-Azhar, will cover about 3 kms. You may prefer to make a separate journey of it, hiring a taxi,

You may already have noticed the City of the Dead as you drove in on the Heliopolis road from the airport; it did not seem inviting. It has the look of a bidonville – hot, dusty, dilapidated, with a quantity of domes. It is in fact the burial ground of the Mameluke Sultans and of others who aspired to their end, and some of its mausolea are as wonderful as anything in the city of the living. Nor is the cemetery without life. There were monasteries and schools, part of the mausolea. And the poor have always made their homes here, and the keepers, while relatives visit the family plots on feast days for a picnic. This is reminiscent of the ancient Egyptian practice of feeding the dead, though it is practiced elsewhere in the Mediterranean, as in Greece where it is more a cheerful popping of the cork and celebration of life.

Mausoleum of Barquq

Follow the road that runs east outside Bab al-Nasr and on reaching the cemetery you will see ahead of you a broad building with two domes and two minarets. This is the Mausoleum of Barquq (149), completed in 1411. Its plan is similar to that of a cruciform madrasa, but the liwans are not vaulted, instead entered through multi-domed arcades. You enter nowadays at the southwest corner and pass through a corridor into the sahn, its vastness once relieved by a pair of tamarisk trees, now only by the fountain. On the eastern side is the sanctuary liwan with a beautifully carved marble minbar, dedicated by Qaytbay. At either end of the liwan are domed tomb chambers, Barquq (removed here from his mausoleum on Sharia Muizz) and his two sons buried in the left chamber, women of the family in the right. These domes are the earliest of stone in Cairo; the zigzag ribbing on their exteriors was to develop into the elaborate polygons of Qaytbay's domed mausoleum. From the outside, the domes are minimised by the surrounding structure, and so inside their marvellous shape and soaring height comes as a surpise.

Go back across the courtyard to the northwest corner and up the stairs. These lead you to the *khanqah* or Dervish monastery, its four storeys a warren of rooms, cells and corridors. For some extra baksheesh the keeper will usually let you go up the northern minaret for a sweeping view of the necropolis itself and all of Cairo from Heliopolis to the Citadel.

Mausoleum of Ashraf Baybars

The Mausoleum of Sultan Ashraf Baybars (121) is south down the dirt road that passes along the front of Barquq's mausoleum. This building is less visited than the other two and finding the keeper may be more difficult; at any monument, here or in the city, apprehend the first child or lounger you see and make it known you want the key – the keeper will usually soon appear. Baksheesh is then of course expected all round.

This was originally planned solely as a khanqah and so is unusually elongated; also it is recognised by its ungainly minaret which too soon comes to a point. This Baybars, whose mausoleum dates from 1432, was a Burgi or Circassian Mameluke and is not to be confused with his namesake who held St Louis to ransom. He neither drank nor swore, though was martial enough and took Cyprus from the Franks in 1426. The appeal of the place is in its few but well-chosen elaborations – the polygonally decorated dome rising above the simple facade through which you pass by a doorway with trefoil arch. The tomb chamber is at the north end of the mosque, dimly illuminated by stained-glass windows subsequently introduced, though the mihrab of mother-of-pearl and marble mosaic is original. But really you have come for the interior view of the dome and its impression alone is sufficient: it ascends effortlessly upwards, almost losing itself to infinity.

Mausoleum of Qaytbay

It is a longer distance down this same dirt road to the Mausoleum of Qaytbay (99), completed in 1474 and a jewel of Mameluke architecture. First, from across the square, look at the ablaq masonry of the facade, the intricate polygonal relief on the exquisitely proportioned dome, and the slender minaret of three tiers (the Mameluke fashion), each tier ornately decorated with columned recesses or raised arabesques or stalactite clusters. Along with the Ibn Tulun and perhaps the Sultan Hassan, this rates as one of the great buildings of Cairo. Unlike them it is free with decoration, but like them it uses its decoration to the highest effect – the frequent play, for example, of filigree flowers upon star-shaped polygons which has been described as "a song for two voices", a geometrical base with floral melody.

Along with al-Nasr, Qaytbay was the grandest of Mameluke builders, emblazoning his cartouche on buildings religious and secular throughout the Middle East, as well as in Cairo and Alexandria. He was also the last Mameluke ruler of strength. Meshullam ben Menahem, an Italian Jew, described him: "He is an old man of about 80, but tall, handsome and as upright as a reed. Dressed in white, he was on horseback, accompanied by more than 2000 Mameluke soldiers . . . Whoever wishes can have access to the Sultan: there is in the town a great and splendid fortress at the entrance of which he sits publicly on Mondays and Thursdays, accompanied by the governor of the city; a guard of more than 3000 Mamelukes surounds him. Whoever has been manhandled or robbed by one of the Mameluke princes or emirs can there complain. Thus the nobles refrain from actions that might carry condemnation." He came up through the ranks, having been bought by Ashraf Baybars, and apart from al-Nasr ruled longer than any other Sultan. The perfection of his mausoleum, however, like the splendour of his reign, marked the final apogee of Mameluke vigour. Decadence ensued; two decades later the Turks were in the city, Bab Zuwayla ornamented by the last Mameluke Sultan, a rope round his neck.

Inside is a cruciform madrasa with vestigial liwans to east and west. The decoration of ceilings, pavings, arches, windows is breathtakingly variegated, yet overall it is measured and subdued. There is deliberate though sensitive contrast with the scale of the courtyard and sanctuary in the immense height of the tomb chamber, its walls drawn into the ascending dome.

Finally, from the sanctuary, you should climb the roof to enjoy at closer hand the tracery of stone carving, as delicate as previous periods had managed in wood and stucco, on the dome and minaret.

PRACTICAL INFORMATION

Mosques still serving as places of worship are open throughout the day and into the evening; otherwise don't count on places being open after 4pm. The Islamic Museum is open in winter from 9am to 4.30pm daily, though closed on Fridays between 11.15am and 1.30pm; in summer it's open from 8.30am to 1pm, but closing at 11.15am on Fridays. The Okel (or Wakala) of al-Ghuri serves also as a permanent exhibition of local crafts and is open from 8.30am to 2pm daily except Fridays when it's closed.

For those with limited time, an **abbreviated itinerary** for the northern quarters of Islamic Cairo should concentrate on the Islamic Museum, a stroll from Bab Zuwayla to the Qalaun complex and a visit to Bayt al-Suhaymi. A separate visit can be made to the Mausoleum of Qaytbay in the City of the Dead.

A **taxi** to al-Azhar or to Bab Zuwayla (the driver may know it better as Bab al-Mitwalli) or to the Islamic Museum (at Midan Ahmed Maher, where Sharia Port Said and Sharia el Qalaa intersect) will set you amidst the major sights of this chapter. Or you can take the **No.66 bus** from Midan el Tahrir to Khan el Khalili. To reach the Northern Cemetery (City of the Dead) you should take the **No.63** or **No.905 bus** from Midan el Tahrir.

Entrance fees are payable at some places, at al-Azhar, the Qalaun complex and (in the Northern Cemetery) the Mausoleum of Barquq (10PT), Bayt al-Suhaymi (25PT) and the Islamic Museum (50PT, valid also for the Gayer-Anderson on the same day). You'll need small change, too, for services.

CAIRO 5: RODA, OLD CAIRO, FUSTAT AND HELIOPOLIS

For Old Cairo and Fustat, you can take the train from Bab el Luq station, east of Midan el Tahrir, getting off at the third stop, Mari Girgis. If you take a taxi, ask for Old Cairo in Arabic – *Misr* (or *Masr) el Qadima*. The distance is about 4 kms, though there are a few places enroute worth noting for those with flexible transport. In any case, Garden City and the northern part of Roda can form a separate excursion, enjoyed on foot.

A river walk The Meridien Hotel at Roda's northern tip can be reached across its own bridge from Garden City, and here you can stop for a drink and a commanding view of the Nile. Gardens run along the western bank of the island to El Gama'a Bridge which crosses over the Nile to the Zoological Gardens. From there you can walk back along the west bank of the river through Dokki, visiting the Papyrus Institute on the way. coming up to the Sheraton and so back to Midan el Tahrir via Gezira.

Manyal Palace But a quarter of the way down Roda, its grounds overlooking the smaller eastern branch of the Nile, its entrance however facing the approach road to El Gama'a Bridge, is the Manyal Palace, built by Mohammed Ali. It is now partly a museum, partly a Club Mediterranée hotel. On view is a reception palace, the palace proper, a private mosque and Mohammed Ali's private hunting museum, which includes a table made of elephants' ears and a hermaphrodite goat. That pretty much sets the tone of the place, which is bizarre kitsch. There is also a garden of banyan trees.

Coming down the corniche from Midan el Tahrir towards Old Cairo, at a point two or three blocks south of your view across to the Manyal Palace on Roda is a traffic roundabout called

The Khalig Fumm el Khalig. This is where the canal, now covered over by Sharia Port Said and its southern extension, left the river. There is a large octagonal tower of stone here, once housing great waterwheels which lifted water from the Nile to the level

The aqueduct of the Mameluke aqueduct which can still be followed almost all the way to the Citadel. At this end, the aqueduct dates only from 1505 and was an extension made necessary by the westward-shifting Nile; the main part of the aqueduct, further east, was built by al-Nasr around 1311.

A further few blocks south is the Malek al-Salih bridge

crossing over to the southern end of Roda. At the lower tip of the island is the Nilometer, dating from the 9th C., though the superstructure with its Turkish-style conical roof dates from Mohammed Ali's time. The stone-lined pit goes down well below the level of the Nile, though the water entry tunnels have been blocked up and you can descend by steps. At the centre of the pit is a graduated column for determining whether the river would rise enough, not enough, or too much, so announcing the expected fertility of all Egypt over the coming year. A reading of 16 *ells* (8.6 metres) ensured the complete irrigation of the Valley. When it reached this level, the Nile crier, attended by boys carrying flags, would broadcast the *Wafa el Nil* or superfluity of the Nile and the dam to the Khalig would be cut amidst great festivity. The Nile used to reach its flood in mid-August, but the High Dam at Aswan now regulates its flow and it keeps a steady level year-round.

The Nilometer

The Nilometer is usually locked but the keeper lives in a small house nearby. If you do not see him, ask one of his children to fetch him; but if he has gone off somewhere, you will have to try your luck another time.

Old Cairo: the fortress of Babylon

You arrive at Old Cairo outside a section of wall and two towers that formed part of the Roman fortress of Babylon, first built around AD 30 in the time of Augustus, added to by Trajan and reformed by the Byzantines. The technique of dressed stone alternating with courses of brick is typically Roman. The portal between the towers was a water gate and excavation has revealed the original quay 6 metres below present street level, but the Nile has since shifted 400 metres to the west.

The Coptic Museum

Now the towers mark the entrance to the Coptic Museum, pleasantly set in gardens. It is a charming building, decorated with wooden mashrabiyyas from old Coptic houses, embracing green courtyards, airy and light within, its spirit in keeping with its collection. The exhibits cover Egypt's Christian era, from AD 300 to 1000, and are both religious and secular, linking the art of the pharaonic and Graeco-Roman periods with that of Islam. The museum is arranged in sections, covering stonework, manuscripts, textiles, ikons and paintings as well as decorated ivories, woodwork, metalwork, and pottery and glass. Often, as in stone carving and painting, the work is crude, though agreeably naive. High artistic achievement, however, is found in the textiles, and there are many fine chemises, tapis and cloths here embroidered with motifs of St George, or graceful women and gazelles.

Coptic churches The oldest Coptic churches sought security within the fortress walls, and usually they avoid facing onto the street and so are indistinguishable from neighbouring houses. Their main entrances were long ago walled up against attack, entry being through a small side door. Their plan is basilical, with a narthex or porch admitting to an aisled nave with an ikonostasis placed across the sanctuary. In seeking out the five churches within the fortress precincts, and also the synagogue, there is interest too in the winding little streets, glimpses within windows and doors, the decorations of the houses, the domes of some as in Upper Egypt, and the atmosphere of remove, of an almost rural village.

Alexandria was the Coptic Rome. This was never a city, never a place of monuments, and it is not a ghetto. Copts live throughout Cairo and all over Egypt, especially in Upper Egypt. But this is an old and holy place, to Jews as well as Copts, and among the 135,000 Moslems living in Old Cairo, within and without the fortress, there are 30,000 Copts and 42 Jewish families, worshipping at 29 mosques, 20 churches and one synagogue.

The Hanging Church The Church of el Muallaqa, the Hanging Church, is so named because it rests on the bastions of the southwest gate into the fortress, its nave suspended above the passage. It is reached by going out from the museum grounds between the two great towers and turning left. Though the church claims origins in the 4th C., it is unlikely that the present structure, which in any case has been rebuilt, would have been built on the walls until the Arab conquest made them redundant. Certainly, it is known to have become the seat of the Patriarchate when it was moved from Alexandria to Cairo in the 11th C. El Muallaqa has a beautiful interior, with pointed arches, cedar panelling and transluscent ivory screens, where services are held in the dead Coptic language sprinkled with some Arabic. On the right, as you come in, is a 10th C. ikon of the Virgin and Child, Egyptian faces, Byzantine crowns. On the same wall is an ancient ikon of St Mark, founder of the Coptic Church. El Muallaqa is dedicated to the Virgin and is properly called Sitt Mariam, St Mary. Its central sanctuary is dedicated to Christ, its left sanctuary to St George, its right sanctuary to St John the Baptist, scenes from the saints' lives decorating their ikonostases.

Now walk back out to the street and turn right so that you pass again the towers and entrance to the museum. Along the Roman wall on your right are some steps leading down to the level of Old Cairo. A narrow street runs southwest and on the left is the Monastery of St George. Further on, you are obliged to turn either left or right: if you turn left and go straight on, you will come to El Adra, the Church of the Virgin, first built in the 9th C. but destroyed and rebuilt in the 18th C. It is known also as Kasriyat er-Rihan, meaning pot of basil, a favoured herb of the Greek Orthodox Church. Al-Hakim's mother had been of that faith and for the duration of his reign it was transferred to Orthodox use. Returning back down the street from El Adra, the Church of Mari Girgis or St George is on your left. The original was built in the 7th C. but burnt down in the 19th, only a later 14th C. hall surviving. The modern church is of no interest.

El Adra

Mari Girgis

Returning to where you had the choice between left and right, you carry straight on, that is as though you had first turned right. You are now at Abu Sarga, the Church of St Sergius, reconstructed during the Fatimid period but with a crypt of much earlier date and reputed to be the halting place of the Holy Family when they fled Herod and came into Egypt. It is entered through a small door at the southwest corner. Inside it is simple stone and plaster, with a high timbered roof supported by marble columns painted with faded saints. Follow some steps to the right of the altar down to the crypt which in the past would fill knee-high with the Nile.

Abu Sarga: associations with the Holy Family

In those Victorian days when people went to Egypt Bible in hand, Abu Sarga was *the* reason for visiting Old Cairo. Flaubert came with his notebook and sharp pen: "Visited the Coptic church in Old Cairo. As M. de Voltaire would have put it: 'A handful of rogues, gathered together in a hideous church, were celebrating with a total absence of style the rites of a religion whose very prayers they cannot comprehend.' From time to time one or another of the acolytes supplies, aloud, the pronunciation of some word the priest cannot read."

Turning right out of the church and then right at the corner, at the end of the street you see Sitt Barbara (St Barbara's) to the left, the synagogue to the right. Sitt Barbara is very similar to Abu Sarga and like it was restored in Fatimid times. Barbara had tried converting her father to Christianity; he responded by beating her to death. Her relics are in a velvet-covered case in a chapel to the right of the nave. In another case, so some Copts claim (and the Copts, as you will find out if you go on visiting their churches and monasteries, are capable of claiming anything), are relics of St Catherine, the Alexandrian martyr broken on the wheel. E.M. Forster says she supposedly died under Diocletian, "but it is improbable that she ever lived; she and her wheel were creations of

Sitt Barbara

Western Catholicism, and the land of her supposed sufferings has only recognised her out of politeness to the French". The famous monastery in Sinai was named for her and did enjoy close relations with medieval monasteries in France to which it exported a prized oil which exuded from her bones.

I said that Old Cairo was no ghetto, and yet here and elsewhere in the Coptic Church there is a sort of ghetto of the mind, lurid phantasms propagated by a religion in retreat – in retreat not so much before Islam as because of its inability to reconcile its mystical conception of Christianity with the materialism of the modern world. Debased mysticism becomes bizarre materialism, as in the possession of macabre relics – or so it seems amidst the mockery of the town. (See Wadi Natrun.)

Synagogue of Ben Ezra

At the Synagogue of Ben Ezra, the mood is more uncertain. It is the neighbourhood temple whose neighbourhood has gone away – left the country or gone to other parts of Cairo. It is a forlorn place, a forgotten outpost, and can be moving. But it does not boggle – unless you encounter Rabbi Cohen.

The synagogue is the oldest in Egypt and resembles in its basilical arrangement an early Christian church. A church did stand here from the 4th to 9th C., but the Copts had to sell it to the Jews to pay Ibn Tulun's tax towards the erection of his mosque. Sources differ as to whether the original church cum temple was subsequently destroyed and rebuilt or whether the early fabric remains in what the Rabbi of Jerusalem, Abraham Ben Ezra, at least renewed in the 12th C. The Jews argue, however, that the synagogue has a longer history than that. On this site, they say, stood the temple of the prophet Jeremiah and it was here that Joseph came to worship with his wife and child. Certainly there was a Jewish community here at that time, explaining why Joseph should have come this way at all; and he was followed, after later political and religious disturbances in Jerusalem, by the apostles Mark and Peter. It makes sense that it was from this Babylon that Peter sent his First Epistle General to Christian communities throughout the East, though many scholars argue that Babylon was no more than a metaphor for Rome. But at Rome there were very few Jews and little reason for Peter to go there; and there is the suspicion that the Western Church appropriated him to that city in order there to crown him pope and martyr. At any rate, the early Christian church eventually sold to the Jews was, it is said, built where the Romans had destroyed Jeremiah's temple.

Ben Ezra's synagogue sits in a small shady garden, its exterior plain, a Star of David in wrought iron over the gate.

Rabbi Cohen lives opposite. Inside there is an arch of ablaq masonry, a small stained-glass window towards the far end and where the ikonstasis would be a Star of David in light-bulbs. Pointed out to you (if Rabbi Cohen is in the mood) will be the Miracle Rock beneath which Jeremiah is supposed to be buried and the spring where (again depending on Rabbi Cohen's mood) either Joseph and Mary drew water to wash the infant Jesus or Pharaoh's daughter plucked Moses from the bullrushes. The synagogue once possessed a library of 100,000 books, all gone; and discovered hidden in the walls at the end of the 19th C. was an ancient Torah, now dispersed throughout the great libraries of the Western world, though you may be shown a fragment.

When I first came to this synagogue in 1967, Rabbi Cohen was already doing a modest trade in black and white post cards of himself. Now with the change in the political climate there is no stopping him. There are piles of post cards inside, in colour yet, most of them still depicting himself, and offer him even 25 piastres for one and you are lucky he does not throw you out the door – $1, even £1 is the asking price, no coins. On my way out, his assistant tapped the side of his head; small consolation for leaving without a colour post card of Rabbi Cohen.

Mosque of Amr

Two or three blocks north of the fortress and one block east of the railway line is the Mosque of Amr, so restored and expanded that nothing remains of the original built here in 642, the first mosque in Egypt and the point from which the country's conversion to Islam began. The short walk here is through a picturesque quarter of potters. But except for its associations, the present mosque is without interest. Its dimensions date to 827, when it was doubled in size, and the last major restoration was in 1798. It is no more than a broken-down courtyard mosque, now being slowly repaired.

Ruins of Fustat

To the east of the mosque and the Fortress of Babylon are the dismal remains of Fustat – that is the foundations and lower walls of the first Arab city in Egypt, destroyed and abandoned in 1168. Once famous for its glassware and ceramics, with water supply and sanitation facilities far more advanced than in Europe until the 18th C., the gradually excavated ruins of Fustat are of interest to archaeologists but probably not to others.

Heliopolis

Another forsaken capital is On, called by the Greeks Heliopolis as throughout ancient times it was the centre for the worship of Re, the sun god. It was even for a time during the predynastic period the political capital of Lower Egypt and it remained a centre of religious and scientific learning until nearly the end of the Ptolemaic period, attracting such distinguished visitors as Solon, Pythagoras and possibly Plato who summed up the Greek impression of Egypt: "We Greeks are in reality children compared with this people with traditions ten times older. And as nothing of precious remembrance of the past would long survive in our country, Egypt has recorded and kept eternally the wisdom of the old times. The walls of temples are covered with inscriptions and the priests have always under their own eyes that divine heritage. The Egyptians continue to transmit to successive generations these sacred things unchanged: songs, dances, rhythms, rituals, music, paintings, all coming from time immemorial when gods governed the earth in the dawn of civilisation."

Herodotus came here to seek information from the priests and seeing four-sided pillars pointed at the top, called them obelisks, meaning little spits. These early Greek travellers did seem to play the role of schoolboy in Egypt, making silly jokes about food: the gigantic monuments spread along the edge of the desert north and south of Memphis they called wheat cakes, or pyramids in Greek.

Ancient Heliopolis is to the northwest of the modern suburb of that name, which is along the airport road. It is about 600 metres north of the one-time village of Matariya where there is a dead sycamore called the Virgin's Tree, much visited by medieval pilgrims, and even more recent ones, in the belief that it was under its branches that the Holy Family paused for shade before the last leg of their journey to Babylon. But even at that time Heliopolis was already in ruins and Augustus was making off with some obelisks. Now nothing remains of Re's temple except a fragment of the enclosure wall, and indeed the only thing standing is an obelisk of Sesostris I (XII Dyn), erected on the occasion of his jubilee marking the thirtieth year of his reign, in 1942 BC. It is 20.4 metres high and weighs around 11,000 kilos.

The Virgin's Tree

Obelisk of Sesostris I

Along the airport road

More entertaining is the taxi ride to or from the airport passing right through modern Heliopolis. The taxi driver will delight in pointing out the lastest Mercedes crashed and overturned by a drunken oil sheikh, and also those villas along the way in which, you are told, certain desert princes keep their Egyptian mistresses. One fantastic mansion, on the right-hand side of the dual carriageway as you head towards the airport, is the deserted 'Hindu Palace' of the Belgian plutocrat Baron Empain, who at the beginning of this century developed this suburb on the edge of the desert, embellishing it with fake Islamic and pharaonic architecture, sports clubs and a race track to draw the wealthy. The exterior of his mansion is an imitation of a temple off the coast of Indonesia, though inside it is furnished to bourgeois taste.

PRACTICAL INFORMATION

If taking a **taxi to Old Cairo,** ask for it in Arabic, *Misr* (or *Masr*) *el Qadima*. Or take the **metro** from Bab el Luk station (on Sharia Mansur, a couple of blocks east of Midan el Tahrir), asking for Mari Girgis.

The churches and synagogue close at 4pm; there are no entrance fees, but all are anxious for donations. The Coptic Museum is open in winter from 9am to 3pm daily but closes at 1pm in summer. Bags and cameras must be checked (no fee).

There are some other museums, exhibits and sights worth visiting in the areas covered by this chapter:

The Cairo Tower on the island of Gezira rises 187 metres and offers marvellous panoramas from its 14th level restaurant, 15th level cafeteria and 16th level observation platform. The ascent costs 40PT.

The Ethnological Museum, Sharia Qasr el Aini, a few blocks south of Midan el Tahrir. Open 9am to 1pm daily, closed Fridays. A small museum with displays of traditional village handicrafts and costumes from all over Egypt.

The Manyal Palace on the island of Roda is open daily from 9am to 1pm. Entry is 25PT

The Papyrus Institute, on a houseboat tied up along Sharia el Nil, is just south of the Sheraton in Giza. Open from 9am to 7pm daily, free. Founded by Prof. Hassan Ragab, this is a workshop, research centre and small museum demonstrating the manufacture and use of this first flexible writing material. Only *cyperus papyrus*, the same plant used by the ancients, is used here (the institute has several commercial imitators, but they use the modern *cyperus alopecuròides* of inferior quality). The institute grows at least some of its own papyrus, and exhibits copies of ancient papyri and sells others. (As you go down the quayside steps, notice on your left the plaque marking the highest level of the Nile during the flood of September 1887.)

The Agricultural Museum and the **Cotton Museum,** next to each other off Sharia Abdel Aziz Radwan, near the exit of the 6 October Bridge in Dokki. Open from 9am to 4pm except winter Fridays when they close from 11am to 1pm, and summer Fridays when they close at noon. Small fee. The Agricultural Museum displays all aspects of present Egyptian rural life, while the Cotton Museum concentrates on the country's single most important crop.

Heliopolis can be reached by **taxi** or **metro:** the station is on Sharia el Galaa near the eastern entrance to the 6 October Bridge.

For **ancient Heliopolis** and the **Virgin's Tree,** ask for El Matariya. **The Palace of Baron Empain** (arabised into *Omban*) is on Sharia el Uruba (the road to the airport) where it is intersected by Sharia el Merghami. Sharia el Merghami runs alongside the Heliopolis Sporting Club and is a curving extension of Sharia el Maqrizi which runs back towards Cairo. Where Sharia el Maqrizi is intersected by Sharia el Matariya (about two-thirds the distance towards Heliopolis from Midan Ramses) is the **Mausoleum of Gamal Abdel Nasser,** the first truly Egyptian ruler of Egypt since the Pharaohs.

PYRAMIDS: GIZA TO THE FAYYUM

Before taking the Giza road out to that desert escarpment where the famous Pyramids of Cheops, Chephren and Mycerinus stand, it is worth knowing something of the period in which they were built, and to know too something of that entire line of Old Kingdom pyramids which extends from Abu Roash to the north of Giza to Meidum near the Fayyum, a line that is 70 kms long and numbers over 80 pyramids. This chapter will refer to the main pyramid clusters, including also the necropolis surrounding the Step Pyramid at Saqqara, and will explain why and how, at the very beginning of recorded history, these most prodigious and enduring monuments in stone were built. "Everything fears time", wrote an Arab physician in the 12th C., "but time fears the Pyramids".

The struggle for unity

Around 3100 BC, Upper and Lower Egypt were united under Menes and the I Dynasty established. It is not certain that Menes was an individual; he may represent a conflation of early warrior-princes, and the conquest of the Delta may not have been a single campaign but a struggle lasting over generations. There is evidence of fighting and rebellion during the I and II Dynasties, and the energies of this period would have been devoted to consolidation. Building was in mud brick and reed, though during the II Dynasty some stone was used underground in tombs.

Mastabas

Below ground these tombs were built like houses: rectangular and divided into chambers. Above ground they had a low, flat-topped form with sloping walls. This mud brick superstructure was sometimes faced with mud plaster and covered with white gypsum stucco. Mariette called them *mastabas,* the Arabic for those stone benches outside the shops and coffee houses of medieval Cairo.

The Old Kingdom

About 400 years after unification, that is c.2700 BC, Egypt entered into a long period of security and order known to us as the Old Kingdom and beginning with the III Dynasty. Awareness of the two Egypts, Upper and Lower, remained acute, as can be read from the ritual of Zoser's Heb-Sed festival at Saqqara, and the village and tribal units up and down the Nile continued to worship their local gods, that prolific pantheon that never disappeared but which eventually was overlayed by a few powerful national cults.

The III Dynasty: building in stone

During the reign of Zoser (III Dyn) there was a sudden use and mastery of stone at Saqqara. His mortuary complex of courts and chapels, 544 metres long and 277 metres wide and surrounded by a wall 10 metres high, was all of stone, beautifully detailed and architectured. And dominating the whole was the first pyramid, over 62 metres high, built in steps. Stone had risen from the darkness of the tomb into the confident light of the sun.

The explanation is not found in technology; stone was not new and tools and construction methods remained as simple as they had been in the past – the lever was used but the wheel and pulley were unknown. Rather there was peace and stability; there was a developing theocratic doctrine that invited the use of stone; and there was a man of genius who knew how to build with it.

The genius of Imhotep

That man was Imhotep, Zoser's grand vizier, chief judge, minister of agriculture and supervisor of building works. He was also high priest at Heliopolis. His range of accomplishment typified the opportunities and needs of a new civilisation, where everything was still to be invented and then organised. He was revered throughout pharaonic history, though recalled as a healer rather than as an organiser, statesman or architect, and he became a mythic figure, a demi-god, and was eventually raised to unqualified divinity – but his contemporary existence is certain from inscriptions found at Zoser's complex.

The doctrine that begged the use of stone was that of the Pharaoh's sole possession of the *ka,* the vital force emanating from the god to his son, the king, who could then dispense it to his subjects. The ka was eternal so long as it was linked to the Pharaoh, and so it was essential that ka and king be given an indestructible container of stone.

The first pyramid

Zoser was built a stone mastaba and this was twice enlarged. Then in three further stages, Imhotep made a qualitative leap, a sudden vertical thrust, and created the world's first skyscraper, the Step Pyramid. Political and cultural revolution in Egypt has always swept down through the Valley, nomadic in inspiration. The mastaba belonged to the earthbound world of the Delta farmers; the pyramid and generally Egyptian architecture thereafter eschewed the enclosure of space and instead posed itself against the sun and the stars. Stone permitted it; Imhotep mastered the physics required; and yearning for the vast and timeless cosmos was its inspiration.

It is interesting and important, though, that Zoser's complex remains human in feeling. Zoser was the son of the god, and even if he was the god himself, he at least relished the life of man, for in the house-like arrangement of chambers beneath his pyramid, with their faience decorations imitating domestic reeding, there is the desire to project his present life

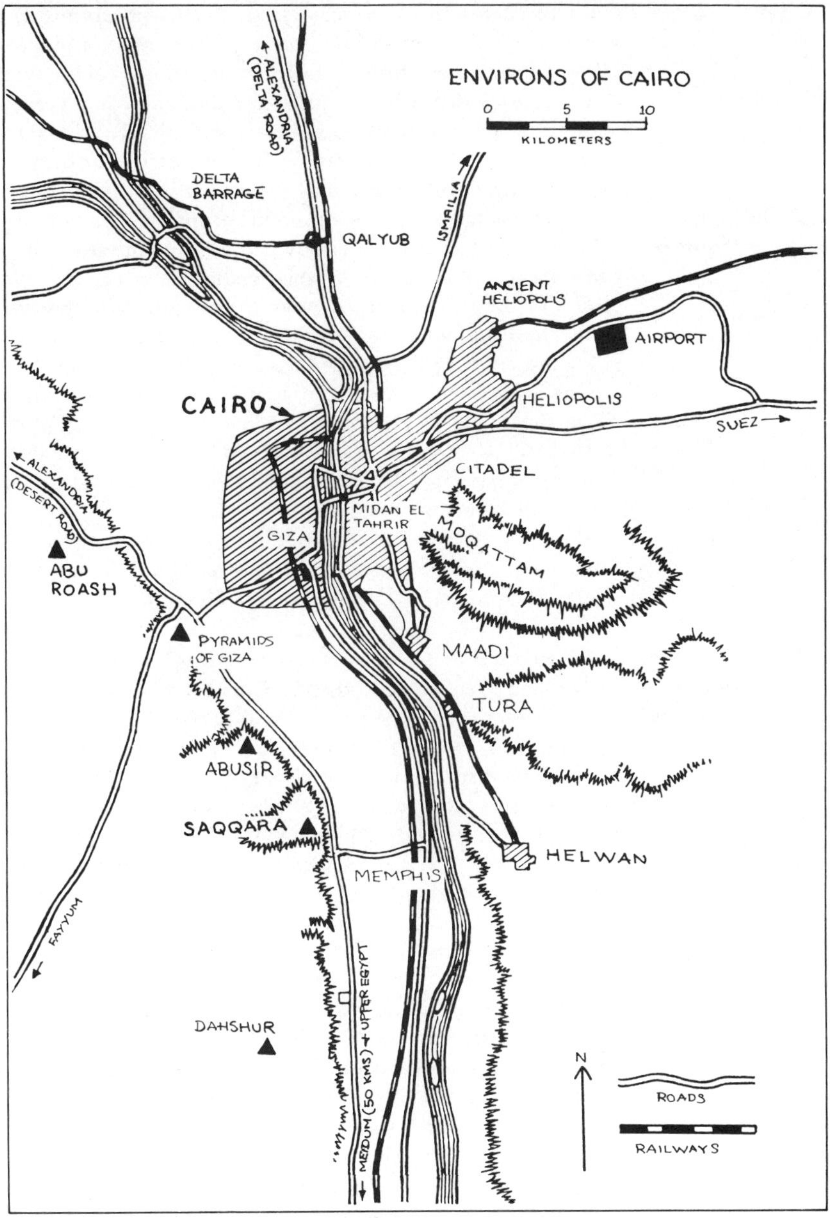
ENVIRONS OF CAIRO
0 5 10
KILOMETERS
ALEXANDRIA (DELTA ROAD)
DELTA BARRAGE
QALYUB
ISMAILIA
ANCIENT HELIOPOLIS
AIRPORT
CAIRO
HELIOPOLIS
SUEZ
CITADEL
MIDAN EL TAHRIR
GIZA
MOQATTAM
ALEXANDRIA (DESERT ROAD)
ABU ROASH
PYRAMIDS OF GIZA
MAADI
TURA
ABUSIR
SAQQARA
HELWAN
MEMPHIS
FAYYUM
DAHSHUR
MEYDUM (50 KMS) UPPER EGYPT
N
ROADS
RAILWAYS

into the hereafter. This sense never again appears inside a pyramid, and rarely at any mortuary structure of a pharaoh throughout Egypt's history. Instead the savouring of the every day was excluded, divinity insisted upon, and ritual became obsessive. There was one exception in the joyous optimism of Hatshepsut's mortuary temple at Deir el Bahri – but then she was an extraordinary woman.

The pyramid revolution

So there was a first revolution, an eruption, in stone. But the second revolution was an adventure even more astonishing and led to the perfection of the pyramid form at Giza. We think of the vastness of Egyptian history and how slowly it must have unfolded, yet from Zoser's complex to Cheops' Pyramid no more time passed than our fast-moving age took to travel from the beginnings of iron construction to the Eiffel Tower – around 75 years in fact. What is more, the age of the great pyramids was over in 200 years. What explains its sudden coming and going, and the intensity, the phenomenal labour, with which it was pursued?

You see that in rushing out to Giza you confront the apogee, but you do not meet the answer. That is found to the south of Saqqara, at Dahshur and at Meidum.

The collapse of the Meidum pyramid

The pyramid at Meidum is about 90 kms by road south of Cairo and even without visiting it you can see it, if you are alert, from the left side of the overnight train back from Luxor soon after it passes El Wasta in the morning. Like all the pyramids, it stands beyond the belt of cultivation on the edge of the desert. It is an amazing sight: a steeply inclined tower rising from a low hill – and that is exactly what it was thought to be by early travellers. In fact it is a pyramid that collapsed. It did not disintegrate over time; near the moment of its completion it collapsed in one instantaneous catastrophe, only a part of the core remaining clear of the mound of debris all around.

This was the first pyramid after Zoser's and it was conceived at first as a step pyramid. A second, larger stepped structure was soon superimposed and finally a true pyramidal shell was added, its smooth sides rising at an angle of about 52°. But there were serious design faults, including the badly squared stones of the outer casing which stood on horizontal limestone blocks embedded in compacted sand instead of on a bedrock foundation given an inward slope. The weight of the pyramid, instead of being directed downwards and inwards, was directed outwards; its lateral forces simply blew it apart.

The mystery of Snofru's pyramids at Dahshur

This disaster leads to an explanation of the pyramid craze that marks the succeeding dynasty to Zoser's. An inscription at Meidum says it was built by Snofru (IV Dyn). But this has disturbed Egyptologists because Snofru was known to have built two pyramids at Dahshur. If the purpose of a pyramid was to provide an indestructible container for the Pharaoh and his ka, why did Snofru need three? Snofru's inscription was explained away as a usurpation of his predecessor's pyramid: "It cannot but seem extraordinary that one and the same king should have built for himself two pyramids of vast dimensions at no great distance from one another . . . and since it is hard to imagine that he erected three pyramids, the one at Meidum is now tentatively ascribed to Huny" (Gardiner). Neatly done! But that left the Bent and Red Pyramids at Dahshur. The Bent Pyramid was disposed of with the argument that it had been deemed unsafe and so Snofru decided to build another. One pharaoh, one ka and one pyramid to suit.

The Bent Pyramid rises for 70 per cent of its bulk at an angle of 52°, the same as at Meidum. It then abruptly alters angle to 43.5°. The Red Pyramid rises at a constant angle of 43.5°. The lower angle of the Red would clearly be safer than the steeper initial angle of the Bent, but it fails to explain why the angle of the Bent should have been changed in mid-construction. If the steep initial angle of the Bent was thought

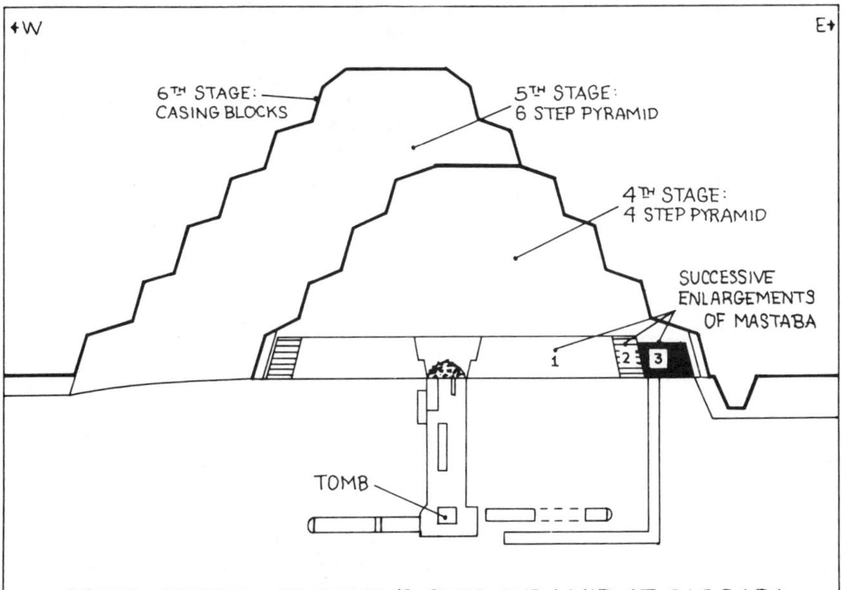

CROSS SECTION OF ZOSER'S STEP PYRAMID AT SAQQARA
SHOWING STAGES FROM MASTABA TO SKYSCRAPER

to be unsafe, why not at once abandon the project? But if changing the angle was thought to make it safe, why build the Red Pyramid? Of course, one could argue that it was thought the change of angle would make the Bent Pyramid safe and that unhappily this proved not to be true – though the pyramid has stood safe and sound for nearly 5000 years.

Eminent Egyptologists have said that the builders of the Bent Pyramid suddenly tired of their task and decided to reduce the pyramid's volume, and hence their labour, by reducing its angle. It has also been said that the bend in the pyramid was predetermined and meant to express a 'double pyramid', that is two pyramids of different angles superimposed, and that this symbolised some unexplained duality. And it has been said that the architect lost his nerve, but the obvious reason for this tantalising possibility – the collapse of the Meidum pyramid at a point when the Bent Pyramid was 70 percent of the way towards completion – has not been countenanced by Egyptologists because it would reintroduce the "unpalatable conclusion that Snofru did possess three pyramids" (Gardiner). The key word there is possess, for it signals the insistence that pyramids were built for the sole reason of providing a container for the Pharaoh's ka, and that Snofru had no business, therefore, building what he believed at that point to be two perfectly good pyramids.

The Egyptologists' evasions could have gone on indefinitely as long as they could have believed that the pyramid at Meidum had belonged to Snofru's predecessor and had merely crumbled with time. But in *The Riddle of the Pyramids,* Kurt Mendelssohn, professor of physics at Oxford, presents hard evidence that Meidum, while nearing completion, came down with a bang as Snofru was already well advanced on his second pyramid – which only then, and for that reason, was continued at a bent angle.

The pyramid production line

So why should several pyramids be built in overlapping succession during the reign of a single pharaoh? It is a fact that more large pyramids were built during the IV Dynasty than there were pharaohs to fill them. The answer is in the scale of the task. Herodotus says it took 20 years to build Cheops' Pyramid and 10 years to build the causeway and the earth ramps that served as a kind of scaffolding, with 100,000 men working a three month shift. Modern calculation of the workforce required does not vary substantially from Herodotus' figure, though it is likely that several thousand men, highly skilled as stone-cutters, masons, surveyors, etc., would have been employed year-round, while the larger requirement for unskilled labour would have been drawn from the fields

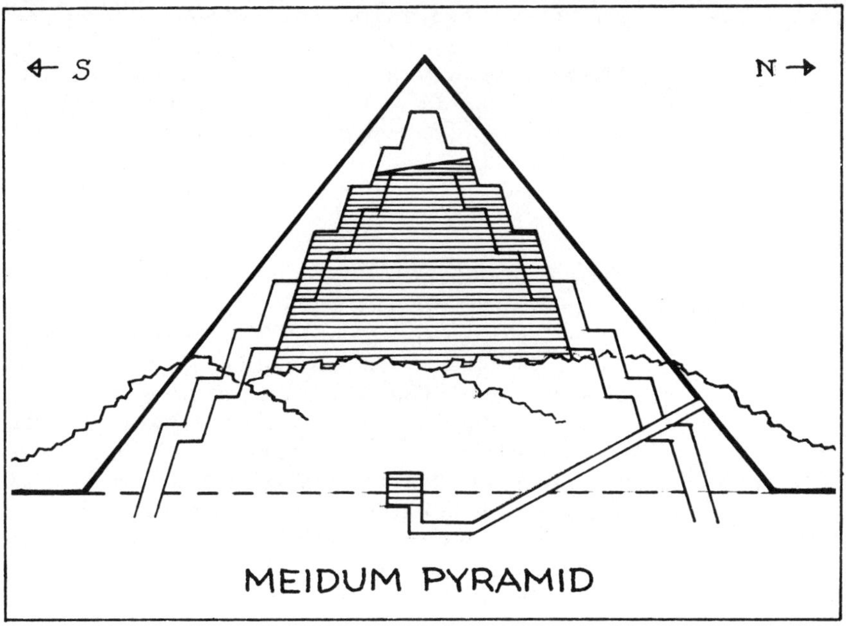

between July and November, the period of the inundation. All of these people needed training and organisation, as well as feeding, clothing and housing, and the logistics of the operation must have been formidable. It is not the sort of operation that is easily or efficiently mounted at the uncertain occasion of a pharaoh's accession, nor is the size of a pyramid and so the time it will take to build readily geared to the uncertain duration of a pharaoh's reign. The suggestion is rather that pyramid construction was continuous and independent of whether or not there would be enough pharaohs to fill them. And this is what the evidence of Meidum and the Bent Pyramid suggests did happen, the overlap accounted for by the fact that as the first pyramid tapered towards completion, the surplus workforce was immediately engaged on starting a second pyramid.

Pyramids and the state

Whether by intention or as a consequence, this pyramid production line must have had two important effects. The first was that the vast levy of men required would have cut across the division of Upper and Lower Egypt and the parochialism of villages and tribes throughout the length of the Valley, the breadth of the Delta. Pyramid building would complete, down to the fibres of society, the unification of the country begun by Menes by force of arms.

The second effect was that whoever was responsible for

pyramid building would see their power enhanced. But production of pyramids surplus to the requirements of any one pharaoh, surplus even to the requirements of an entire dynasty, demanded a transcending organising authority. Imhotep's own career suggests the composition of that authority: in part the power of the Pharaoh, but also that of the bureaucracy and the priesthood. Pyramids created the apparatus of the state.

Symbolism of the pyramids

There is then the pyramidal form. One can see how constructionally the pyramids began with the mastaba, Zoser's pyramid in fact a stepped mastaba. The achievement in architecture of the pure abstract pyramidal form came, briefly, at Meidum, when before it collapsed its steps were being sheathed in planes. If anything, the disaster was a spur to the technical perfection of the pyramidal symbol. That symbol preceded construction rather than technology dictated symbol seems likely. In Egyptian creation myths there is a primal hill which rises above the waters, and from it ascends the sun. And until the High Dam at Aswan finally put an end to the annual inundation, that was very much the scene in Egypt: villages huddled on mounds to avoid the flood, then its subsidence and the sun drawing from the mud the harvest. This myth is referred to at Medinet Habu and Hermopolis; Heliopolis also claimed a primal hill, the *benben,* a tapering megalith, a word whose root, *bn,* is bound up with the notion of shining, brilliant, ascending. It is depicted in II Dynasty inscriptions, that is before the pyramid age.

Variations on the pyramidal form continued to be popular throughout Egyptian history, as for example the obelisks whose points or pyramidions were sheathed in electrum, a mixture of silver and gold. Pliny the Elder described obelisks as petrified rays of sunlight, and more than one modern writer has remarked on the pyramid-like form of a burst of sunlight through the clouds after a rare Egyptian rain.

The building of pyramids then would have been no mere drudgery inflicted on the population by some megalomaniac pharaoh. The symbolism would have been appreciated throughout all levels of society, and it is quite likely that far from being built by slave-labour, as Herodotus claims, they were built willingly and with a shared sense of exalted purpose which at the time would have seemed far more important, and certainly would have been more conscious, than creating new political forms.

The end of the pyramid age

But as Robin Feddan says, "Here the gods have died sooner than the works of men". And those works included not only the pyramids, but the creation for the first time in human history of an organisational principle, the state, that was to serve Egypt until her absorption into the Roman Empire, and is the basis of human organisation to this day. Once the pyramid production line had achieved this, their symbolism could be carried on in lesser forms, such as obelisks; in any case, it was no longer necessary to build pyramids, and apart from some inferior examples in later dynasties, by 2500 BC the age of the pyramids was over.

Visiting the Giza Pyramids

Half a day should be allowed for the visit to the Giza Pyramids, though you should return again at night. They are approached along a broad straight road, originally built for that same Empress Eugénie who attended the opening night at the Opera House, so that she could cover the 11 kms from Cairo in her carriage. This Sharia el Ahram or Road of the Pyramids once passed across fellahin's fields which would flood with the rising of the Nile, but nowadays most of the route has been built up. There is therefore, at first, something ordinary about the approach, as though you were off to a funfair on the edge of town, expecting at any moment the distant screams of roller coaster passengers as they plunged down papier-maché mountains. Nor is the notion so far-fetched: "Egypt's most ambitious tourist development is the Pyramids Plateau complex in Giza by the Great Pyramids," wrote *The Times* in 1977. "The 10,000-acre complex, to be developed by a Hong Kong firm, Southern Pacific Properties, and the Egyptian General Company for Tourism, will have 10,000 beds, 5800 villas, 5100 flats, parks, artificial lakes, golf courses and even a giant glass pyramid for a museum and archaeological centre." One year and $7,000,000 later, following attacks in the Egyptian press and People's Assembly, the project was mercifully abandoned.

But even the Pyramids themselves initially conspire to deflate anticipation. One of the savants accompanying Napoleon described his approach: "Seen from a distance they produce the same kind of effect as do high mountain peaks. The nearer one approaches, the more this effect decreases. Only when at last you are within a short distance of these regular masses is a wholly different impression produced; you are struck by surprise, and as soon as you have reached the top of the slope, your ideas change in a flash. Finally, when you have reached the foot of the Great Pyramid, you are seized with a vivid and powerful emotion, tempered by a sort of stupefaction, almost overwhelming in its effects".

Even so, you might just as easily be overwhelmed by touts

urging you to ride their donkey, horse or camel, and by numberless 'guides' and 'watchmen' who gather about you like mosquitoes, endlessly trying to lure you into ruined little temples with the promise of an undiscovered mummy or reliefs of pharaonic pornography. In the old days, visitors would come with a dragoman who wielded a big stick for which you are bound to develop the greatest nostalgia. Mark Twain, who led a party of tourists here in the 1860s, attempted escape by climbing to the top of Cheops' Pyramid but was pursued by an Arab whom he offered $1 if he could race to the top of Chephren's Pyramid and back to the top of Cheops' within nine minutes, in the hope that the man would break his neck. Three dollars later an exasperated Twain, now joined by the man's mother, offered them each $100 if they would jump off the Pyramid head first.

The best times to visit the Pyramids are at dawn, at sunset and at night when they form as much a part of the natural order as the sun, the moon and the stars. Flaubert recalled the view from the top of Cheops' Pyramid: "The sun was rising just opposite; the whole valley of the Nile, bathed in mist, seemed to be a still white sea; and the desert behind us, with its hillocks of sand, another ocean, deep purple, its waves all petrified". My first visit was at night. I had gone to the son et lumiere, the Arabic programme, so that I would not have to listen to any of the usual tourist drivel, but could instead enjoy the play of lights to the eerie accompaniment of this booming, gutteral but poetic language. The programme over but some floodlights on, I walked up past the Sphinx and stood between the Pyramids of Cheops and Chephren. And then suddenly the lights went out. Black night. The great stones rising on either side, picked out by the moon and stars. The feeling, as Napoleon said here to his army, of "forty centuries of history looking down upon us", feeling it in the most awesome way.

Statistics

The road arrives at the Mena House Hotel and then curves sharply to the left, mounting a gentle slope and finishing at the north end of the plateau, almost directly opposite the Great Pyramid, that of Cheops. This is the oldest of the group and the largest, and the others, Chephren and Mycerinus, stand in descending order of age and size along a southwest axis, each identically oriented 8.5° west of magnetic north; when built they were probably aligned precisely with the North Star, their entrance corridors aiming straight at it. At first the second pyramid, that of Chephren, seems largest, but that is because it stands on higher ground and retains its casing towards its peak. Its present height is 136.4 metres (originally 143 metres) and its volume is 2,200,000 cubic metres; this compares with a height of 137.2 metres (originally 146.6 metres) for the Great Pyramid of Cheops, which has a volume of 2,550,000 cubic metres. This pyramid was built of over 2,500,000 enormous blocks of limestone cut from the Moqattam and locally, though about 170,000 have been removed by Arabs and Turks since the founding of Cairo. Mycerinus is much smaller, rising only to a height of 65.5 metres, though it is still imposing, and it contributes to the satisfying arrangement of the group. Napoleon astonished his officers with the calculation that the stones from these three pyramids would be sufficient to build a wall 3 metres high and 0.3 metres thick around the whole of France.

But the Pyramids do not have this rocky ledge entirely to themselves. There are smaller attendant pyramids, some at least for royal wives, and suburban rows of mastabas for nobles and princes of the blood. There are the remains of temples and causeways; there are solar boat pits; and there is the Sphinx. A pyramid was never merely a self-sufficient geometrically shaped tumulus of masonry raised above a royal burial; it was the culminating point of a vast funerary area comprising, apart from the pyramid itself, three parts. First, near the desert edge and overlooking the cultivation so as to be accessible by boat in

A pyramid complex

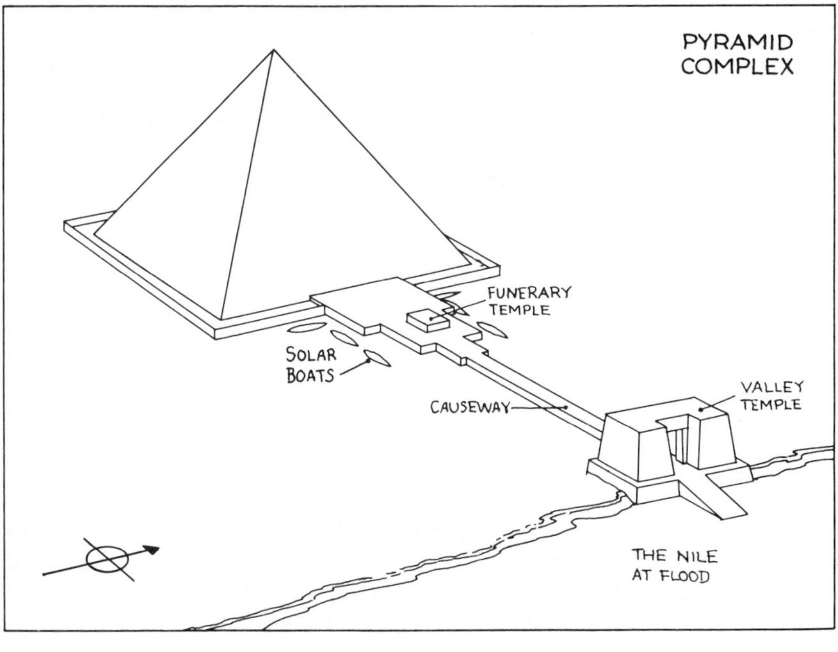

the inundation season was a modest *valley chapel*. From it led a walled-in *causeway,* as long as 500 metres, upwards to the *funerary temple* proper, this abutting on to the east side of the pyramid, where a false door permitted the deceased Pharaoh to emerge in order to partake of the offered feasts. Also, on several sides of a pyramid, set in pits, *wooden boats* have been found. Whether these were only symbolic or actually used is not known; some have supposed they enabled the Pharaoh to follow the sun god across the skies, but as they have been found facing all four points of the compass they could as easily have been intended to enable the Pharaoh to go wherever he desired. For convenience, however, they will be referred to here as solar boats.

Climbing the Great Pyramid

The polished casing to the Pyramid of Cheops (Khufu) is entirely gone and so you are presented with the tiered courses of limestone blocks, an invitation to climb to the platform at the top, 10 metres square. This used to be a fairly easy and entirely safe thing to do, as guides would simply haul you up, one at each arm, a third shoving from below. Climbing the Pyramids is now technically forbidden, however, which leaves the field open to the more adventurous or the more foolhardy to make the attempt unassisted, though a Beduin will often miraculously appear when you get into trouble. The ascent is best made at the northeast corner, each 'step' in fact a metre-high block, and will take 15-20 minutes. If anything, it is more difficult on the way down. At 7 am one morning I saw the body of a man who had fallen and bashed himself against the blocks all the way down, his brain spilled out, his face gone.

Going inside

The squeamish might content themselves with going inside. Here the only thing to fear is fear itself, in the form of claustrophobia and difficulty for some in breathing due to inadequate oxygen, and also the possibility that you might get locked in, which in fact happened one night to my brother (more on the very real dangers of being sealed up, temporarily and even permanently, in ancient tombs when you read about Saqqara and Thebes).

The descending corridor

You *enter at the north face* (1) through an opening made by Caliph al-Mamun in his search for treasure (though it is probable that this pyramid had been robbed as early as the First Intermediate Period), and soon come to the *original corridor* which descends for 100 metres to a depth of 30 metres beneath the surface of the bedrock. It reaches an *unfinished chamber* (2) of no interest, and as this corridor is constricted (1.3 metres high, one metre wide) and slippery, it is not usually open to the public. Why this lowest chamber was never finished is not known; Herodotus said it was subject to flooding by the Nile.

The ascending corridor

Instead, about 20 metres from the entrance along the descending corridor you come to a block of granite designed to prevent access to the *ascending corridor* (3), though al-Mamun merely hollowed out the rock to the left and you soon find yourself crouching your way upwards (height again 1.3 metres, width one metre) for 40 metres. The gradient is 1 in 2, and so can be quite tiring, but arrival at the Great Gallery at least permits a stretch. Here there is a *shaft* (right) which winds down to the descending corridor – purpose unknown. There is also a *horizontal corridor,* again only 1.3. metres high for most of its length, which leads to the so-called *Queen's Chamber* (4), nearly square with a pointed roof of gigantic blocks. But best by far is the ascending *Great Gallery* (5), 8.5 metres high, 47 metres long, a marvel of precision masonry, of which it has been said that neither a needle nor a hair can be inserted into the joints of the stones.

The Queen's Chamber and Great Gallery

The King's Chamber

This gives on to the principal tomb chamber, commonly called the *King's Chamber* (6), 42.5 metres above the surface of the bedrock, 5.22 metres wide and 10.44 metres long, that is a double square, aligned east-west. On the north and south walls, a metre above the floor, are the rectangular mouths of

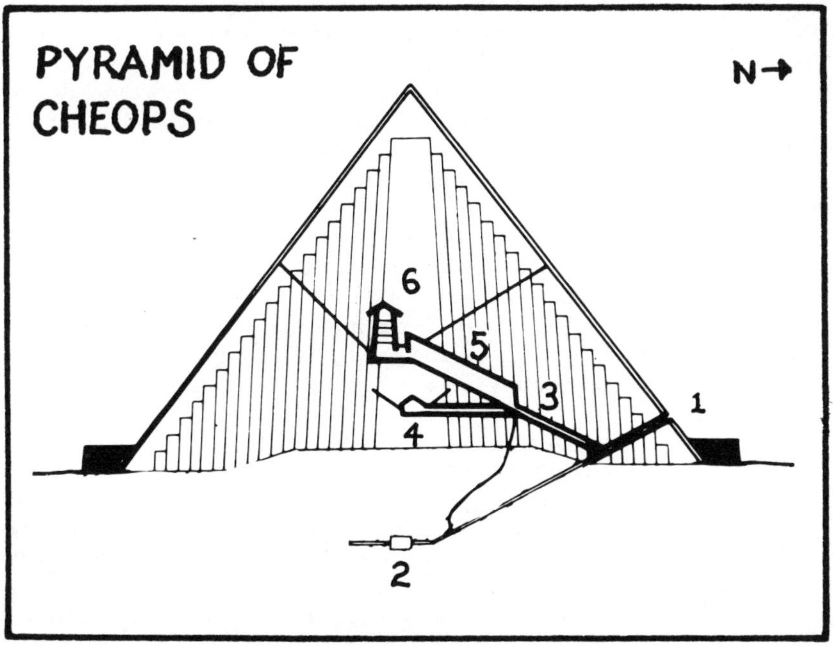

the two *ventilation shafts* which extend to the surfaces of the pyramid. The chamber is built entirely in pink Aswan granite and roofed over with nine huge granite slabs laid horizontally, and above these (seen by means of a ladder leading to a passage in the upper south wall of the Great Gallery) are four more granite layers, each separated by a *relieving chamber,* possibly meant to distribute the full weight of the pyramid away from the King's Chamber, though in fact this job is accomplished by the topmost pointed roof of limestone blocks. It was in these relieving chambers that the only inscriptions in any of the Giza Pyramids were found – the cartouche, traced several times in red, of Khufu, Cheops. His mummy, if it found its way to this pyramid at all, would have been placed in this King's Chamber; the sarcophagus is empty.

It is here that you might think about the great weight upon you. Over your head is 95 metres of solid pyramid, more than enough to squash you very thin for a very long time. Unlike the Meidum pyramid, however, the Pyramid of Cheops has been shown by Swiss engineer H. Roessler (1952) to be exceptionally stable. The building blocks are far larger than those used for earlier pyramids and they are precisely fitted together, while the casing blocks overlaying the basic step structure rest upon foundations slotted into the bedrock. The weight of the pyramid itself contributes to its stability, but not simply its dead weight; the stepped inclined buttresses throw much of this weight towards the centre. At every level the pyramid's horizontal thrusts are directed towards the central core, while 35 percent of the vertical thrusts are transmitted to the inner core (that is the line running from the top of the pyramid *through you* to the base), only the remaining thrusts being carried down into the bedrock. In fact the bigger the pyramid the more stable it becomes.

Around Cheops' Pyramid

Coming out of the pyramid you can see on the north side, also on the east, the remains of the original *enclosure wall,* about 10 metres from the base. Backing against this wall on the east side is the basalt paving of Cheops' *funerary temple,* about all that remains of it, and only occcasional traces too of the *causeway* that would have come up from the valley temple. The *three small pyramids,* from 15 to 20 metres high, probably belonged to Cheops' queens or sisters: the southernmost is certainly Henutsen's, daughter of Snofru, sister and perhaps wife of Cheops. She became identified during the XXI Dynasty with Isis and her mortuary temple, to the east of her pyramid, was enlarged as the shrine of the 'Mistress of the Pyramids'. Also in the vicinity of the smaller pyramids and the funerary temple are *boat pits.* A *solar boat* is being pieced back together on the south side of the Pyramid, within a glass and concrete structure not yet open to the public.

The Sphinx An outcrop of hard grey and soft yellow limestone, useless as building material, was left standing in the quarry from which Cheops cut many of the blocks for his pyramid. His son Chephren had the happy idea of shaping it into a figure – lion's body, god's face, though perhaps Chephren's own, and wearing the royal headdress with uraeus. The Egyptians would have regarded it as a symbol of strength and wisdom combined, but the Greeks applied their word sphinx to it, recalling a lion's body but the breasts and head of a woman given to putting riddles to passers-by, and so this most famous Sphinx has acquired an air of mystery quite foreign to its intention.

Nevertheless, some mysteries are associated with it. Neither Herodotus nor any other classical writer until Pliny the Elder mentioned the Sphinx, presumably because it was

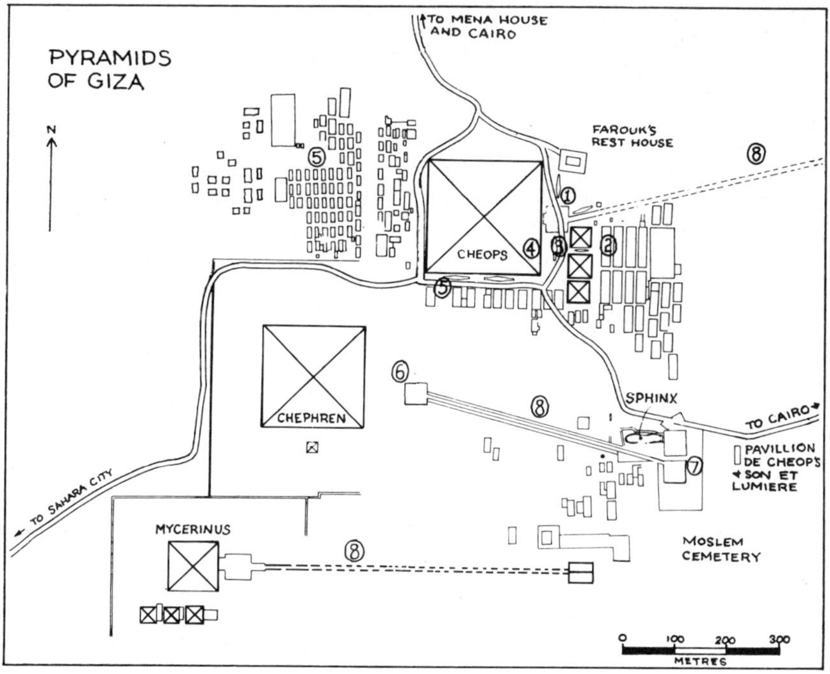

1. Cheops' mortuary temple
2. Pyramids of Cheops' Queens
3. Boat pits
4. Solar boat
5. Mastabas of IV and V Dynasties
6. Chephren's mortuary temple
7. Chephren's valley temple
8. Causeways

buried in sand. Prints and photographs of recent times show its features looming from an engulfing sea of sand, but this is all too assiduously cleared today, some mystery swept away with it. The future Tuthmosis IV (XVIII Dyn) dreamt here that if he was to become Pharaoh he must clear away the sands: his stelae between the Sphinx' paws commemorate this first known restoration. During the Turkish domination the Sphinx was used for target practice and its nose, which originally had been cemented on, fell off and is now in the British Museum; 18th C. drawings show that it was missing long before Napoleon was supposed to have done the damage. In the son et lumiere programmes, the Sphinx is given the role of narrator which it performs, as I have said, much better in Arabic when you cannot understand a word. This is in fact one of the best times for viewing it or, after the programme, having a drink on the terrace of the Pavillion of Cheops, for then it gains in perspective against the more distant Pyramids. It may not otherwise seem as large as you have imagined: it is 20 metres high and 48.5 metres long, much of its bulk crouched within the quarry so that only its head overtops the horizon.

Immediately in front of the Sphinx and associated with it is a IV Dynasty temple, one reason for believing the face on the Sphinx is a god's and not Chephren's, for the Egyptians did not build temples to their kings. Adjacent and to the south is

Chephren's Valley Temple

Chephren's Valley Temple, facing east. This is the only IV Dynasty sanctuary to retain its grandeur, its exceptional state of preservation owing to having been buried in the sands and not discovered until 1853 by Mariette. The material is pink Aswan granite, majestically and simply assembled in strong verticals and horizontals, square monolithic pillars supporting massive granite architraves. It was here that Mariette discovered the magnificent diorite statue of Chephren (Room 42, Ground Floor, Egyptian Museum). The purpose of this temple is uncertain, or rather certain for some and contradicted by others. One view is that valley temples were used for mummification; others think the site too exposed and that embalming would have been done either at the Pharaoh's Memphis palace or at the base of the pyramid, in the funerary temple. There is at least more general agreement that here was

'Opening of the Mouth' ceremony

performed the 'Opening of the Mouth' ceremony at which the ka entered the deceased's body. The ka always required a secure residence, hence pyramids and immutable bodies, though it would also inhabit the mortuary statue of the Pharaoh, such as that one in the Egyptian Museum, one of 23 that sat round the main T-shaped chamber.

Chephren's Funerary Temple and Pyramid

You should now follow if you can the traces of Chephren's causeway up to his Funerary Temple at the base of his pyramid. More of this temple survives than of Cheops', the walls formed of possibly the largest blocks ever used in building, one of them 13.4 metres long and weighing 163,000 kilos. To the south of the pyramid is a ruined small pyramid, probably of a queen.

The Pyramid of Chephren (Khafre) compares to Cheops' in size, seemingly exceeds it in height and is also capped with its original casing. But its interior is less interesting, while the ascent is much more difficult, requiring an hour to get to the casing, progress being very dangerous thence upwards because the smooth surface offers no hold. One of the earlier explorers and snatchers of antiquities was Belzoni, born in Italy but first achieving fame for his 'human pyramid' act on the stage of the Sadlers Wells in London. He was the first European to enter this pyramid (1818) and promptly emblazoned his name on the south wall of the burial chamber. When Flaubert entered the chamber 33 years later he recorded: "Under Belzoni's name, and no less large, is that of a M. Just de Chasseloup-Laubat. One is irritated by the number of imbeciles' names written everywhere: on the top of the Great Pyramid there is a certain Buffard, 79 Rue Saint-Martin, wallpaper manufacturer, in black letters; an English fan of Jenny Lind's has written her name; there is also a pear, representing Louis-Philippe".

When the Egyptians built their pyramids it was with a feeling for the sublime power of the plane, without reliefs, inscriptions or any detailing whatsoever. Once the polished limestone casings were set in place, the pyramids both literally and symbolically repulsed the touch of mortals – well, that was the idea, anyway. One of the high points of a visit to the Pyramids in Roman times was the spectacle of men from a nearby village shinning up from the ground to their very tips; while one Roman woman scribbled on a casing stone, "I saw the Pyramids without you; sadly I shed tears here", a lament copied down by a 15th C. pilgrim, when the casing was more extensive than now.

Pyramid of Mycerinus

The Pyramid of Mycerinus (Menkaure) has only one-tenth of the volume of the other two pyramids and effectively marks the end of the pyramid age. The last Pharaoh of the IV Dynasty built a quite different sort of tomb at Saqqara, while the pyramids of the next dynasty were small and shoddy. Though last of the great pyramids, Mycerinus' was built well, with granite used for the lower courses and a casing that remained intact until the 16th C. An attempt was made by the Caliph in 1215 to destroy all the Pyramids and his workmen started with Mycerinus'. After eight months they gave up. "Considering the vast masses that have been taken away, it might be supposed that the building would have been completely destroyed, but so immense is the pile that the stones are scarcely missed. Only on one of its sides can be noticed any trace of the impression which it was attempted to be made", wrote the historian Abd el Latif. Though you can enter, the interior is not interesting. Opposite the south face are three small pyramids, while against the east are the remains of Mycerinus' funerary temple.

Mons Venus

Herodotus recorded a belief in Greece that this pyramid was in fact built by Rhodopis, a beautiful courtesan from Thrace who flourished in Egypt, charging a building stone for her services. The Pyramid of Mycerinus is built of at least 200,000 granite and limestone blocks. But it is not only for that reason that the story is untrue.

To Saqqara and Memphis

Saqqara is 32 kms by road from Cairo and 21 kms south of the Giza Pyramids. The necropolis extends about 7 kms north to south along the desert plateau and looks down over the palm groves that cover the site of Memphis, about 6 kms to the southeast in the valley of the Nile. Memphis was the capital of the Old Kingdom, its palaces and shrines of that period built of mud brick for the span of the living and now vanished; Saqqara, built of stone to endure eternity, survives.

The Saqqara road is a left turn off the Road to the Pyramids at the traffic lights immediately after a canal about 1500 metres before the Mena House Hotel. It is a pleasant country road with glimpses to the right of the Libyan Desert and the V Dynasty pyramids of Abusir. (You can also ride across the desert by camel or horse from the Giza Pyramids in about three hours.) You come first to the turning, on your right, for Saqqara; or you can carry straight on for the left-hand turning to the Memphis site. Alternatively, you can take the bus from the Giza Pyramids to Badrashein and can ask to be let off at Memphis. It is best to visit Saqqara early in the morning to avoid the heat, and so to call on Memphis afterwards. But for context, Memphis will be mentioned first.

History of Memphis

Memphis probably began as a fortress by which Menes controlled the land and water routes between Upper and Lower Egypt and kept the conquered inhabitants of the Delta in subjection. By the III Dynasty it must have become a sizeable capital, as the Saqqara necropolis suggests, but it may not have been fixed. The IV Dynasty Pharaohs built their pyramids to the North at Giza and would probably have had their palaces near there too. One can imagine Memphis developing in stages like Arab Fustat and its successors, decamping northwards. Whether it was the Mediterranean breezes that attracted, or the growing dominance of the sun cult at Heliopolis, so closely associated with pyramid development, is not known. By the VI Dynasty, however, the old site of Memphis had been reoccupied, its attraction the venerable sanctuary of Ptah. From the court of Pepi and its associated monuments came the name *Men-nefru-Mire,* The Beauty of King Mire (Pepi), later abbreviated to Menfe, in Greek Memphis.

Although no longer capital, in the New Kingdom Memphis rivalled Thebes in grandeur, embellished in particular by Ramses II's mania for building. During the 5th C. BC when the Persians ruled Egypt from here and Herodotus visited the city, it was a great cosmopolitan centre, a foreshadowing of Alexandria, with many Greeks and Jews, Phoenicians and Libyans among its population, as full of oriental spectacle as Cairo is today. Herodotus, in his hydrology of Egypt, which fascinated him, wrote that "when the Nile overflows, the whole country is converted into a sea, and the towns, which alone remain above water, look like islands in the Aegean. At these times water transport is used all over the country, instead of merely along the course of the river, and anyone going from Naucratis to Memphis would pass right by the Pyramids . . . The priests told me that it was Menes, the first king of Egypt, who raised the dam which protects Memphis from the floods . . . On the land which had been drained by the diversion of the river, King Menes built his city and afterwards on the north and west sides of the town excavated a lake, communicating with the river". As late as the 12th C., Abd el Latif could write that "the ruins still offer, to those who contemplate them, a collection of such marvellous beauty that the intelligence is confounded, and the most eloquent man would be unable to describe them adequately". But towards the end of the Mameluke period the dikes around Memphis fell into disrepair and at every inundation the level of the ground was raised.

Memphis today

Today the centuries of Nile mud have swallowed Memphis entirely, so much so that it is impossible to stand here and soliloquise on how the once mighty has fallen – there is, simply, so little to stir reflection. And even had the dikes been maintained, the more ancient stratas of Memphis would have been lost. Herodotus exactly describes those conditions, persisting until the building of the High Dam at Aswan, which annually drowned the Valley and the Delta and gradually covered the past with mud, so that settlements built upon themselves, one strata upon another, to form what in Arabic are known as *tells*. The earliest mud brick houses, palaces and sanctuaries have long since disintegrated beneath the wash of the annual flood, explaining why so much is known of the Egyptian dead, who dwelt in stone on high desert ground, while so little is known of the living. At Memphis there is a friendly alabaster sphinx dating from the New Kingdom set up in high grass, and the faint remains of the vast Temple of Ptah, and alabaster mummification beds where the Apis bulls (see the Serapeum at Saqqara) were prepared for burial. And there is a modern building erected for the sole purpose of roofing over a supine colossus of Ramses II, brother to the one outside the Cairo railway station. This Ramses is the victim of monumental indifference: the Egyptian government gave him to the British Museum – which failed to collect. He lies here with his right fist clenched, like a cataleptic Gulliver, bound down by brain seizure rather than ropes. A keeper, perhaps to make sure Ramses does not collect himself and stalk away, stands guard with an old rifle, its last probable use at Omdurman.

Saqqara

The Saqqara site has a far more desert feel than Giza; the sands wash about your feet nearly everywhere. Also it is dotted with untended holes left by excavators, some of terrific depth and rarely enclosed. It would be dangerous for children on the loose, and adults should mind their step. Many tombs, once discovered and examined, have been closed again and some have even sanded over. The most comfortable way to explore the site is to go first to Zoser's funerary complex, visiting also the Pyramid of Unas nearby, and then to drive round to the refreshment tent (or walk across the sands to it) from where you can visit the Mastaba of Akhti-hotep and Ptah-hotep, the Mastaba of Ti and the Serapeum.

Saqqara, from Sokkar, the Memphite god of the dead, was a necropolis from the unification of Egypt through the Ptolemaic period, and it is the site also of a Coptic monastery destroyed by the Arabs c.960, so that discoveries here span 4000 years. In historical range and the quantity and value of what has been found here – monuments, works of art, texts and vases – there can be few archaeological sites in all the world, let alone Egypt, to compare with Saqqara. Even so, serious examination of the site only began in the mid-19th C. and what remains to be discovered is incalculable. Considering its proximity to Cairo, it is surprising how infrequently it is visited, and how briefly, with organised tours usually allowing only one to two hours. Though the heat is best avoided by an early morning visit, a full day's stay is compensated for by the early departure of tour groups when you will have the place almost entirely to yourself.

Discovery

Except for Zoser's Step Pyramid, Saqqara was ignored, its revelations unsuspected, until 1851 when Auguste Mariette discovered the Serapeum. Even the funerary complex immediately surrounding the Step Pyramid went undiscovered until 1924, and its restoration, to which Jean-Philippe Lauer has given a lifetime, continues to this day. Cecil M. Firth's campaign of 1924-7 overturned accepted notions about the origins of Egyptian architecture in stone which, because of the gigantic blocks used at Giza, was thought to have developed from megalithic monuments. Instead, at Zoser's complex, one sees a stone architecture which replicates the use of brick in its size and courses, and which also is full of imitative references to rush matting, reed and wood forms. One of the greatest achievements of Egyptian civilisation was to sever stone from the rock and to make of it a building material unsurpassed to this day. It happened here, for the first time, at Saqqara, with some hesitancy in the new technology but astonishing artistic brilliance.

Zoser's funerary complex: the enclosure wall

Zoser's funerary complex, dominated by the Step Pyramid, is 544 metres from north to south, 277 metres from east to west, and enclosed by a magnificent panelled and bastioned *wall* of fine limestone. It still survives to a height of 4.7 metres at some places along its south side, while on the east side, near the southeast corner, it has been rebuilt with stones found in the sand to its original height of 10.48 metres. This vast white wall in itself, once easily visible from Memphis, must have conferred enormous prestige on Zoser and his architect Imhotep. Lauer was himself at first an architect and was called in by Firth when it was realised that the complex could be accurately reconstructed using the original stones.

Entrance colonnade

Though there are many *false doors* in the enclosure wall for the ka to come and go, there is only one *entrance* (1) for the living, at the southeast corner. The narrow passage is through a fortress-like tower and gives onto a vestibule where you can see on either side the leaves of a *simulated double door* thrown open, complete with hinge pins and sockets. Ahead of you is a *colonnaded corridor* (2), its columns engaged and ribbed in imitation of palm stems (the protective ceiling is modern concrete.) At the far end is a broad *hypostyle hall* (3) with four pairs of engaged columns, and on your right as you enter the court a half open ka door. This is where the statue base bearing Imhotep's titles was found. Before leaving the hall, notice that the columns are comprised of drums seldom exceeding 25 cms in height, one of many details of the masonry which betray Imhotep's hesitancy in working with this new material, stone.

Great South Court

You now emerge into the *Great South Court* (4), and along the wall to your left is a section of rebuilt wall with a *frieze of cobras* (5). The cobra, *uraeus* in Latin, was an emblem of royalty and an instrument of protection, always appearing on the Pharaoh's headdress and able to destroy his enemies by breathing flames. The cobra was worshipped in Lower Egypt, and so here in this early dynasty it also emphasises Zoser's mastery over the conquered peoples of the Delta. Near here is a shaft leading to Zoser's *southern tomb* (6), similar in its faience decoration to that beneath the Step Pyramid. There is a relief here of Zoser running the Heb-Sed race (see below). One explanation for two tombs is that early Pharaohs thereby demonstrated their connection with the two Egypts, so a southern and a northern tomb. Possibly the canopic jars containing Zoser's viscera were placed here, the body beneath the pyramid (where in fact a foot was found).

Zoser's Step Pyramid

The *Step Pyramid* (7) and its place in the development of pyramid building has already been referred to at the beginning of this chapter. Now you have a first-hand opportunity to examine its features. Despite its 62-metre height, it was built of fairly small limestone blocks, far smaller than those enormous blocks at Giza. Though working with stone, Imhotep was still thinking in terms of mud brick. But even in the enlargement of this monument from mastaba to pyramid you can detect signs of Imhotep's growing confidence in the new medium: at the southeast corner where the casing has come away you can see the smaller stonework of the *mastaba,* as you can if you walk along the east face of the pyramid. Also note how regularly the courses are laid, both of the mastaba and the pyramid as a whole, and how well shaped and fitted the stones are. In technique, Imhotep was without fault. The last enlarged mastaba measured 63 metres each way and a little over 8 metres high. Recall that the first pyramid erected over this mastaba rose four steps; the further pyramid of two additional steps increased the total volume by more than four fold. The entire monument was then sheathed in fine limestone from Tura, just to the south of modern Cairo, as were the Giza Pyramids.

FUNERARY COMPLEX OF ZOSER

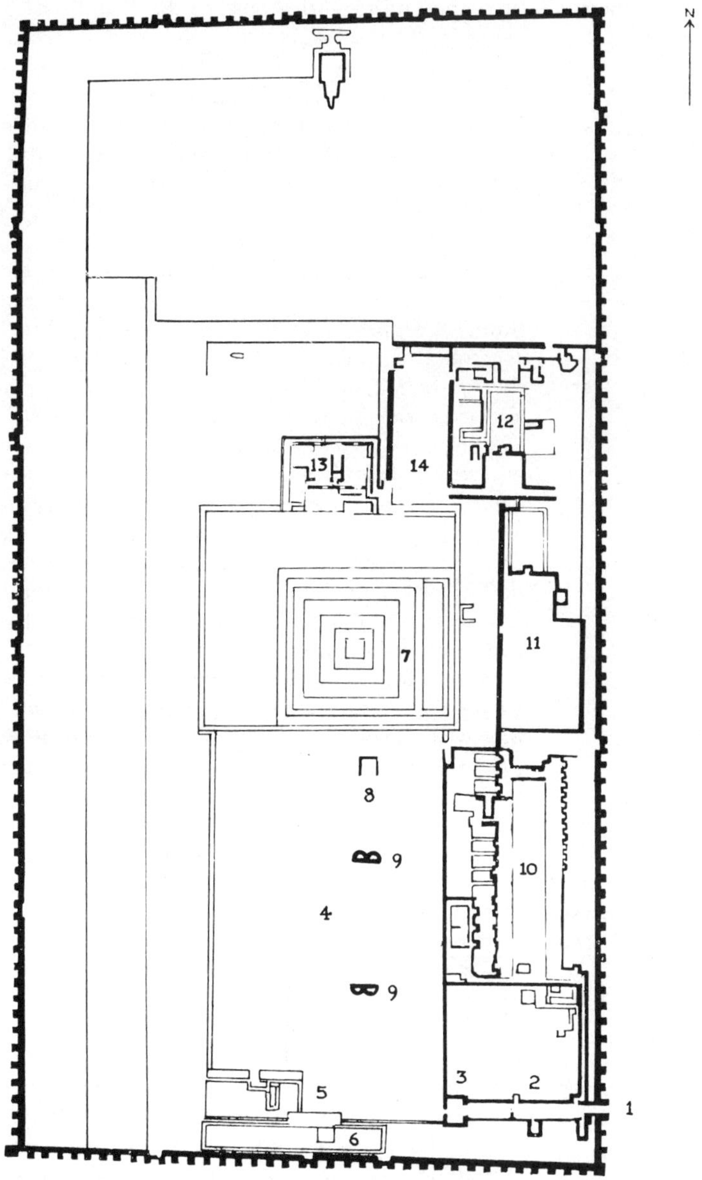

Saite Gallery: entrance to the pyramid

The original entrance to the Step Pyramid was at the north face, but in the XXVI Dynasty, known as the Saite period for its dynasty's origins at Sais in the Delta, a *gallery* (8) was dug from the Great South Court to the chambers beneath the pyramid. Permission and keys will have to be asked for at the office of the Inspector of Antiquities to the northeast of the Pyramid of Teti. The Saites admired the works of the Old Kingdom and it is quite possible they tunnelled their way into the pyramid out of sheer archaeological curiosity. After 60 metres you come to the main central shaft from where there are impressive views up into the pyramid and down towards the *burial chamber* which is sealed with a huge granite plug.

The Heb-Sed race

Emerging once again into the Great South Court, you see two *B-shaped constructions* (9) near the centre. These marked the limits of Upper and Lower Egypt, the gap between them symbolically spanned by Zoser in the Heb-Sed race. (A *relief* in the southern tomb shows Zoser in full stride, the two B-shaped constructions to the rear and fore.) The Heb-Sed race was one of the ceremonies during the five-day jubilee which occurred in the thirtieth year – that is at the interval of one generation – of the Pharaoh's reign. It is possible that at some earlier period, power was granted only for 30 years, the chieftain then deposed, perhaps killed, to spare the land from declining because of his failing strength. This jubilee, therefore, was a renewal of the vital forces of the Pharaoh and his ka, and so of all Egypt.

Significance of the Heb-Sed Court

Also at his jubilee the Pharaoh re-enacted his coronation, sitting first on the throne of Upper Egypt, then on the throne of Lower Egypt, each time presenting gifts to the various priesthoods before they returned to their provinces. Participation in the festival obliged the priests to recognise the supremacy of the Pharaoh over their own local deities. These ceremonies, however, including the ritual race, would not have taken place here but at Memphis. The funerary complex was meant as a cosmic 'stand-in' for the actual jubilee site – it perpetuated the regenerating Heb-Sed in eternal stone. This explains the extraordinary film set quality of the Heb-Sed Court.

Colour plate: Zoser's Step Pyramid at Saqqara (top); the Hypostyle Hall at Karnak (bottom left); children at a fishing village on the shores of Lake Mareotis (bottom right).

The *Heb-Sed Court* (10) in the southeast part of the complex is rectangular and flanked to east and west by *shrines*, each one representing a province. They are hardly more than facades, as in a Hollywood Western. Access to the offering niches is by circumventing a screen wall, disguising the lack of depth, for the tall buildings are mere dummies, filled with rubble. Half open doors with hinges, imitations of the wooden originals, receive immortality in stone. In actuality, these shrines would

Colour plate: relief at Kom Ombo showing a Ptolemaic king receiving the crowns of Upper and Lower Egypt (top); a truck decorated with talismans against the evil eye (mid-left); the market street in Luxor (bottom left); Islamic Cairo, with the minarets of the Barquq and Qalaun mosques (bottom right).

have been tents with wooden poles and cross-supports. The chapels are not uniform; some have a curved cornice, as though the underlying frame represented flexed wood; other roofs are horizontal with the outward curve of the cavetto cornice that was to become so familiar a feature of Egyptian architecture, and torus molding. Drawing on earlier building materials, Imhotep here invented the language of stone architecture, Cornices, torus mouldings, stone corner posts and columns and a variety of capitals appear for the first time in history at Saqqara. All the more astonishing that the effect is so delicate and beautifully proportioned.

A stone *platform* at the south end of the court is probably where the two thrones of Egypt stood for the re-enactment of the coronation, while at the north end of the court, to the left, is a *base with four pairs of feet*, most likely those of statues of Zoser, his wife and two daughters.

House of the South

North of the Heb-Sed Court is another spacious court and the *House of the South* (11) with engaged proto-Doric columns. Though found again about 1200 years later at Hatshepsut's mortuary temple, these Doric-style columns were never popular in Egypt where planes and hence smoothly-rounded columns were preferred to the Aegean play of light and shadow. There is the peculiarity of the door being placed asymmetrically, owing to the prototype facade being no more than a curtain, the door therefore needing to abut a column for support. As with the shrines in the Heb-Sed Court, the House of the South and the House of the North would actually have had wooden frames. They may have been sanctuaries, or possibly they represent government buildings of Upper and Lower Egypt.

First tourist graffiti

Inside the corridor are the first known examples of tourist graffiti, written in a cursive form of hieroglyphics and dating from the New Kingdom. The visitors, scribes from Thebes, express their admiration for Zoser's achievement, though here and elsewhere some settle for the ancient equivalent of 'Kilroy was here', while one smug crackpot, taking exception to some illiterate graffiti he must have seen, scribbled: "The scribe of clever fingers came, a clever scribe without his equal among any men of Memphis, the scribe Amenemhet. I say: Explain to me these words. My heart is sick when I see the work of their hands. It is like the work of a woman who has no mind".

House of the North

The *House of the North* (12) is similar to that of the South except here the columns have the form of a papyrus plant, the shaft the triangular stem, the capital the fanning head.

The *mortuary temple* (13) at the north face of the pyramid is largely in ruins. The original entrance to the burial chamber

The serdab

beneath the pyramid led from this temple. To the east of the temple is the *serdab* (14), as startling now as it was to Firth when he uncovered it. It is a masonry box, tilted slightly back and with two small holes drilled through its north face. A window at the side, put there by the excavators, allows you to peer in. And there is Zoser! A life-size painted *limestone statue* as you realise after the initial surprise, but for all the world like a strapped-in astronaut in his space capsule, his eyes fixed through the holes on the North Star, awaiting blast-off and immortality. The circumpolar stars and the North Star itself were "those that know no destruction" or "those that know no weariness", for they never set and so never died; this was the place of eternal blessedness for which Egyptians longed. And there is Zoser. It is absolutely convincing. It is this which impresses about the ancient Egyptians again and again, how they gave as well as they could mechanical effect to their illusions. They put California body-freezers to shame. Alas for poor Zoser, the unbelieving Mr Firth removed the original statue to the Antiquities Museum in Cairo; this is a copy. But then again, the substitution probably does not bother Zoser's ka, and it lives here still, and at dark of night it rockets starwards and mingles with the universe.

Pyramid of Unas

Unas was the last Pharaoh of the V Dynasty. About 350 years mark the distance between Zoser's Step Pyramid, the Great Pyramids at Giza, and this heap of rubble that is Unas' pyramid. These monuments graphically portray the rise and decline of the Old Kingdom sun cult.

The Pyramid of Unas was approached by a kilometre-long *causeway,* part of which has been reconstructed, including a very short section of its walls and roof, for it was entirely enclosed. A slit in the roof allowed the sunlight to illuminate the inscribed walls which were lively with everyday scenes.

Along the causeway

The *tombs of nobles* lie on either side, but most of these are closed or even sanded over – there are, anyway, better tombs to see elsewhere in the necropolis. On the south side of the causeway there are impressive *boat pits.* Also, about 150 metres to the south are the sanded over ruins of the *Monastery of St Jeremias,* founded in the second half of the 5th C. and destroyed by the Arabs around 960. Practically all of its paintings and carvings have been removed to the Coptic Museum in Old Cairo.

The *pyramid* looks like a pile of dirt, certainly when approached from the east. On the west side its stones are more evident, but are disarrayed. Even originally it rose only about 18.5 metres; its core was loose blocks and rubble, its casing alone of hewn limestone. Nevertheless, the pyramid has proved of immense historical importance, for when Gaston Maspero entered the tomb chamber in 1881 he found the walls covered with inscriptions, the *Pyramid Texts,* which are the earliest mortuary literature of Egypt. These are hymns and rituals that preceded and accompanied the interment of the body; prayers for the release of the *ba* or soul; another section listing offerings of food, drink and clothing for use in the afterlife. Until this time, pyramids had gone unadorned. Thereafter, funerary literature underwent considerable elaboration and embroidery, culminating in that collection – or rather genre, for no such definitive compilation existed – of New Kingdom literature known to us as the Book of the Dead.

The Pyramid Texts

Entering the pyramid

Despite its exterior, the pyramid remains internally sound and you can creep down the 1.4-metre high corridor, entered from the north face, past three enormous slabs of granite meant to block the way. Unlike the New Kingdom texts which were full of advice on how to steer a course clear of the forces of evil, which in effect emphasised the dangers that preceded safe arrival in the afterlife and were the tools of the trade of a blackmailing priesthood, the Pyramid Texts celebrate eternal life and identify the deceased Pharaoh with Osiris. Nevertheless, there is anxiety in the prayers. The confident era of the sun cult was waning; a personal god and a note of redemption marked the rising cult of Osiris. The state was weakening; the troubled times of the First Intermediate Period were approaching.

Refreshments and Mariette's house

You can now trudge across the sands or drive to the refreshment tent which stands near the site of Mariette's house, where he stayed during those first serious explorations of Saqqara. The beer is cold and in the heat goes straight to your head. You can walk around the rest of the necropolis in a state of intoxication. When visiting the Serapeum, you may be grateful for that.

Mastaba of Akhti-Hotep and Ptah-Hotep

But first you can visit some mastabas. The *double Mastaba of Akhti-Hotep and Ptah-Hotep* is to the southeast of the tent, along your way if you are walking between Zoser's or Unas' complex and a beer. Ptah-Hotep describes himself as a priest of Maat and he may have held other positions too. At any rate, he seems to have been a very important official during the reign of Djedkare (V Dyn), predecessor of Unas. His son Akhti-Hotep was vizier, judge and chief of the granary and treasury. Their mastaba is smaller than that of Ti's, which we come to next, but is more developed and is particularly interesting for the reliefs which are in various stages of completion.

Reliefs in progress

You enter from the north and come into a *corridor*. On its left wall are preliminary drawings in red with corrections by the master artist in black. On the right wall are various stages of low relief. The background is cut away first to yield a silhouette and then the details are pencilled in and cut. In the lower registers, servants carry fowl in their arms towards Ptah-Hotep who stands at the far end of this right-hand wall. Though somewhat stylised, with his shoulders squared but with head and limbs in profile, the detailed musculature shows the artist's sound sense of anatomy.

At the top end of the corridor you turn right into a *pillared hall* and then left, passing through a *vestibule*, into *Ptah-Hotep's tomb chamber*. The ceiling imitates the trunks of palm trees while the mural reliefs, still retaining some colour, are the finest preserved of the Old Kingdom, surpassing even those in the more famous Mastaba of Ti.

Ptah-Hotep's tomb chamber: finest Old Kingdom reliefs

On the *right wall* are two door-shaped stelae, representing the entrance to the tomb. Between them is Ptah-Hotep, depicted in the panther-skin of a high priest, seated at a cornucopian table of offerings, a goblet raised to his lips. In the upper register, priests make offerings; in the lower three rows, servants bear gifts. They are lucky to get off so lightly; during the I Dynasty they were sacrificed and interred around their master's mastaba. On the *far wall* Ptah-Hotep is again at table, this time with a stylised loaf of bread before him and copper basins and ewers alongside so that he may cleanse himself before eating. In the upper register women representing various estates bring him the products of his farms, while in the second register animals are being thrown and slaughtered. The reliefs on the *left wall* are the finest and most interesting, a catalogue of events in the life of the deceased. On the right, according to the text, Ptah-Hotep is inspecting the "gifts and tribute that are brought by the estates of the North and South"; boys are wrestling and running, caged

Places mentioned in the text

A Zoser's funerary complex
B Causeway of Unas
C Boat pits and nobles' tombs
D Monastery of St. Jeremias
E Pyramid of Unas
F Refreshment tent
G Mastaba of Akhti-Hotep and Ptah-Hotep
H Mastaba of Ti
I Greek Statues
J Serapeum

Other sites

a Tomb of Horemheb
b Unfinished Pyramid of Sekhemkhet
c Pyramid of Userkaf
d Pyramid of Teti
e Mastaba of Mereruka
f I Dynasty tombs
g Mastaba of Hest

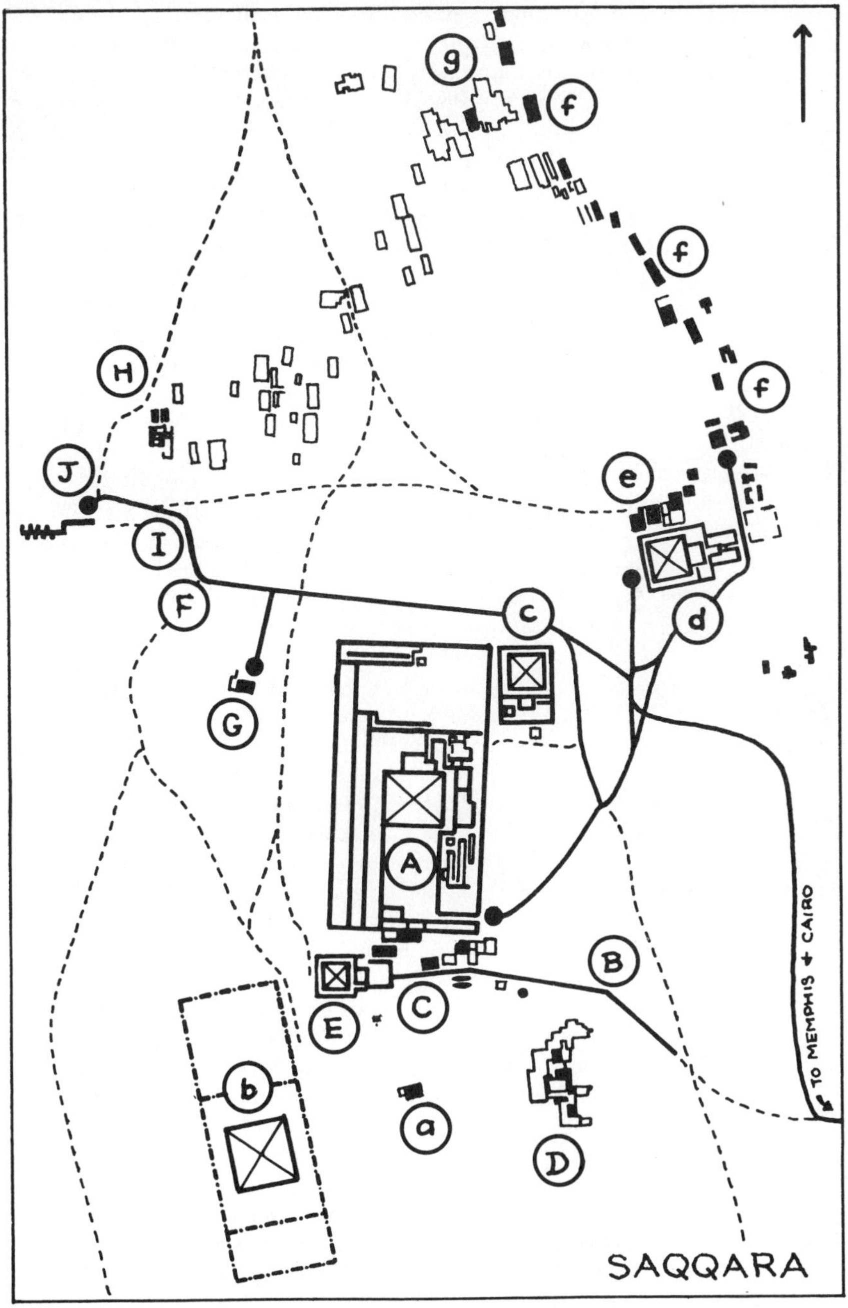
g
f
f
f
H
J
I
F
G
c
e
d
A
B
C
E
b
a
D
TO MEMPHIS + CAIRO
SAQQARA

animals (lions, gazelles, hares and hedgehogs) are drawn up, and a cow is giving birth, a peasant guiding the calf into the world. The bottom register shows domestic poultry and the text claims that Ptah-Hotep possessed "121,000 geese of one variety, 11,210 of another variety, 120,000 small geese, 111,200 goslings and 1225 swans". On the left of this wall Ptah-Hotep "witnesses all the pleasant activities that take place in the whole country". In the top registers, boys and girls are playing; there is one episode of two boys seated and facing each other as their friends vault over them. This game, called *Khaza la wizza,* is still played today in Lower Nubia. The third register is devoted to aspects of viticulture; the fourth shows animal life (note the hare emerging from its hole with a cricket in its mouth); the fifth is a hunting scene, the cow tied as bait for the lion; the fifth and sixth registers show marsh and boating scenes.

Above the entrance is a faded mural, but you can make out Ptah-Hotep preparing for his day, a manicurist at his hands, a pedicurist at his feet, musicians entertaining him, greyhounds beneath his chair and a pet monkey held by his valet. The sophistication of this scene is all the more striking when you recall that it depicts daily Egyptian life, albeit at the very top of the social ladder, nearly 4500 years ago, that is when Europe and most of Asia were still in the Stone Age.

The purpose of tomb reliefs

The purpose of these reliefs was to provide food, indeed a complete experience of life, for the ka. They began during the IV Dynasty as it was realised that relatives and descendants did not always provide fresh offerings; the reliefs are imitative magic against default. But one can also imagine the great pleasure they must have given the tomb owner, an assurance that he was going to take it all with him, and to his relatives when they did gather in his tomb. I think of some of the more elaborate marble tombs in Greek cemeteries today; they are like small shrines with an inner chamber for the deceased and an outer chamber with seats for the living, and they are the cheeriest places, often attracting bountiful picnics. Unas, a generation later was already worried about his relationship with Osiris; but here there is not a single god, no judgement, no doubt – afterlife follows on from life as assuredly as day follows day, and without even an intervening night.

Now returning to the pillared hall you turn left for the *chamber of Akhti-Hotep,* similarly though less finely decorated. A passageway leads out of the side of this and opening off it, on your left, is a chamber containing an *anonymous mummy.* The pasageway leads back to the pillared hall and the entrance corridor; while negotiating it I tripped over a skeleton, perhaps belonging to a 20th C. AD tourist who had got locked in.

Getting yourself entombed

I have already mentioned that my brother got himself locked into the Great Pyramid; at Saqqara a friend got himself locked into the Serapeum for half an hour with the lights off (an experience that would have turned me instantly into a skeleton); and I got locked into the Mastaba of Ti, and would have spent the night there but for a ladder left providentially in the open court. If you lack Ptah-Hotep's confidence in the coming day, make certain the keeper knows you are there and looks like the sort of fellow who would let you out.

The Mastaba of Ti

The Mastaba of Ti is to the north of the refreshment tent and you can follow the road that leads to the Serapeum part of the way there. The mastaba was discovered by Mariette in 1865 and has been well restored by the Egyptian Department of Antiquities. It originally stood above ground but is now entirely sunk in the sand. Its reliefs rival those in Ptah-Hotep's tomb chamber and exceed them in variety. Ti was a parvenu and royal hairdresser during the early V Dynasty; he was also overseer of several royal mortuary temples and pyramids and controller of royal ponds, farms and stock from which he evidently enriched himself. His wife was related to the royal family and his children bore the title 'royal descendant', to which Ti himself was not entitled. Ti's wife and eldest son were also entombed here, but some later would-be arriviste made off with the goods and disposed of the bodies.

Outline of the plan

In plan, the entrance is from the north, a two-pillared vestibule leading to a spacious open pillared court at the centre of which a flight of stairs descends to a subterranean passage ending in an antechamber and the tomb chamber. Otherwise, a corridor leads out from the rear of the open court and passes a chamber on the right, arriving at the funerary chamber and the serdab.

Once through the open court, whose reliefs have been badly damaged by exposure, the walls of corridors and rooms are finely decorated with familiar scenes. The most interesting room, with the most beautiful reliefs, is Ti's *funerary chamber*.

Funerary chamber

Through the slot in the far (south) wall you can see Ti (this is a cast of the original statue now in the Cairo Museum) staring vacantly northwards from his serdab, lacking, I am afraid, Zoser's look of adventure. Needless to say his hair, or rather his wig, is well done. Most enjoyable are the *reliefs on the near (north) wall,* all concerned with life in the marshes of the Delta. Look particularly at the central relief of *Ti sailing through the marshes.* This is a classic representation of a hippopotamus hunt; the hippopotamus, to the lower right, has seized a crocodile which, meanwhile, is desperately trying to bite the hippo's leg. Ti is shown larger than his huntsmen who, from another boat, are harpooning the hippo. Below the boats are fine Nile fish of different species, identifiable as favoured catches in the river today. On the right, in a small boat with a curiously truncated stern, a fisherman is about to club a large schal fish over the head. Above Ti, among the papyrus clusters, birds are being attacked in their nests by carnivorous animals, the reeds bending with their weight. In the register below is a line of *elegant female bearers,* their transparent coloured dresses surrendered to time, their nakedness and varied poses freshly pleasing.

Tea in the desert

By way of making amends for having locked me in Ti's tomb, the keeper afterwards invited me to his little concrete hut for a glass of mint tea. It was clearly his eagerness to retreat here, out of the blistering heat, that caused my incarceration in the first place. We sat on a reed mat on the floor while he manipulated various soda cans over his burner – some of the cans for storing the water, one for boiling it, others for decanting the tea – and we smoked his hubbly-bubbly meanwhile. This he lit with bits of dried corncob he kept for the purpose and brought to a glow in the burner flame. The surrounding necropolis, my temporary entombment, the sand and heat were all forgotten in this humble private place where tea and tobacco were prepared and consumed with meticulous ritual. The keeper fussed and bubbled and tasted and grunted with the fullness of it all, and as we drank the thick sweet tea, so satisfying, and enjoyed the relaxation of the waterpipe, we looked out as from a serdab upon the desert wasteland and he called this tea and this tobacco his friends.

The weirdest place in Egypt

The Serapeum is the weirdest place in Egypt. A temple once stood here amidst the sands but what remains are the long underground galleries cut through the rock where the Apis bulls were buried. This was Mariette's great discovery in 1851 which began the serious excavation of Saqqara that has continued ever since. Entry is to the west of the refreshment tent; you follow the road which first bends right towards Ti's mastaba and then turns left. At this second bend was Mariette's house, and immediately by the roadside, on your left and under a protective roof, is the surprising sight of several Greek statues arranged in a semicircle. These and their unlikely connection with bull burial requires some explanation.

The huge tombs of these Apis bulls were previously known only from references to them by various writers of antiquity.

Apis bulls For instance, Herodotus wrote: "The Apis is the calf of a cow which is never afterwards able to have another. The Egyptian belief is that a flash of light descends upon the cow from heaven, and this causes her to receive Apis. The Apis-calf has distinctive marks: it is black, with a white diamond on its forehead, the image of an eagle on its back, the hairs on its tail double, and a scarab under its tongue". Apis thus miraculously conceived was considered to be an incarnation of Ptah, the god of Memphis. Worshipped as such during his lifetime within a special sanctuary in the Temple of Ptah, he was mummified after his death on those alabaster beds you can still see among the few surviving stones of Memphis. Then, identified with Osiris under the name Osiris-Apis, he was taken with great pomp to these underground galleries at the Serapeum and placed within a gigantic sarcophagus.

Sacred bull cults go back into the prehistory of Egypt, and during the I and II Dynasties a bull would wander across the field of the Heb-Sed race, symbolically fertilising the two lands. But animal cults enjoyed an astonishing popularity during the Late Egyptian Period as the old beliefs degenerated. It is reminiscent of the mysticism of the Copts degenerating into the veneration of trunkloads of bizarre relics. Herodotus, attempting to demonstrate the madness of Cambyses, the Persian ruler of Egypt, records that "the priests brought Apis and Cambyses, half mad as he was, drew his dagger, aimed a blow at its belly, but missed and struck its thigh. Then he laughed, and said to the priests: 'Do you call that a god, you poor creatures? Are your gods flesh and blood? Do they feel the prick of steel? No doubt a god like that is good enough for the Egyptians; but you won't get away with trying to make a fool of me' ", and he had the priests whipped and forbade the cult, but when finally Apis died of his wounds he was buried by the priests without the knowledge of Cambyses. In this instance, at least, Cambyses sounds quite sane, but it is understandable that the once mighty priesthood should cling to some tangible shred of belief as the old order was being attacked by foreign rulers. The Ptolemies were more shrewd and flattered the priesthood, encouraged their cults, built temples and ruled Egypt for 300 years.

The galleries of the Serapeum date from three periods, the earliest to the reign of Ramses II (IXX Dyn), enlarged by his son Khaemwas; a second to the reign of Psammetichus I (XXVI Dyn); and the main gallery to the Ptolemies. It was the Greek Ptolemies who encouraged an identity between Osiris and Dionysos, and Plutarch comments that "as for what the priests openly do in the burial of the Apis when they transport its carcass on a raft, this in no way falls short of Bacchic revelry, for they wear fawn-skins and carry thyrsus-rods" – a staff tipped with a pine cone, in short a phallus – "and produce shouts and movements as do the ecstatic celebrants of the Dionysiac orgies". (Recall the sarcophagus of the dwarf in Room 49 on the ground floor of the Cairo Museum.) It is from the Ptolemaic period that the semicircle of Greek statues of poets and philosophers dates. Homer is at the centre, Pindar plays the lyre at the far right, and at the far left is a base inscribed with the name of Plato. They must be turning over in their graves.

Statues of Greek poets and philosphers

Mariette was led to the Serapeum by recalling a quotation from Strabo (24 BC): "One finds at Memphis a temple to Serapis in such a sandy place that the wind heaps up sand dunes beneath which we saw sphinxes, some half-buried, some buried up to the head, from which one can suppose that the way to the temple could not be without danger if one were caught in a sudden wind-storm". Mariette had found one such head at Saqqara, and removing the sand in the area found an entire avenue of sphinxes leading to the Greek statues and to the Serapeum galleries. The avenue has since sanded up again.

Mariette's description of his discovery of the Serapeum

Saqqara can seem strange enough today. When Mariette was excavating here, he described the conditions in his house: "Snakes slithered along the floor, tarantulas or scorpions swarmed in the wall crevices, large spider webs waved from the ceiling like flags. As soon as night fell, bats, attracted by the light, entered my cell through the cracks in the door and kept me awake with their spectral flights. Before going to sleep, I tucked the edges of my mosquito net beneath my mattress and put my trust in God and all the saints, while outside jackals, hyenas and wolves howled around the house". Of entering the Serapeum, Mariette wrote: "When I first penetrated into the sepulchre of the Apis, I was so overcome with astonishment that, though it is now five years ago, the feeling is still vivid in my mind. By some inexplicable accident one chamber of the Apis tombs, walled up in the thirtieth year of Ramses II, had escaped the general plunder of the monuments, and I was so fortunate as to find it untouched. Three thousand seven hundred years had had no effect in altering its primitive state. The finger mark of the Egyptian who set the last stone in the wall built up to cover the door, was still visible in the mortar. Bare feet had left their traces on the sand strewn in a corner of this chamber of the dead; nothing had been disturbed in this burying-place where an embalmed ox had been resting for nearly fourteen centuries".

The Serapeum galleries

My own recollection was of Robin Fedden's words: "One has the impression of a terrifying moronic force at work, for the tombs reveal the endemic stupidity of man". You descend a ramp slipping under the formless desert surface and reach a corridor leading off to left and right. Down to the left it meets a transverse gallery and left into that, on the left, within a vault, is a massive pink granite sarcophagus with panels and across the top edge hieroglyphs – on the right an Apis bull is depicted with the characteristic black markings. The rest of this gallery is blocked off by a grate.

You now reverse direction, heading down a 150-metre gallery, lit at lengthy intervals by dim yellow lights which in the murky darkness cast a greenish glow. At some places, the lights will have gone out and you will have to walk through blackness. On either side, in alternating succession, are more vaults, in all but one of which squats a monstrous black sarcophagus – bull-size. In the silence and the dim light, this repetition of vaults and sarcophagi becomes like a bad dream you cannot awake from, and you just walk on, with literally no light at the end of the tunnel. It is macabre, and with your capillaries shot full with beer you achieve enough perspective to find it utterly incredible that the Ptolemies, whose gallery this is, could have perpetuated anything so repulsive and outlandish. The finest sarcophagus of all is perversely placed at the very end of this gallery, on the right, with carved decoration and polished to a glassy lustre. You can climb down into its pit and stand on a step at the back to peer inside. But it is not this sarcophagus that is worth the walk; it is the walk that is worth the walk, if only to be astonished, and for want of being able to assimilate the insanity of human belief to laugh, as finally I did in the darkness.

The finest bull sarcophagus

It was not here, but in the Rammesid gallery, now inaccessible, that Mariette found the one untouched Apis tomb, a mummified bull inside, and also in the gallery the mummy of Khaemwas, who had been appointed by his father Ramses II High Priest of Ptah. And there he found those ancient footprints. You notice footprints in the sand in this Ptolemaic gallery too, of more recent visitors, and they bring to mind, as so often encounters with Egypt's pharaonic past do, our own voyages into the cosmos, those footprints left in the dust on the surface of the windless Moon which may remain for millions of years undisturbed.

Secondary gallery

Retracing your steps from the end of the main gallery, turn to the left and then to the right. An empty sarcophagus almost blocks the route. A little further on is its lid. It seems to have been abandoned before the interment of the sacred bull, suggesting the cult was abruptly ended.

The search for Imhotep's tomb

This account of Saqqara has covered only the most major points of interest to the layman. There is a search now going on for Imhotep's tomb which is thought to be to the northeast of the Serapeum and the Mastaba of Ti. In this area have been found the Anubieion, sacred to Anubis, with a gallery for dogs; the galleries of the Bubasteion, sacred to Bastet, filled with mummified cats; the Temple of Thoth, its galleries piled with thousands of mummified ibises, baboons and falcons; and the Isieion, the Temple of Isis, with underground galleries containing the sarcophagi of the sacred cows that had given birth to the Apis bulls. It is possible that these stacks of smaller mummified creatures were brought over hundreds of years by pilgrims as offerings to a favoured god, or as supplication by those seeking a cure. It is because of these associations with healing cults that Imhotep's shrine and tomb might be here; he was later worshipped as the god of medicine, the Egyptian equivalent of Asclepios. These cults continued into the Roman period and were only finally suppressed several centuries into our era by the victory of Christianity over paganism.

The Bent and Red Pyramids at Dahshur

The necropolis of Dahshur is a few kilometres to the south of Saqqara. Of its four pyramids, two date from the Middle Kingdom and are badly ruined – they are likely to be of interest only to the specialist. Snofru's Bent and Red Pyramids, already referred to at the beginning of this chapter, are the chief attraction. The distance between them is 2 kms and can be managed on foot; interiors of both can be visited, but a powerful light and a ladder, or at least a rope, will be necessary, and care must be exercised. But it is enough just to stand here in the desert, undisturbed by tourists or the debris left by excavations, and to see these great pyramids resting upon an endless plain confronting only the cosmos.

One way of getting here is by donkey or camel across the sands from the refreshment tent at Saqqara; the complete journey will take two to three hours. The main road from Cairo enters a military area south of Saqqara and foreigners are not permitted along it, so if travelling by car you should turn right off the main road and head towards the desert, as though for the Saqqara necropolis, but about 250 metres before reaching the necropolis you should turn left (south) and drive along the near side of a small canal into the village of Saqqara. Through the village and past its palm groves the road continues south for Meidum, but instead at the end of the groves you turn right, following the canal and skirting the desert. You are now within close view of the four pyramids of Dahshur and can carry on by foot or road to the northerly Red Pyramid or the Bent Pyramid to the south.

The desert road to the Fayyum

Meidum and the Fayyum can be visited by continuing south, but this almost certainly will be a separate excursion and the easiest, most direct approach to the Fayyum, and also the most striking, is by the desert road from Giza. You drive out of Cairo as though to the Giza Pyramids but before reaching the Mena House Hotel you turn right onto the desert road for Alexandria. Follow this for a few kilometres and then take a side road on the left which dips through a wadi and then rises across a plateau. After 76 kms you approach the edge of the depression at Kom Aushim, the ancient Karanis, on your left. From here there is a fine panorama over the whole of the Fayyum, a surprise of green cultivation and blue lakewater surrounded by rocky hills and expanses of sandy desert. (Without a car you could take the train to El Wasta and then the branch line to Medinet el Fayyum; there is also a public bus service from Cairo, but this is usually very crowded and not at all comfortable. Once there, a taxi can be hired at Medinet el Fayyum. Alternatively there are organised tours from Cairo.) An excursion to the Fayyum can be accomplished in a day, starting early in the morning. For a longer stay, it is most agreeable to overnight at one of the hotels on Lake Qarun – though advance reservations are recommended as the Fayyum is a popular resort with Egyptians, especially at weekends and holidays.

An oasis which is not an oasis

The Fayyum is a near-level basin of abundant harvests, fleshed with fields of vegetables and sugar cane, watered by hundreds of capillary canals. Groves of almonds, apricots, oranges, lemons, pomegranates, figs and olives screen the horizon, while tall acacias, tamarisks and eucalyptus trees cast dappled shadows on the grass. There are vineyards and poultry farms, water buffalo drawing the ploughs and white egrets wading in the bright crystal greeness of the rice paddies. The lake is brackish, sometimes muddy and marshy and not suitable for swimming, but it is rich with fish and migratory birds, including the pink flamingo; its pearly surface is blackened in winter by thousands of ducks.

This lake, now filling only the northwest edge of the depression, once covered the whole and was fed by the Bahr Yusef (River of Joseph – so named by the Copts) where it left the Nile at Deirut. In the last century this life-giving waterway was extended further south to Assiut by the construction of the Ibrahimiya Canal to provide improved irrigation for the lower reaches of the Valley. Fed by the Nile, the Fayyum therefore is not a true oasis, though the Bahr Yusef frequently silts up or changes course and the Fayyum survives too on spring water while the millenial battle between man and nature to maintain and regularise the flow continues.

History of the Fayyum

The shores of Qarun were inhabited already in the prehistoric period by hunters and fishermen, but it was the Pharaohs of the XII Dynasty who turned the depression (some 45 metres below sea level at the present surface of the lake) into the garden of Egypt and a regulator of the Nile's flood by building an extensive system of canals, dikes, locks and sluices. From the XIII Dynasty on, the Fayyum became a favourite resort of pharaohs, and Amenophis III (XVIII Dyn) built a palace at El Lahun for Queen Tiy (at their palace at Thebes he built her a lake). Evaporation caused the lake to contract while the cultivable area was extended, reaching its greatest extent during the Ptolemaic period, Greek and Macedonian veterans being settled on the land. The variety of the Fayyum was sacrificed to the Roman demand that it supply Rome with corn and the harsh imperial taxes led to the irrigation system silting up. The desert slowly crept back. In modern times the trend has been reversed, though the Fayyum still does not occupy the extent it enjoyed in ancient times. But its abundance, even more than its ancient remains, make it worth the visit.

Karanis

If you have come along the desert road from Giza, your first stop will be Kom Aushim, the Ptolemaic Karanis, still in the desert, with a small museum and behind this the remains of two temples, the agora and some houses. It is the view of the cultivated basin below that is appealing. Entering the Fayyum proper, you can continue westwards along the southern shore of the lake, its far shore desert but on this side cultivated. Here you will find the Auberge du Lac, a famous old inn though now run down, and the Pavillion de Chasse; there is also a café nearby and waterwheels.

The lake

Either by driving along backroads south of the lake via Sanhour or retracing your route part way to Karanis and then turning south on the main road to Medinet el Fayyum, you will arrive at the large village of Sennouris. The countryside becomes considerably more verdant. Sennouris stands on high ground, its minarets and domes standing out against the sky. Continuing on the road south to Biyahmu, at 4 kms from Sennouris you can turn off to the right to briefly see the site where Ammenemes III (XII Dyn) erected two colossal seated figures of himself to mark the northern boundary of the cultivable land. Herodotus saw these from a distance, rising above the flooded fields, and thought they must have been

The colossi of Ammenemes III

sitting atop pyramids. In fact they stood on either side of a lakeside harbour. One of them was seen as recently as the 17th C. by Europeans, but now only the 8-metre bases remain – the statues rose another 12 metres above these, which would have made them as high as the famous Colossi of Memnon, erected 400-odd years later.

Medinet el Fayyum

Medinet el Fayyum, which means Town of the Fayyum, is the capital of the province and a major market centre. For centuries the water from the Bahr Yusef has been distributed here throughout the canals of the basin, and at the centre of town three waterwheels still perform this task, a café nearby where you can listen to their groaning. El Medina (as it is more briefly known) had earlier this century a sizable Greek population and there are a number of handsome mansions and several churches, including a large Coptic one, while its mosques include one built by the side of a bridge over the Bahr Yusef by Qaytbay in the 15th C.

Crocodile cult

A settlement stood here already in early pharaonic times and was the chief centre for worship of the crocodile god Sobek. The Greeks named it Crocodilopolis, though Ptolemy I, in converting the town to a Hellenic centre with Greek temples and schools and even a Greek-speaking population, named it for his deified sister-wife, Arsinoe. In abandoning its crocodile cult, the town has lost what was once its greatest draw; in Ptolemaic and Roman times, tourists came from all over the Mediterranean and Europe to feed the sacred beast with specially prepared food – how much more exciting than pigeons in Trafalgar Square.

Today El Medina is a dusty place and to its northwest are the rubbish dump remains of the ancient city. It requires an extraordinary imagination to conjure up any vision of its past. Not only time and treasure-hunters, but also the *sebakhin* have made a mess of it. This is an interesting example of how Egypt lives upon its past. In a land where wood is a rarity, animal dung has traditionally been used for fuel and so other fertilisers have been sought. One of these has been the debris mounds of ancient towns which yield a kind of earth, called *sebakh*, containing as much as 12 percent potassium nitrate, sodium carbonate and ammonium chloride.

You now drive southeast towards Beni Suef, passing along the narrow corridor of cultivation which attaches like a stem the bud of the Fayyum to the Nile. At Hawarat el Makta, 7 kms from Medinet el Fayyum, a track runs northwards to the dilapidated mud brick pyramid of Ammenemes III. Its surrounding complex is no more than an expanse of rubble,

The Labyrinth

though at the south of the pyramid was once the vast mortuary temple, now all but vanished at the hands of stone robbers, which so excited ancient travellers and which they called the Labyrinth. Herodotus, who seems to have enjoyed describing in fantastic terms sights he had never seen, said it had 3000 chambers, half below ground, half above; but Strabo, who did come here in AD 24, gives a more sober account of a still vast low building divided into sections for each nome, "a work as important as the Pyramids" with "long covered passages, intersecting each other and thus forming such a winding path that a stranger cannot find his way into or out of each court without a guide". From a cemetery nearby, and also from Philadelphia to the north, came the painted wax portraits of mummified Romans which make such a striking impression now in the Cairo Museum. At the Nile end of the corridor, in the desert a short distance to the north, is the Lahun pyramid, that of Sesostris II (XII Dyn), a predecessor of Ammenemes III. It also was built of mud brick and cased in limestone.

Getting to the Meidum pyramid

On reaching the main Cairo road, turn north for El Wasta. While the Meidum pyramid is still ahead of you, look for an asphalt road (sign in Arabic) heading across the fields towards the desert. This brings you parallel with the southern face of the pyramid; slightly past it there is a road which will lead you up past the west face and then finally a dirt track, a bit further to the north, cuts back to the structure itself. This was the first attempt at a true pyramid and, as reviewed at the beginning of this chapter, the lessons learnt from its monumental failure led to the successful completion of those greatest pyramids of all at Giza. For that reason, but also for the spectacle of this abrupt tower on the desert's edge, the Meidum pyramid is as much worth visiting as any.

PRACTICAL INFORMATION

THE GIZA PYRAMIDS:

The *Practical Information* section at the end of the *Cairo I* chapter contains information on accommodation and eating places by the Pyramids, travel to them, and the Sound and Light show. However, for convenience, some of that information will be repeated here and additional information supplied.

To replenish yourself during a visit to the Pyramids, drinks, light meals and full meals can be had at the Vue des Pyramides at the southeast corner of the Pyramids Road/Alexandria Desert Road; at the rest house (built in the style of a pharaonic temple by King Farouk) to the northeast of the Pyramid of Cheops; and at the Pavillion de Cheops facing the Sphinx.

From Cairo to the Pyramids should cost no more than LE2 by **taxi**; a **service (shared) taxi** from Midan el Tahrir will cost about 30PT per person. Also from Midan el Tahrir are the Nos. 800 and 900 **buses,** departing every 10 minutes for the Mena House Hotel.

Although you can have a general view of the

Pyramids and Sphinx at any time of day or night, **access** to the Sphinx, tombs and valley temples, and **entry** into the chambers of the Pyramids is from 8am to 4.30pm daily. The only **fee** is to enter the Pyramids; tickets (50PT) should be bought at the kiosk at the top of the road coming up from the Mena House Hotel towards the north side of the Pyramid of Cheops. Con men may attempt to extort money from you for simply staring at the monuments, while others will press their services upon you as guides or try to sell you fake antiquities and other rubbish. All are to be ignored, and if necessary the Tourist Police invoked. You should accept assistance and agree a price only if you want help in climbing the Pyramids.

You can **ride on horseback or camelback** across the desert from the Pyramids to **Saqqara.** The journey will take at least 3 hours in each direction, and spending just a little time at Saqqara means an 8-hour expedition in all. For this reason you should resist offers of hire by the hour and negotiate a price for the entire day. Camels will cost about LE5, horses a bit more. The best camel man is an old Christian called Louka, with his camel Moses. There is some dispute as to which animal is better; most people prefer horses over longer distances. Either way, all but the most hardened rider can expect to end the day feeling pretty sore.

The **Sound and Light** show starts nightly (except Fridays) at 7.30 and lasts 1 hour. The English-language programmes are on Mondays, Wednesdays and Saturdays; the French on Tuesdays and Sundays; the German on Sundays (at 8.30pm); the Arabic on Thursdays. Admission is LE2 except for the Arabic programme which is 50PT. Seating is on a terrace facing the valley temple of the Pyramid of Cephren, ie by the Sphinx. Bring a sweater; it can get cool on the edge of the desert, even in summer.

Almost any taxi driver will know what you mean if you say Sound and Light; if you want him to wait for you (thus avoiding any difficulty in getting a ride back), offer LE2 to LE3 per hour. Also there are the service taxis and buses mentioned above, but these will take you to the Mena House Hotel and you'll have to walk back down the Pyramids Road till you reach the Sound and Light sign (on the right as you face Cairo) and then walk to the right, through the village on the edge of the desert escarpment. Or if you are alert you can alight at the sign (it's about 1000 metres before the Mena House Hotel), saving yourself some shoe leather. Another alternative is to take a tour, which will include admission and the ride out and back for about LE9. This works out at about as much as it would cost one person to take a taxi and keep it waiting; for 2 or more people it's better to take the taxi.

MEMPHIS AND SAQQARA:

You can reach Saqqara by **horse or camel from the Giza Pyramids** (see above), though you won't be left with much time to explore the site. Also there are **tours** or a **taxi** from Cairo. But there are **cheaper ways:**

1) The Tourist Information Office recommends taking a bus to the Pyramids and hiring a taxi from there for LE4 return. I haven't tried this and suspect that with keeping the driver waiting and competing with the lure of suckers willing to pay LE2 for the one-way ride from the Pyramids into Cairo, you'd have to pay more.

2) Service (shared) taxi from the south end of Midan el Tahrir: find one going to Badrashein, the village near Memphis.

3) There are trains from Mahattat Ramses to Badrashein, though these are uncomfortable and very crowded.

4) Ask at the Mena House Hotel or the Tourist Police for the bus to Badrashein; then ask to be let off at Memphis or Saqqara.

DAHSHUR:

Dahshur is in the midst of a **military area** and certain approaches are off-limits to foreigners. It would be a good idea to check in advance with the Tourist Information Office on Sharia Adli in Cairo; if necessary, permission can be obtained from the Ministry of the Interior. (See main text for present routing.)

Tours do not normally include Dahshur with Memphis and Saqqara, but ask, eg at Thomas Cook, if it can be included for a bit extra.

Camels or donkeys can be hired at the refreshment tent at Saqqara; the journey will take 2 to 3 hours. Camels are infinitely preferable to donkeys.

THE FAYYUM:

There are numerous **tours** to the Fayyum, permitting you to see the entire area in a day. Also there is a **bus** from Midan el Tahrir, third class and jam-packed.

If intending to **stay overnight** in the Fayyum, you should reserve in advance at one of **the hotels on Lake Qarun, eg the Pavillion de Chasse – doing so through a travel agent.**

MEIDUM:

Some **tours** going to the Fayyum also take in the pyramid and Labyrinth at Hawarat and the pyramid at Lahun, both along the corridor of cultivation leading towards Beni Suef. To my knowledge, nobody advertises a pause at the Meidum pyramid, though they might be induced to.

Otherwise, you can take the **train** to El Wasta and a **bus** from there to Meidum. See the *Background* chapter for train schedules.

UPPER EGYPT 1: THE VALLEY

Lower Egypt is the Delta; Upper Egypt is the Valley where the desert and mountains encroach on either side. But the Valley only finally loses its grip on the Nile at Cairo, the Moqattam hills a last reminder, yet Upper Egypt still lies some distance to the south for it is not defined in geographical terms alone. An ancient text expresses the bewilderment of an exile finding himself in a foreign country: "I do not know what separated me from my place. It was like a dream, as if a man of the Delta were to see himself in Elephantine, or a man of the northern marshes in Nubia". Culture and horizons place Upper Egypt along the thin papyrus stem of fields and river before it bifurcates, the full flower of the Delta to the north, the bud of the Fayyum to the west.

Beni Suef

At this place, unpromisingly, is a dull-looking town, Beni Suef (124 kms from Cairo), celebrated for its linen manufacture in the Middle Ages and now at once crumbling and jerking into new forms as modern factories and housing blocks go up. From here two roads strike out across the Eastern Desert for the Monastery of St Anthony and the Red Sea; another Egypt, another time. You travel through it in another chapter, *The Desert and the Sea*. But following the Nile southwards you are – as nearly as geography and chronology in Egypt coincide – travelling from the Old Kingdom into the New.

Travelling up the Valley

For the traveller flying from Cairo to Luxor, the change is fairly abrupt. Less than 90 minutes intervene between the Memphite pyramids and your first glimpse of the sprawling Theban temples below. Along the way there is the amazing and beautiful sight of the long blue ribbon of the Nile snaking through the scorched desert bringing a few kilometres, sometimes only a few metres, of land to life on either side. A life fragile like the delicate green wheat which waves against vast sand plateaux, a life – if you were close enough to know it – heavy with the mass of burnt-backed fellahin whose survival has depended on the varying generosity of the river's annual flood and the constancy of their own unending field labours.

The traveller through time is isolated from the moment. From the air, this isolation seems no more than standing back from a charming tapestry to appreciate its overall effect. Travelling overland you are closer and you see the threads and knots; you long to feel for texture. You are probably travelling by train, sensibly in an air-conditioned carriage. Outside the sealed windows, sealed against the sand, sealed against the heat, sealed against fragrance and life, Egypt passes in a series of tableaux vivants.

Station signs, road signs, all are in Arabic. They might as well be in hieroglyphs. The pattern of older villages is a vestige of living 10,000 years with annual inundations: they sit on low mounds beyond the reach of a river which for a decade or more has ceased to rise. Their mud brick houses pack against and on top of one another, a dense metropolis in embryo. At first their roofs are flat like houses of the Delta, but as you run southwards under the sun you see the dome and barrel roofs of Upper Egypt which so admirably deflect the heavy fall of heat.

Ochre, rectangular, severe like a temple, really a landowner's country house – a former landowner anyway – embellished with a cavetto cornice, but awaiting further decoration, awaiting a new dynasty. It stands alone, enclosed by a walled garden.

Camels, carts, donkeys and women troop along the road, enduring the flame-blue sky.

An old man stands up to his knees in an irrigation ditch, washing himself, naked to the passing eyes and years, no longer ithyphallic Min.

All this passes beyond touch, beyond sound. I am an air-conditioned pharaoh riding with the sun, uncontaminated, unliving, kept company through eternity by wall paintings.

The train goes slowly and stops often. At one station I am surprised by a knock at my window. Suspended from the roof of a third class train, children are knocking, laughing.

Minya and Mallawi

Beni Hassan, Hermopolis and Tell el Amarna all lie near Minya (247 kms from Cairo) and Mallawi (295 kms). Though Mallawi is closer to Tell el Amarna, travellers might prefer to stay at Minya with its attractive and winding corniche along the west bank of the Nile and its better accommodation.

Middle Kingdom tombs at Beni Hassan

Beni Hassan, on the east bank of the Nile and equidistant from Minya and Mallawi, is a Middle Kingdom necropolis of 39 rock tombs belonging mostly to XI and XII Dynasty nomarchs. The excursion, taking in four of the tombs most worth visiting, will take about half a day.

The tombs are exceptional for their architecturally refined interior columns, including a fluted style designated by Champollion as 'proto-Doric', and the excellence of their paintings, done on stucco. Unfortunately, the paintings are either damaged or obscured and in need of delicate restoration if their brilliant colours are to be realised. Agricultural, craft, hunting and sports scenes are usual, and occasionally military scenes, for the princes of this nome were powerful in their own right. *Tomb 17 of Kheti* has the best preserved paintings. *Tomb 15 of Baket,* Kheti's father, has lost its columns, but *Tomb 3 of Khnumhotep* contains 'proto-Doric, columns and also paintings evidencing Khumhotep's wide-ranging authority. He was also governor of the Eastern Desert and is shown receiving a gift of eye-paint from a caravan of Semites, gaudily dressed and befeathered, who have crossed into Egypt with their women, their children and their goats and asses in tow. The porch of this tomb and of *Tomb 2* is extant; they were once preceded by an open court. In columns and paintings, *Tomb 2 of Amenemhat* is similar to *Tomb 3.*

Speos Artemidos

On the way down from the necropolis you pass the entrançe to a wadi on the left. About 500 metres along its south side is the rock chapel of Pakhet, the lioness goddess, assimilated by the Greeks to Artemis so that the chapel is better known as Speos Artemidos. Inside are scenes of offerings to various deities, but the chief interest of the shrine is the inscription over the entrance in which Hatshepsut (XVIII Dyn) implies that she has rid Egypt of the Hyksos invaders. That she certainly did not only heightens the belief that Hatshepsut desired to be seen as the restorer of stability and the old ways of the Middle Kingdom in her struggle against Tuthmosis III's imperial ambitions (see Deir el Bahri). As it extends deeper into the forbidding desert landscape, the wadi is cut with numerous other grottoes, once anchorite cells and early Christian tombs.

Hermopolis

Hermopolis, near the village of El Ashmunein on the west bank of the river, lies off a secondary road between Minya and Mallawi. The remains of the Middle and New Kingdom cities here are no more than uncertain mounds of earth and rubble, though a later Ptolemaic agora has been restored and the surrounding palm grove lends a picturesque effect. An early association with Thoth, whom the Greeks identified with Hermes, accounts for its familiar name. Originally known as Khmun, meaning city of the eight primordial forces, it was said to have been built upon the primal hill from which the sun first rose above the waters to create the world out of Chaos – though the same claim was made for Medinet Habu and Heliopolis. The primal name, if not the hill or city, has tenaciously survived: from Khmun derived the Coptic Shmun, whence the Arabic Ashmunein.

Tuna el Gebel, at the end of a road running into the Libyan hills from Ashmunein, marked the western limits of

Akhenaton's new city of Akhetaton. This side of the river was reserved for villages and farms. A boundary stela remains *in situ,* carved from the top of a cliff, showing the heretic Pharaoh, Nefertiti and three of their daughters with upraised arms in adoration of the solar disc. A necropolis to the south is riddled with underground passages used the by the inhabitants of Hermopolis for burying mummified ibises and dog-headed baboons, sacred to Thoth. The most important building here is the Ptolemaic tomb of Petosiris, chief priest of Thoth at Hermopolis. It imitates the pronaos of a temple and is entered through a vestibule of four columns with floral capitals painted red, blue and turquoise though bleached where exposed to the sun. Inside, the reliefs portray traditional Egyptian themes but Petosiris and his family wear Greek clothing.

The Amarna revolution

The beauty of Old Kingdom art and architecture lay in its restraint, in its simplicity and its confident mastery of form. There was a moment of discovery, of harmonisation and integrity, and if the First Intermediate Period had instead marked the termination of pharaonic civilisation we might now more eagerly respond to what had been lost. But the centuries rolled on and too often carried with them only the embalmed culture of the past, integrity reduced to repetition, mastery to facility, the spirit salved with interminable formulae, authority justified and reassured with bombast. Even when using the old forms, there were brilliant exceptions as will be seen here and there further upriver. But the general impression of tedium weighs heavily on the traveller. The breathtaking impact, then, of the Amarna period is all the more powerful, the sense of something wonderful, tragic and lost all the more acute.

The sensitivity and delight, the reverence and forcefulness conveyed in the paintings, reliefs, sculpture and hymns of Akhenaton's reign are probably best appreciated in museums and books, for at his capital city of Akhetaton few of these things remain. Nevertheless, its site should be visited – in homage, perhaps; for the interest it does hold; and for its own beauty, spared the incursions of large numbers of tourists.

Akhenaton's city

Akhetaton, or Tell el Amarna as it is known, is on the east bank, 67 kms south of Minya, 11 kms south of Mallawi. Once a boat has carried you across, you must pursue your exploration of this extensive site by foot or donkey, allowing a full day for the visit.

Tell el Amarna conflates the name of a local village, El Till, and the tribal name of the Beni Amran bedouin who live here.

In wrongly supplying Tell for Till it gives the impression that a mound created of centuries of human habitation and debris *(tell)* identifies the spot. It does not, and that is what makes Amarna archaeologically so interesting. It is all one layer, the largely mud brick remains of a complete royal city begun in the fourth year of Akhenaton's reign, his residence from about his sixth year, and abandoned for all time soon after his death in the eighteenth year of his reign.

The ancient name Akhetaton means 'Horizon (or Resting Place) of the Disc', so that just as Amun dwelt at Thebes, Ptah at Memphis and other gods at their favoured places the Pharaoh Akhenaton offered this as home to Aton. On boundary stela he inscribed: "Akhetaton belongs to Aton my Father like the mountains, the deserts, the fields, the islands, the upper lands and the lower lands, the water, the villages, the men, the animals and all those things to which Aton my Father will give life eternally. I shall not neglect the oath which I have made to Aton my Father for eternity". From a strip of palm-spiked fields along the Nile, a plain, 12 kms from north to south, swells against a crescent ridge of the Arabian plateau. Sand fills the greater part of the arena, the remains of temples, houses and palaces trace upon it in bare outline. It is a lonely spot, of melancholy beauty, one of the most attractive in all Egypt.

From the village of El Till the ancient *Royal Road* runs southwards to the administrative centre of the city. Folk memory recalls the grandeur of this thoroughfare with the modern name Sikket-es-Sultan, Road of the Sultan. On your left (east) is a Moslem cemetery and traced in part beneath it is a vast rectangle, stretching 800 metres back towards the ridge, marking the *Great Temple of Aton.* It was deliberately desecrated and destroyed after Akhenaton's death and its foundations later quarried by Ramses II for his temples at Hermopolis. Further along on your left are the faint outlines of the temple's *magazines.* Then there are three clearly excavated rectangles, again on the left. The first was an extension of the royal palace and was the *residence of Akhenaton* and his queen, Nefertiti. It was divided into a walled garden (northwest quadrant), private apartments (southwest quadrant) and storerooms (the east half). Near the bedroom was found the celebrated picture now in the Ashmolean Museum of Akhenaton and Nefertiti seated upon an embroidered cushion, face to face, surrounded by their six daughters. The entire residence was decorated with lively scenes, and the ceilings painted with ducks and other aquatic birds flying in all directions.

The royal residence was linked by a *bridge* across the Royal Road to the *main palace complex* on your right (west), now partly erased by tillage. Set within the bridge was a Window of Appearances where the royal family showed themselves before the public, as often depicted on reliefs and tomb paintings. (Indeed it is to the detailed and realistic tomb paintings at Amarna that so much knowledge of the city's original appearance is owed.) The next rectangle to the east marks the *Sanctuary of Aton* used by the royal family, and the rectangle beyond it the *magazines* associated with it.

Along a parallel road to the east and immediately behind the royal residence stood the *'Foreign Office'* where the famous Amarna Letters, cuneiform tablets received from Asian princes, were found. This road continues southwards in the direction of the village of Hagg Kandil through *residential quarters*. You should seek out the houses of such dignitaries as General Ramose, Vizier Nakht (neither are to be confused with their namesakes at the Theban necropolis) and Panehsi (see Tomb 6, below), and the workshops of the sculptor Tuthmosis where the exquisite bust of Nefertiti, now in the Berlin Museum, was found. There is a model of an Amarnan house in Room 8 on the ground floor of the Cairo Museum. Other quarters, palaces and temples are scattered throughout the plain, their seemingly aimless distribution probably dictated by available well water, but exploration is unlikely to prove meaningful without the company of an archaeologist familiar with the site.

The Amarna necropolis

The *necropolis* at Amarna is in the eastern cliffs. Unlike at Thebes, the tomb decorations do not concern themselves with the afterlife: the Judgement of Osiris, for example, is absent, while instead there are vivid scenes of the everyday. Many of the tombs were never finished and only a few reveal signs of burial, as if the collapse of the Amarna revolution outpaced mortality. Akhenaton's body has been vainly sought both here and at Thebes; one imagines him disinterred at the restoration of Amun and left to rot like Cromwell. The *royal tomb* lies far back in the wild valley, the Darb el Malik, dividing the north and south faces of the cliff. On founding Amarna, Akhenaton proclaimed: "My tomb will be hollowed in the Eastern Mountain, my burial will be made there in the multitude of jubilees which Aton my Father has ordained for me, and the burial of the Great Royal Wife Nefertiti will take place there in the multitude of years". Instead, like an ominous cloud on the Amarna horizon, it was their young daughter Makitaton who first died and was entombed here. Akhenaton and Nefertiti, joyful children of the solar disc, are shown on the walls of Makitaton's sarcophagus chamber in sad mourning. The tomb is closed to the public.

There are 25 tombs along the base of the cliff face, Nos. 1 to 6 to the north of the Darb el Malik, Nos. 7 to 25 to the south. Both to see the wall carvings and to avoid tumbling down the shafts leading to the burial chambers, a flashlight should be brought. The tombs are preceded by an open court, as at Thebes, and then usually run through two or three chambers, sometimes with papyrus-bundle columns, ending at a recess in the rear wall where a statue of the deceased would have been placed. The lyrical 'Hymn to the Sun' composed by Akhenaton is frequently incorporated into the decorations. The tombs most worth visiting are *No. 1 of Huya,* superintendent of the royal harem and steward to the queen mother, Tiy; *No. 4 of Merire,* high priest of Aton; *No. 6 of Panehsi,* servant of Aton with responsibility for his granaries and herds and also vizier of Lower Egypt; *No. 9 of Mahu,* chief of police; and *No. 25 of Ay,* royal confidant, Akhenaton's scribe and successor to Tutankhamun as Pharaoh of Egypt. The outstanding tombs are the last two.

Mahu's tomb (No. 9) is one of the best preserved and is interesting for the detail it gives of his duties. He was responsible for certain desert frontier posts and is shown receiving a report of a nomadic incursion. Three offenders are brought before Mahu and the vizier for interrogation; the chief of police is true to his timeless type in accusing them of being "agitated by some foreign power".

Ay's tomb (No. 25) is the finest in the necropolis. In one scene, Ay and his wife are shown receiving golden collars from Akhenaton and Nefertiti while guards and onlookers outside the palace react to the honour and excitement of it all. There are street scenes, closely observed and marvellously true to life, and peeps of palace intimacy, with a lady of the harem having her hair done, some girls playing the harp and dancing, while others prepare the food and sweep the floor. Also, on the right-hand side of the doorway is the most complete and probably the most correct version of Akhenaton's hymn. Here are some excerpts.

Akhenaton's 'Hymn to the Sun'

> At dawn you rise shining in the horizon, you shine as Aton in the sky and drive away darkness by sending forth your rays. The Two Lands awake in festivity, and men stand on their feet, for you have raised them up. They wash their bodies, they take their garments, and their arms are raised to praise your rising. The whole world does its work.

> The cattle are content in their pasture, the trees and plants are green, the birds fly from their nests. Their wings are raised in praise of your soul. The goats leap on their feet. All flying and fluttering things live when you shine for them. Likewise the boats race up and down the river, and every way is open, because you have appeared. The fish in the river leap before your face. Your rays go to the depths of the sea.
>
> You set the germ in women and make seed in men. You maintain the son in the womb of the mother and soothe him so that he does not weep, you nurse in the womb. You give the breath of life to all you have created. When the child comes forth from the womb on the day of his birth, you open his mouth and you supply his needs. The chick in the egg can be heard in the shell, for you give him breath inside it so that he may live. You have given him in the egg the power to break it. He comes out of the egg to chirp as loudly as he can; and when he comes out, he walks on his feet.

Like the wall reliefs, the hymn portrays in remarkable detail and variety the cumulative incidents that give wonder to life. Convention, myth and abstraction are dispensed with, replaced by the sensate reality of Aton which creates, embraces and expresses existence.

For a moment, Egypt was offered spiritual and philosophical renewal. Akhenaton broke with a past whose search for stasis was leading to sterility. The sun and soul were recovered from their long dark voyage through the underworld and set in brilliant transit across the horizons of this life. Whether it was monotheism is uncertain and probably irrelevant; the universe was alive again. More important is whether Atonism was ever anything more than a royal cult. Akhenaton's hymn, phrased in demotic, suggests his intention was to place his revelation before all mankind. Yet when he died, his religion was soon suppressed, and what is more, all mention of the heretic Pharaoh was proscribed from the king lists and he went unknown until the 19th C. of our era. Can it have been just a political reaction? Dynastic infighting led Tuthmosis III to obliterate all images and cartouches of Hatshepsut, but her memory remained. It seems as if Akhenaton offered something far more than a political threat – and more than the military and administrative failures he has been accused of. Possibly Egypt had so far lost its faith in life that it could accept no substitute for its long investment in death. That may explain the empty tombs at Amarna; cold comfort, for all their paeans, to a civilisation lost to the hocus-pocus of formulae and solar boats. It is significant that with the coming of the Ramessids, tomb decorations concentrated less on the quality of this life or the next but on the rigmarole of passing from one to the other.

Like Akhenaton himself, those pharaohs who followed him and had shared at some time in their lives in the worship of Aton – Smenkhkere, Tutankhamun and Ay – were proscribed from the king lists at Saqqara and Abydos, and from that of Manetho. Akhetaton was never built on again, Horemheb's reign marked the full force of the reaction and cleared the decks for Seti I's classical renaissance. Something of Amarna art is found, straitjacketed and reduced to mannerism, in the works of Ramses II, especially in the fluid beauty accorded the female form, a touch of Nefertiti's Florentine elegance in those portraits of Nefertari, Ramses' queen, on the tomb walls at Biban el Harem at Thebes and inside the Temple of Hathor at Abu Simbel.

Nefertiti stayed on at Amarna after her husband's death. Living in exile at the north end of the plain, she had carved on the walls of her palace the names of Akhenaton and herself. And this palace she called without compromise the House of Aton.

Manfalut

Manfalut, 54 kms upriver from Mallawi, is the seat of a Coptic bishop. It was the gathering point for the Egyptian army sent to the Peloponnese in 1825 under Ibrahim Pasha, Mohammed Ali's son, to suppress the Greek revolt against the Turkish Sultan – a task which the sickly but disciplined Egyptian soldiers all but accomplished, the Greeks saved only at the eleventh hour by the British destruction of the Egyptian and Turkish fleets at Navarino.

The Crocodile Grotto

On the opposite (east) side of the river, 5 kms northeast of the village of El Maabda, is the Crocodile Grotto contemptuously dismissed by Baedeker as "hardly worth visiting, as practically nothing is to be seen except the charred remains of the mummies of crocodiles". Not only crocodiles, but human mummies too, and those of snakes, fish, eggs, birds and all sorts of animals. Flaubert was enthusiastic: "A hole, down into which we climb; we have to crawl. Sand; then very soon stones; they are large, black, slippery, sharp, hard, painful to the knees – everything oozes bitumen: we have to drag ourselves along flat on the ground – exhausting . . . Here they all are, one on top of another, packed together, undisturbed; their bones break under your feet; put down your hand and pick up an arm. How deep would you have to go to reach the earth? There are as many here as the place can hold". Flaubert returned to France with a human foot and kept it in his study as he wrote *Madam Bovary;* one day his servant shined it up with shoe polish.

Flaubert's friend, Maxime du Camp, emerged with a head and a pair of hands and feet. Du Camp later wrote: "When you are standing on this bed of corpses, precautions cannot be too stringent: a bit of flame falling from a candle could instantly set fire to the dry debris, full of inflammable material, and then flight would be impossible and even useless. About 20 years ago an American visited the grotto with his dragoman and a guide. Some time after he went down, a loud noise was heard, and then black smoke poured from the opening. Neither American nor dragoman nor guide was ever seen again; the fire lasted 18 months and burnt itself out; for several years no one dared venture into the dangerous cave". Once again, dear reader, I advise you to illuminate your way by flashlight.

Assiut Assiut (378 kms from Cairo) lies in the midst of an extensive and fertile plain on the west bank of the Nile. To the west of the railway line is the old town; to the east, running down to the tree-lined corniche, are the newer districts. It is the largest town – swelling now into a city of nearly a quarter of a million – in Upper Egypt and the effective capital of the region. Once at the head of a great caravan route to the oases of the Libyan Desert and across the Sahara, it is still a centre of trade and crafts as a walk through its bazaars will confirm. Pottery, inlaid wood and ivory carving are much overshadowed though by wheat and cotton exports, and spinning. A university has recently been established, with a strong faculty of agriculture.

Assiut's importance, like its name, goes back to pharaonic times, though it never achieved political dominance. Tombs of the Middle Kingdom, its period of ancient glory, are cut in the mountain, 2 kms to the southwest, and nearby is a Moslem cemetery with hundreds of domed mausolea. Yet higher up is the Convent of the Virgin Mary with a commanding view of the town and plain below.

Near the station, to the west of the railway line, is a carpet-making school open to visitors and in the American College the small Museum of Pharaonic and Coptic Antiquities.

Plotinus (AD 204-262), the great Neo-Platonist, was probably born in Assiut: "No one could find out for certain because he was reticent about it, saying that the descent of his soul into his body had been a great misfortune, which he did not desire to discuss" (Forster).

The barrage at Assiut, built in 1898-1902, formed part of the British plan, which included the old dam at Aswan, for controlling the Nile. From here the amount of water entering the Ibrahimiya Canal is regulated for the irrigation of the Valley right the way down to Beni Suef. A road crosses the barrage and continues along the east bank of the river, but the main road and the railroad follow the west bank with its broader cultivation and more frequent towns and villages. One of these towns is Sohag (470 kms from Cairo); a few kilometres along a dusty road are the dilapidated Red and White Monasteries.

The Red and White Monasteries

One tradition has it that the Red Monastery was founded by St Helena, peripatetic mother of the great Constantine, but the Copts insist it was dedicated to a robber named Bishoi who found greater reward in prayer and fasting. Its basilical church is built of dark red Roman brick; a 10th C. Pantokrator is painted on the half-dome of the central altar but is blackened by the smoke of incense and candles. The White Monastery once housed a colony of 2000 monks within its high limestone walls with a cavetto cornice like an Egyptian temple. Inside are more early Christian paintings going to pot. It was founded about 400 by Shenoudi, Coptic saint, father of the Egyptian Church and a ferocious disciplinarian who once flogged an erring monk to death. But by the 17th C. a European visitor, Father Vansleb, found that the monks spent their time "seeking for the philosopher's stone and in works of Chymistry – an excellent employment for such as have left the world and forsaken their riches".

Qena

At Nag Hammadi (556 kms from Cairo) the Nile sweeps round in a great bend to the east and the main road and railroad go over a bridge to the other side. First Qena (612 kms from Cairo) on the east bank: from here a main road crosses the desert to Port Safaga on the Red Sea. Flaubert journeyed by camel through the devouring heat to Quseir, to the south of Safaga, in four days; on returning to Qena he sank into a bath and then into the arms of a prostitute: "Dark eyes, much lengthened by antimony; her face held up by velvet chinstraps; sunken mouth, jutting chin, smelling of butter, blue robe". But the major starting point for caravans from pharaonic to

Qift

more modern times was Qift (633 kms from Cairo), the ancient Coptos. Expeditions such as Hatshepsut's (see Deir el

Bahri) would have set out for the Red Sea from around here and then continued by ship to the land of Punt, while throughout antiquity and until the Portuguese found their way around Africa Coptos thrived on trade with Arabia and India. The Eastern Desert was once a busy place, criss-crossed by the Egyptians, and later the Romans, in search of gold, emeralds, granite and porphyry. The Romans turned it into a highway and maintained staging posts a day's march from each other along the way charging a levy which rose from 5 drachmas for an able seaman or shipyard hand to 108 drachmas for luxury traffic like prostitutes. The Suez Canal, which made transshipment between the Red Sea and Alexandria no longer necessary, dealt the final blow to Qift's fortunes. There is now nothing of interest or of licence to detain you, and from here it is only another 43 kms to Luxor.

Along the way we have missed out Abydos (reached via Baliana, 40 kms west of Nag Hammadi) and Dendera (6 kms west of Qena), both on the west bank of the Nile. The express sleepers and shuttle jets between Cairo and Luxor spoil us, make it seem hard to explore the route described from Beni Suef, and so these famous temples are usually visited as day-trips by taxi or air-conditioned tour bus from Luxor. They are mentioned here out of geographical integrity but will probably be footnotes to your stay at Luxor – and historically that is not altogether untrue.

Abydos

The local god of Abydos had been a patron of the dead and the identification of Osiris with him towards the end of the Old Kingdom was both natural and rapid. The crucial role Osiris played in the Egyptian conception of the afterlife soon turned Abydos into a natural shrine. Rather like Mecca is to Moslems today, it became the goal of all Egyptians to visit Abydos during their lifetimes, or failing that, between death and burial. Frequently on the tomb walls at the Theban necropolis you see the mummy of some notable making the voyage by river to Abydos. Some were even buried here as Old, Middle and New Kingdom tombs testify. The appeal was to lie for eternity at that very spot where the head of Osiris was buried after Seth had cut him to pieces and scattered his remains (see Philae).

It is a measure of Akhenaton's assault on the established religion that not only did Aton supplant Amun but that the Judgement of Osiris did not appear on the tomb walls at Amarna. After Akhenaton and his successors were proscribed and Horemheb restored the old ways, the XVIII Dynasty was replaced by the XIX Dynasty from the south (so often the

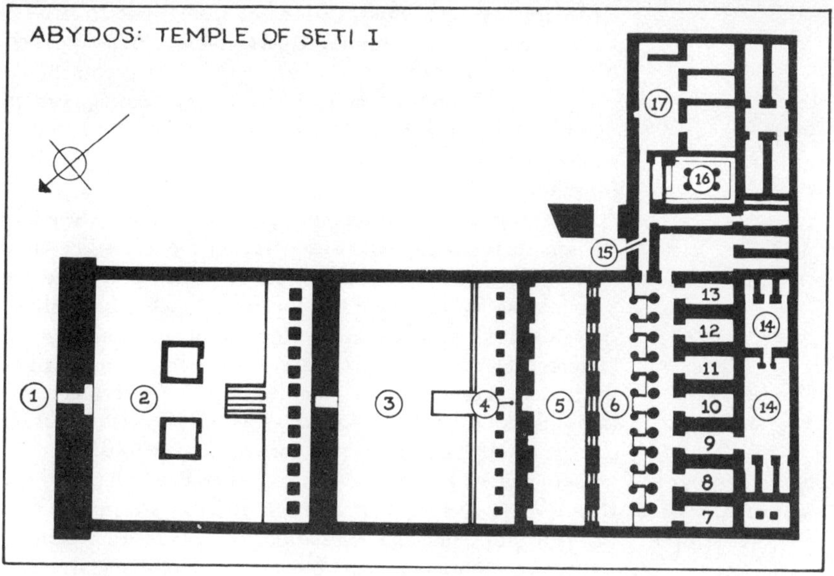

1. Pylon (destroyed)
2. First court (destroyed)
3. Second court (largely destroyed)
4. Present entrance
5. First hypostyle hall
6. Second hypostyle hall
7. Sanctuary of Horus
8. Sanctuary of Isis
9. Sanctuary of Osiris
10. Sanctuary of Amun
11. Sanctuary of Re-Herakhte
12. Sanctuary of Ptah
13. Sanctuary of Seti
14. Inner Sanctuaries of Osiris
15. Gallery of the Kings
16. Sanctuary of the Boats
17. Hall of Sacrifices

source of zeal) – by the brief reign of Ramses I and by Seti I who now had to consolidate. Ironically, Seti bore the name of Osiris' mortal enemy – his sensitivity on this point is demonstrated at Abydos where his cartouche reads Menmare Osiris-Merneptah rather than Menmare Seti-Merneptah – and both to remove any doubts about his loyalty to the past, and to identify his dynasty with the national god, Seti built a temple of fine limestone at Abydos. But Seti was more than a reactionary; he declared a renaissance, and in art he ignored both Akhenaton's expressionism and the overblown style of the XVIII Dynasty empire. His bas-reliefs at Abydos are finely formed and beautifully coloured Old Kingdom revivals – though perhaps a touch effete: it is these one comes to see.

Seti's mortuary temple

The pylon of Seti's mortuary temple has collapsed and the walls of the first and second courts are reduced almost to foundation level. You enter the temple by the central door of seven (the three on either side were sealed by Ramses II) and pass through the first hypostyle hall into the second. The seven doors are explained by the unusual feature of seven sanctuaries lying beyond, dedicated, from right to left, to Horus, Isis, Osiris, Amun, Re-Herakhte, Ptah and Seti himself. But it is in the *second hypostyle hall* that you should pause, for this contains the remarkable *reliefs*. Seti appears in distinctive profile, a stylised but close likeness as can be determined by comparison with his mummy at the Cairo Museum.

Also unusual is the wing built onto the temple to the left of the sanctuaries. The first passageway on the left is known as the *Gallery of the Kings* for its famous list of Seti's predecessors. Though the list is incomplete the 76 cartouches from Menes onwards have assisted archaeologists in determining the correct order of pharaonic succession. The list is on the right wall, and represented as revering their ancestors are Seti himself and his son, the future Ramses II, with youthful side-lock and holding up two papyrus prayer rolls.

Seti's cenotaph and Ramses' temple

Immediately behind the temple is the Cenotaph of Seti I or the Osireion. It stands on lower ground and was sunk within an artificial mound, an association, perhaps, with a creation myth (see Hermopolis and Medinet Habu). Funerary texts decorate the interior, and across the ceiling of the fine transverse chamber is a beautiful relief of Nut, goddess of the sky. Her arched body is supported by Shu, god of the air. She is swallowing the winged disc at the end of day, but the birth of morning is already seen in the winged ball at her feet. The temple of Ramses II is 300 metres to the right of Seti's but is almost wholly destroyed above foundation level. The fine-grained limestone, architectural details picked out in red and black granite, and the bas-reliefs (Ramses normally employed sunk relief) suggest a standard of execution higher than was to be bothered with later in Ramses' prodigal reign.

Colour plate: the court and minaret of the Ibn Tulun mosque (top); the Delta-style facade and reused classical columns of the Terbana Mosque in Alexandria (left); St Simeon's monastery near Aswan (mid-right); a Luxor mosque illuminated for Ramadan (bottom right).

The primitive roots of Egyptian religion – an animal fetishism that it never quite escaped and at the end, as seen at Saqqara, retreated to – are illustrated in Hathor, the cow goddess, goddess of joy and love and identified by the Greeks with Aphrodite, despite her bovine features. One thinks of the Dinka, a still primitive people of the southern Sudan, whose entire culture is based on cattle. The cow to them is the epitome of beauty; it is tended for its milk and aesthetic satisfaction, never for its meat unless it dies. The Dinka have contempt for agriculture, the nomad's disdain for those tied to the land. Perhaps it was so with the pre-dynastic Egyptians as their grasslands were swallowed by the desert and they were forced to labour for their existence along the Nile – a yearning for a stolen way of life expressed through Hathor, one of the

most ancient and revered of their gods. At any rate, the worship of Hathor at Dendera went back to the earliest times. Cheops built, or rather rebuilt, here, as did numerous pharaohs throughout the Old, Middle and New Kingdoms. By Ptolemaic times the ancient cosmology had become much simplified. Deities, concepts and aspects were often assimilated to the dramatis personae of the Osiris myth. Through the incestuous working of mythology the fertility goddess Hat-Hor, literally Castle of Horus, first suckled the son of Osiris and then lay with him at Edfu in culmination of a great pageant issuing each year from Dendera. As it was important that each pharaoh should trace his ancestry back to Horus (see Philae), it was especially necessary that the foreign Ptolemies should stress their links with the Osirid trinity and with the wet-nurse and bed-mate of Horus. The Temple of Hathor at Dendera was part of this Ptolemaic assertion, and the Romans too found it expedient to contribute stones to the story.

Dendera

Cosmological simplification and single-mindedness of political purpose – and perhaps a Greek concern for harmony – gave unity to Ptolemaic temples in contrast to the sprawling accretions of earlier dynasties. The old motifs in architecture and decorations were retained to gratify the priesthood in exchange for their absorption into the machinery of Alexandrian rule, and perhaps to impress the populace – though not to include them, as the abstruseness of Ptolemaic inscriptions makes clear. Non-pharaonic nationalism was shut out, though it intruded in the protesting defacings of later centuries.

The Temple of Hathor

The temple *facade* (1) is a pylon in outline, relieved by six Hathor-headed columns rising from a screen. A winged disc hovers at the centre of the huge cavetto cornice, an inscription above it from the reign of Tiberius – the facade and pronaos are Roman works. A central doorway admits to the *pronaos* (2), a great hypostyle hall, again with Hathoric columns. Its ceiling decorations include the signs of the Egyptian zodiac, the various deities traversing the heavens in their sacred boats amidst bursts of stars. The successive chambers become smaller, lower, darker. The *second hypostyle hall* (3) of six columns is decorated with scenes concerning the temple foundation rites: turning the first spadeful of earth, laying the first stone, etc. Beyond this is the temple proper, the sanctuary at its centre surrounded by a corridor lined with chapels. But first you pass through the Hall of Offerings and the Hall of the Ennead.

Colour plate: the vaulted ceiling in the tomb chamber of Ramses VI in the Valley of the Kings, showing the goddess Nut (top right); during the heat of the day in Luxor (top left); evening at Aswan (mid-left); the mortuary temple of Hatshepsut in the Theban necropolis (bottom).

The *Hall of Offerings* (4) marks the scene of the daily cult ritual in which offerings were laid out before the sanctuary, and from where the divine images were carried in New Year processions up the staircases to the roof to a kiosk where they made contact with the rays of Re – a spiritual emergence from darkness into light. The processions are depicted ascending and descending on both stairway walls.

The *Hall of the Ennead* (5), immediately before the sanctuary, contained statues of Hathor's nine consorts, these being the primal elements or deities following on the creation (eg air, moisture, earth, sky) as opposed to the pre-creation forces (see Medinet Habu) – that is, the elements of cosmic order rather than the elements of cosmic disorder.

The *sanctuary* (6) itself would normally be bolted and in complete darkness. It was opened and illuminated by torchlight to permit the Pharaoh to adore the goddess, and for her consorts to dine in communion with her. These rituals are depicted on the inner walls. The surrounding *chapels* each had their different ritual and ceremonial functions. Most interesting are the three chapels immediately behind the sanctuary: at the centre the Per-Ur (7), to its left the Per-Nu, and to its right the Per-Neser. The *Per-Ur chapel* was the starting point for the New Year procession and its decorations include the Pharaoh offering the goddess a drink of intoxicating liquor, as Hathor was the goddess of joy. From the *Per-Nu chapel,* Hathor embarked on her annual voyage to Edfu and congress with Horus. In the *Per-Neser chapel* the goddess is represented in her terrible aspect, for example as a lioness goddess (by Ptolemaic times Hathor had assimilated the lioness goddess Sekhmet and the cat goddess Bastet, reflecting the terrible and gentle aspects of her nature).

Reliefs of Cleopatra

On the outside rear (south) wall of the temple colossal *reliefs* show Caesarion, son of Julius Caesar, with his mother, the great Cleopatra and the last of the Ptolemies, behind him, making offerings to a head of Hathor. The carvings are entirely conventional and in no way portraits. It is odd seeing Cleopatra in this anonymous form – for domestic consumption – when she is so much better known, or imagined, in flesh and blood, the centre-page fold-out who bedded the two most powerful Romans of her day.

Birth houses

The birth house is a particular feature of Ptolemaic temples and served to legitimise the dynasty through its ritual association with the birth of Horus (see Philae). At Dendera there are three birth houses. The *Temple of Isis* (8), to the rear (south) of the Hathor temple was built by Augustus and is in ruins; *a second monumental birth house* (9), also built by Augustus, with reliefs completed under Trajan and Hadrian, is to the front of the Hathor temple court (a Coptic church (10) built of stones from this birth house is squeezed between them); *a third* (11),

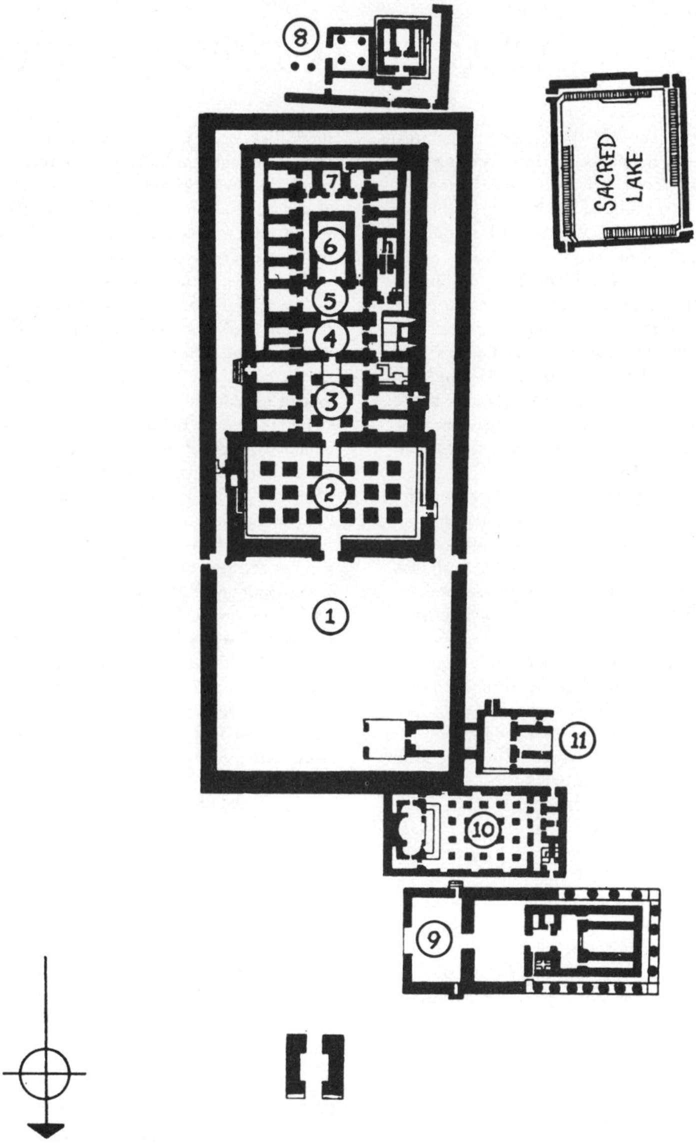

DENDERA: TEMPLE OF HATHOR

bisected by the west wall of the court, was begun during the reign of Nectanebos I (XXX Dyn) and completed under the Ptolemies.

PRACTICAL INFORMATION

Distances between major points in this chapter are by rail and so are less than those for road or river travel. The boat journey between Cairo and Luxor follows the Nile for 740 kms; by road the journey is 730 kms; while by rail the journey is 676 kms.

To cover the distance by **boat** means joining a Swans or Bales cruise (see *Background* chapter) for the complete voyage, lasting at least 14 days, and visiting the most famous places – Beni Hassan, Amarna, Assiut, Abydos and Dendera. Most of the effort and all of the planning are taken out of your hands; the voyage is comfortable and restful, the river scenery beautiful and ever-changing.

The overnight sleeper or day express **train** between Cairo and Luxor takes about 11 hours. The day train permits you to see the scenery enroute and is recommended in at least one direction. But rail travel is also a good way to see the Valley in stages (for train schedules, see the *Background* chapter).

The main **road** follows the railway, keeping to the west bank of the Nile between Cairo and Nag Hammadi (which lies between Abydos and Dendera) before crossing over to the east bank to continue to Luxor and Aswan. There are also alternatives, a minor road along the east bank between Assiut and Nag Hammadi, and another along the west bank between Nag Hammadi and Edfu. The main road is good along the entire length of the Valley; the drive from Cairo to Luxor will take 2 days, with an overnight stop at Minya.

Road and rail travel in Egypt have not received their due. Local trains, buses and service (shared) taxis operate throughout the length of the Valley, and cars with drivers can be hired. Service taxis are particularly recommended as a quick, inexpensive and not uncomfortable way of getting from town to town. Using Minya, Assiut and Qena as bases, you can explore out of the way places at your own pace.

There are no bridges across the Nile between El Wasta and Assiut, and so to get to sites on the east bank (eg Beni Hassan and Amarna) means taking a boat across (there are regular ferry services at all towns) and continuing on foot or by donkey.

Before starting out on a tour of the Valley, it would be worthwhile talking with the Tourist Information Office on Sharia Adli in Cairo. They can advise on the best means of travel in each locality and provide contacts and up to date information. In some cases you should call on the Department of Antiquities in the area you are visiting. Also Misr Travel might be able to advise you on local accommodation.

For the less fussy, the local no-star hotels will do. The **hotels** recommended to tourists, however, will be starred and these are found only at Minya and Qena. **At Minya** there are the 2-star **Lotus,** a modern pink building on Sharia Port Said, with a roof restaurant and bar, and bath, toilet, telephone and air conditioning in all rooms. A double room costs about LE6. And there is the 1-star **Ibn Khaseeb** on Sharia Ragheb, costing about LE3.50 double. (For more information on Minya, phone the Tourist Office: 2044 or 2155). **At Qena,** the 1-star **New Palace Hotel** is in the station square and costs about LE3.50 double. There are no **youth hostels** until you reach Luxor.

UPPER EGYPT 2: LUXOR

Luxor, Karnak and the Theban necropolis

At Luxor the Nile flows north-northeast and the town and the temples in the area take the river as their axis, but to simplify matters it will be assumed here that the river flows north and that the temples therefore lie along one or other of the cardinal axes of the compass. The name Luxor is loosely applied by travellers to include three distinct places: the town of Luxor on the east bank of the Nile (676 kms south of Cairo), the village of Karnak and its immense temple 4 kms north on the same bank, and on the west bank of the river opposite Luxor and Karnak the Theban necropolis. Accommodation is in Luxor, the base of your explorations.

The landscape all about is placid and horizontal, with a broad cultivated plain on either side of the river. The desert to the east rises gently to the Arabian plateau, while to the west a low range of hills, the Theban Mountain, interpose themselves between the cultivation and the Libyan Desert. The Nile is majestic, at sundown an implacable lava flow. By day, feluccas seem to stride upon its surface like pond insects, and distant palms rise from the level stillness, distinct and exactly outlined in the clear air and brilliant light. "The palm – an architectural tree. Everything in Egypt seems made for architecture – the planes of the fields, the vegetation, the human anatomy, the horizon lines" (Flaubert). For the ancient Egyptians, the richness and never-failing fertility of this landscape was a source of wonder. As capital of the New Kingdom it was the focus of architectural activity so grand, and still so well preserved, that it can lay just claim to being the world's greatest outdoor museum.

History

The name Luxor derives from the Arabic *el qasr,* meaning castle or military camp (hence the Alcazar, the Moorish palace in Seville). The Arabic derived in turn from the Latin *castrum,* and may have referred to the Roman base here, though possibly to the appearance of the town to the end of the 19th C. when it lay largely within the remains of the Temple of Luxor. The ancient Egyptian name for the settlement was Weset, though it is best known by the Greek name Thebes, "where the houses are full of treasures, a city with a hundred gates" (The *Iliad*). At the height of its glory during the XVIII and XIX Dynasties, Thebes covered all the ground of Luxor and Karnak, and may have had a population as high as one million. During the Old Kingdom, however, when the capital was at Memphis, Thebes was only one of four humble townships in the nome – Tod and Armant to the south, Medamud to the

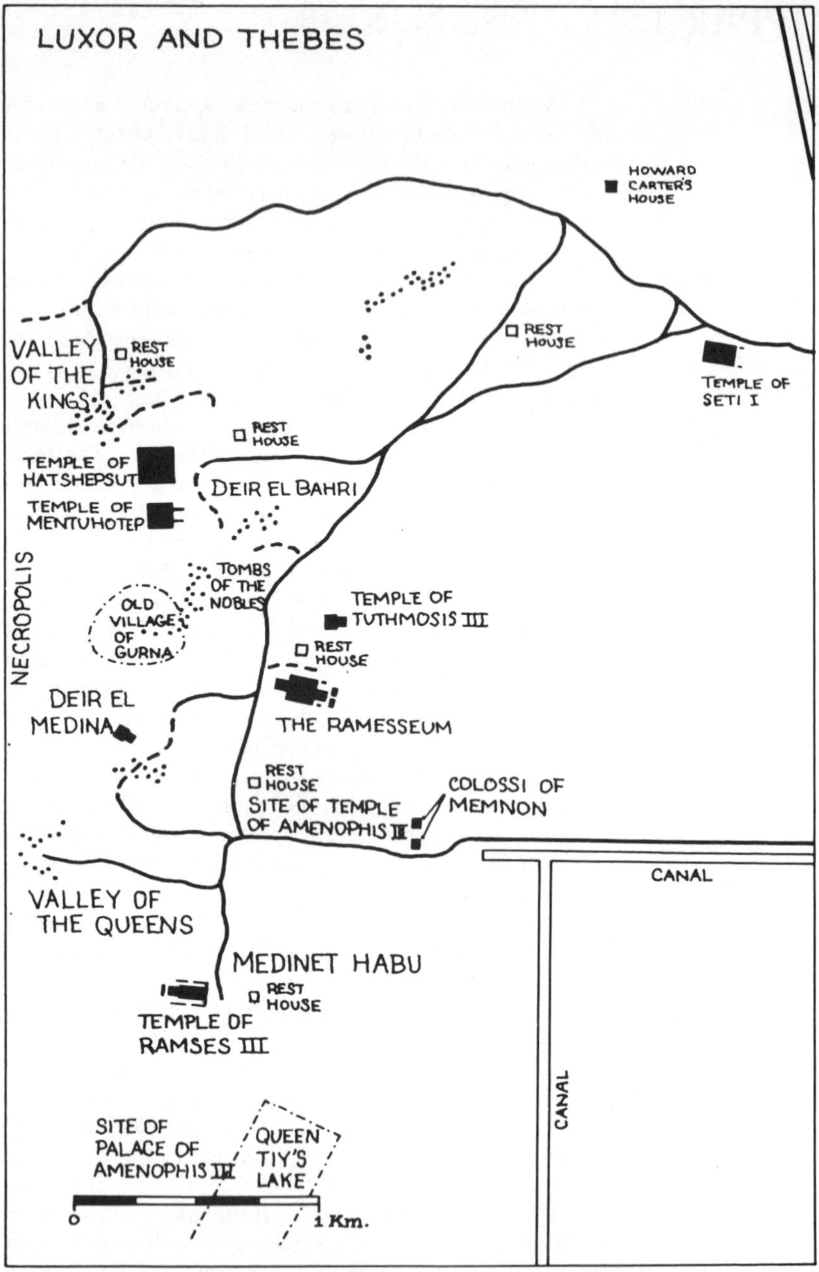
LUXOR AND THEBES
HOWARD CARTER'S HOUSE
REST HOUSE
VALLEY OF THE KINGS
REST HOUSE
TEMPLE OF SETI I
REST HOUSE
TEMPLE OF HATSHEPSUT
DEIR EL BAHRI
TEMPLE OF MENTUHOTEP
NECROPOLIS
TOMBS OF THE NOBLES
OLD VILLAGE OF GURNA
TEMPLE OF TUTHMOSIS III
REST HOUSE
DEIR EL MEDINA
THE RAMESSEUM
REST HOUSE
SITE OF TEMPLE OF AMENOPHIS III
COLOSSI OF MEMNON
CANAL
VALLEY OF THE QUEENS
MEDINET HABU
REST HOUSE
TEMPLE OF RAMSES III
CANAL
SITE OF PALACE OF AMENOPHIS III
QUEEN TIY'S LAKE
0
1 Km.

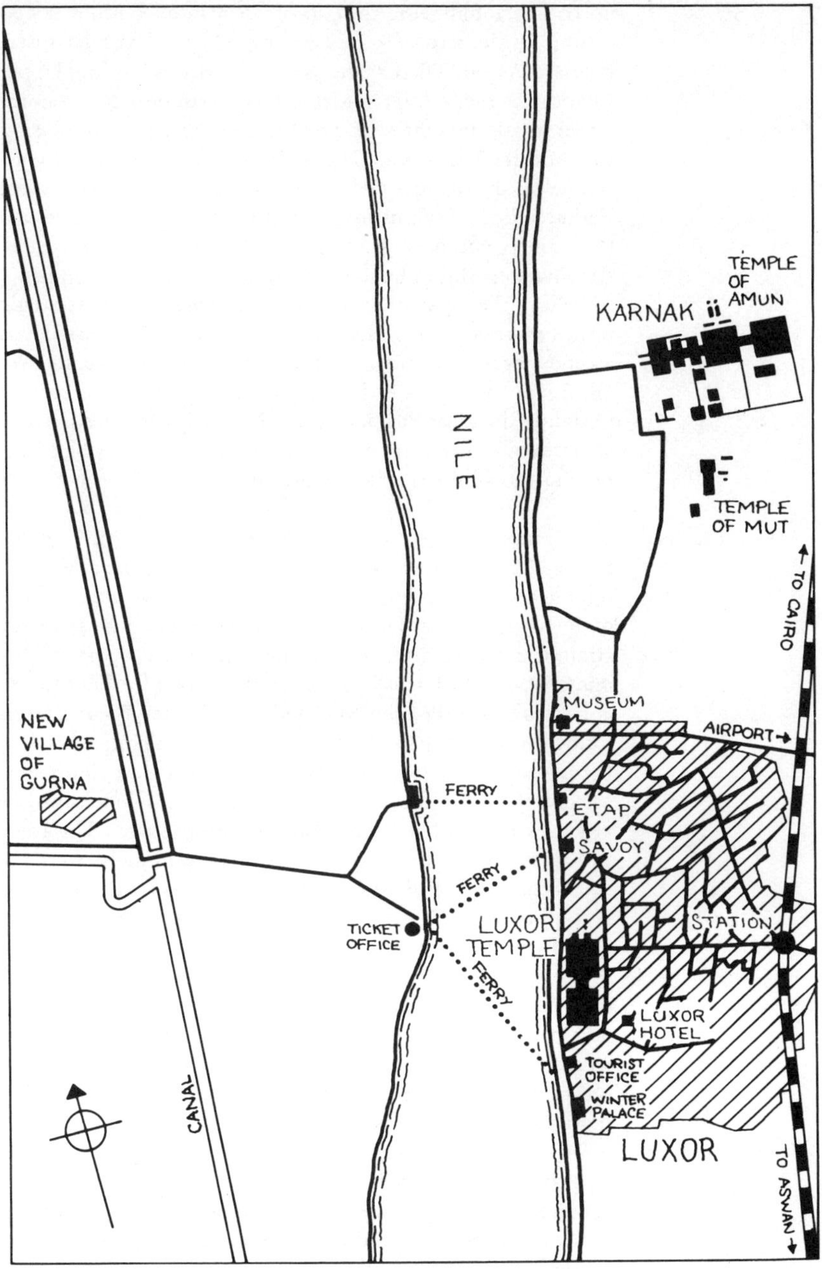

TEMPLE
OF
AMUN
KARNAK
NILE
TEMPLE
OF MUT
TO CAIRO
MUSEUM
AIRPORT
NEW
VILLAGE
OF
GURNA
FERRY
ETAP
SAVOY
FERRY
TICKET
OFFICE
LUXOR
TEMPLE
STATION
FERRY
LUXOR
HOTEL
TOURIST
OFFICE
WINTER
PALACE
LUXOR
CANAL
TO ASWAN

north – each following the cult of falcon-headed Mont, a god of war. In the retreat to regional rule during the First Intermediate Period, Thebes emerged as the power binding Upper Egypt together. After a struggle it re-united the country under its administrative and religious authority, inaugurating the Middle Kingdom. Thebes repeated the pattern when following the disintegration during the Second Intermediate Period and the Hyksos invasion of Lower Egypt, it liberated the country and now also became the permanent residence of the Pharaohs throughout the New Kingdom. It is tempting to believe that apart from its prowess in war and its strategic position between the Delta and the Cataracts, Thebes achieved ascendancy over the townships of its nome and eventually over all Egypt because of the special beauty of its situation. Certainly the great Pharaohs of the New Kingdom responded, sometimes sensitively, sometimes grandiosely, to the architectural possibilities of the landscape.

Orientation The Temple of Luxor is on the Nile, only the corniche road, Sharia el Bahr (Nile Street), separating it from the river. The temple and the gardens lying along its west side are the focus of the town. All roads meet here. From the station, it is a short straight carriage ride (the usual means of transport) to the gardens with the Luxor Hotel on the left. A bit further and you are on the corniche, the New and Old Winter Palace Hotels immediately to the south, the Savoy and Etap Hotels north of the temple. The Etap and New Winter Palace are unimaginatively modern; the others were the grand hotels of the twenties and thirties and retain an atmosphere. The town proper extends on either side of the street running between the station and the gardens; the corniche with its hotels and touts is a quite separate world. Nowhere in Egypt, except at the Giza Pyramids, are the touts so much a plague as here along the corniche – insisting that you take their carriage, sail in their felucca, buy their home-made mummified ibis or at any rate give them baksheesh – and on the other side of the river where a mob of car and donkey drivers will harrass you to accept the worst deal at the most outrageous price. The irritation comes close to spoiling Luxor altogether.

Tour schedule The briefest possible tour of the area requires two days, one on either side of the Nile. Three or four days are required for a comprehensive impression, though still only an impression, of ancient Thebes and its necropolis. You must bear in mind that outside of winter, mid-afternoons get very hot (around 40° C); also, that year round the temples and tombs on the west bank close at 4pm. On the east bank there is the enjoyment of carriage rides; on the west bank the choice is between donkey or car, the latter being infinitely preferable. Best of all for the sound of limb, and cheap, breezy and free of constraint, is to hire a bicycle in Luxor and use it on both sides of the river. Karnak and the Temple of Luxor can be visited on the same day, the latter best seen in the late afternoon as it glows in the rays of the sinking sun, or at night when it is unsparingly and intelligently floodlit. Rising as early as possible, the whole of the second day should be devoted to the west bank, and the third day too, if you have the time. A fourth day will allow you to revisit Karnak, and perhaps one or two temples or tomb clusters on the necropolis side, and will allow you greater leisure to shop in Luxor and visit the museum there.

The Temple of Luxor

Close to the hotels and landing stages for the Nile cruise boats, a visit to the Temple of Luxor can be casually arranged following a more rigorously organised morning. The temple is appealing: it is well preserved, its unity clearly stated; yet there is the intriguing irregularity of its plan that has given rise to several explanations and speculations. The temple was built largely under Amenophis III (XVIII Dyn) on the site of an older sanctuary. He also built the Third Pylon at Karnak and began the Hypostyle Hall there, and erected an enormous mortuary temple on the west bank of which only the Colossi of Memnon remain: he was the first Pharaoh of the New Kingdom to go in for the gigantism that broadcasts the imperial pretensions of the period. He would have been delighted with the reaction of the French army in 1799: while in pursuit of the Mameluke Muradbey it rounded a bend in the Nile and came suddenly upon the temples of Karnak and Luxor. "Without an order being given, the men formed their ranks and presented arms, to the accompaniment of the drums and bands", wrote a lieutenant.

Since 1885 when excavations began here, the temple has been gradually cleared of the village once within it, the rubble blocking the pylon entrance, and the kom to the north which

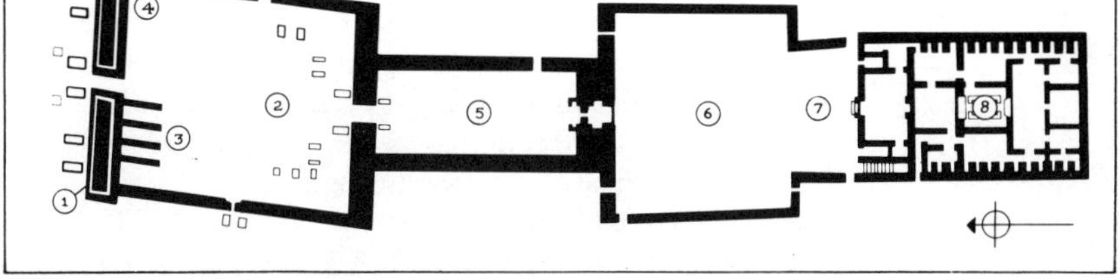

has revealed the *forecourt* and *avenue of sphinxes* leading to Karnak. It was from Karnak that Amun came during the annual Opet festival, but by water, amidst a floating procession of great splendour to this Harem of the South with his wife Mut and their son the moon god Khonsu. The forecourt wall is the work of Nectanebos I (XXX Dyn), as are the sphinxes which are set at a lower level to the excavated remains of post-pharaonic houses on either side. In the northwest corner of the forecourt is the restored *Serapeum* dedicated by the Emperor Hadrian on 24 January AD 126, his birthday.

The pylon

Now turning south to look at the *pylon* (1): this and the court behind it were additions by Ramses II (XIX Dyn), the pylon a gigantic billboard advertising Ramses' dubious victory over the Hittites at Kadesh. The west (right) tower shows the Egyptian camp within a circle of shields and Ramses on his throne holding a council of war while beneath him two spies are being interrogated by beating. In the right light, or by floodlight, you can see that Ramses has been reversed on his throne, now facing east where he once faced west. (The floodlighting also attracts bats which enjoy fluttering to rest upside-down within the deeper incisions of the drama.) The east (left) tower shows Kadesh on the left, surrounded by the waters of the Orontes, while to the right an heroically proportioned Ramses in his chariot is pursuing the broken enemy. In vertical lines below these scenes on both towers is the *Poem of Pentaur* (see Abu Simbel for partial translation), comparison of which with Hittite sources, and also taking into account the contemporary situation, including the superior iron weaponry of the Hittites to the Egyptian bronze, suggests that the battle was less glorious for the Egyptians than Ramses made out. The vertical grooves along the pylon facade were for supporting flagstaffs, the apertures above to receive the braces securing the staffs and to admit light and air to the interior. Except at the corners above the entrance passage, the cavetto cornices are missing. Originally the pylon stood 24 metres high; its width is 65 metres.

In front of the pylon were six *statues of Ramses,* two sitting, four standing. Only the two seated figures on either side of the entrance and the westernmost standing figure remain, and these are all badly damaged. Also there were two *obelisks* of exceptionally fine detail standing on plinths decorated with dog-headed baboons in relief. Mohammed Ali offered the pair, plus one at Alexandria, to France. It is said that the French desire for an obelisk was first expressed by Josephine to Napoleon before he embarked for Egypt: "Goodby! If you go to Thebes, do send me a little obelisk". Napoleon left Egypt under circumstances that denied Josephine the pleasure. In celebration of the Bourbon restoration, Louis XVIII renewed the idea. In the event, the task proved so difficult and lengthy that Champollion's identification of the west obelisk as the finest in Egypt left the French satisfied with it alone, and in 1836 it was erected in the Place de la Concorde. As the obelisk was lowered at Luxor, Ramses' name was found engraved on the underside of the shaft; his titles, his achievements, his piety had already been carved on the four sides of each obelisk, but being a great ursurper of other pharaohs' monuments, he knew well the value of this secret protestation of ownership. Standing before the temple in 1850, Flaubert wrote: "The obelisk that is now in Paris was against the right-hand pylon. Perched on its pedestal, how bored it must be in the Place de la Concorde! How it must miss its Nile! What does it think as it watches all the cabs drive by, instead of the chariots it saw at its feet in the old days?" One hundred years later, Cocteau was more caustic: the plinth of the obelisk removed to Paris "was surrounded by low reliefs of dog-faced baboons in erection. This was not thought to be proper and so the monkeys' organs have been cut off".

The Court of Ramses II

The *entrance passage* through the pylon is decorated with carvings of the XXV Dynasty, a period when Egypt was ruled by Ethiopian or Cushite pharaohs, one of whom, Shabaka, is shown on the east (left) wall wearing the white crown of Upper Egypt, running a ritual race in the presence of an ithyphallic Amun-Re. The *Court of Ramses II* (2), entirely surrounded by a double colonnade of bud-capital papyrus columns, lies within. Belying the seemingly universal symmetry and regularity of Egyptian architecture, it is immediately obvious that this court does not lie on the same axis as the Colonnade of Amenophis III, which in turn is out of line with the temple proper, but these are very slight divergencies while that of the court of Ramses II is striking. An explanation is found in the northwest corner of the court, a small *temple to Amun, Mut and Khonsu (3)* built by Tuthmosis III and Hatshepsut 100 years before Amenophis, 200 years before Ramses. The granite columns are original, while the carvings were redone by Ramses II who integrated the temple into his court, aligning his court to suit. However, the outré French archaeologist Schwaller de Lubicz rejected this opportunist interpretation, arguing instead that temples were precalculated generations in advance, that the various axes here have a meaning, part of the wealth of symbolism found in the architecture, texts and figurations of the ancient Egyptians, and that the purpose was didactic, to encode and transmit a "geodetic, astronomical and physiological knowledge surpassing that which Egyptology has hitherto been able to concede". He spent years measuring and drawing the position of the paving stones in the temple, and then by shading in some but not others was able to 'prove' that they formed a pharaonic profile with the top of the skull sliced off; and also he superimposed a skeleton on the temple plan to demonstrate a close similarity in its proportions to that of the human frame. Certainly Schwaller de Lubicz proves that if you have enough dots, and spend enough time connecting them, you can come up with any picture you like. Cocteau, however, was very impressed when he met the archaeologist whose mathematical interpretation of the temple launched Cocteau on a poetic and more perceptive vision.

"A tourist soon tires of the unchanging positions of the gods, goddesses and royal personages. Not to look beyond this deceptive decoration, is to be like a pupil looking up from morning to night at a school board covered by algebraic signs and to think it is a pretty picture. The stones say more than the inscriptions on them and the inscriptions more about static movement than about the story of ritual or of valour in the field.

"The octopus-temples twist about, the pachyderm-temples walk, and the colossi move their legs forward, while a slight deviation from complete balance on the left gives them a start in that direction."

By 'static movement' Cocteau means: "An everlasting operation by means of which the abstract becomes the concrete and the void is translated with deep intensity into stone . . .

"The Pharaohs wish to live whatever it may cost, willy-nilly (not to survive), to live as they did on earth but eternally to translate themselves into the less and less translatable, to vibrate in one extreme gesture, to slip from a court ceremony on a throne in the centre of which all lines cross each other, to be digested and absorbed through a labyrinth of deep-rooted viscera.

"In a word, they decide to allow of no static pomp because the universe itself is time and movement. It is to perpetual movement that they aspire."

In the northeast corner of the court, surviving the clearance of the old village within the temple, is the *mosque and mausoleum of Abu Haggag* (4), a local holy man.

The interior walls of Ramses' court are adorned with reliefs. Especially interesting is the *representation of the pylon facade* at the west end of the south wall, complete with colossi, obelisks and fluttering banners. Approaching this, along the west

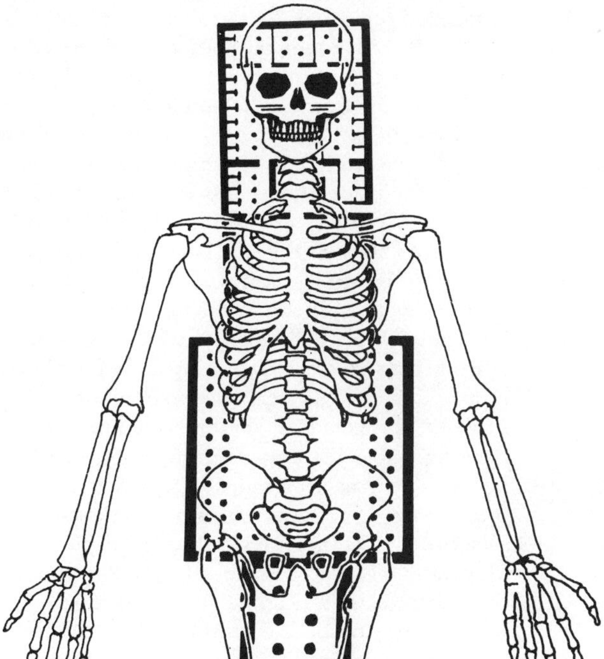

TEMPLE OF LUXOR: LUBICZ'S INTERPRETATION

wall, is a procession led by 17 of Ramses' sons (he fathered over 100 in his 90-odd years) and followed by priests and sacrificial oxen. The unnaturally long hooves indicate the oxen have been fattened in their stalls for the occasion, while the model of an African's head between the horns of the fifth ox and the Asiatic head with long pointed beard between the horns of the sixth symbolises the Egyptian triumph over Africa and Asia. The southern half of the court is further embellished with standing *colossi of Ramses,* while the triumph motif is repeated round the bases of the black granite seated colossi on either side of the southern doorway: the shields and bound figures of vanquished Asiatics on the east base, of Africans on the west.

Colonnade of Amenophis III

Passing between these last two guardians of Ramses' memory, you enter the imposing *Colonnade of Amenophis III* (5). The 15.8-metre high papyrus columns with calyx capitals bearing massive architraves contribute greatly to the serene profile of the temple when viewed from the river. Originally, however, this columnar rhythm would have been lost behind flanking walls, the upper three-quarters of which have collapsed. The remaining courses bear fine and fascinating *reliefs from the reign of Tutankhamun,* a celebration of the re-establishment of the Amun orthodoxy, depicting the god with Mut and Khonsu accompanied by the Pharaoh and priests on their voyage from Karnak to Luxor at the height of the inundation period. Crowds of common folk follow by land, and there are scenes of rejoicing, of musicians and dancers, and of sacrifice. The series begins at the northwest corner with Pharaoh sacrificing to the boats at Karnak, and continues with the water-borne procession and, at the southwest corner, the arrival at Luxor. Starting at the southeast corner, the procession returns 24 days later to Karnak.

Court of Amenophis III

The colonnade leads into the *Court of Amenophis III* (6), once enclosed on east, north and west by double rows of clustered papyrus columns with bud capitals, an ensemble that appeals through its harmony. The east and west sides are well preserved and still carry their architraves. On the south side is the *Hypostyle Hall* (7) with four rows of eight columns. On either side of its south wall are reliefs of the coronation of Amenophis by the gods. To the left of the central aisle, between the last two columns, is a Roman altar dedicated to Constantine. Cocteau noticed a more recent intrusion: "Suddenly, in the hypostle hall, I was struck dumb. What could that be? High up, on the top of the wall, Rimbaud had carved his name. He carved it, at the height of a man, and now that the temple is cleared, it shines forth like a sunflower. It blazes out, royal and sunlike, above suspicion, dreadful in its solitude".

Now you enter the *temple proper*. A central chamber, its roof once supported by eight columns, was stuccoed over when turned into a chapel of a Roman Imperial cult, but this has now mostly been removed to reveal reliefs of Amenophis. The side chambers were dedicated to Mut (east) and Khonsu (west). Through the central chamber is the Offering Chapel with four columns, and beyond that the *Sanctuary of the Sacred Boat of Amun* (8).

The Sanctuary and Birth Room

The sanctuary consists of a chapel open to north and south set within a chamber. The chamber walls are decorated with reliefs of Amenophis, while the chapel was rebuilt by Alexander the Great and both its exterior and interior walls bear reliefs of him before Amun and other gods. A room to the east of the sanctuary has badly damaged scenes of Amenophis' coronation and on the north wall Pharaoh hunting in the marshes. Immediately to the north is the *Birth Room* with reliefs on the west wall referring to Amenophis' divine birth. At the left of the lowest register, Khnum is moulding the infant Amenophis and his ka on a potter's wheel. Moving from left to right across the middle register, Thoth foretells to Mutemuia, mother of Amenophis, the birth of her son; the pregnant Mutemuia is conducted by Isis and Khnum; her confinement; Isis presenting the infant to Amun; and Amun with the infant in his arms. The top register shows Amenophis and his ka nurtured by the gods and presented to Amnun; to the far right, in the corner, Amenophis has become Pharaoh. The remaining rooms at the south end of the temple are without present interest, though the central chamber was a sanctuary once containing the intriguingly described 'divine image of millions of years'.

The temple of Luxor is experienced most intensely at night when the floodlights throw the carvings into deeper relief and the black night rests like a roof on the brightness of the stone, enclosing you. On the dome of the mosque of Abu Haggag, cursive green neon proclaims 'Allah'. Once a year the saint's boat is carried in procession as was Amun's 3500 years before.

Ramadan celebrations

At Ramadan the mosque is the focus of the nightly festivities. Hundreds of men gather in the gardens, some off to the sides playing cards, gambling, smoking hashish, many more listening raptly or dancing wildly to the drums, tambourines, ouds and violins, and to the teasing, climaxing, repeating passages of the imam's songs. They are religious songs, but passionate, or occasionally playful: a boy and girl are walking down a street hand in hand, they enter a house, they 'go to God together'. The audience laughs and shouts, but the lyrics are always secondary, and it is the narcotic beat and wailing of the music and the imam's exquisite phrasing that draws cries from the crowd. The imam twirls and sings, his eyes closed, his head shaking violently from side to side. A policeman in baggy khakis embraces him, rushes into the crowd to collect fistfulls of paper money and presses it into the imam's hands. Two or three dozen men begin to dance, arranging themselves in facing rows. First half-whirls, to the right, to the left, then hopping up and down, now jackknifing, eyes closed, bodies sweating, shouting, whirling, hopping and jackknifing in unison, beyond exhaustion. An onlooker intervenes to ask a young boy, an old man, to rest. But they all dance until they can barely stand, can merely twitch, or until they collapse.

It was less surprising that these men were killing themselves dancing than that others could resist joining the frenzy. I asked one onlooker why he did not dance. "I am angry." Then he showed me a photograph of himself taken five months earlier. He was bearded then. "Now I have no beard because I am angry." At first I thought he *was* angry, he said it with such emphasis, but he meant sad. His wife had died five months ago. "I was happy with my wife, I loved her. I enjoyed sex with her, she washed my clothes, I gave her money to buy things." How did she die, I asked? "One morning I woke up and she was still in bed. I said to her, wife, you must get up and make my breakfast. But she did not get up, and I saw that she was dead." But what did she die of? Had she been sick? "No, she was not sick. She just died that morning." But she must have died of something. For what reason? "My God took her away. Maybe in two years I will look at women, but now I do not look at women. I am very angry."

The Luxor Museum

The Museum of Ancient Egyptian Art is along the corniche to the north of the Etap Hotel, and unlike many in Egypt is well arranged, with some well chosen objects lit to best advantage. The exhibits include jewellery, furniture, pottery and stelae, but most outstanding are the stone *statues and busts.* The latter are most finely represented by granite and basalt works identified by the cartouches as Tuthmosis III, Amenophis II, Amenophis III (all XVIII Dyn) and Sesostris III (XII Dyn), any of which could stand in place of another for all they depict an individual (except for that of Sesostris with big ears). The craftsmanship is excellent, however, and the enjoyment of working with the graceful curves of crowns, necks and waists is clear. There is a marvellous alabaster statue of Sobek with crocodile's head and man's body, and one of Amenophis III, usurped by Ramses II by altering the cartouche – which shows how little the figure itself served to identify. A series of scenes in sunk relief on limestone blocks found within the Ninth Pylon at Karnak show *Akhenaton and Nefertiti worshipping Aton,* but also the most ordinary daily palace tasks. At least when Akhenaton attacked the Theban priesthood, he obliterated images of their god Amun; the post-Amarna counter-revolutionaries reverted to the traditional method of defeating a predecessor's bid for immortality: for example, *exhibit 150* is a block showing Akhenaton worshipping Aton – so clearly understandable and evidence of his heresy – yet it is defaced only to the extent that his cartouche is gouged. Always the name, the sign, rather than the idea.

The walls of the dining room of the Savoy Hotel are painted with scenes of finches sitting on snow-covered pine branches. The forest, brook and mountain landscapes of northern Europe are common decorations in all classes of Egyptian eating places. Riding back in a carriage from Karnak, enjoying the clear blue sky and the rich orange sundown light on the palms and the facades of pastel houses, I thought how we all have our exotica. Do Egyptians wax romantic about Lapland? Take a carriage along the corniche to the First Pylon of the main temple at Karnak, but when leaving ask the driver to return you to Luxor by the road which passes the Gateway of Euergetes and which continues past these pastel facades, offering you a glimpse of village life too easily missed in bustling from one ancient site to another. Somewhere deep beneath this present roadway of your return journey lies the old sacred way, lined with sphinxes that joined the temples of Karnak and Luxor, visible now only at either end, where it leaves Euergetes' gateway, and where it enters the forecourt of the Temple of Luxor.

Carriage to Karnak

The Karnak site covers an enormous area, sufficient to accommodate ten European cathedrals. The Hypostyle Hall alone is large enough to contain Notre Dame. At least two half-day visits are required to see the entire complex; if you can manage only one, then you will have to be content with walking through the main temple, that of Amun. A return can be made at night for the *son et lumiere,* though one could do without the *son.* The size and complexity of the site, the arrangement of its structures on both an east-west and north-south axis, the multiple extensions to several of these structures by successive pharaohs, and in some areas its ruinous state, contribute to the lack of unity and proportion at Karnak. But this has probably always been so, even in its days of completeness. Karnak astounds, but does not awaken the sensibilities. When Egypt stood at the height of empire, when Thebes ruled over Egypt, and when Amun was supreme over all, his temple here possessed 81,000 slaves and their families, 240,000 head of cattle, 83 ships, and from 65 cities and towns their vast annual tribute in gold, silver, copper and precious stones. "Every breath that wanders down the painted aisles of Karnak seems to echo back the sighs of those who perished in the quarry, at the oar, and under the chariot wheels of the conqueror" (Amelia Edwards). It is a grandiloquent and overbearing monument to power without spirit.

History of Karnak

Apart from its size, Karnak represents a vastness of historical time. The main Temple of Amun, from the foundations of the original Middle Kingdom temple to the First Pylon built (probably) during the XXV Dynasty, saw construction over 1300 years. Comprehension of the site requires a brief historical review. Although the war god Mont, associated with Thebes during the Old Kingdom, continued to be worshipped at Karnak, Amun achieved pre-eminence by the beginning of the Middle Kingdom and was honoured during the XII Dynasty by a series of temples facing west, the principal orientation throughout subsequent periods. All that remains of these are the alabaster foundations of what was to become the most venerable part of the extended Temple of Amun, and limestone blocks belonging to the White Chapel of Sesostris I, recovered from the foundations of the Third Pylon and re-erected in the 'open air museum' to the north of the Great Court. With the expulsion of the Hyksos from Egypt and the elevation of Amun to victorious national god, the early Pharaohs of the XVIII Dynasty set about turning Karnak into the principal sanctuary of their kingdom. Amenophis I and his son Tuthmosis I built chapels around the Middle Kingdom temple, while in front of it (to the west) the latter built the Fourth and Fifth Pylons and erected a pair of obelisks. Hatshepsut added two further obelisks between those of her father, chambers with carved decorations in front of the original temple, and initiated the north-south axis of the complex by building south. Her nephew Tuthmosis III continued building along the north-south axis with the Seventh and Eighth Pylons, and constructed the Festival Hall behind (to the east of) the Middle Kingdom temple.

In the century that passed between the Asian conquests of Tuthmosis III and the reign of Amenophis III, artistic and architectural restraint gave way to an overblown imperial style, expressed at Karnak by the Third Pylon built by Amenophis and his start on the great Hypostyle Hall. Empire introduced foreign influences and new wealth to the country, required an enlarged bureaucracy, and upset the status quo. Amun, who had lent his sword to Pharaoh's victories, saw the coffers of his priesthood and of the old aristocracy from which it was drawn swell with tribute, and so their power grew. But another class, which owed its very existence to empire, grew up around Pharaoh. Tuthmosis IV married an Asian princess, and her son Amenophis III married Tiy, an Egyptian commoner. Tiy was given unusual artistic prominence alongside her husband, and her parents, Yuya and Tuyu, were buried in splendour in the Valley of the Kings. Pharaoh and temple no longer represented identical interests. Before decamping to Amarna with his court of parvenus, Amenophis IV (Akhenaton as he became) did some building at the east of Karnak, where several of his statues now in the Cairo Museum were found, while some blocks now in the Luxor Museum were re-used in the foundations of later pylons and the Hypostyle Hall.

But the Amarna revolution did not survive the death of Akhenaton, and the reign of Tutankhamun marked the beginning of the counter-revolution which proceeded with a vengeance. The power of Amun was reaffirmed, and as though to sweep away all memory of heresy, internal conflict and the diminution of empire associated with the last Pharaohs of the XVIII Dynasty, Seti I of the XIX Dynasty declared his reign the era of 'the repeating of births', literally a renaissance. Both he and his son Ramses II outdid all that had gone before, both in architecture and in military propaganda, to make good any deficiencies in this assertion. Between them they completed the Hypostyle Hall. It remained only for later dynasties to build the Great Court and the First Pylon for Karnak to assume the form it has today. The Ptolemies embellished, and the Copts cut crosses in stones.

The XIX Dynasty made its peace with Amun, but the cost in sacrificed wealth was greater than could be borne for long without Pharaoh becoming a mere creature of the priesthood. The Hypostyle Hall, the Ramesseum, Abu Simbel, may all have glorified Ramses II, but only through Amun who long survived that long-lived Pharaoh. By the time Ramses IV (XX Dyn) came to the throne, that is 200 years after Akhenaton's resistance and only 60 years after the death of Ramses II, the Temple of Amun owned at least 7 percent of the population of Egypt and 9 percent of the land, with some estimates trebling those percentages, while the family of the High Priest of Amun directly controlled the collection of Pharaoh's taxes and management of Pharaoh's lands. Pharaoh had become no more than an instrument of a ruling oligarchy, and Karnak was its juggernaut.

Tour: the Temple of Amun

You approach the maw of the beast along a short *processional way* (1) lined with ram-headed sphinxes with figures of Ramses II in mummy wrappings between their forelegs. This exactly expresses the new enveloping relationship between god and Pharaoh, for the ram was identified with Amun. A now filled-in canal once linked the temple with the Nile, giving egress during the Opet festival for gods, priests and Pharaoh aboard their boats. The *First Pylon,* 113 metres wide and 43 metres high, is the largest at Karnak and nearly twice the size of the entrance pylon at the Temple of Luxor. It was probably built during the XXV (Ethiopian) Dynasty, a trumpeting echo of XIX Dynasty bombast, but left unfinished, the south tower higher than the north and neither bearing any decoration. The north (left) tower can be climbed for magnificent views over Karnak and the surrounding countryside.

The Great Court

The *Great Court* (2) was built by the rulers of the XXII Dynasty but encloses earlier structures. Columns with papyrus bud capitals line the north and south sides of the court, while a tall doorway in the southeast corner leads to the south end of the *Second Pylon* on which is cut a scene commemorating the victory of Sheshonk I (Shishak of the Bible) over Rehoboam, son of Solomon. The pylon itself was built by Horemheb, an XVIII Dynasty general who became military dictator and finally last Pharaoh of the dynasty he had served. Like the Ninth and Tenth Pylons, also built by Horemheb, the Second Pylon made use of blocks that had once formed temples to Akhenaton's god, Aton. Continuing the palimpsest of politics, Ramses I and II cut their names on the pylon over that of Horemheb, and Ramses II had two *colossal figures* of himself in pink granite stand on either side of the pylon entrance. Of the one on the left hardly anything remains; nor does that sector of the avenue of rams which once ran through the area that became the court, to continue beyond the First Pylon towards the Nile. Instead, at the centre of the court Taharka (XXV Dynasty) built a *kiosk* (3) with ten enormous columns 21 metres high with papyrus calyx capitals, only one still standing. In the northwest quadrant of the court is the *Temple of Seti II* (4), a simple arrangement of three chapels facing south, the one at the centre to hold the sacred boat of Amun, those to the left and right hold the boats of Mut and Khonsu, during preparations for the Opet festival. The *Temple of Ramses III* (5) intersecting the south wall of the court similarly served as a station chapel during processions and is a fine example of a simple pharaonic temple. Its pylon, facing north, is decorated with the obligatory triumphal scenes on the outside and with jubilee scenes, assuring the Pharaoh a long life, on the inside. An open court leads to a pronaos of four columns and then to a hypostyle hall of eight columns beyond which are the three boat chapels, Amun's at the centre.

A doorway on the north side of the court leads to the *'open air museum'* (6) where blocks and architectural fragments from around the site have been gathered for study. The reconstructed *White Chapel* of Sesostris I and the alabaster *Chapel of Amenophis I* are the finest 'exhibits', but entrance to the museum requires a special permit from the Director of Antiquities at Karnak. No permit is required, however, to ascend the outside staircase at the north end of the First Pylon for views from the top.

View from the First Pylon

Passing through the Second Pylon, you enter the *Hypostyle Hall* (7), certainly one of the most spectacular sights in Egypt. It is the height and massiveness of the columns that is overwhelming rather than spaciousness or even rhythm or repetition of form, for on either side of the central aisle the columns are packed tightly together in overgrown forests of stone. The eye is permitted no perspective and is incapable of taking in more than a glimpse of the whole at any one moment. It is best to come early in the morning or late in the afternoon when the effect of the columns is heightened by the black diagonals of their shadows. Tourists wander round the column bases as priests and pharaohs once wandered, like ants, and the idiot in us all is enthralled. An American woman is told by a guide that the columns are fitted drums, no mortar. She pushes against a drum to observe that the column does not fall – "Wow!" she says.

The Hypostyle Hall

The columns are in fact composed of semi-drums, the 12 along the central aisle (probably originally 14) rising to 23 metres and with a girth of 15 metres. It requires six men with outstretched arms to span one of these columns. Like the papyrus columns forming the Colonnade of Amenophis III at the Temple of Luxor, these also have calyx capitals and were probably erected as a processional way. But Seti I and Ramses II elaborated on the plan by adding a further 122 columns with bud capitals, creating extensive wings on either side. The entire hall was roofed over and the 10-metre difference in height between the central and wing columns was accounted for by raising stone lattice windows from the architraves of the wing columns closest to the nave, providing lateral support for the higher central roof otherwise resting on the taller columns. Several of these windows, in a better or worse state of preservation, remain in place.

The central columns are richly painted and cut in sunk relief

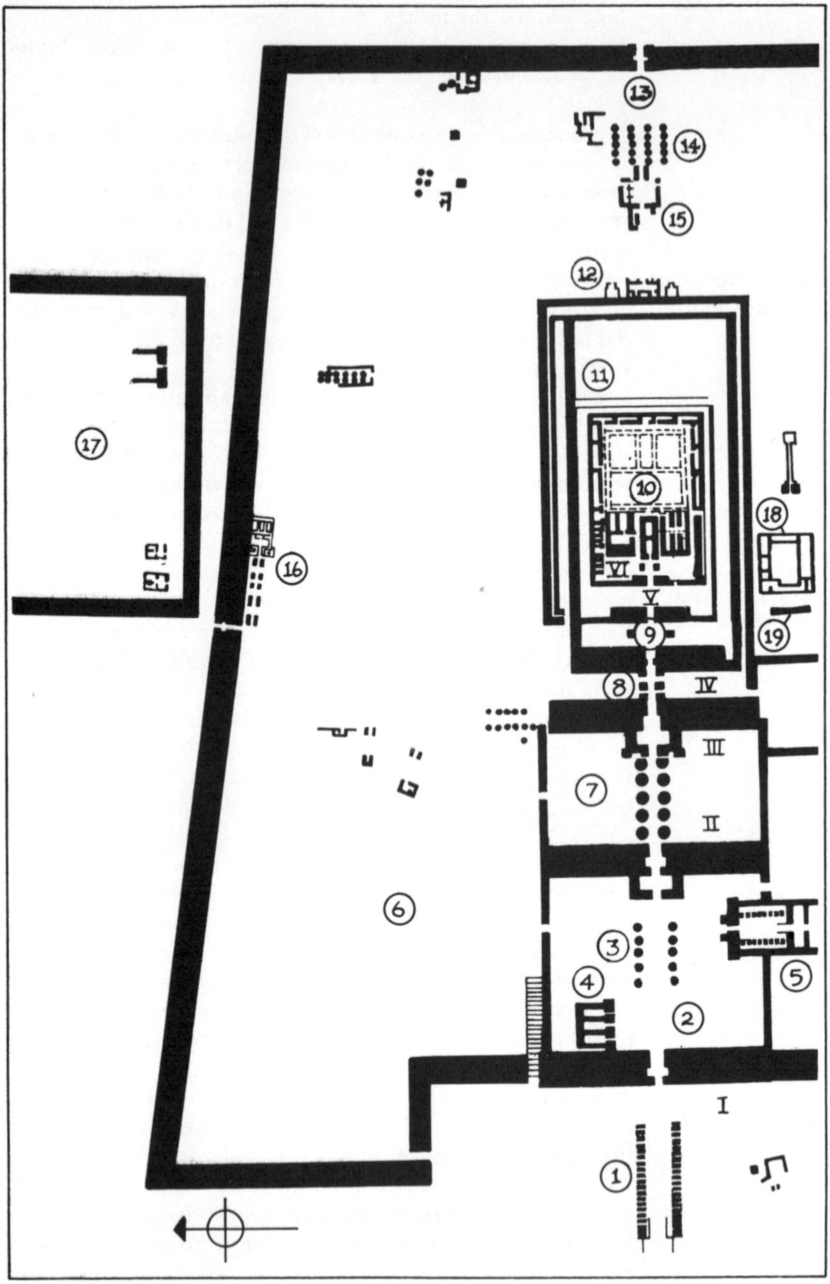
13
14
15
12
11
10
VI
V
9
8
IV
III
7
II
6
3
4
2
5
I
1
17
16
18
19

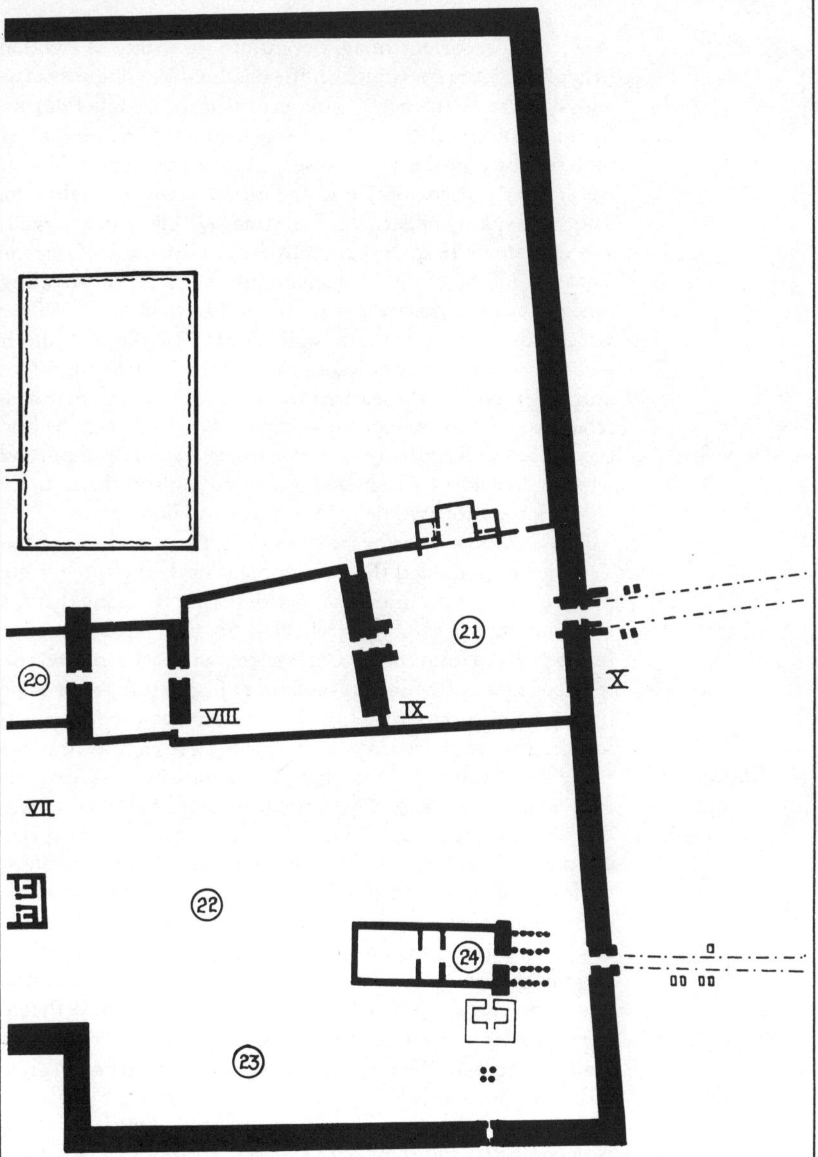

KARNAK: PRECINCT OF AMUN

with standard temple themes, most often Pharaoh making various offerings to Amun and other Theban gods. These *cult scenes*, with recurrent images of Amun in a state of erection (ithyphallic), are continued on the phallus-like columns of the wings, those in the north wing executed in bas-relief during the reign of Seti I, those in the south wing in the sunk relief preferred by Ramses II. The inside walls of the Hypostyle Hall are similarly decorated, but the *outside walls* proclaim the military exploits of Seti I in Palestine and Libya (north wall) and of Ramses II against the Hittites (south wall). Of some romance in the study of ancient history is a *stele* standing upright against the west wall of the Court of the Cachette which runs into the south wall of the Hypostyle Hall: it records a treaty between Ramses II and the Hittite king. Not only is it one of the earliest codifications of international relations, but its cuneiform version was found inscribed on clay tablets at the Hittite capital across the Mediterranean and when independently translated served to confirm the accuracy of the labours of philologists in the two languages.

The intimate relationship between the structure of the Temple of Amun and the development of the Egyptian state has already been outlined. It is worth noting the irony that the great columns of the Hypostyle Hall stood on bases formed of re-used blocks from the time of Akhenaton (since removed and replaced mostly by concrete) and that these in turn stood on no firmer foundation than sand. Pretension was careless of the future, though a century of archaeological engineering has made good the past. Yet though grandiosity so suited the Pharaohs of the XIX Dynasty, it is arguable that it was dictated by the temple itself. It was a canon of Egyptian temple architecture that as you approached the innermost sanctuary, perspective should narrow – that pylons and columns should get smaller, ceilings lower, and that even the temple platform should rise so that you walked upwards towards the sanctuary as walls and ceilings funnelled in around you. Once Amenophis III decided to build his Third Pylon, it had to be larger than the one before, and the Hypostyle Hall, the Second Pylon and finally the First Pylon had to grow more massive still.

Pattern of Egyptian temples

A constricted *court* lies between the *Third Pylon* of Amenophis III and the *Fourth Pylon* of Tuthmosis I, a narrow gap of space and time between traditional and imperial Egypt. When the Fourth Pylon still marked the entrance to the temple, two pairs of *obelisks* (8) were erected before it by Tuthmosis I and III. Only one obelisk survives. Of the pink granite pair raised by Tuthmosis I, originally tipped with

Obelisk of Tuthmosis I

electrum (a natural alloy of gold and silver), one fell as recently as the 18th C., some of its parts lying nearby, and the other leans a little but is still stable. Beyond the Fourth Pylon the outline of the temple becomes difficult to follow. The successive pylons are closely set, and the buildings have undergone repeated alterations and suffered extensive damage. But many beautiful details reward your exploration, and the absence of both overwhelming architecture and overwhelmed tourists encourages tranquil reflection.

The numerous columns in the open space behind the Fourth Pylon suggest that this, at least in part, was a hypostyle hall. It was built by Tuthmosis III and may have been part of his extraordinary attempt to disguise the existence of Hatshepsut's two magnificent *obelisks* (9). The lower shaft of one of these remains on its base, the upper shaft lying near the northwest corner of the Sacred Lake where you can closely examine its inscriptions. The second obelisk is *in situ,* the tallest completed obelisk in Egypt and of ancient obelisks second in height only to the Lateran obelisk in Rome. It stands 29.5 metres high and was covered in electrum not only at the pyramidion but also down half its shaft, so that as its inscription tells, "Hatshepsut made as her monument for her father Amun two great obelisks of enduring granite from the south, their upper parts, being of electrum of the best of all lands, seen on the two sides of the river. Their rays flood the two lands when the sun-disc rises between them at its appearance on the horizon of heaven". Step-mother to Tuthmosis III and originally regent to the young Pharaoh, Hatshepsut soon proclaimed herself Pharaoh and relegated Tuthmosis to the shadows for the remainder of her life. He later showed his resentment by chopping out her name wherever he found it, and here at Karnak went to the absurd length of building a now removed sandstone structure around her obelisks to a height of 25 metres.

Obelisks of Hatshepsut

The *Fifth Pylon* was also built by Tuthmosis I and leads almost immediately to the badly ruined *Sixth Pylon,* the smallest of all, built by Tuthmosis II. In the *court* beyond it he erected two tall pink granite pillars. Carved in high relief on their north and south sides are three lilies (south pillar) and three papyrus flower (north pillar), the heraldic plants of Upper and Lower Egypt, beautifully stylised. At the north end of the court are two colossal sandstone statues of Amun and his 'grammatical consort' Amonet in the likeness of Tutankhamun. Further along the main axis of the temple, on the spot where Hatshepsut's Red Chapel once stood (its quartzite blocks engraved with scenes of the procession of the sacred boats are in the 'open air museum'), is the granite *Sanctuary of the Sacred Boats* built by the half-brother of Alexander the Great. The interior decorations in bas-relief and the exterior ones in sunk relief are finely worked and vividly coloured in yellow, red and blue. High though the standard is, however, its mock-traditional Egyptian terms were adopted by the Ptolemies for political expedience and are sadly inferior to the terms governing the greatest period of Greek art only 100 years before.

The Sanctuary

On the north side of the sanctuary, where there was much rebuilding, a *wall* erected by Hatshepsut was found concealed behind a later wall of Tuthmosis III, thus preserving the original freshness of its colouring. The wall has now been removed to a nearby room, and shows Amun, his flesh painted red and with one foot in front of the other, and also Amun in the guise of ithyphallic Min, a harvest god often amalgamated with Amun, his flesh painted black. The wall of Tuthmosis, known as the *Wall of Records,* was erected after the battle of Megiddo (Armageddon) in northern Palestine, fought in April 1479 BC. Breasted wrote of Tuthmosis that "he was the first to build an empire in any real sense; he was the first world-hero. He made, not only a world-wide impression upon his age, but an impression of a new order". Modern political history, insofar as it tells the story of territorial imperialism, began that April day when Tuthmosis, instead of destroying his enemies, organised the vanquished into agencies of tribute and annually recorded on this wall the share that was due to Amun.

Walls of Hatshepsut and Tuthmosis III

The original temple

The open space beyond the sanctuary marks the site of the original *Middle Kingdom temple* (10), its plan suggested by the remaining alabaster foundation stones.

Festival Temple of Tuthmosis III

To the east of the original temple is the *Festival Temple of Tuthmosis III* (11), and running north-south within it the Festival Hall of many columns and pillars where Tuthmosis celebrated his jubilees, those reinvigorations of temporal power and divine spirit (see Saqqara). The pillars form a rectangular cloister around a central and taller colonnade. The two rows of ten columns are unique in Egypt, affecting the form of tent poles or upturned tree trunks (as in Minoan Crete), broader above than below. The capitals, like bells or inverted calyxes, are incised and painted in patterns of overlapping leaves or of vertical stripes. The architectural suggestion is of an outdoor tent or, as echoed in stone at the Heb-Sed Court at Saqqara, of a temporary timbered building. Early in the Christian era the hall was converted into a church, and the occasional haloed saint may be discerned on its columns.

A chamber at the southwest corner of the hall contained, until taken to the Louvre, the *Table of Karnak,* a list of 57 predecessors of Tuthmosis. It is probable that statues of ancient pharaohs carried in procession were also kept here. From the northwest corner of the hall, an antechamber leads into a corridor lined with fine *reliefs* of Tuthmosis in the presence of Amun. Without the hall but in the northeast area of the Festival Temple is a small room with four papyrus bundle columns with bud capitals still supporting the architraves, though the roof is gone. This is popularly known as the *Botanic Garden* for its bas-reliefs of plants and animals seen in and perhaps brought from Syria by Tuthmosis.

Towards the east enclosure wall

A footbridge leads east across the remains of *enclosure walls,* and against this wall, on the axis of the main temple, is a *counter-temple* (12) facing east. Beyond this is the *east gateway* (13) to the Karnak complex, set in an outer wall of mud brick and built by Nectanebo I (XXX Dyn). From the avenue of rams before the First Pylon to this gateway, it is half a kilometre. Before exploring the breadth of the complex, have a look at the two structures standing between the counter-temple and the east gateway. The one to the east is a ruined *portico* (14) built by the same Taharka who built the kiosk in the Great Court; he placed similar structures at the north and south ends of the site, so covering the four cardinal points. Adjacent to this to the west is a small *temple* (15) built by Tuthmosis III. On the centre line of this temple is a large square base on which once stood the world's largest obelisk, the *Lateran obelisk* in Rome.

The Lateran obelisk

It was a considerable achievement for the French to get the 22.5-metre high obelisk of Ramses II from the Temple of Luxor to the Place de la Concorde in the 1830s, yet the giant 32.2-metre obelisk that stood at this small temple at Karnak was removed by order of the Emperor Constantine in the 4th C. AD, consigned originally to Constantinople but having its course changed upon the Emperor's death and delivered to Rome instead where it was erected in the Circus Maximus in AD 357. It fell or more probably was toppled some centuries later, but in 1588 was re-erected in the Piazza San Giovanni in Laterano. Hieroglyphs on its shaft state that Tuthmosis III "made as his monument for his father Amun-Re, Lord of the Thrones of the Two Lands, the setting up for him of a single obelisk in the Upper Court of the Temple in the neighbourhood of Karnak, on the very first occasion of setting up a single obelisk in Thebes". It is stressed that the erection of a single obelisk was unusual, and it is probable that the Lateran obelisk comes from the same quarry of pink granite as that in which the great unfinished obelisk at Aswan still lies, and that the unfinished obelisk, until faults in the stone were discovered, was intended to complete the pair.

North complex area: the Temple of Ptah and the Precinct of Mont

The Temple of Ptah and the Precinct of Mont at the north end of the Karnak complex are reached by a winding path that leads from the north wall of the Great Court of the Temple of Amun. The ground is overgrown and barely excavated. Against the north enclosure wall and shaded by palms, the *Temple of Ptah* (16) is approached through an east-west series of five doorways. If the inner doorway is locked, call to what looks like a sentry tower atop the mud brick wall. Shout. The keeper is probably asleep and will have to put on his galabiya before coming down to let you in. Each of the doorways is carved with scenes and texts of the Ptolemaic period. The fifth doorway leads into a columned vestibule; to the rear is a small pylon marking the entrance to the temple proper. Beyond the antechamber are three chapels dating from the reign of Tuthmosis III, and most unusually the cult statue of Ptah (with head missing) is still in the middle chapel; while in the chapel to the right is the startling apparition of Sekhmet, her bare-breasted body surmounted by the head of a lioness. The keeper will close the doors to enhance the eerie effect of the single shaft of sunlight from an aperture in the roof casting a greenish glow within.

A gateway (also often locked) leads through the enclosure wall to the *Precinct of Mont* (17), god of war, its structures largely dilapidated and only of specialist interest. The main temple, totally ruined, was built by Amenophis III.

The south complex area

Exploration of the south end of the Karnak complex can begin at the *Sacred Lake,* recently restored and cemented. A grandstand at its east end is where visitors sit for the culmination of the *son et lumiere.* Near the northwest corner is a giant *scarab* dedicated by Amenophis III to Atum, the god of the rising sun. Also here is the base with underground chambers of an *Osireion* (18) built by Taharka, and the broken-off top of Hatshepsut's other *obelisk* (19). On the pyramidion a kneeling Hatshepsut is being blessed by Amun: his figure was recut by Seti I within the gouge caused by Akhenaton's attempt to obliterate the god of his priestly opponents.

At the south ends of the Third and Fourth Pylons of the Temple of Amun begins the second (north-south) axis of the Karnak complex, a *processional way* consisting of a series of open courts bounded by walls along their east and west sides and separated from each other by pylons. The Seventh and

Eighth Pylons led originally to a Middle Kingdom temple and a temple of Amenophis I which both stood in what is now the Court of the Cachette. The temples were taken down by Tuthmosis III, but not before he had erected the Seventh Pylon. A large votive pit in the *Court of the Cachette* (20) was excavated early this century and found to contain several thousand bronze statues and 800 of stone. The best are on display in the Cairo Museum.

Considerable restoration work is being carried out along the north-south axis and the pylons may be closed off to the public. Nevertheless, the keepers will not hesitate to show you around for some baksheesh, and will lead you up the inner stairways to the tops of the pylons, or encourage you to follow them as they leap like goats across deep gaps in the towers and walls.

The Seventh Pylon

Seven *statues of Middle Kingdom pharaohs* stand or sit before the north face of the Seventh Pylon, while on its south side are the remains of two *colossi of Tuthmosis III.* On the outside of the east wall between this and the Eighth Pylon is an interesting *relief of the High Priest Amenophis,* his arms raised as though adoring Ramses IX (XX Dyn), who extends his palm in a reciprocal gesture. The very presence of the High Preist, adoring or not, is unusual, but it is revealing that the priest is as large as the Pharaoh and is even the focus of the composition. The relief is a vivid illustration of how much priestly power and arrogance had grown within a century after the reign of the great Ramses II.

The Eighth, Ninth and Tenth Pylons

The *Eighth Pylon* was built by Hatshepsut and, though the oldest part of the north-south axis, is well preserved. On its south side a relief shows Amenophis II slaughtering his enemies, while of the original six colossi on this side of the pylon, four remain, the figure of Amenophis I, on the left, the most complete. The *Ninth and Tenth Pylons* were built by Horemheb in part with blocks from buildings erected by Akhenaton in honour of Aton. In front of the north side of the west tower is a stele erected by Horemheb proclaiming the restoration of the Amun orthodoxy. On the east side of the court between the Ninth and Tenth Pylons is a small *temple* built by Amenophis II, probably for his jubilee, with a graceful portico of square pillars. The fine bas-reliefs inside the hall, some of their colouring well preserved, show Amenophis before various deities. On the *interior wall of the court* between this temple and the Tenth Pylon, Horemheb is shown in relief leading captives from Punt bearing gifts for the Theban triad, and to the right of this he appears with fettered Syrian captives. Both claims of foreign triumph are almost certainly false, at best mere conventions, for Horemheb is known to have spent most of his energies imposing law, order and the old religion on post-Amarna Egypt, while there is no evidence at all that he led his armies abroad.

The Precinct of Mut

From the Tenth Pylon an *avenue of sphinxes* (21) runs for several hundred metres to the *Precinct of Mut,* still not entirely excavated and all the more picturesque for its ruins rising from the overgrown scrub. Consort of Amun and originally a vulture goddess, Mut was depicted during the New Kingdom with the skin of a vulture on her wig. Approached through a propylaeum cut with Ptolemaic cartouches, her badly ruined temple, built by Amenophis III, consists of two courts, a hypostyle hall and sanctuary. All around it, rising from the scrub, are figures of Sekhmet, the lion goddess, beautifully worked and with care taken to use the pink veins in the bluish granite to highlight certain features such as the *ankh* sign or the goddess's breasts. A *sacred lake* enwraps the temple and across it, to the west, is a temple of Ramses III. Another temple, of Amenophis III, is in the northeast corner of the precinct.

The Temples of Khonsu and Opet

But still within the main Karnak enclosure, in the south west corner, is the *Temple of Khonsu* (22), the moon god son of Mut and Amun. It faces south towards the Gateway of Euergetes and so towards the avenue of rams which disappears beneath village houses before emerging again before the entrance pylon of the Temple of Luxor. For the most part in a good state of preservation, its simplicity and clarity of layout make it a classic of New Kingdom architecture. It was started by Ramses III, though possibly completed and certainly almost entirely decorated by his successors down to Herihor (XXI Dyn), who like Horemheb rose from the army to seize power as Pharaoh, and went one better by making himself High Priest of Amun as well. The pylon is small but well proportioned, and decorated with a variety of religious scenes. On the rear wall of the first court, to the right, is a carving of the temple facade, banners flying. To the left is Herihor performing rites before the boats of the Theban triad. Beyond this is a small transverse hypostyle hall leading to the dilapidated sanctuary. Walking through its centre chapel once containing the sacred boat of Khonsu, you come to a small hall of four columns with reliefs of Ramses IV, but also, on either side of the entrance, Augustus. From the southeast corner of the sanctuary a staircase leads up to the roof, from which there are good views of the ruins.

Immediately to the west is the smaller *Temple of Opet* (23), a hippopotamus goddess and mother of Osiris. It was left unfinished by Eurgetes II, though otherwise finely decorated throughout the Ptolemaic period and into the reign of Augustus.

You can now leave the Karnak site through the *Gateway of Euergetes I* (24), its concave cornice adorned with a winged sun disc.

Visiting the West bank

Because of the intense heat of the afternoon, it is usual to cross over to the west bank of the Nile very early in the morning and to complete your explorations by about one o'clock. If you do not mind the heat, there is no reason not to stay until the tombs close at 4 o'clock. Certainly you will have fewer fellow tourists to contend with, and if pedalling your own bicycle the breeze and dry air will evaporate the heat away. The disadvantage of a bicycle is the long incline to the Valley of the Kings, and then not being able to walk over the escarpment and down to Deir el Bahri, the Temple of Hatshepsut. So that expedition is best done by car: the driver will leave you at the Valley of the Kings and collect you later at Hatshepsut's temple. All the rest of the west bank should be covered by bicycle if you are up to it; it leaves time on your hands and frees you from the impatient harrassment of your driver. Distances can be long and donkeys are recommended only for those seeking the perversely picturesque.

Speaking of which, I do recommend Mohammed Aboudi's *Guide Book,* on sale at Aboudi's shop along the corniche, though I fear Aboudi himself, a former Cook's dragoman, has long since joined his ancestors. The book is near to useless and vastly entertaining. It contains "a few useful phrases" such as "Open your eyes!" *(Iftah enek!)* and "Hold your tongue!" *(Iskut!),* and also liberal helpings of Aboudi's own poetry.

> O East is East and West is West in Luxor or in London town;
> But Aboudi, our faithful Aboudi, will never let us down.
> Through all the plagues of Egypt, donkey-boys, the flies, the sand,
> This trusty modern Moses leads us toward the Promised Land.
> Weird tales of long dead ages come tripping from his tongue,
> With him through tombs and temples we pass in wondering throng.
> And when foot and brain are weary with the sights we've come to see,
> He calls our patient donkeys up to bear us home to tea.

Surely in future ages the tourists all will stand,
An unabridged edition of Rosetta in each hand,
And read the hieroglyphics which proclaim how
Pharaoh's Cook,
By his henchman, great Aboudi, mighty hosts
through Egypt took!

o o o

There's one thing more, if you can stick it:
The law of this land is very intricate.
At each temple gate is an Arab picket,
So please don't forget your little ticket;
And galloping donkeys is not allowed!

Ferries, and car and donkey hire

Before leaving the east bank, it is a good idea to ask at Thomas Cook or one of the other travel offices about the going rate for car and donkey hire on the other side to prepare yourself for the bargaining that is about to come. The 'tourist ferries' leave from the corniche opposite the main hotels and disembark you at the ticket kiosk downstream on the west bank. If you take what the locals call the 'people ferry', you will be landed near a village a bit upstream from the kiosk. Either way, you will have to decide as soon as you land what tombs and temples you want to see and purchase the appropriate tickets by the river bank: you cannot buy them at the sites. While you are doing this, you will be accosted by every car driver and donkey-boy in sight. Strike what you know to be a fair bargain, and do not pay until your visit is complete.

Outline of the tour

A tour of the necropolis involves following a north-south arc, starting at either end. If you want to follow the path from the Valley of the Kings to Deir el Bahri, you should start at the north, visiting first the Temple of Seti I, continuing thence to the Valley of the Kings, Deir el Bahri, the Tombs of the Nobles, the Ramesseum, the Valley of the Queens, Medinet Habu and back to the river via the Colossi of Memnon. This guide describes the tour in that order.

And dangers enroute

While not wishing to inhibit the curiosity of travellers, it is worth mentioning that on either side of the river here, as at Saqqara, care should be taken at excavations and you should not get off the beaten track if exploring on your own. I cite a recent newspaper report: "The mystery of a Canadian woman's disappearance 2 years ago at Luxor was unravelled this week when police located her remains in an archaeological ditch. Before dying she had scribbled on a postcard that she fell inside the labyrinth after losing her way, and she was preparing herself for death from thirst and hunger. The police located her skeleton this week, her clothes still on, in a distant area behind the pharaonic temples where archaeological digs were underway".

The village of Gurna

From the west bank landing stage the road runs to the new village of Gurna and continues on past the Colossi of Memnon towards the Theban Mountain. At the village another road runs north towards the Temple of Seti I. Built in the late 1940s, the new village, with plumbing, theatre and recreation centre, was designed to lure the modern Thebans down from their old village of Gurna spread across the nobles' tombs. Until recently, all enticement failed, and even now only ill is spoken of new Gurna. Constructed in the traditional way out of mud brick, the houses fall down and are infested with scarabs say the villagers. Nor are they as cool in summer as the rock tombs which serve as convenient extensions to many of the older houses. It seems the familiar argument between new and old, but there is a twist. Over the past 3000 years or more, easy access to the Theban tombs has provided villagers on the west bank with an extra source of income. It was partly to check this that the new village was built, and for this same reason that new Gurna is so much resented. Old Gurna at the foot of the Theban Mountain has not yet been entirely abandoned, nor entirely has been tomb robbing.

Modern tomb robbing

There are a least 900 tombs built into the rock. The authorities say all have been checked and locked. But there are constant rumours of secret finds beneath the houses and even the wall paintings in known tombs are occasionally removed. The modern heydey for tomb robbers was a century ago with the explosion in Europe and America of archaeological and tourist interest in ancient Egypt. Luxor saw a roaring trade in tablets, statuettes and scarabs, both real and faked – home-made scarabs were fed to turkeys to "acquire by the simple process of digestion a degree of venerableness that is really charming", wrote one visitor. Mummies were dragged out of their tombs and unrolled, stripped of their valuables, broken up and left to crumble in the sands. In earlier centuries, mummy cases were chopped up for firewood, and from at least the 13th C. through to the 19th C. 'mummy' was highly regarded in Europe for its medicinal properties, the export demand sometimes proving so great that Egyptians often substituted modern corpses. In *The Innocents Abroad,* Mark Twain wrote of the Egyptian railways: "The fuel they use for the locomotive is composed of mummies three thousand years old, purchased by the ton or by the graveyard for that purpose. ...Sometimes one hears the profane engineer call out pettishly, 'Damn these plebeians, they don't burn worth a cent – pass out a king' ".

Not that the humble quest for loot has always been without its larger benefits, or that even the poorest Egyptians have not sometimes shown respect for the objects of their peculations. In an effort to save their royal masters from contemporary tomb robbers, priests in the XXI Dynasty removed the mummies from their tombs in the Valley of the Kings and stacked them, 30 in a shaft, in a nearby rocky cleft. In 1875, Abdel-Rasul, sheikh of Gurna, found the cache and kept it secret for six years, selling off bits and pieces as he needed money. Archaeologists traced these clues to their source, and the mummies are now those on display in the Mummy Room of the Cairo Museum. As these long-dead Pharaohs sailed down the Nile by steamer, fellahin lined the banks at village after village, the women ululating in lament, the men firing their rifles in homage.

A case of looting in pharaonic times

Under the powerful Pharaohs of the XVIII and XIX Dynasties local officials were closely supervised and tomb looting kept in check. But under the weaker rulers of the XX Dynasties were robbed. A picture of surprising detail can be built up from surviving papyri of the necropolis workers enduring food shortages and late payments of wages, of riots, pay disputes and strikes. There are also documented accounts of bribery and collusion amongst workers, priests and officials. One papyrus describes a major Theban law case during the reign of Ramses IX (XX Dyn) in which the mayor of Thebes brought to the vizier's attention stories of tomb robbing at the necropolis. The matter was investigated by the chief of the necropolis police and the stories denied; the vizier then ensured that the mayor of Thebes was disgraced for making malicious and politically inspired accusations. Some years later, however, as the tomb robbings continued, the case was reopened and it became clear that both the vizier and the chief of police were up to their eyeballs in corruption. Examined by birch and screw, the stonemason Amun-pa-nefer admitted tunnelling into a royal tomb and stripping the Pharaoh and his Queen of gold, silver and precious stones. "And we made the gold which we had found on these two gods - from their mummies, amulets, ornaments and coffins - into eight shares. And two kilos of gold fell to each of us."

Amun-pa-nefer then described the chain of corruption: "We then crossed over to Thebes. And after some days, the agents of Thebes heard that we had been stealing in the west, so they arrested me and imprisoned me at the mayor of Thebes' place. So I took the two kilos of gold that had fallen to me as my share, and gave them to Kha-em-Opet, the District Clerk of the harbour of Thebes. He let me go, and I joined my companions, and they made up for me another share. And I, as well as the other robbers who are with me, have continued to this day in the practice of robbing the tombs of the nobles and people of the land who rest in the west of Thebes. And a large number of the men of the land rob them also". Presumably the bribe was shared out amongst other officials higher up the ladder, though no share falling to the mayor of Thebes who was either an honest man or complained because he was being cut out of the action.

The case has its anecedotal interest, but it throws light too on the causes underlying the enfeeblement of the New Kingdom from the XX Dynasty on. In describing Karnak it was mentioned how an ever greater proportion of the nation's wealth went to the priesthood; much gold and silver was also literally buried underground in the tombs, taken out of circulation. Yet it was precisely at this time that the world was shifting from the Bronze Age to the Iron Age, and while Egypt had copper mines, she had no iron – the essential metal for weapon superiority. Under the Empire, iron could be expropriated abroad; as the rule of the Pharaohs weakened and the Empire shrank, Egypt was forced to buy iron abroad, payment to be made in gold and silver. The value of these precious metals rose during the period 1160 to 1110 BC (Ramses V through Ramses X, approximately). Food shortages and wage delays followed; the necropolis workers struck and many of them turned to tomb robbing. The bonanza of precious metals and stones they clawed back from the tombs and put into circulation – however corrupt the channels might have been – soon relieved the situation. By that time, however, the Empire was finished, the moral authority of the administration had been sapped, and power fell to Herihor, a general who became military dictator, assumed the High Priesthood of Amun and made himself Pharaoh and founder of the XXI Dynasty. His power extended only over Upper Egypt however, Lower Egypt was ruled by merchant princes at Tanis and the country was never long united again.

Iron Age economic crisis

Even moreso than Karnak, the tombs and mortuary temples of the Theban necropolis tell of the rise and fall of the New Kingdom and the Egyptian Empire.

Mortuary Temple of Seti I

The Temple of Seti I (XIX Dyn) lies off the road to the Valley of the Kings and is usually bypassed by tourists in haste. This in itself should recommend it; also that the works of Seti's reign – most famously his temple at Abydos – are amongst the finest and most restrained of the New Kingdom. The temple was founded in honour of Amun, but also devoted to the worship of Seti's father, Ramses I. The first two pylons and courts have been destroyed; what remains is the temple proper and a tour of it is made both at ground level and, the better to see certain reliefs, by leaping goatlike after the resident guide, from architrave to broken architrave.

A colonnade facing east towards the Nile admits, through a central door, to a hypostyle hall with six columns decorated with reliefs of Seti and Ramses II making offerings to divinities. On either side of the hall are small chapels with very fine reliefs of Seti, his ka, his sacred boat, Thoth and Osiris, as he offers sacrifices and performs ceremonies enroute to the afterlife. The sanctuary, once containing Amun's sacred boat, lies beyond. Reliefs show Seti offering incense before the boat. To the left (south) of the hypostyle hall is the chapel of Ramses I. On the side walls of the central chamber, Seti is again depicted offering incense to Amun's boat, and anoints a statue of Ramses I with his finger. The chambers on either side were given inferior reliefs by Ramses II. The right (north) side of the temple is ruinous; a larger hall, dedicated to Re-Herakhte, was built by Ramses II and decorated with crude reliefs.

The obsessive appropriations of Ramses II and their inferior quality stand out amongst the works of Seti I who consciously sought a renaissance in taste and values. But then Seti's own reliefs suffer from the New Kingdom preoccupation with gaining access to the afterlife: they are reassuring encounters with the gods at death, but do not concern themselves with the quality of life. If not yet in empire, certainly in spirit Egypt was in retreat.

To the Valley of the Kings

The flat alluvium suddenly quits and it is utter desert to the Valley of the Kings. On a barren hill where the road from Seti's temple is joined by the road from Deir el Bahri sits a large domed boulder of a house where Howard Carter lived during his search for the tomb of Tutankhamun. The road climbs towards the oven of white sand and sun that is Biban el Muluk – the 'Gates of the Kings'. Unblinking tomb entrances stare vacantly from the close valley walls. Each ramp is cut and swept, each doorway numbered in order of discovery. The most exclusive suburb in the world, where the mightiest dead once lay in silent, motionless expectation of awakening. Anxious priests, covetous archaeologists, and robbers caring more for life than life after, carried them away. Anubis and Osiris remain, paintings on the walls.

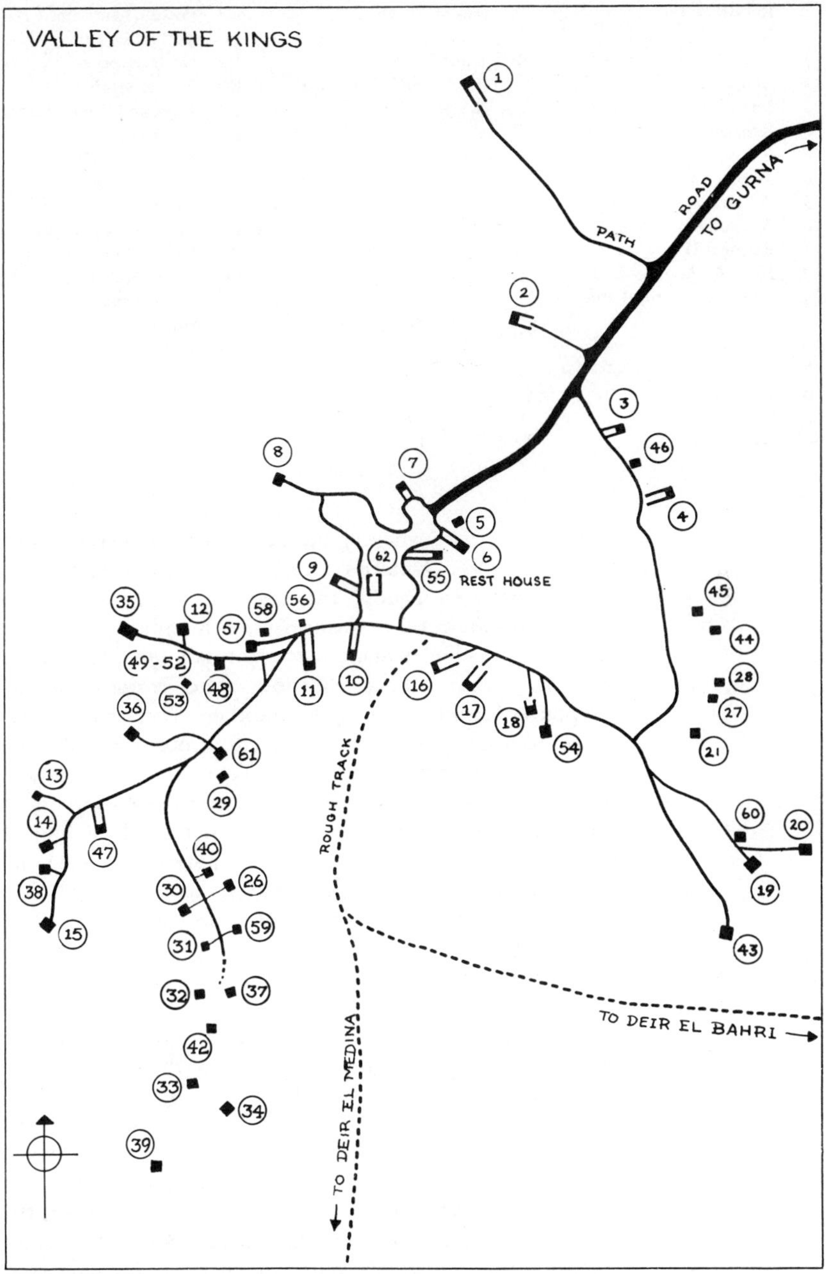

See over for key.

1. Ramses VII
2. Ramses IV
3. Intended for Ramses III
4. Ramses XII
5. Intended for Ramses II
6. Ramses IX
7. Ramses II
8. Merneptah
9. Ramses VI
10. Amenmeses
11. Ramses III
12. No inscriptions
13. Intended for royal functionary
14. Tausert, wife of Seti II
15. Seti II
16. Ramses I
17. Seti I
18. Ramses X
19. Son of Ramses IX
20. Hatshepsut
21. Unfinished
22. Amenophis III (in the Western Valley)
23. Ay (in the Western Valley)
24 & 25. No inscriptions (in the Western Valley)
26 to 33 Unfinished
34. Tuthmosis III
35. Amenophis II
36. Maherpra, fan-bearer to Hatshepsut (contents in Cairo Museum)
37. No inscriptions
38. Tuthmosis I
39 to 41. No inscriptions
42. Possibly Tuthmosis II
43. Tuthmosis IV
44. No inscription
45. Private tomb
46. Yuya and Tuyu, parents of Queen Tiy, wife of Amenophis III (contents in Cairo Museum).
47. Siptah
48. Vizier Amenemopet
49 to 54 No inscriptions
55. Tiy or Smenkhkare
56. No inscriptions
57. Horemheb
58. Tutankhamun annex
59 to 61 No inscriptions
62. Tutankhamun

Burials at the Valley of the Kings date from the XVIII through the XX Dynasties, with Tuthmosis I being the first to select the site. Though the Pharaohs and, rarely, certain exalted but non-royal personages were entombed here, offerings to the dead were made at the mortuary temples built on the plain. The tombs therefore were entirely private receptacles for the sarcophagus, and their decoration concentrated exclusively on the formulae efficacious in transferring the deceased from this world into the next. The tombs and their decorations can be impressive, and their contents of course were staggering, but they do not speak of life, of humanity, or even of personal death and resurrection – they are monuments of state and of ideology, and less vivid, less revealing than the tombs of the lesser dead elsewhere in the Theban necropolis.

Tomb construction and decoration

A similar pattern of construction and decoration is followed in each of the tombs. Three corridors lead to an antechamber giving onto the main hall with its sunken floor for receiving the sarcophagus. The tombs were cut into the soft limestone by two teams of 25 men working alternating ten-day shifts. They normally lived at Deir el Medina, but when on shift stayed in huts within the valley. Construction of a tomb began at the beginning of a reign and never took more than six years to completion. Once the interior surfaces were prepared, the designs and inscriptions were sketched in black; the designs filled in, the hieroglyphs outlined, in red; the decorations carved and finally painted. In some tombs, notably that of Horemheb (57), these various stages of decoration are evident.

Decorative themes The dead Pharaoh, absorbed in the sun god, sailed through the underworld at night in a boat, with enemies and dangers to be avoided along the way. This is the recurrent theme of the decorations, the inscriptions being extensive quotations from the Amduat or Book of the Underworld and the Book of the Gates which provide instructions for charting the course. Pictorially, there are three registers, the middle one showing the river of passage, the top and bottom registers depicting the shores with their inhabitants of deities and demons. The registers are divided into 12 sections for the 12 hours of the night. The Book of Day and Night is also sometimes employed: after this nocturnal voyage the naked body of the goddess Nut gives birth each morning to the sun. This is beautifully represented in the sarcophagus hall of the tomb of Ramses VI.

Visiting the tombs In all, 62 tombs are known in the Valley of the Kings. A few of these were known and visited by tourists in Ptolemaic times as indicated by Diodorus and Strabo and the occasional Greek and Latin grafitti. Most are of little interest except to scholars and are closed to the public. Only tombs 6, 8, 9, 11, 16, 17, 35, 57 and 62 have electric lighting, and most visitors will be content to see those of *Tutankhamun (62), Ramses VI (9)* and *Seti I (17),* and then possibly the tombs of *Amenophis II (35)* and *Horemheb (57).* Not all of even these tombs will necessarily be open when you visit. The identity of all 62 tombs is given on the accompanying map, but only those electrically lit are described below.

Tomb 6: Ramses IX (XX Dyn). A flight of steps on either side of an inclined plane leads you down to the tomb door, its lintel decorated with the solar disc, the Pharaoh worshipping it on both sides. Behind him stands Isis (left) and Nephthys (right). The tomb is of near-model design: three corridors, an antechamber, but then a pillared hall and short passage before the final sarcophagus chamber. The decorations are similar to those in Tomb 9.

Tomb 8: Merneptah (XIX Dyn). Pharaoh of the Exodus, Merneptah's tomb descends steeply through corridor steps. Such descents are typical of XVIII and XIX Dynasty tombs; those of the XX Dynasty are shallower. Over the entrance, Isis and Nephthys worship the sun disc, while the entrance corridors are decorated with scenes from the Book of the Gates and other texts. In the small antechamber is the huge granite lid of the outer sarcophagus; a further flight of steps leads down to a pillared hall with barrelled roof containing the pink granite lid of the inner sarcophagus. Carved on the lid is the recumbent figure of Merneptah as Osiris.

Tomb 9: Ramses VI (XX Dyn). Though decorated in sunk relief of workmanship inferior to that of the previous dynasty, the colouring remains fresh. The tomb was originally constructed for Ramses V and ended with *Chamber E.* On the left walls of this part of the tomb is the complete text of the Book of the Gates with a summary of the creation of the world on the left part of the rear wall of *E.* Another text, the Book of Caverns, decorates the right walls, while the ceilings of *C, D* and *E* are decorated with the Book of Day and Night. *Corridors F and G* show the hours from the Amduat on their walls. In *Chamber H* are portions of the Book of the Dead; on the left wall is chapter 125, the declaration of innocence. The pillared *Chamber I* contains fragments of the great granite sarcophagus. Its vaulted ceiling is splendidly painted with the Book of Day and Night, the sky goddess Nut appearing twice, back to back, framing the Book of Day on the entrance side, and on the far side the Book of Night.

Ramses VI

Tomb 11: Ramses III (XX Dyn). One of the largest tombs in the valley, the second half is ruinous and not illuminated. Once again the decorations are inferior sunk relief, but they are exceptionally varied and remain freshly coloured. This is sometimes called the 'Harpers' Tomb' after the two harpers playing to divinities in the last of four small chambers opening off the left-hand side of the second corridor. This tomb is unique in having ten side-chambers off its entrance corridors; where they do occur in tombs, they were for receiving tomb furniture.

Tomb 16: Ramses I (XIX Dyn). Though founder of his dynasty, Ramses I reigned for only a year or two and was interred in a simple tomb. A sloping corridor and steep flight of steps leads to a single almost square chamber containing the open sarcophagus. The decoration – painted, not carved – is brilliantly coloured on grey ground. The Pharaoh is variously shown with Maat, Ptah, Osiris, Anubis and other deities, and portions of the Book of the Gates are depicted (on the left wall, notice the 12 goddesses representing the hours of the night).

Tomb 17: Seti I (XIX Dyn). At 100 metres, this is the longest tomb in the valley. Its reliefs are wonderfully preserved and so beautifully executed that they rival the famous decorations in Seti's temple at Abydos. Beneath a ceiling painted with vultures flying towards the back of the tomb, the walls of *Corridor A* are decorated on the left with Seti before the falcon-headed Re-Herakhte, god of the morning sun. The sun in other forms, as disc, scarab and ram-headed god follows, and the text of the Sun Litany continues on the right wall. This and other texts are continued in *Corridor B* with staircase. On

Seti I

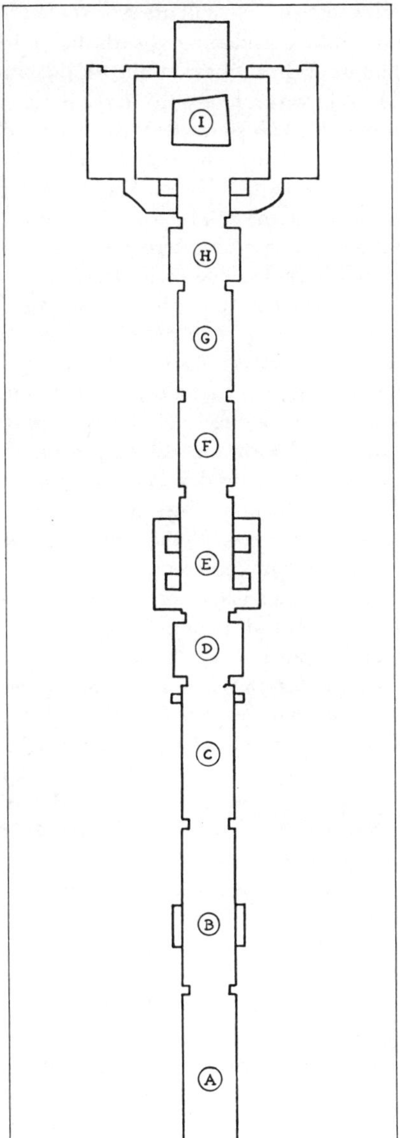
I
H
G
F
E
D
C
B
A
TOMB 9:
RAMSES VI

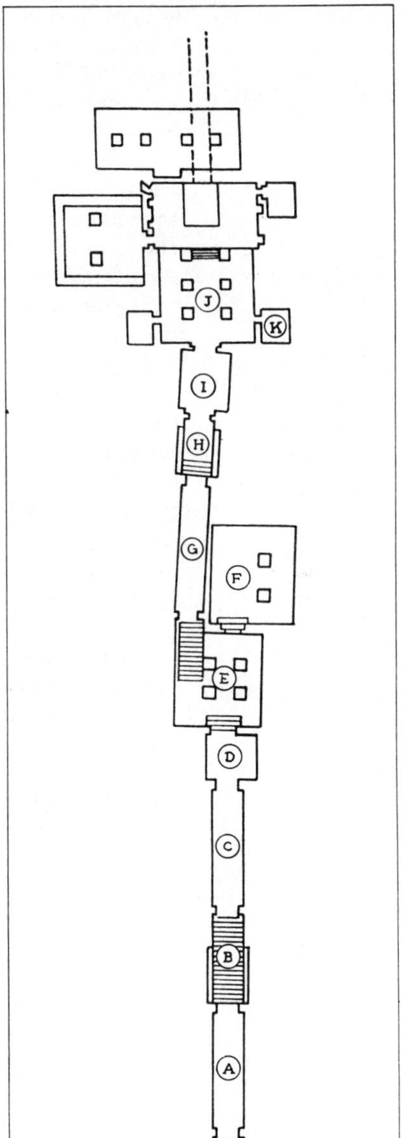
J
K
I
H
G
F
E
D
C
B
A
TOMB 17:
SETI I

the upper part of the recess in the left wall are represented 37 forms of the sun god. *Corridor C* is decorated with the fourth (right) and fifth (left) hours of the night from the Amduat. In *Chamber D* the Pharaoh is shown on four walls in the presence of various deities. *Chambers E and F* show the Pharaoh on each side of the square pillars with a deity. The wall decorations are various hours from the Book of the Gates. The pattern of construction and decoration of the tomb so far is now in a general sense repeated, with *G, H* and *I* corresponding to *B, C* and *D. Corridors G and H* are decorated with the Ritual of the Opening of the Mouth which ensured that the mummy's organs were functioning, particularly to permit eating and drinking. The decorations in *Chamber I* are similar to those in *D. Chamber J* is in two parts, the first a pillared hall with hours from the Book of the Gates on the walls, the second with the Amduat on the walls and astronomical figures on the vaulted ceiling. The sarcophagus rested in the depression in this second part; a passage behind runs for 46 metres, apparently to nowhere. A side room, *K,* to the right, is known as the Chamber of the Cow for its representation of the sky goddess Nut in the form of a cow. The texts here recount the myth of the destruction of mankind, the Egyptian equivalent of the Mesopotamian and Biblical story of the Flood.

Tomb 35: Amenophis II (XVIII Dyn). Discovered and opened by the French during Napoleon's expedition, this tomb is unadorned except for the sarcophagus chamber, approached by a long corridor and steep flights of steps. A shaft at *A* is crossed by a modern gangway leading to *Chamber B* with unfinished walls. The walls of the Sarcophagus *Chamber C* are painted yellow in imitation of papyrus and bear the complete text of the Amduat as though inscribed on a continuous scroll. The blue ceiling is painted with yellow stars. Amenophis' mummy was found *in situ,* a floral garland still round its neck, and was only removed to the Cairo Museum in 1934. The quartzite sarcophagus was left in the tomb. Three mummies were found in side room *D,* and nine royal mummies, hidden there by priests, were found in room *E.* These last included Tuthmosis IV, Amenophis III and Seti II, now all in the Cairo Museum.

Tomb 57: Horemheb (XVIII Dyn.) The plan is almost identical to that of Tomb 17 (Seti I) and some of the decorations are finely executed. The principal interest, however, is in the partially finished work, showing the various stages of decoration.

Tomb 62: Tutankhamun (XVIII Dyn). This most famous of Egyptian tombs is neither large nor impressively decorated. It

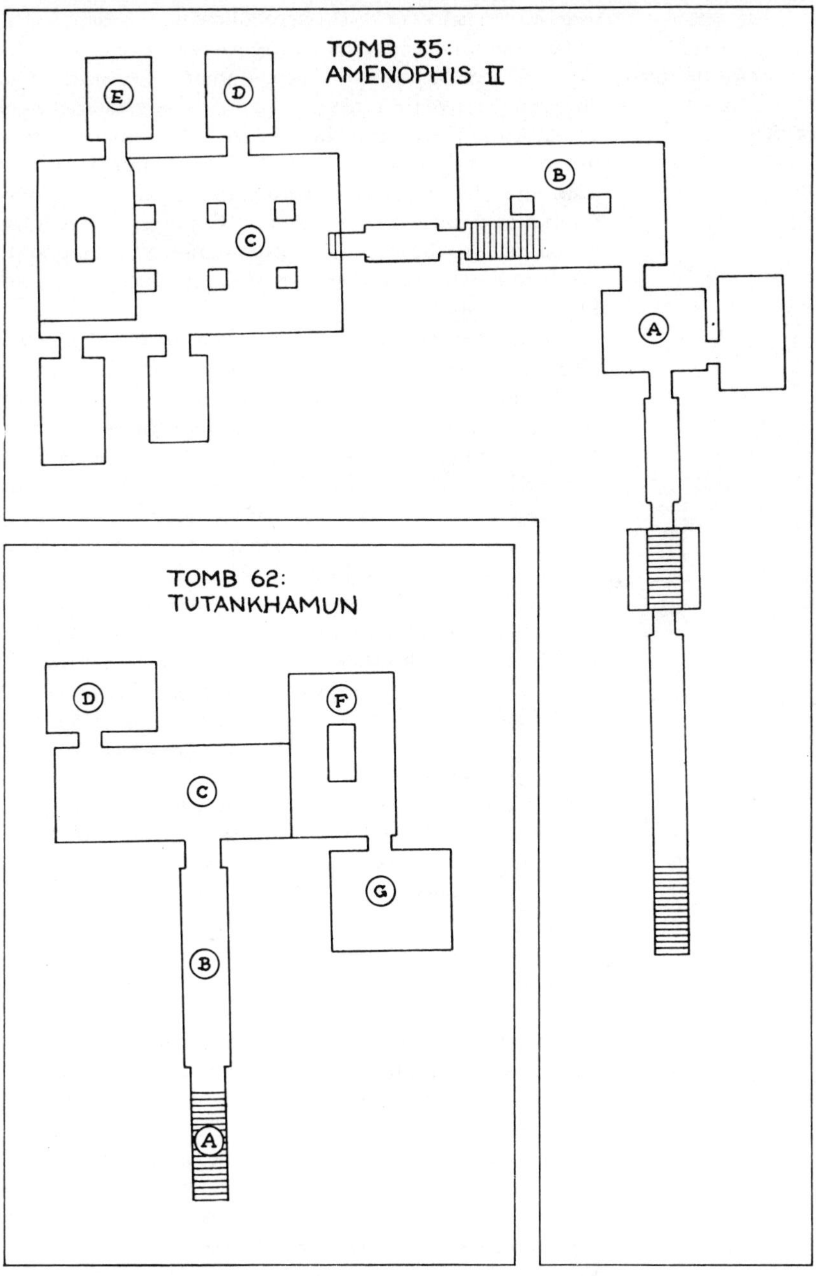
TOMB 35:
AMENOPHIS II
E
D
B
C
A
TOMB 62:
TUTANKHAMUN
D
F
C
G
B
A

bears all the marks of hasty burial following the early death of Tutanhkamun in about his nineteenth year. Even its fabulous contents, seen by millions of people around the world, cannot have compared to the funerary treasures of far greater pharaohs entombed in the valley. This relative lack of importance of a briefly reigning puppet pharaoh of the Amun priesthood's counterrevolution probably assisted in the long secrecy of the tomb's existence and whereabouts. Also, nearly above it, was the entrance to the grander tomb of Ramses VI (Tomb 9), the debris from which early on covered the entrance to the young Pharaoh's tomb.

Tutankhamun

The tomb was discovered on 4 November 1922 by Howard Carter and opened by him and his patron Lord Carnarvon on 26 November in the presence of experts from New York's Metropolitan Museum of Art – or so the official story went. But in a last great irony in the history of looting at the Valley of the Kings it has recently been revealed by Thomas Hoving, ex-director of the Metropolitan Museum, in his book *Tutankhamun, the Untold Story* that between discovery and public entry, Carter and Carnarvon sneaked into the tomb, stole 35 items, and then walled it up again.

The door at the bottom of the entrance stairway *A* was found walled up and sealed with the royal seal. The entrance corridor *B* was found filled with stone debris through which a tunnel had been dug soon after interment in an unsuccessful attempt to rob the tomb. The undecorated *Chambers C, D* (now walled up) *and F* contained most of the funerary objects now on display at the Cairo Museum. *Chamber E,* originally walled off from *C* and at a lower level, contained the four gilded wooden shrines, one inside the other, within which lay the rectangular stone sarcophagus, then three mummiform coffins, the innermost of solid gold, and then finally the mummy of Tutankhamun himself. The wall has now been replaced by a railing beyond which visitors cannot venture.

From here you can view what remains in the tomb: the sarcophagus, the largest of the mummiform coffins within it, and, unseen within that, the badly decayed mummy of Tutankhamun. This chamber was the only one decorated, its paintings betraying signs of haste. On the right wall, the coffin is transported on a sledge. To the rear from right to left, Ay, the young king's successor, performs the rite of the opening of the mouth; Tutankhamun sacrificing to Nut; again the young Pharaoh, this time with his ka, before Osiris. On the left wall is the sun god's boat, while on the all but impossible to see entrance wall, Tutankhamun, accompanied by Anubis and Isis, receives life from the goddess of the West.

You can leave the Valley of the Kings by the road you came, that same ancient road along which the bodies of the Pharaohs were drawn here on sledges. Or you can leave on foot, climbing the path to the right of Tomb 16, opposite the rest house. As it gains the ridge, there is usually a donkey boy waiting but the donkeys should be declined. Almost certainly, a guide will fasten himself on you in hope of baksheesh. He can be useful for those who are not foot sure, but otherwise he is not necessary either. On the ridge, the path divides. One heads south, rising slowly over the mountain; the other runs to the left and level along the ridge. The first leads to Deir el Medina and is the same path the workmen used when returning home from their shift at the tombs. There are sweeping views of the Nile valley, magnificent in the afternoon with the sun in the west. The second path soon creeps high along the edge of the amphitheatre of Deir el Bahri and offers changing angles and elevations of Hatshepsut's temple, and views towards the Nile. You continue along until you are above the old Cook's rest house at Deir el Bahri and then pick your way down, to be met by your driver after visiting the temple. Both walks are highly recommended, but the second (about 30 minutes) is a must for a full appreciation of Hatshepsut's architectural achievement.

Mountain paths to Deir el Medina and Deir el Bahri

Hatshepsut's mortuary temple at Deir el Bahri

The mortuary temple of Hatshepsut at Deir el Bahri is the finest building in Egypt. Elegant, revolutionary, it satisfies and provokes in whole and in detail. Along with the Parthenon, the Taj Mahal, the interiors of Chartres and Hagia Sophia, it is one of the great buildings of the world. Not that the temple has received its fullest due: though far older than the others, it was unknown in modern times until Mariette made preliminary excavations in the third quarter of the 19th C. The temple was only entirely cleared in 1894-96 and since then has undergone sporadic restoration, still in progress today.

Hatshepsut's reign

Interpretation of the events following the death of Tuthmosis I (XVIII Dyn) is marked by controversy amongst archaeologists which mimics, even if it does not rival, the original dynastic struggle played out between Hatshepsut, his daughter, and Tuthmosis III, his grandson. By any interpretation, Hatshepsut emerges as one of the most formidable figures in Egyptian history, only the third woman to rule as queen, the first to rule as king. In the ruthlessness and romance the story implies, and the high policy at stake, parallels between the reigns of Hatshepsut and Elizabeth I easily suggest themselves to the imagination.

Hatshepsut married her father's son and successor, Tuthmosis II, and during the lifetime of her husband her full titles were 'Pharaoh's daughter, Pharaoh's sister, god's wife and Pharaoh's great wife'. But Tuthmosis II died before Hatshepsut could bear him a child, and it was one of her husband's secondary wives who became 'Pharaoh's mother' to Tuthmosis III. But for her sex, Hatshepsut's claim to the throne through her father was at least as good as Tuthmosis III's and through her mother she was descended from the Ahmose family who had thrown the Hyksos out of Egypt. But as Tuthmosis was later to advertise, his future as Pharaoh was proclaimed by no less a god than Amun who while Tuthmosis I was sacrificing at Karnak stood the young prince in the place usually occupied by the sovereign. This conveniently has Tuthmosis III designated heir in the lifetime of his own father, but betrays the more pedestrian likelihood that the priests of Amun eventually sided with the army in its support of Tuthmosis and his imperial designs against Hatshepsut and her party in the civil service who preferred a peaceful domestic policy.

The struggle with Tuthmosis III

Tuthmosis III, when finally he became sole Pharaoh well into his manhood, launched Egypt upon her period of conquest abroad and bloated magnificence at home so often celebrated in stone at Thebes. Yet as powerful a pharaoh and warrior as he was to become, Tuthmosis was no match for Hatshepsut in her prime. In the first few years following her husband's death, Hatshepsut reigned as widow-queen, but she soon took the momentous step of assuming the title of Pharaoh, co-reigning with but entirely overshadowing her stepson. She went so far as to pose and dress as a man – at least on reliefs – and to wear the pharaonic beard. In this way she ruled for about 20 years.

Hatshepsut's favourite, Senmut

Elizabeth I had her Essex; Hatshepsut had her Senmut, a man of modest birth who rose to occupy a score of high offices, including Steward of Amun, probably giving him control over the vast wealth of the Karnak temple, and Minister of Public Works, with the suggestion that he was the architect at Deir el Bahri. As such favourites often do, Senmut overstepped the mark. He used his royal mistress's temple for his own purposes, introducing reliefs of himself in niches that would be concealed behind opening doors, and though building himself a tomb at Gurna, planned secretly to be buried within the great court at Deir el Bahri. Most of his reliefs were hacked out and his sarcophagus smashed, yet in his secret tomb the name of Hatshepsut was left untouched, suggesting the destruction was wrought not by Tuthmosis III, who in malice destroyed so much that was Hatshepsut's, but by Hatshepsut herself in rage at this attempt to extend familiarity into the eternal. The last record of Senmut comes about five years before the end of his mistress's reign. In those last years she was alone.

How Hatshepsut's reign ended is not known. Perhaps she fell victim to a coup d'etat, or merely died a natural death. In any case her inward-looking peace policy was suddenly eclipsed and Tuthmosis III, obliterating her name and her image wherever he found them, within 75 days of her death was leading his army into Palestine.

Conception of Hatshepsut's temple

Into the rugged eastern flank of the Theban Mountain nature has cut an immense amphitheatre facing Thebes. Its sheer golden walls embrace the site like the wings of some mighty hovering solar disc. Just off centre, to the left and rising from the cliffline, is a pyramidal peak. A magnificent backdrop, it invites a performance, and would condemn any but the most brilliant to insignificance before it. The Middle Kingdom Pharaoh Mentuhotep II (XI Dyn) built a temple here; you can see its ruins to the south of Hatshepsut's. What impression it made cannot fairly be judged from its remains. Like Hatshepsut's temple, it rose in terraces but then was surmounted by a pyramid, a Memphite legacy perhaps. Mentuhotep II and III were both entombed here. But a pyramidal structure set against the pyramidal peak seems superfluous, and any structure vying with the cliffs for beight can only have been overwhelmed.

Mentuhotep's temple was already in ruins when 500 years later Hatshepsut was drawn to the holy site. (Whether out of convenience or some similar feeling of awe, Hatshepsut's temple was taken over by early Christians as a monastery: Deir el Bahri, the Northern Monastery). She was obviously influenced by the earlier temple, and in all probability would have replicated it on a larger scale: the foundations suggest a pyramid was intended. One purpose of a pyramid is to protect the tomb, but her father Tuthmosis I had abandoned this idea for the greater security of discreet entombment in the Valley of the Kings. It remained necessary therefore to build only a mortuary temple at which the appropriate ceremonies would be performed. At some point Hatshepsut decided to build wide instead of high.

If it is true that circumstances dictated this decision, or suggested that the alternative was now pointless, it is no less true that the new form was seized upon with conviction and executed with genius. The terraces of Hatshepsut's temple emphasise the stratification of the cliff behind and the line between rock and sky. At the same time, the bold rhythm of the pillared colonnades, vertical shafts of light-reflecting stone framing and contrasting with the shadowed ambulatories, reflect the dark gashes of gullies and fissures in the cliff face itself. Even the peak seems brought into the conception: a pyramid offered by nature. The temple mediates between the wildness of the mountain and the cultivation of the Valley. The power and contradiction of the landscape is gripped and tamed with a confidence and elegance that is breathtaking, and then played throughout the structure so that as you walk round the temple you feel it, never too much, but to a measure that insists on the spiritual nature of man.

Tour of Hatshepsut's temple: the Lower Terrace

The main temple complex may originally have been preceded by a valley temple near the Nile; if so, it has been lost beneath the tilled alluvium. From this temple ran a promenade lined with sphinxes to the *Lower Terrace,* a zone of transition between the profane and the sacred. This was a garden with myrrh trees and fountains, as though a foretaste of that life which endures in the desert of the other world. A pair of lions (the left-hand one survives) stood at the bottom of the ramp leading up to the Middle Terrace and another pair (the right-hand one survives) stood at the top. These were at once guardians of the temple and witnesses to the rising sun, proof of rebirth. *Colonnades* are on either side of the ramp, to the north and to the south. On their pillars are simple devices stating a variation of Hapshepsut's name surmounted by the solar falcon wearing the double crown. Within the colonnades, the retaining walls of the Middle Terrace are decorated with vividly coloured reliefs. Not all of the original courses have survived, and where they have, the decorations have suffered deliberate defacement, first by Tuthmosis III, later by Akhenaton. Representations of Amun were restored at the counter-revolution, but Hatshepsut remains obliterated; the Pharaoh seen is Tuthmosis III, who, as co-ruler, had been included in the original decorations. The carvings within the *North Colonnade* depict an idealised country life, continuing the theme established by the gardens of the Lower Terrace. Of the greatest delicacy are the scenes (right) of water birds being

1. Lower Terrace
2. Colonnades
3. Lower ramp
4. Middle Terrace
5. Birth Colonnade
6. Chapel of Anubis
7. Punt Colonnade
8. Chapel of Hathor
9. Upper ramp
10. Upper Terrace
11. Sanctuary of Amun
12. Sanctuary of Hatshepsut
13. Sancturary of the Sun

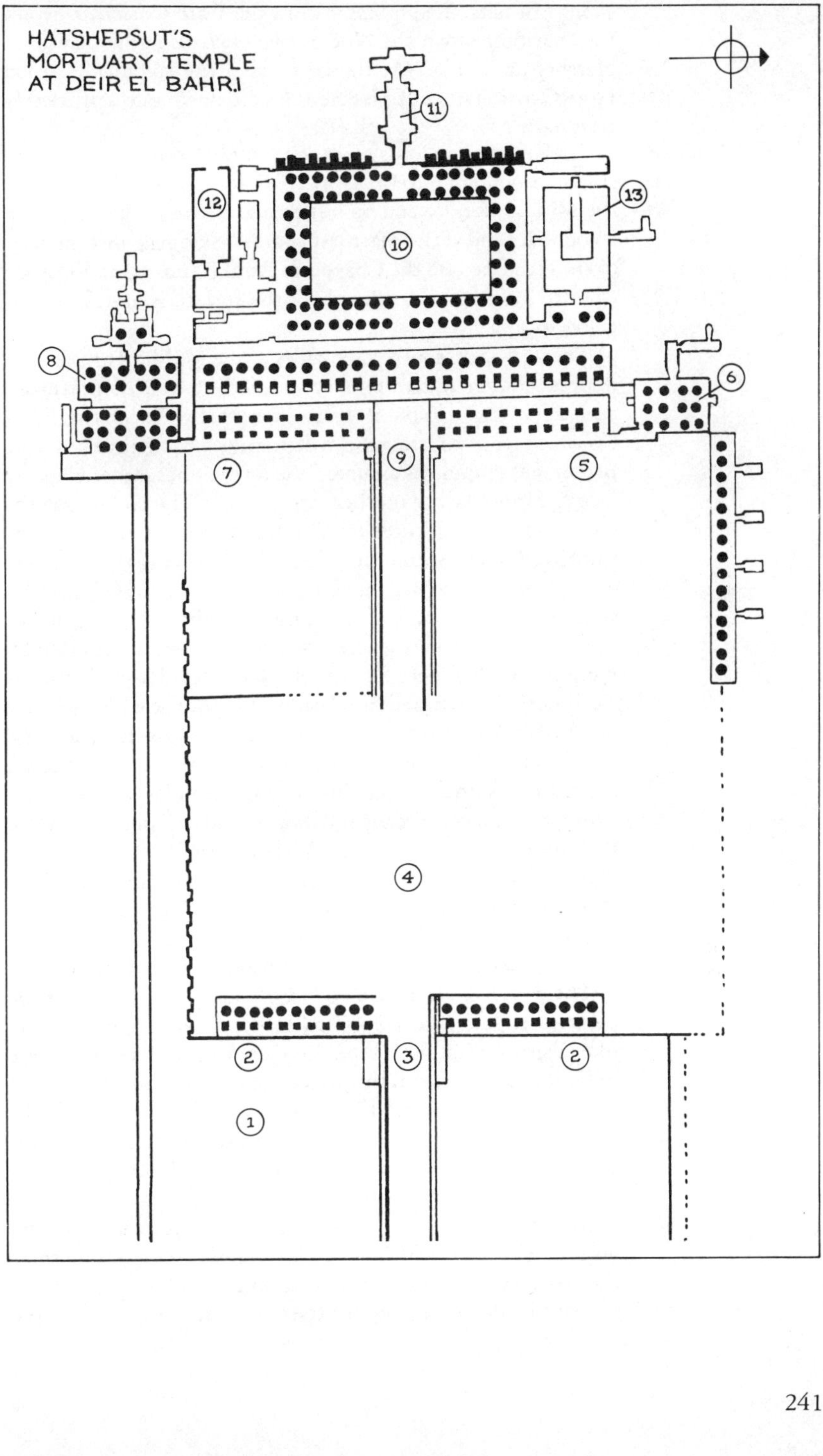
HATSHEPSUT'S
MORTUARY TEMPLE
AT DEIR EL BAHRI
1
2
3
4
5
6
7
8
9
10
11
12
13

caught in nets. The reliefs within the *South Colonnade* depict the transport down the Nile of two obelisks cut at Aswan at Hatshepsut's order. At the far ends of the colonnades stood large Osiris statues of Hatshepsut (the north one imperfectly restored).

The Middle Terrace

The lower ramp leads up to the *Middle Terrace*. At its centre rises a second ramp to the Upper Terrace. Again, at the rear of the Middle Terrace and on either side of the second ramp are colonnades and at their farthest ends, pressing against the rock of the cliff face, are the Chapels of Anubis (north) and Hathor (south). Along the north side of the terrace is an unfinished colonnade.

The north and south colonnades of the Middle Terrace have double rows of square pillars, simple but well-proportioned and achieving a modest grace. On the walls of the *Birth Colonnade* (north) are reliefs depicting Hatshepsut's divine parentage: Amun has assumed the form of her father who sits facing Ahmosis, her mother, on a couch. The couple gaze at one another, their knees touching in a scene at once conventional and reserved and yet sensitively conveying their ardour. The Queen is led to the birth chamber, accompanied by strange deities, a smile of suffering and delight playing on her lips. The child, conventionally shown as a boy, is fashioned by Khnum on his potter's wheel, and also its ka. Just as Tuthmosis III justified his claim to the throne with the story of Amun's selection of him at the Temple of Karnak, so these reliefs serve the same purpose for Hatshepsut. Not that we should think that either Pharaoh was simply cynical; overriding the political propaganda was probably a sincere belief in their diving birth, and these reliefs certainly have all the delicacy and feeling of a belief honestly integrated in Hatshepsut's character, sustaining her in her rule. On the lateral faces of the pillars, Tuthmosis is shown with Amun; on front and back it is Hatshepsut (defaced) with Amun.

The facade of the *Chapel of Anubis* continues the line of the colonnade, but with columns (fluted, with simple capitals, like Doric columns). From a distance, the columns are indistinguishable from the pillars, but stand in the northwest corner of the terrace and look along the facades towards the ramp: that almost unnoticed variation creates a subtle yet entirely harmonious contrast. There is a touch of Greece here, and in the discreet widening of the distance between the central columns as if inviting the visitor into the sanctuary within. The walls of the hall are brilliantly coloured and show the co-rulers (Hatshepsut hacked out), Anubis, protector of the dead, and facing each other at either end, the falcon-headed sun god (north wall) and his wife Hathor (south wall). Cut into the rock in a series of right angles are serveral *chambers* with vaulted roofs of brick, though lacking the wedge-shaped keystones of true weight-bearing vaults which do not appear in Egypt until the 8th C. BC (and not universalised until taken up by the Romans).

On the south side of the ramp is the *Punt Colonnade,* named for the decorations on its rear wall of the expedition to the land of Punt (probably the coastal region of the modern Somali Republic) instigated by Hatshepsut. Amun had told her: "It is a glorious region of god's land, it is indeed my place of delight; I have made it for myself in order to divert my heart". Hatshepsut's ancestors had often sent expeditions there to procure the precious myrrh necessary for the incense in temple services, but now, as she recorded, Amun desired her "to establish a Punt in his house". So the purpose of the expedition was to obtain for the first time living myrrh trees; to plant the terraces of this temple dedicated to Amun with them.

The walls illustrate and relate the story. After presumably crossing the desert to a Red Sea port, the expedition sailed southwards in five ships. The Egyptians are shown being greeted on the shore by the chief of Punt and his extraordinarily corpulant wife – a rare instance of humourous caricature, the rolls of fat from her body reaching right down to her ankles. In exchange for gifts, the beached ships are laden "very heavily with marvels of the country of Punt; all goodly fragrant woods of god's land, heaps of myrrh resin, of fresh myrrh trees, with ebony and pure ivory, with green gold of Emu, with cinnamon wood, with incense, eye cosmetic, with baboons, monkeys, dogs, with skins of the southern panther, with natives and their children. Never was the like of this brought for any pharaoh who has been since the beginning". Back at Thebes, Tuthmosis III and Hatshepsut are shown offering incense to Amun's sacred boat, his offering paltry compared to hers. But later he had Hatshepsut defaced; Tuthmosis' portrait, however, is beautifully carved, his individuality realised in a way lacking in the idealised representations on the pillars.

At the far south end of the colonnade it is the *Chapel of Hathor* that continues the facade. This time there are pillars, not columns, but still, and unnoticed from any distance, they differ from the rest in having the cow-eared head of Hathor serve laterally as capitals. Beyond the first pillared chamber, and then the second, decorated with a procession of boats along the Nile, is the *Sanctuary of Hathor* with vaulted roof. After all the hacking out of Hatshepsut's figure you yearn to see one intact and here, in the furthest recess of the sanctuary, that desire is satisfied. Either because the room was sealed or because at least here in Hathor's sanctuary Tuthmosis respected Hatshepsut's right to some modest remembrance, she survives, albeit in stylised and masculine form. She meets Amun, she suckles regenerating milk from Hathor, and above a recess in the left wall she and Tuthmosis III are shown kneeling, she to the left with an offering of milk, he to the right with wine. Also within this chamber, in a little alcove on the right and towards the floor, is a figure of Senmut, Hatshepsut's favourite.

(It is possible that Hatshepsut has been identified 'in the flesh': one of the mummies found in the tomb of Amenophis II proved to be that of a woman aged from 35 to 45 bearing a strong resemblance to the mummies of Tuthmosis II and III. Most significantly, her left arm is flexed and lies across her chest with the fist clenched, as though she had been buried holding one of the symbols of royal office. Future X-raying of the head may confirm her identity. The face is well preserved and the head is covered with long curls of brown hair reaching down to the bottom of her shoulder blades. There is a photograph of her in *X-raying the Pharaohs.*)

The Upper Terrace

The second ramp leads to the *Upper Terrace,* badly ruined and currently being restored (it may be closed). A portico of Osiris pillars stood a short distance from the edge; their restoration is well underway. On what remains of the rear wall are reliefs of boats accompanied along the Nile banks by a festive procession of soldiers, and of the Festival of the Valley during which Amun visited the necropolis.

Passing through the last wall against the cliffs is a granite doorway leading into the *Sanctuary of Amun* hewn out of the rock. The walls are decorated as elsewhere in the temple but are blackened with smoke. In Ptolemaic times the sanctuary was cut deeper and was dedicated to the healing cults of Imhotep, counsellor to Zoser, and Amenhotep, son of Hapu, counsellor to Amenophis III.

At the left (south) end of the Upper Terrace is the *Sanctuary of Hatshepsut.* The reliefs are of high quality and show processions of priests and offering-bearers. At the right (north) end of the terrace is the *Sanctuary of the Sun,* an open court with an altar in the centre. A flight of steps on its west side permitted a priest to mount the altar gaining a magnificent view of the Valley and river below and the rugged horizon to the east, and to await the rising of the sun. The seclusion of this sanctuary and its emphasis on worship of the rising sun suggests a private royal communion above and beyond the convolutions of the evolved and traditional state religion, and may have influenced Akhenaton in his attempt to destroy mythology and present Aton to the world.

The noble tombs

Over 400 private tombs are accessible in the Theban necropolis, and as many as 100 of these hold some interest for the non-specialist. But to see that many would require three to five days. This Guide concentrates on only four of the most outstanding tombs, all close to the old village of Gurna (Sheikh Abd el-Gurna) and requiring an hour or so to see: *Nakht (52), Menna (69), Ramose (55)* and *Khaemhat (57).*

The private tombs are interesting because they often give a vivid picture of contemporary life instead of the impersonal ritual decorations of the royal tombs. The artists have been more free to express themselves and the sensitivity of their work has been greater. The limestone on this side of the mountain is of poor quality, not suited to carving; the decorations are generally paintings on stucco walls of white, grey or yellow ground. The tombs date from the XI Dynasty through to the XXVI Dynasty, but most belong to the New Kingdom and the four described here are XVIII Dynasty. The tombs are, strictly, mortuary chapels; a filled-in shaft led to a deeper chamber containing the sarcophagus.

Tomb 52 (beside the road from Deir el Bahri to the Ramesseum): Nakht was a scribe and astronomer of Amun in the middle of the XVIII Dynasty. A short passage leads to a transverse first chamber, the only decorated part of the tomb. The paintings are brilliantly preserved and depict country life: the supervising of field labours by Nakht; the deceased and his wife banqueting and making offerings. The chamber beyond, as was the custom, contained a statue of the dead man with his wife, but this was lost while being shipped to America. A shaft here runs down to the sarcophagus chamber.

Tomb 69 (on the north side of the hill, at the bottom): Menna was an estate inspector under a mid-XVIII Dynasty pharaoh, and like the previous tomb the emphasis is on country life. The paintings are finely executed and excellently preserved. In the entrance passage, Menna, his wife and daughter are shown worshipping the sun. In the left wing of the first chamber are a variety of rural scenes, while the right wing depicts various ceremonies, with the dead man and his wife receiving offerings, Anubis facing Osiris, Re and Hathor. A lively hunting and fishing scene occupies the centre of the right-hand wall of the second chamber, though generally mourning and burial scenes are depicted.

Ramose's tomb

Tomb 55 (near the mayor's house in the village): a relatively grandiose structure with wall carvings, the unfinished tomb of Ramose is one of the most fascinating in the necropolis. Ramose was governor of Thebes and vizier in the early years of Amenophis IV's reign and took pains to honour himself with two hypostyle chambers (only the first is open) decorated in the most exquisite classical style. From an open court you enter the first chamber and follow the decorations from the near wall of the right wing: classical reliefs show Ramose and his wife in several offering ceremonies (A). These scenes are continued along the near wall of the left wing. The groups of seated figures are friends or relatives of the dead man (B). Continuing clockwise, the south wall (C) bears a painting of the procession to the tomb with bearers of offerings, mourning women and priests; to the right, the dead man and his wife worshipping Osiris; and below, four representations of the dead man before his tomb. The west wall in the left wing resumes the reliefs (D) and shows Ramose four times offering flowers to Amenophis IV seated under a canopy with the goddess Maat. At the very south (left) end of this wall you can see that prior to cutting the relief the figures were drawn in black outline over a red grid, suggesting the usual artist's concern to transfer the scene in the same detail and proportions as it appeared on the (perhaps smaller) original sketch. Now passing across the closed entrance to the second chamber you come to the north end of the west wall and suddenly the style has changed from the classical to the Amarnan (E). The explanation is that while Ramose was working on his tomb, Amenophis IV had become Akhenaton, introducing both Aton and a new art. Ramose never did finish his tomb here because he followed Akhenaton to Tell el Amarna. This wall shows Akhenaton and Nefertiti at their palace window under the rays of Aton, receiving homage from Ramose. In sketch form you can see Ramose receiving a decoration (a gold collar, as at Ay's tomb at Amarna) and acclaimed by courtiers and representatives from Nubia, Libya and Asia, and also Ramose receiving bouquets in the temple. It is interesting to compare these new-style portraits of Ramose to his classical portrait at the north side of the east wall. And it is significant to note that not only Akhenaton and Nefertiti are depicted with elongated heads, but now Ramose (though not quite so much) is too – in some measure countering the argument that Akhenaton and his family were portrayed in this way because they were afflicted by some deforming disease or gene.

Tomb 57 (to the south of Ramose's tomb): Khaemhat was a royal scribe and inspector of granaries in Upper and Lower

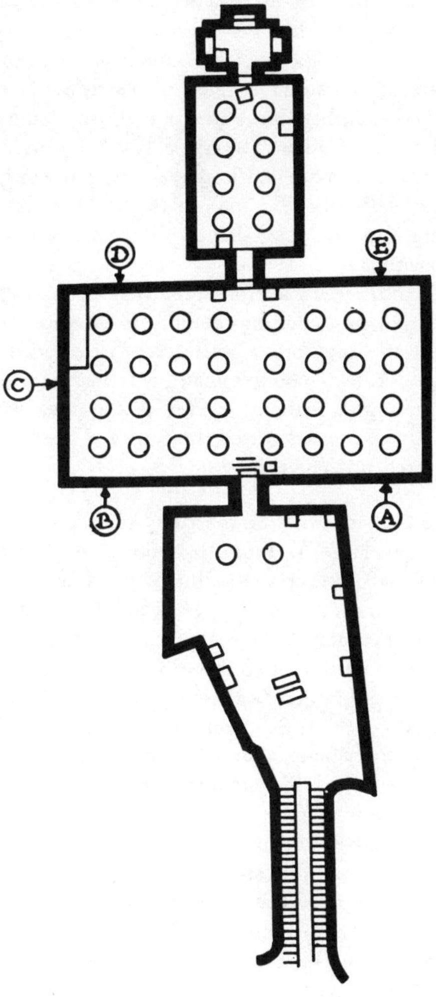

NOBLE TOMB 55: RAMOSE

Egypt under Amenophis III. His is another carved tomb, as fine and even firmer in style than that of Ramose. In the entrance court, to the right of the doorway, are reliefs showing the complete set of instruments employed in the opening of the mouth ceremony, while to the left is Khaemhat adoring Re. The first chamber presents scenes of country life and, particularly, aspects of Khaemhat's official life: unloading of boats, an amusing market scene, cattle herds, the harvest. The second chamber shows the funeral procession and ceremonies in honour of Osiris. The chapel beyond contains several statues with finely modelled heads; in the left wing, on the right-hand wall, the dead man in the act of worship; in the right wing, on the right-hand wall, the cast of a portrait of Khaemhat.

A coffin was traditionally carried through a banquet, giving the lie to an unending feast of life. Macabre it might seem to us; to the Egyptians it must have carried with it some promise against time: "You live again, you live again for ever, here you are young once more for ever" – the final benediction of the priests as the dessicated mummies of these titled dead were interred in their tombs.

The Rameseum

The Ramesseum, the mortuary temple of Ramses II, is part of a still larger rectangular complex enclosed by its original brick wall. The area was filled with vaulted brick storehouses, now entirely ruinous, which were once invaded, as is known from an extant papyrus, by desperate tomb workers who had not been paid for two months: "We have reached this place because of hunger, because of thirst, without clothing, without oil, without fish, without vegetables! Tell Pharaoh, our good lord, about it, and tell the vizier, our superior. Act so that we may live!" So that the great Ramses should live forever this grandiose temple was built, and enough of its stones remain piled atop one another to remind us of *his* hunger. Diodorus was impressed. Coming upon the granite colossus of Ramses he fancifully interpreted its inscription, corrupting the Pharaoh's praenomen, User-maat-Re, as he went: "I am Ozymandias, king of kings. If any would know how great I am, and where I lie, let him excel me in any of my works". To which Shelley offered time's reply:

> I met a traveller from an antique land
> Who said: Two vast and trunkless legs of stone
> Stand in the desert...Near them, on the sand,
> Half sunk, a shattered visage lies, whose frown,
> And wrinkled lip, and sneer of cold command,
> Tell that its sculptor well those passions read

Which yet survive, stamped on these lifeless things,
The hand that mocked them, and the heart that fed.
And on the pedestal these words appear:
"My name is Ozymandias, king of kings:
Look on my works, ye Mighty, and despair!"
Nothing beside remains. Round the decay
Of that colossal wreck, boundless and bare
The lone and level sands stretch far away.

You approach the temple at its north flank and so to reach the *First Pylon,* measuring 67 metres across, you must turn left through the ruined First Court. The outer wall of the pylon is as intelligible as a quarry face, but on the pylon wall facing the court there are excellently carved reliefs, albeit of Ramses' all to familiar exploits against the Hittites (see the Temple of Luxor). A double colonnade on the south side of the court formed the facade of the *royal palace* of which little remains. A colonnade of Osiris pillars runs along the north side of the court. At the far (west) end a flight of steps leads to the Second Court; on the left, as you ascend, is the fallen *Ozymandias.* Weighing nearly 500 kilos and once standing at 17.5 metres, this was one of the largest free-standing statues in Egypt, surpassed by the Colossi of Memnon only by virtue of their pedestals. The index finger alone is a metre long.

The inner surface of the north tower of the *Second Pylon* is decorated, again, with the battle of Kadesh, though the top register more peacefully portrays the festival of the harvest god Min. The front and back of the court is lined with Osiris pillars, and where three stairways rise to the west portico, another *granite colossus,* not quite so large as the first, lies in fragments, the head in good condition with only the nose smashed. On a nearby throne, next to the name of Ramses, Belzoni carved his name. An Italian artist and one-time seminarian, in the early years of the 19th C. Belzoni appeared on the stage of Sadler's Wells and elsewhere in England with his famous human-pyramid act, "bearing on his colossal frame, not fewer, if we mistake not, than 20 or 22 persons". He later turned serious explorer and succeeded in removing from the Ramesseum the giant bust of Ramses II now in the British Museum.

On the rear wall of the portico, between the central and left-hand doorways, are three rows of *reliefs:* the bottom register shows 11 of Ramses' sons; the middle shows Ramses with Atum and falcon-headed Mont who holds the hieroglyph for 'life' to the Pharaoh's nose, while to the right Ramses kneels before the Theban triad and Thoth inscribes the

Pharaoh's name on a palm branch; the top shows Ramses sacrificing to Ptah, and to the right offering incense to an ithyphallic Min. Against the outside north wall of the portico and the Great Hypostyle Hall are the scant remains of an earlier *temple of Seti I,* its alignment probably accounting for the overall alignment of the Ramesseum which accordingly skews to the south instead of fitting squarely within the rectangular walls of the complex.

The *Great Hypostyle Hall* had 48 columns of which only 29 still stand. It was similar to the one at Karnak (to which Ramses II made a major contribution), a higher ceiling over the central aisle allowing illumination through windows set upon the architraves of the adjoining rows of shorter columns. The *First Small Hypostyle Hall* of eight papyrus bud columns still retains its ceiling, decorated with astronomical signs. Only four out of eight columns survive in the *Second Small Hypostyle Hall,* while of the shrine beyond nothing remains.

Here, as elsewhere beneath the glaring sun of Egypt, the columns, the reliefs, the sculptures are streaked with white. Ramses boasted and Shelley cut him down to size; and Flaubert dispassionately observed: "Birdshit is Nature's protest in Egypt; she decorates monuments with it instead of with lichen or moss".

Deir el Medina

Seven hundred metres or so to the west of the Ramesseum is Deir el Medina, the 'monastery of the town', for the small *Ptolemaic temple* here amidst the ruins of the ancient tomb workers' village was occupied by monks during the early centuries of Christianity. Dedicated to Maat and to Hathor whose head adorns the pillars between the outer court and pronaos, this elegant temple is worth visiting if you have the time, though other more considerable Ptolemaic temples await you upstream at Edfu, Kom Ombo and at Philae.

The Valley of the Queens

In the *Valley of the Queens,* Biban el Harem, there are over 70 tombs of queens, princes and princesses of the XVIII though mostly XIX and XX Dynasties. These dead, however, were not gods and so their tombs were not built on the same scale as those of the Pharaohs. Nor did the friable limestone at this end of the Theban Mountain permit much carved decoration; the tombs are more often only painted, though many were left unfinished and have merely the appearance of caves. Those open are 43, 44 and 55, all belonging to sons of Ramses III, and *Tomb 52 of Queen Titi,* wife of one of the Ramessid pharaohs. Queen Titi's tomb, and that of *Amun-her-khopshef (55)* contain the freshest paintings. The *outstanding tomb (66)* in the valley, however, *is Nefertari's,* celebrated wife of Rames II. Unfortunately, it has suffered from landslides and you will probably find it closed. There are several striking portraits of Nefertari; one, on the left wall of the antechamber, shows her beneath a canopy playing a board game, her wig covered with the skin of a vulture, the protective symbol of Maat. Above the door to the corridor leading to the burial chamber is Maat herself, wings extended in protection about the cartouche of the Queen.

Medinet Habu

Though built by Ramses III of the XX Dynasty, the temple complex of *Medinet Habu* is in the great building tradition of the XIX Dynasty Pharaohs and has many points of similarity with the Ramesseum and is better preserved. Not long after the reign of Ramses III, the power of the Pharaohs declined and Egypt herself became divided once more. Medinet Habu is the last major architectural work of the pharaonic period. Though Egypt was threatened by foreign invaders early in Ramses' reign and a palace conspiracy against him and the succession of his son was uncovered, the greater part of his 30-odd years of rule seems to have passed in peace. A papyrus, probably part of the palace archives here, declares: "I caused the woman of Egypt to walk freely wheresoever she would unmolested by others upon the road. I caused to sit idle the soldiers and the chariotry in my time, and the Sherden and the Kehek [Sardinian and Libyan prisoners, or their children, who were recruited to the royal bodyguard] in their villages to lie at night full length without any dread".

In nomen and praenomen, Ramses III imitated his great predecessor of the XIX Dynasty and the designers of Medinet Habu freely borrowed from the Ramesseum. They sometimes cut reliefs celebrating triumphs by Ramses III over Asian foes who had either long since perished on the field of history, or who since the reign of Ramses II lay beyond the enfeebled might of Egypt. This motif is echoed in the lofty gatehouse, a unique feature in Egyptian architecture, through which you enter the site. It was meant to resemble one of those Syrian fortresses which the Egyptian armies had met with so often in their Asiatic campaigns, but here the purpose was not military, the upper stories serving as a resort where the Pharaoh could amuse himself with the women of the harem. The carved heads of captured prisoners enlivened the view from the east window above, reached now by a staircase on the south. Scenes inside the top apartment show Ramses waited on by harem girls, their bodies bared of even their transparent dresses once suggested by a light wash of paint. To the left of the west window the Pharaoh is stroking one of the girls under the chin.

To the north (right) of this gateway is an earlier *XVIII Dynasty temple* built and partly decorated by Hatshepsut. Her image and name were obliterated, as elsewhere, by Tuthmosis III; Akhenaton scratched out all reference to Amun but Horemheb and Seti I replaced them; and Ramses III then decorated the north and south walls to suit his own purposes.

The primeval hill

This temple stood on one of the most sacred spots in Egypt, the primeval hill which first rose clear of the receding waters of Chaos. An inscription identifies it as the burial place of the four primal pairs – Ocean and Matter, the Illimitable and the Boundless, Darkness and Obscurity, and the Hidden and Concealed ones – who preceded even the creator god, Re-Atum. While preserving this older temple, Ramses III levelled the ground behind to build his own mortuary temple dedicated to 'Amun united with Eternity', and a palace and other structures, set within gardens, surrounded by walls, and linked to the Nile by a canal.

Through the gateway and to the south (left) are the *mortuary chapels of the Divine Adorers,* princesses who were the chief priestesses of Amun at Thebes. The chapels are late additions, dating from the XXIII through the XXVI Dynasties.

Straight ahead (to the west) is the First Pylon of Ramses' mortuary temple. The pylon would have almost the same dimensions as that at the Temple of Luxor except that it has lost its cornice. A stairway at the north end leads to the top for

View from the First Pylon

an excellent view across the temple towards the Theban Mountain. The pylons, columns and chambers are smaller as you gaze westwards; the platforms at each stage of the temple are higher; an architectural funnel pointing towards the final sanctuary – as at Karnak, and with the Egyptian temples generally.

The reliefs on the pylon towers depict campaigns against the Nubians and Syrians, campaigns never fought by Ramses III and probably copied from the Ramesseum. But in the eighth year of his reign, Ramses III was in desperate struggle with the Sea Peoples, a coalition of northerners including Sardinians, Cretans, Philistines and others, not all of whom have been identified, who by sea and by ox-carts carrying their women and children overland were bent on permanent settlement in the rich Delta pasturelands. One group, whom the Egyptians called the Danu, the Danaoi of the *Iliad,* here emerged into history for the first time. The invasion is

Sea battle relief

recorded in dramatic detail along the *north outer wall* of the mortuary temple (walk round to it before passing through the pylon) and should not be missed. It is the only Egyptian relief portraying a sea battle. An inscription graphically describes the outcome: 'A net was prepared for them to ensnare them, those who entered into the river-mouths being confined and fallen within it, pinioned in their places, butchered and their corpses hacked up'. In a single sweeping picture the artist has combined the various phases of the engagement: the Egyptians stand on their decks in steady order; an opposing vessel is held fast with grappling irons, the enemy in confusion, many of them falling into the water; while from the shore Ramses standing upon the heads of captives joins with his archers in shooting volleys of arrows at the invaders. In places, deep grooves have been cut into the wall by ancient visitors seeking to obtain stone dust from this sacred place for use in magical charms.

The *First Court* was the scene of ceremonies and entertainments which would have included sword fights and wrestling. The east wall celebrates Ramses' victory in his eleventh year against the Libyans: trophies of enemy hands and genitals are counted by scribes and soldiers are rewarded for their valour. The Pharaoh himself might have distributed rewards from the window in the south wall, decorated on either side with reliefs of prisoners' heads. This was the facade of the *royal palace;* its central hall surrounded by six columns was for holding audiences; the private apartments were on the south side.

The mortuary temple continued in use for only 200 years, though the smaller temple of Hatshepsut remained a place of worship right through Ptolemaic times. In the Ptolemaic and Roman periods, the First Court was filled with houses and a monastery, the *Second Court* with the principal church of what was now a town of some size. *Traces of the church* can still be seen, for example the base of an octagonal font on the south side. Osiris figures against the pillars along the east and west sides were removed in building the church, and the central pillar on the north side was removed to make way for the apse. A few of the Osiris figures remain at the north end. Along the west colonnade, which is also the facade of the temple proper, the colours on the reliefs are especially bright. In the central register on either side of the doorway, Ramses is shown variously with Atum and Mont entering the temple; being crowned in the presence of the Theban triad; and being purified before receiving the emblems of his rank from the gods of Heliopolis. In the lower register on either side, Ramses' name is written in alternation with figures of his sons. None of their names, however, is inscribed as there appears to have been some uncertainty over the succession. On the

Early Christian church

architrave over the doorway is a brightly painted winged solar disc.

Beyond is the *First Hypostyle Hall,* roofless now but once with a raised ceiling over the central aisle as at the Ramesseum and Karnak. To the right are a series of *sanctuaries,* the first for the cult of the living Pharaoh. To the left are *treasure chambers,* still with their original roofs. The central chamber of these shows the weighing of gold on its south wall; sacks of gold on the west wall; and precious stones on the east wall. Off to the left of the *Second Hypostyle Hall* is the funerary chamber of Ramses III with Thoth represented on the south wall inscribing the Pharaoh's name on the sacred tree of Heliopolis. In the *Third Hypostyle Hall,* on either side of the central aisle, are statues of Ramses with Maat and with Thoth. At the west end of this hall are three *sanctuaries;* to the right, that of Mut; to the left, Khonsu; between them, the sanctuary of Amun, once finished with electrum, its doorway of gold, the doors themselves of copper inlaid with precious stones. The granite pedestal, now to one side of the sanctuary but originally at its centre, supported Amun's sacred boat.

Sanctuaries of the Theban triad

You should now walk back through the temple to the First Pylon and turn to the right to view the reliefs along the *outer south wall.* Above, Ramses is shown hunting various desert animals; below, most vividly, he is shown impaling with his hunting spear writhing bulls in a marsh.

The works of Amenophis III

The remaining sights on the west bank of the Nile are associated with Amenophis III (XVIII Dyn) who ruled over Egypt at the height of her prosperity. He began the penchant for the grandiose, and though it later served pharaonic bombast, in the works of Amenophis there is always a more tolerable touch of grandeur and opulence. It is unlikely that he was ever personally engaged in any military exploits, though some inscriptions make this claim by way of convention; rather he comes across as a man who enjoyed life to the full, and had the means to enjoy it more fully than any other man of his times. A smile of contentment plays upon his lips as he sits with Queen Tiy in the colossal group at the Cairo Museum; a stela found at Amarna and now at the British Museum shows him in later years, his weary frame and jaded expression suggesting that he had known pleasures beyond even his ability to enjoy them.

Though the ancient Egyptians built their temples of stone, their homes and even their royal palaces were built merely of mud brick and so have barely survived the millenia. Amenophis' palace lies about a kilometre south of Medinet

His palace Habu. Though badly ruined and rarely visited, it is one of the few royal residences in Egypt of which substantial portions remain. Where traces of plastered walls survive, there are lovely paintings of birds and water plants prefiguring the art of Akhenaton. The palace contains living and state apartments for Amenophis, a separate residence for Tiy, a large festal hall built for the Pharaoh's jubilee and quarters for courtiers and for the harem.

Though Tiy clearly enjoyed her husband's love and confidence, and was often represented as his equal in size, Amenophis did not deny himself the delights of an extensive harem. The dowry of a Hittite princess whom Amenophis married as a secondary queen included 317 damsels for most of those other nights of the year. Another text shows that having already married the sister of a Babylonian king, he was now clamouring for the king's daughter as well. And in his old age Amenophis is known to have married one of his own daughters by Tiy. Little wonder he called his palace the 'House of Joy'.

Tiy's lake To the east of his palace Amenophis shared his bounty by digging for Tiy an enormous lake, 370 metres broad by 1940 metres in length, whereon the imperial couple might sail in the royal barge named 'Aton Gleams' – again suggesting that in spite of his indulgence Amenophis played some role, insensible though he might have been of the effect, in raising his son to Aton and bringing religious revolution to Egypt. Amenophis claimed, improbably, that the lake was dug in 15 days, though signs of haste are apparent in the mounds of excavated earth still lying along its western boundary. An aerial photograph of the site in Room 48 on the ground floor of the Cairo Museum gives a clear impression of the scale and features of the project.

Amenophis also built a mortuary temple which has now vanished beneath ploughed fields between the Ramesseum and Medinet Habu. Responsibility for its principal destruction lies with Merneptah, Pharaoh of the Exodus, who used it as a quarry for building his own temple immediately to the north. All that remains are the two famous Colossi of Memnon which once guarded its outer gates.

The Colossi of Memnon The Colossi are along the road leading back to the new village of Gurna and are visible from some distance. They are in fact gigantic statues of the enthroned Amenophis himself, rising 19.5 metres from the plain. At one time they wore the royal crown and were even higher. Both are damaged and are lacking their faces; the one on the right (north) broke at the waist during an earthquake in AD 27 and was later crudely repaired, the top having been sawn into blocks. Cocteau described them as victims of rainless thunder storms: "Crucified, sitting against great crosses; the lightning has left nothing untouched except their legs".

If it was lightning that crucified them, it was Greek and Roman tourists who cut grafitti into the legs of the figure on the right. The inscriptions reach as high as a man can stretch and were usually cut by visiting notables, including eight Roman governors. The Colossi had early on been accorded the wonder due to the divine, perhaps because of their imposing size, perhaps because Amenophis was recognised as both Pharaoh and god. But their cult status was to elaborate: a commoner, Amenophis, son of Hapu, was architect of his Pharaoh's mortuary temple and raised the Colossi. The vast undertaking impressed both king and public, and like Imhotep at Saqqara, he was divinised. In Ptolemaic times the Colossi this son of Hapu erected and the wise sayings attributed to him attracted followers throughout the Graeco-Roman world. All memory of Amenophis III was forgotten, and the Greeks decided the statues were of Memnon, son of Tithonus, a legendary king of Egypt, and Eos, the Dawn, who went to fight in defence of Troy and was slain by Achilles.

But it was the north Colossus that eventually attracted so much curiosity, for after it was shattered by the earthquake it would sometimes emit a musical note as the sun rose over the eastern mountains. The Emperor Hadrian came in AD 130 with his wife and a large retinue, and camped for several nights at its feet to hear the phenomenon. He was at last rewarded with three performances on a single morning and was declared to have been exceptionally favoured by the gods. The association with Memnon was now expanded to account for the sound: fallen at Troy, he now greeted his mother Eos with a sweet and plaintive sound when she appeared at dawn, and she in turn wept tears of dew upon her beloved child. Nowadays it is thought that the rapid change in temperature as the sun rose caused splittings off of quartzite particles which resonated within the fractures. Certainly, once the Colossus was repaired in AD 199, it cried out no more.

The last time I visited the Colossi I climbed upon the pedestal of the northern one to get a closer look at the inscriptions. As I stood knee high to the diminutive figures of Amenophis' mother Mutemuia on the left and Queen Tiy on the right, a voice began to sing. Hadrian may have heard a few squeaks, but this was a beautiful and passionate love song, and I recognised the voice of Oum Khalsoum, until her death Egypt's greatest singer. The appearance from around the other side of a young Egyptian with a portable radio revealed the source of this singing Memnon. After days of wandering around the tombs and temples of the necropolis, I realised that with the possible exception of Hatshepsut's temple at Deir el Bahri, I would rather hear that marvellous voice than see all the stones of Thebes.

At evening at a cafe on the Luxor embankment you watch the Nile and sky go black, infinity lost in the sensual embrace of the goddess Nut, her breasts sparkling with stars, the moon rising along her thighs. Ouds, drums and tambourines pulse through the body of her night. A dancer ties a long scarf round his waist, the knot at one side; it writhes in orgiastic rhythm but his head is high and motionless like a woman's bearing water. Time is led a dance through coils of music. A censer is swung across your table to drive away the evil that covets and holds.

PRACTICAL INFORMATION

ACCOMMODATION

Luxor's winter high season (October through May) puts a strain on accommodation, and a room in the hotel of your choice can be difficult to get. It's best to make reservations in advance, either in Cairo (through a hotel or travel agent) or abroad (see *Background* chapter). The prices below are for double rooms (except where noted) in the high season; singles are generally 10% less. Low season prices are from 5% to 10% less. Meals are additional, some hotels making half board compulsory, which can greatly add to your bill. Also, service and tax will add about 14% to the total.

The Winter Palace Hotel (5-star), Sharia el Bahr. Tel: 2222. Telex: 92160 WINTER UN. Located at the southern end of the corniche, this is now 2 hotels, the New Winter Palace and the Old Winter Palace. The latter dates back to the heyday of leisured travel earlier this century and remains the most elegant hotel in Luxor. Its rooms have been tastefully refurbished and air conditioning added. At the rear, the rooms overlook a well-planted garden, while the Nile-side rooms offer beautiful views across the river and towards the Theban Mountain. Unfortunately, the Old has been joined by the New Winter Palace, a characterless modern edifice with rooms to match; and worse, meals must be taken at the new hotel, a voluminous mess hall with third-rate food and service. Half board is compulsory year-round, adding at least LE6 per person to the bill. There is a swimming pool, a bar, a terrace (all at the new hotel), a bank and shops, while the arcades on either side of the drive leading up to the Old Winter Palace are lined with more shops and agencies. Double rooms are about LE23.

The Etap Hotel (5-star), Sharia el Bahr. Tel: 2011. Telex: 92080 ETAPLX UN. Along the corniche to the north of the Temple of Luxor, this is the newest hotel in town, a large air-conditioned mausoleum, though with several redeeming features. All rooms face the Nile and have small balconies; there's a good bar; half board is not compulsory, and the restaurant food and service are better than at the Winter Palace; 3 nights a week there is entertainment, including belly dancing; and there is a pool. Also, in the lobby, there are several shops, including an Hachette bookshop. Doubles are about LE26.

The Savoy Hotel (4-star), Sharia el Bahr, between the Temple of Luxor and the Etap. Tel: 2200. After the Old Winter Palace, this is my favourite hotel in Luxor. It too dates from the grand days of travel, with large, high-ceilinged rooms, not all of them air-conditioned, but usually cool all the same. Those overlooking the Nile have balconies and beautiful views. Unfortunately, the place is being allowed to run to seed and refurbishment is called for. In the garden are a number of bungalows, newer, better-appointed, all with air conditioning, but without the Nile view and atmosphere of faded glory. Half board is compulsory year-round, but at least the restaurant is agreeable, the food good and the service too. A meal will cost around LE4. Best of all (and you don't have to be a guest to enjoy it) is the terrace on either side of the main entrance, a convivial gathering place for afternoon tea or drinks at night. Bungalow doubles are LE17; in the main building they are LE11 with bath, LE9 without.

The Luxor Hotel (3-star), in its own grounds facing the Temple of Luxor. Tel: 4205. This dates from the same period as the Savoy and Old Winter Palace, and like the Savoy is running to seed – though refurbishment has begun and its class (and prices) may soon be upgraded. It's built in Moorish style, or a '20s version of it, with ablaq arches and columns along the verandah, the lobby darkly decorated in black, green and wood, and with art deco pharaonic prints on the walls. There's a good African-style bar and a bank for changing money. Half board is compulsory year-round. Doubles with air conditioning and bath are LE13; a reduction applies to rooms without air conditioning. All prices should be treated with caution, as refurbished rooms may cost more.

The Nile Belladona (3-star), south of the Winter Palace on the banks of the Nile. This is a new and unusual venture, a hotel consisting of American camper units and prefabs arranged in terraces with peaceful views over the river. There is a restaurant, with compulsory year-round half board, and in the garden a tent with bar and nightclub. Distance from town means you'll often want to take a carriage. Doubles are about LE17.

Hotel Philippe (2-star), Sharia Nefertiti, off the corniche just after the Etap. Tel: 2284. A new hotel with a good reputation. There's a downstairs restaurant and bar and a rooftop garden. Rooms to the rear are air-conditioned; those to the front, with a glancing view of the Nile, have small balconies. Doubles are LE12, with air-conditioning extra.

Horus Hotel (1-star), right off Sharia el Mahatta (the road running down from the station) as it reaches the Temple of Luxor. Tel: 2165. Gaudy from the outside, simple and decent within, the Horus offers a range of rooms and prices, so you should ask to be shown a few first. A restaurant serves basic meals. Doubles are around LE3 without bath, LE5 with.

The New Karnak Hotel, Midan el Mahatta (Station Square). A no-star hotel on the left side of the square, favoured by young backpackers. A clean but noisy place to stay, and it's hot in summer. There's a restaurant next door and meals on the roof in winter. Bring your own soap, towels and toilet paper; and if it gets too hot, you can rent a fan. Doubles without bath are about LE2; singles range from around LE1 to those with bath at LE3.

The Radwan Hotel, second left off Midan el Mahatta, to the right of the New Karnak Hotel. Tel: 2214. Run by Romani Hanna, this is another no-star place and very much better (I have stayed here too) than the New Karnak. Rooms lead onto a central garden where inexpensive meals are served beneath the minaret of a neighbouring mosque. If space permits, you can have a room to yourself; otherwise, accommodation is dorm-style. But the atmosphere is pleasant, the place clean, and at no more than LE1.50 per night you can't go wrong.

There is a **youth hostel** costing about 75PT on Sharia el Manshia in Luxor (Tel: 2139); and, on the **west bank** of the Nile, there are three small (no-star) hotels, the **Habu,** near the entrance to Medinet Habu; the **Sheikh Ali** (known also as the **Mersam Hotel**), opposite the Department of Antiquities at the intersection past (ie behind) the Colossi of Memnon; and a place of no name across the road from the Colossi themselves. They are all very simple.

EATING PLACES AND ENTERTAINMENT

As many of Luxor's hotels require that you take lunch or dinner at their restaurant, independent restaurants catering to visitors are few. The **Etap** and **Savoy** offer better meals than the rest, and the Etap's come with entertainment, including belly dancing, 3 nights a week. Meals at the **Winter Palace** are as mediocre as they are expensive.

Atop the Tourist Bazaar building next to the New Winter Palace is the **Marhaba Restaurant** with beautiful views, air conditioning in summer and moderate prices. A meal will run to LE3 or so. The menu is Egyptian, a change from the bland Western fare at the hotels.

There are several agreeable cafés, a bar and a restaurant/bar along the riverbank by the Temple of Luxor. A complete meal at the **Chez Farouk** will set you back about LE3, and you can also stay on here into the night drinking beers and listening to the music. The **Café Nil** is a simpler place, sometimes with very good

Egyptian music and dancing. An Egyptian will come up to the musicians, give them some money, reel off a list of people to whom he dedicates his dance, and then dance – usually alone and oblivious to onlookers. The dances are regional, some Nubian, some of Luxor, occasionally one from Suez where many Nubians work on the Canal.

The **Savoy** has a terrace on either side of its entrance which is a very pleasant place to while away a late afternoon or late evening with a drink or other light refreshments.

There is a certain earnestness about Luxor: so many antiquities lying on either side of the river, requiring early risings to see them before the day grows too hot, and so visitors go to bed early too and nightlife is limited. There is a **disco** at the **Etap's bar.**

SHOPPING

The principal market street in Luxor is **Sharia el Birka,** to the right off Sharia el Mahatta (the station road) as it comes to the gardens behind the Temple of Luxor. It is less extensive and varied than the market streets in Aswan, but does sell galabiyyas, spices and other items of interest to visitors.

Along the front of the Old Winter Palace are arcades of agencies and shops selling the usual souvenirs. Here you will find **Aboudi's shop** (see main text) with his ridiculous guide for sale – a must. Next to the New Winter Palace is the **Tourist Bazaar,** a soulless concrete building. Arcades in the Etap have brighter **boutiques,** and there is also an **Hachette bookshop** there.

Touts on both sides of the river will importune you *ad nauseum* with their phoney pharaonic relics. If you want one of these, be sure to knock the price right down, offering perhaps a tenth of what is asked. Decent replicas of **antiquities** are on sale in the arcades by the Old Winter Palace, and sometimes even the real thing – but be sure the shop has a licence from the Department of Antiquities and is prepared to offer a certificate of authenticity for what you buy. Genuine antiquities cost less in Luxor than in Cairo.

OF INTEREST

East bank:

Temple of Luxor, open from 7am to 5pm (50PT), and from 7pm to 10pm, illuminated (LE1).

Luxor Museum, open winter from 4 to 9pm, summer from 5 to 10pm (50PT).

Karnak, open from 7am to 5pm (75PT). **Son et lumiere** starts at 7.30pm daily. Performances in English on Mondays, Wednesdays and Saturdays; in French on Tuesdays, Fridays and Sundays; in German on Thursdays – all these cost LE2. There is also a Thursday Arabic performance, 25PT. The **carriage ride** to Karnak should cost no more than 50PT one way; for LE1 the carriage will take you there and back and wait an hour or two.

West bank:

All the sites on the west bank are open from 5am to 4pm, though the funerary temples may stay open an hour or two longer.

Tickets are required for the major sites and must be purchased in advance, ie from the ticket kiosk at the tourist landing on the west bank. Fees are:

Valley of the Kings (Biban el Muluk)	LE1
Mortuary Temple of Hatshepsut (Deir el Bahri)	50PT
Tombs of the Nobles (Sheikh Abdul Gourna)	75PT
Mortuary Temple of Ramses II (Ramesseum)	50PT
Valley of the Queens (Biban el Harim)	25PT
Mortuary Temple of Ramses III (Medinet Habu)	50PT
Mortuary Temple of Seti I	25PT

Tickets are date-stamped and good only on the day of purchase.

If you're with a tour, you'll probably board the **tourist ferry** in front of the Winter Palace or Savoy Hotel and go straight to the tourist landing on the other side. However, just south of the Savoy, down an earth bank, is the more frequent **Egyptian ferry** (the *people* ferry, as it is called, in contrast to the mere tourist ferry). The fare is 10PT return. This will land you a couple of hundred metres south of the tourist landing and ticket kiosk, but smack amidst the taxi drivers and donkey boys. You negotiate a price, travel to the kiosk to buy your tickets, and you're off.

Bicycles, hired for about 75PT per day in Luxor, are the best way to get around, if you're fit (see main text). They can be taken on the ferry free. Otherwise, you'll have to bargain for a taxi or donkey.

Donkeys are uncomfortable and best avoided. Donkey boys, in any case, can be bastards: they have a nasty habit of agreeing to a price, then increasing it as you trot along, and tossing you off the donkey if you don't given in. My first time in Luxor I was de-donkeyed 3 times enroute to the Valley of the Kings, finally agreed to an extortionate price, and when I got back to the Nile, leapt onto the ferry and left the donkey boy screaming on the west bank for his money. The maximum you should pay for a donkey is LE1.50 per day.

Taxis are about LE3.50 for 4 hours. The cost of bargaining them down to the proper price is that they'll try to find other ways of making money – for example, the driver may refuse to be exclusive to you, constantly darting off in search of quick fares while you visit a temple. That doesn't matter as he'll show up again when you need him.

It's very important that you agree clearly on the price beforehand and that you do not pay a single piastre until the donkey boy or taxi driver has completed his side of the bargain. You should also, before setting out for the west bank, call in on Thomas Cook or the Tourist Information Office to learn the proper up to date rates – and then stick to them, come what may.

An **abbreviated itinerary** for the west bank should include, at the very least, the Valley of the Kings and the Mortuary Temple of Hatshepsut.

INFORMATION

The **Ministry of Tourism** (Tel: 2215) is in the Tourist Bazaar building near the New Winter Palace. They are very helpful, providing information, for example, on the proper charges (set by the government) a carriage or taxi driver or donkey boy can make. They can also help find accommodation if things get difficult.

Thomas Cook, American Express and **Misr Travel,** all in the arcades by the Old Winter Palace, can also provide a variety of information and assistance.

TRAVEL

Travel to the sites on the east and west banks is covered above, under the *Of Interest* heading.

A very pleasant time can be had by **sailing** about the Nile in a felucca. Bargain with any of the boatmen along the river and expect to pay about LE2.50 per hour. You can sail all the way up the Nile to Aswan, though you'll probably get a better price coming downstream from Aswan (see Aswan). At Luxor, ask for Gomal Ali Doma, an enterprising young boatman who hangs out in front of the Winter Palace Hotel.

Another way of covering the distance between Luxor and Aswan, and being able to stop along the way, is to take a service (shared) **taxi.** The taxis depart from the north end of the gardens behind the Temple of Luxor. You can go from Luxor to Esna, Esna to Edfu, Edfu to Kom Ombo and Kom Ombo to Aswan, each leg costing about 50-60PT and usually requiring a change of taxi.

Trains and **planes** link Luxor with Cairo and Aswan. For rail schedules, see the *Background* chapter. The **Egyptair** office is in the arcade by the Old Winter Palace Hotel. Also here are **Thomas Cook, American Express, Misr Travel** and **Eastmar** – all of these offer tours, but mostly they handle groups and are rather poor at arranging individual travel. You can often join a group tour by going to one or the other of these agents the evening before and asking if there's space.

For the Luxor-Aswan Nile **cruise** you should already have made arrangements in Cairo, or from abroad (see the *Practical Information* at the end of the *Cairo 1* chapter, and the *Background* chapter), though you can try at one of the above agents on the off chance.

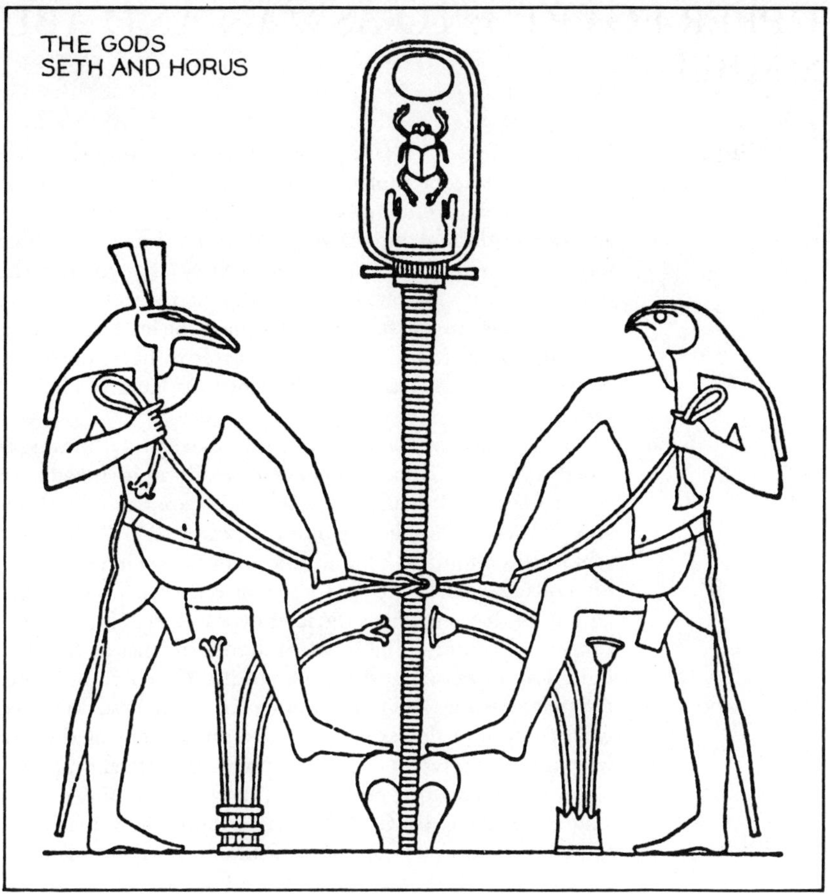
THE GODS
SETH AND HORUS

UPPER EGYPT 3: TO ASWAN AND ABU SIMBEL

Ptolemaic temples

Like a string of citadels extending Alexandrian power towards Nubia, the Ptolemies built temples along the Nile at Esna, Edfu and Kom Ombo. Cruise boats ply between Luxor and Aswan throughout the year and offer the most agreeable way of enjoying the lush Valley scenery and visiting the temples enroute. By car, Esna and Edfu, on the west bank, are a half-day's excursion from Luxor. Esna is the least interesting temple, however, and it would be better to base yourself at Aswan for the half-day excursion down to Kom Ombo and Edfu.

Esna

At the centre of Esna (54 kms from Luxor), with its tight and dirty streets, is the temple, deep within a pit. It had been covered over with houses; now it is laid bare behind railings and you descend a staircase into the excavations. Ptolemy VI rebuilt this temple to Khnum, the god who fashioned man on his potter's wheel, over the ruins of earlier structures, but almost all that remains is the later hypostyle hall built by the Emperor Claudius. The facade is similar to that at Dendera but is less impressive and has worn badly. The columns within the pylon outline and rising from a screen are here decorated with composite flower capitals. The intact roof of the hall within is supported by 24 columns with 16 different capitals. The carvings are third-rate. In fact, there is something depressing about these 1st C. AD remains, built by Romans in a foreign style that was already anachronistic. You feel it was not worth pulling down even these houses to see what lay beneath.

In fact, for me the appeal of Esna lies entirely in some small pieces of literary pornography, the letters and travel journals of Flaubert. It sounds like the town was a dump when Flaubert passed through in 1850, but it did then have one redeeming feature in his eyes: by an edict of Mohammed Ali's in 1834 prohibiting prostitution and female dancing in Cairo,

The learned women of Esna

the *almehs* (literally 'learned women') of Egypt had concentrated in Qena, Esna and Aswan. Flaubert entertained a mystique about prostitution: "A meeting place of so many elements – lust, bitterness, complete absence of human contact, muscular frenzy, the clink of gold – that to peer into it deeply makes one reel. One learns so many things in a brothel, and feels such sadness, and dreams so longingly of love!"

At Esna he was propositioned aboard his boat by an *almeh*

followed by her pet sheep, its wool spotted with yellow henna. He went with her to the house of Kuchuk Hanem, "a tall, splendid creature, lighter in colouring than an Arab; she comes from Damascus; her skin, particularly on her body, is slightly coffee-coloured. When she bends, her flesh ripples into bronze ridges. Her eyes are dark and enormous, her eyebrows black, her nostrils open and wide; heavy shoulders, full, apple-shaped breasts". She danced the Bee, which required that the musicians be blindfolded, and slowly removed her clothes. "When it was time to leave I didn't leave. I sucked her furiously – her body was covered with sweat – she was tired after dancing – she was cold – I covered her with my pelisse, and she fell asleep with her fingers in mine. As for me, I scarcely shut my eyes. Watching that beautiful creature asleep (she snored), my night was one long, infinitely intense reverie – that was why I stayed. I thought of my nights in Paris brothels – a whole series of old memories came back – and I thought of her, of her dance, of her voice as she sang songs that for me were without meaning and even without distinguishable words. That continued all night. At three o'clock I got up to piss in the street – the stars were shining...As for the *coups,* they were good – the third especially was ferocious, and the last tender – we told each other many sweet things – towards the end there was something sad and loving in the way we embraced."

Back in France, while he was writing *Madame Bovary,* he wrote to Louise Colet, his jealous mistress: "You tell me that Kuchuk's bedbugs degrade her in your eyes; for me they were the most enchanting touch of all. Their nauseating odour mingled with the scent of her skin, which was dripping with sandalwood oil. I want a touch of bitterness in everything – always a jeer in the midst of our triumphs, desolation even in the midst of enthusiasm". And he reminded Louise that "you and I are thinking of her, but she is certainly not thinking of us. We are weaving an aesthetic around her, whereas this particular very interesting tourist who was vouchsafed the honours of her couch has vanished from her memory completely, like many others. Ah! Travelling makes one modest – you see what a tiny place you occupy in the world".

Unfortunately Kuchuk Hanem is gone and the stupid temple remains.

Edfu Edfu (105 kms from either Luxor or Aswan) creates a different impression. The Temple of Horus is on the western outskirts of the present town, at a spot where Horus and Seth met in titanic combat for the world. The temple is suitably monumental and the best preserved in Egypt. Construction began under Ptolemy III Euergetes and it was completed, down to its decorations, by the mid-1st C. BC. It is therefore hardly a century or two older than the many technically superior imperial ruins in Rome. But you forget this and applaud the Ptolemies' phoney archaic style, for this is pure theatre. Remembering Justinian's boast that with Hagia Sophia he had surpassed Solomon's temple, at Edfu despite a mouthful of popcorn you cry out, "Cecil B. DeMille, they have outdone you!"

On the pylon towers Neos Dionysos, in New Kingdom gear, snicker-snacks amongst the Bandersnatch, while in the colonnaded court, against the elaborate floral columns of the pronaos, is the Jabberwock itself – the survivor of a pair of granite falcon-Horuses which stood on either side of the entrance. You walk through a series of ever smaller, ever darker halls and chambers to the sanctuary of the god, weirdly illuminated through three small apertures in the ceiling by a dim green Nilish light. The reliefs on the lower row on the right-hand wall within show Philopator entering the sanctuary and worshipping Horus, Hathor and his deified parents.

Leaving the sanctuary and walking back towards the pronaos, you first pass through one antechamber and then enter another with a staircase on either side leading to the roof. As at Dendera, the residing deity required at least an annual dose of sunshine, a reimpregnation of soul from the sun. This occasioned the New Year procession up to the roof, and the decorations along the staircase walls reproduce the ceremony in full detail.

Other rites celebrated annually were the conjugal visit of Hathor (see Dendera); the triumph of Horus over Seth (see the inner face of the east enclosure wall); the coronation in the main court of a live falcon as the living symbol of Horus on earth; and the re-enactment of the divine birth of Horus and the Pharaoh at the Birth House outside the pylon (with episodes of the ceremony carved on its walls).

Southwards beyond Edfu the palms and cultivation on the east bank give way to the Arabian Desert and at Silsileh (145 kms from Luxor) the Nile passes through a defile, now with only hills on either side but once thought to mark a cataract.

1. Pylon
2. Court
3. Pronaos
4. Hypostyle hall
5. Antechamber (staircases to roof)
6. Antechamber
7. Sanctuary of Horus
8. Relief of Horus slaying Seth
9. Nilometer

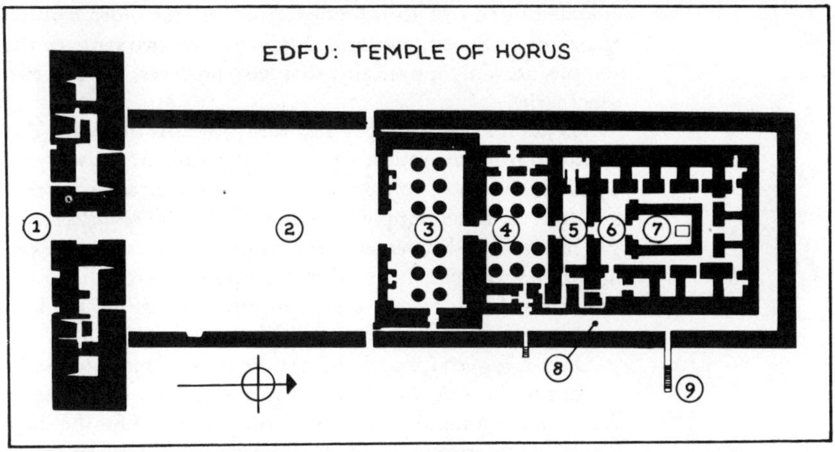

The rock bed of Egypt changes here from limestone to the harder sandstone used in almost all New Kingdom and Ptolemaic temple building. During the reign of Ramses II the Silsileh quarries were worked by no fewer than 3000 men for the Ramesseum alone.

The Silsileh quarries

Above Silsileh the mountains again recede from the river and the desert is kept at bay by canals. Irrigation and the fellahin bring harvests of cane and corn to the fields. The reclaimed land on the east bank around Kom Ombo (164 kms from Luxor, 46 kms from Aswan) supports a large Nubian population displaced from their homeland by the rising waters of Lake Nasser. The village is on the Luxor-Aswan road; nearby is a sugar refinery supplied by barges landing near the temple 4 kms to the west.

Kom Ombo

The temple stands on a low promontory overlooking the Nile. Its elevation, its seclusion, the combination of sun and water flowing past as though in slow but determined search for the Mediterranean, at last suggests something of Greece. It has ruined well, and there is something in its stones of that Hellenic response to light, the uncompromising noonday glare, the soft farewell to the setting sun without fear of night.

The usual Ptolemaic (and Roman) appeasement of the fossilised Egyptian priesthood is apparent, however, as soon as you abandon mood for detail – even Marcus Aurelius must stoically appear on an outer corridor wall in pharaonic garb offering a pectoral to Sennuphis, divine wife of Haroeris. The naos was begun by Ptolemy VI Philometor; the hypostyle hall and pronaos were added by Neos Dionysos; and Augustus added the court, the outer enclosure wall and the now destroyed pylon. It is a symmetrically twin temple, the left side dedicated to falcon-headed Horoeris (the older Horus), the right to Sobek, the crocodile god. The two parts of the temple are only physically divided, however, at the two sanctuaries.

The temple faces more or less west, towards the Nile. You approach from the south, past a massive ruined *gateway* built by Neos Dionysos. In front of you, between an ancient brick wall and the outer temple wall, is a small *chapel of Hathor*, the gift of a wealthy Roman woman. Through its gratings you can see sarcophagi and the piled up mummies of crocodile – not belonging here, merely tossed in after being dug up in a nearby cemetery.

Only a few courses of the temple *pylon* remain, and the stumps of the 16 columns once surrounding the *court* – at its centre is the stone altar used in sacrifices. Except for the three centre columns framing the dual passageways leading to the twin sanctuaries, the *pronaos* facade has lost the upper parts of its columns where they rise above the screen. But there is no loss of effect. The surviving columns burst in floral capitals, and above them, across the remaining section of the cavetto cornice, are two winged discs emphasising again the duality of the divine presence here. Within the pronaos the ceiling is decorated with flying vultures and the supporting capitals proclaim the unity of Upper and Lower Egypt, some the lily, some papyrus – and one eccentrically a palm. On this side of the screen are *reliefs* of various Ptolemaic pharaohs receiving the blessings of Egypt's high gods and the double crown of Delta and Valley.

In the hypostyle hall beyond, and in the three rising antechambers after that, are more *reliefs*. One, between the doors into the sanctuaries, shows Ptolemy Philometor and his sister-wife before Sobek, Haroeris and Khonsu who inscribes the Pharaoh's name on a palm stalk, the equivalent of St Peter confirming entry into heaven. Philometor wears a full Macedonian cloak, a rare exception to the traditional guise. Little is left of the *sanctuaries,* but they are all the more revealing for that. Between them, at a lower level, is a crypt which communicates with a chapel to the east. The crypt is now exposed but was once covered with a sliding slab. It is not difficult to imagine someone creeping down there from the

1. Gate of Neos Dionysos
2. Chapel of Hathor
3. Pylon (destroyed)
4. Court
5. Altar
6. Pronaos
7. Coronation reliefs
8. Hypostyle Hall
9. Antechambers
10. Sanctuary of Haroeris
11. Sanctuary of Sobek
12. Inner corridor
13. Stairway in centre chapel
14. Outer corridor
15. Roman wells
16. Birth House

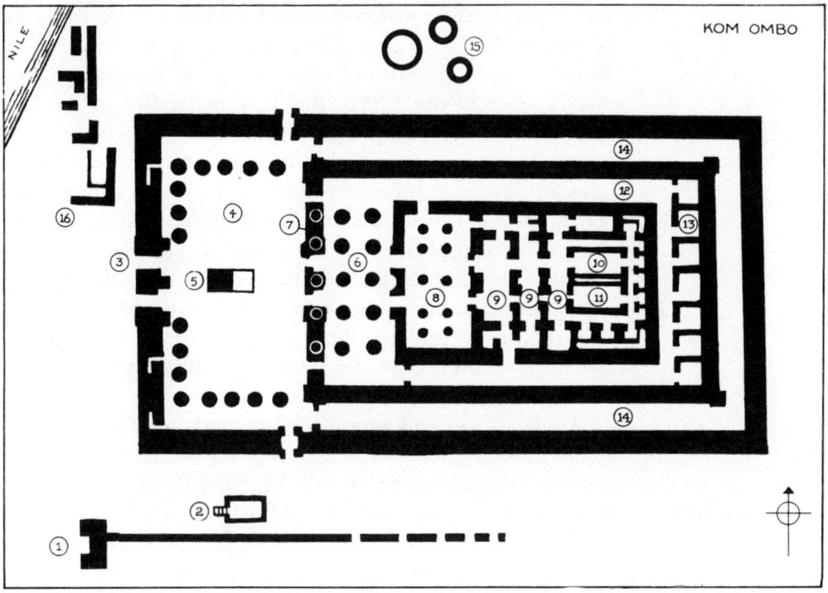

chapel to make spectral noises at appropriate moments – the priests to fool Pharaoh, or one of Pharaoh's men to fool the priests? Probably the priests fooling each other, the Ptolemies having the last laugh.

Beyond the rear wall of the naos are seven *chapels* leading off the *inner corridor*. A stairway in the centre chapel leads upwards for a view over the temple. The chapels are at various stages of decoration. An *outer corridor,* entered from either end of the court, is decorated with Roman reliefs.

Along the north flank of the temple are two *Roman wells* in which, perhaps, the sacred crocodiles were kept. At the north-east corner of the temple is what is left of the *birth house,* much of which has fallen, along with its portion of the terrace, down to the Nile. It is Egypt reclaiming her own.

Aswan Aswan (210 kms from Luxor, 886 kms from Cairo) is where the Valley closes upon the river, no more buffer of cultivation on either side, instead a universe of desert sundered by the pulsing Nile flowing out of Africa. At this point the Nile is only 87 metres above sea level, so low a height for so massive a river, you would think it would disdain the 87-metre inducement to go further, but there is a continent of water behind, urging it on through the cataract above Aswan, and the current is strong. The layer of sandstone covering Upper Egypt from Edfu southwards is ruptured here by the thrust of underlying granite which the river has hewn into the rocks and islands of the First Cataract. Even before construction of the British dam at the turn of the century and the giant hydroelectric dam in the 1960s, this is where traffic on the Nile stopped. Camels transported cargoes round the rocks while lightened boats took their chances through the granite passage. The more intrepid passenger might stay aboard: "We see the whole boat slope down bodily under our feet. We feel the leap – the dead fall – the staggering rush forward. Instantly the waves are foaming and boiling up on all sides, flooding the lower deck, and covering the upper deck with spray. The men ship their oars, leaving all to helm and current; and, despite the hoarse tumult, we distinctly hear those oars scrape the rocks on either side" (Amelia Edwards).

Frontier outpost

Aswan is where Egypt ends. Beyond lie Nubia and the Sudan, and the traditional routes of invasion and trade. The ancient Egyptians garrisoned the 500-kilometre stretch of river to the Third Cataract, and a fleet patrolled the Nile between the First Cataract and the Second at Wadi Halfa. An uprising or an attack on a caravan, and signal fires relayed the summons for help to Aswan. Two thousand years and more later, Aswan marked the southernmost margin of the Roman world, and when Juvenal fell into disfavour at Rome for writing satirical verses against the Emperor's court, it was to Aswan that he was posted, to guard the Empire he had mocked. It is the High Dam that accounts for the modern military presence. Its breach would send a tidal wave down the whole length of the Nile Valley and inundate half of Cairo. But that presence and the object of its protection lie out of sight some kilometres south of the town, which for all of its growth and the influx of workers in recent years retains an atmosphere of remoteness and tranquillity.

Over the centuries the Tropic of Cancer has shifted slightly to the south, but in classical times it fell across Aswan, proved by a famous well into which the sun's rays plunged perpendicularly at midday during the summer solstice, leaving no shadow. Hearing of this, Eratosthenes (276-196 BC) of the Mouseion at Alexandria concluded that the earth was round and had a diameter of 12,560 kms – an error of only 80 kms. A triumph of constructive thought inspired by a place whose genius lies in the inducement to idle contentment. Following the day's fierce sun and dry desert heat, there is the beauty at evening of sand, sky and water fading impercepitably through deepening violet, a lift of breeze on the Nile, a movement of palms, a flight of ibis, and the graceful glide of swallow-tailed feluccas. The final pleasure is to know that when morning comes at Aswan there is so little to do. Those who insist on doing it can easily do it all in a couple of days. Those who want to do nothing will want to stay far longer.

Climate Long favoured as a winter resort with daytime temperatures around 23° to 30°C, the increase and changing style of tourism in Egypt has led greater numbers of travellers to challenge the summer heat which usually ranges from 38° to 42°C during the day, though it can climb much higher. Air conditioning and a siesta during early afternoon, and the low humidity, make even the hottest July and August days bearable. The older hotels without air conditioning but with high ceilings and louvred shutters are often as comfortable as the artificially polar and sometimes mechanically noisy environments of the modern places.

Orientation The station is at the north end of town, some distance back from the river. The temperature, often 10°C higher at Aswan than in Cairo, hits you as you step off the train, and darker skins, lighter builds, introduce you to the tropics. A taxi, or better yet a carriage, will take you to your hotel and provide you with your first glimpse of the setting. As you emerge onto the corniche, you see a bare hill rising from the opposite bank and cut into its face the small dark openings of the ancient tombs of Aswan's governors and princes.

Along the corniche The facades at this end of the corniche are new and concrete, but the sweep of the Nile is impressive. The older town lies behind. A few streets back, running parallel with the corniche, is the best bazaar outside Cairo, alive with Arabs and Nubians and blacks trading in gum, spices, ivory, ebony and other exotic prizes out of Africa, as well as local weaves and manufactured goods. Although Aswan is not the crossroads of trade it once was, and the days of the caravans are gone, the flavour remains and the imagination recalls magnificently shawled and turbaned guards, huge scimitars dangling at their sides, accompanying a hundred camels laden with elephant tusks out of Ethiopia, driving the dust before them in clouds. The picturesque inner town deserves exploration, especially at evening. There are a few simple but good restaurants, and a large Coptic church.

In ancient times this area was known as Syene and famous for its nearby quarries of pink granite, but it was always secondary to the main commercial and administrative settlement of Yebu, which stood at the southern end of the long palm-covered island on your right. Yebu was Egyptian for elephant, and the island today bears the Greek translation, Elephantine. Perhaps in the earliest millenia of their history, before the desert had crept down to the Nile, the Egyptians first encountered elephants here, though it is more likely that Yebu owed its name and much of its importance to the ivory trade from the south. The most obvious feature at this northern end of Elephantine is the unfortunate bulk of the Aswan Oberoi Hotel, like a control tower without an international airport. On the far side of Elephantine, and largely obscured by it, is Kitchener's Island; it was from Aswan that Kitchener set out to conquer the Sudan in 1896-98 and the island is a botanical garden begun by him.

Continuing along the corniche, the Philae Hotel is on your left, and after it the Grand Hotel of faded glory, second only to the Old Cataract as the favoured place to stay between the wars. It is along this quayside that the Nile cruise boats tie up when visiting. Ferries leave from here to Elephantine. Further on at the roundabout with the Egyptair office, the road from the airport enters town. Ferries also leave from here to Elephantine, and to the Amun Island Hotel in mid-river, and feluccas may be hired. One arm of the Nile runs through the narrow channel between the massive embankments of ancient Elephantine town and the great doughlike outcrops of pink granite on the east bank, the road rising round the shaded public gardens that overlook the river here. Surmounting the outcrop is the Old Cataract Hotel; near it is the New Cataract, and beyond that the Kalabsha Hotel. Devotees of nostagia must make a pilgrimage to the Old Cataract, a russet pile atop a loaf of pink granite, surrounded by gardens, with beautiful views along the Nile in either direction and across the tip of Elephantine to the Mausoleum of the Aga Khan and against the distant desert horizon the old Monastery of St Simeon. John Fowles in *Daniel Martin* describes the interior: "Pierced screens, huge fans, tatty old colonial furniture, stone floors, silence, barefooted Nubian servants in their red fezzes; so redolent of an obsolete middle class that it was museum-like". The exterior features in the film of Agatha Christie's *Death on the Nile*; the terrace, cocktail in hand, amidst the calm, is the perfect place to plot an elegant murder.

The Old Cataract Hotel

Elephantine Island

The purposeful excuse for visiting Elephantine Island is to see the scant ruins, the ramshackle museum and the ancient

1. Station
2. Cataract Hotels
3. Nobles' tombs
4. Mausoleum of the Aga Khan
5. Monastery of St Simeon
6. Fatimid cemetery
7. Obelisk
8. Quarries
9. Aswan Dam (built by British)
10. The new Philae
11. The High Dam
12. New harbour (for Wadi Halfa)
13 · Kalabsha temple

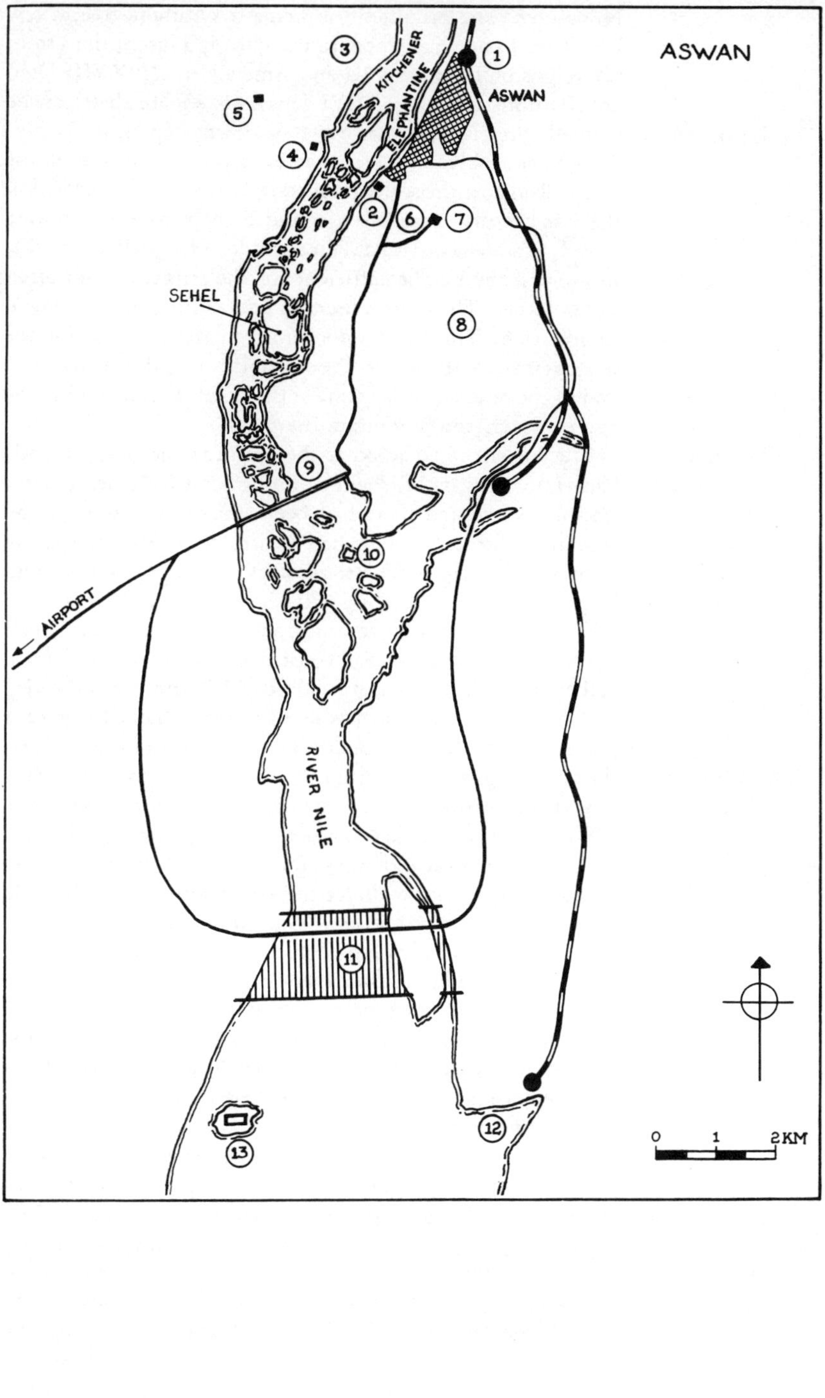
ASWAN
1
ASWAN
2
3
KITCHENER
ELEPHANTINE
4
5
6
7
8
SEHEL
9
10
AIRPORT
RIVER NILE
11
12
13
0
1
2KM

Nilometer. The Nilometer is under a sycamore tree, a few boat-lengths north of embankments bearing inscriptions from the reigns of Tuthmosis III and Amenophis III (XVIII Dyn) and Psammetichus II (XXVI Dyn). Its square shaft can be entered directly from the river or down steps from above. Though probably dating from an earlier period, it was rebuilt by the Romans, the scales marked in Greek. It was restored in the last century, when Arabic and French inscriptions were added. Strabo records that "on the side of the well are marks, measuring the height sufficient for the irrigation and other water levels. These are observed and published for general information. This is of importance to the peasants for the management of the water, the embankments, the canals, etc., and to the officials on account of the taxes. For the higher the rise of water, the higher are the taxes".

The Nilometer

The ancient town

The ancient town stood at the southern end of the island. Excavation began at the beginning of this century after evidence suggested there had been a sizeable Jewish colony here in the 6th C BC, but there is little to see that makes any impression on the amateur. Most of the remains are of mud brick and the dusty ground is littered with shards. There are the foundations of three temples, and the fragments of a small temple down by the water reconstructed with the aid of much yellow brick. The island was home to Khnum, a ram-headed god of the cataracts who was said to have fashioned man on a potter's wheel. Rams sacred to the god were mummified, and the sarcophagus of one, with mummy, is in the museum. This is a verandahed old house on high ground overlooking the ruins and set in well-kept gardens. Inside, anything that can rot or crumble away is doing so unmolested. Temporarily, and maybe forever, that includes the ram mummy, which along with all other mummies has been dumped in a back room. There remains on view a golden bust of Khnum with brown peaceful eyes, and an assortment of jewellery, pots, granite statues of island governors, weapons, bronze mirrors and beautiful slate palettes for cosmetics in the form of fish, birds, buffalo and hippopotamus – all of them local finds dating from the predynastic through Byzantine periods, and labelled in English and Arabic.

The museum

The greatest pleasure of the island, however, is to follow the pathways which wander off through fields and luxuriant palms to the three Nubian-speaking villages of the island. The houses are pale yellow or brilliant blue, the eyes of the young girls alluringly black. A brass woman's hand serves as a door knocker, a ring on one finger. Some doorways are carved with crocodiles at the foot, fish in the middle and a man on top, the woman's hand between fish and man, a statement of ideal proximities. The Kaaba, the sacred black cube at Mecca, is painted on some housefronts to show that its owner has been on the hajj, and sometimes to show how he got there a boat will be added, or fancifully a single-engined propeller plane with open cockpit, or more likely a wide-bodied chartered jet. At the north end of the island is that big hotel again, behind a 3-metre high cordon sanitaire, erected I first thought to keep the Nubians out, but on second thought almost certainly to keep the air-conditioned people in.

Botanical gardens

On the way to Kitchener's Island, Aswan disappears behind Elephantine Island and you could be almost anywhere along the Nile, except that few stretches of the river are as lovely as this. Kitchener was presented with the island when he was Consul-General in Egypt and here he indulged his passion for flowers, ordering plants from India and all over the Middle and Far East. It attracts birds of remarkable pattern and colour, but is a trifle too formal to be exotic. At the south end there is the odd sight of hundreds of white ducks paddling about in a closed-off cove, a research station for duck breeding.

Noble tombs

The noble tombs are on the west bank of the Nile opposite the north ends of Elephantine and Kitchener. They are modest structures, mostly dating from the end of the Old Kingdom through the First Intermediate Period and the Middle Kingdom. Ascending steps from the landing stage, you come to the tombs numbered from south to north. The first of interest are *Nos. 25 and 26, the tombs of Mekhu and his son Sabni.* These are of the VI Dynasty, a period of decline, and are crude both in construction and decoration; it is the entrance (blocked) of No. 26 that is noteworthy, for an inscription on it states that Sabni, governor of Elephantine, mounted an expedition against the Nubians who had killed his father; that he recovered the body which was then mummified by embalmers sent by the Pharaoh; and that Sabni went to Memphis to thank him and offer presents. Apart from instancing an occasion of Yebu's military role on Egypt's southern border, the inscription shows how múch importance was attached to the outpost by Memphis. *Tomb No. 31 of Sirenput,* also a governor, and son of Satet-Hotep, is one of the largest and best preserved. It was constructed in the XII Dynasty, the apogee of the Middle Kingdom, when Egypt extended its power beyond the Second Cataract. Paintings of Sirenput alongside Osiris statues of the deceased in the corridor, and in the recess of the second chamber, are delicately executed and still vivid.

The unnumbered *tomb of Heka-ib,* immediately to the north of No. 35, was only cleared in 1947. It has a handsome facade with two columns and inside good reliefs depicting fishing, hunting and bulls fighting. *No. 36 is the tomb of Sirenput,* son of Sat-tjeni, and is about 60 years earlier than No. 31, but also XII Dynasty. A limestone doorway leads to a six-columned courtyard decorated with the makings of a contented afterlife: a large figure of the deceased followed by his sandal-bearer and two dogs; another of his bow-bearer, dog and three sons; and others of fishing, women bringing flowers and two men gambling.

Moslem shrine

The summit of the hill is crowned with the Kubbet el Hawa, the shrine of a local sheikh and holy man, and commands a magnificent view of the Nile Valley, the cataract and the desert that more than compensates for the difficult climb. A path runs from here across the desert to St Simeon, about 45 minutes by foot.

Mausoleum of the Aga Khan

An easier way of reaching St Simeon is by landing below the Mausoleum of the Aga Khan. The walk from here is about 20 minutes, though a donkey, or preferably a camel, can be hired. But first you should visit the mausoleum, principally for the view, built above the Aga Khan's white villa where until his death in 1957 he spent the winter months and where the Begum still does. Apart from its beauty, I have heard a story that he associated himself with the spot after he found a cure here for his leg trouble by immersing himself up to the waist in the sand. The restrained proportions and the granite and sandstone of the domed mausoleum are entirely in keeping with the surroundings. The tomb within is of white Carrara marble. Each morning in winter the Begum lays a red rose on the tomb, and the ritual is taken over in summer by the gardener. There is another story that one July not a single rose was to be found in Egypt and on six successive days a red rose was flown in by private plane from Paris.

Aga Khan III, in addition to his fondness for horses, was also spiritual leader of the Ismailis, a Shi'ite sect. He is succeeded by his son Aga Khan IV.

Monastery of St Simeon

The Monastery of St Simeon (in Arabic, Deir Amba Samaan) with its towers and walls looms like a Byzantine fortress on a ridge at the head of a desert valley once cultivated with fields and gardens down to the Nile. Founded much earlier but largely built in the 8th C, it is the finest example of an original Christian monastery in Egypt, and is highly evocative. Little is known of St Simeon – he was not the Stylite – but the death, perhaps martyrdom, in 304 of Bishop Hadra occasioned the founding. The Copts base their calendar from that year. The bishop's tomb may have been here, a pilgrims' rest and monastery growing up afterwards. The monastery actively survived into the Middle Ages, but in 1321, 11 churches were destroyed by the Arabs in Aswan, the St Simeon monks were killed or driven out, and though the monastery was left intact it remained abandoned thereafter.

St Simeon was built on a grand scale, with dressed stone walls 10 metres high. A small city lay within the walls, with cells for 300 resident monks and dormitories for several hundred pilgrims, as well as bakeries and workshops to support the community. The hills and desert roundabout offered solitude and godly communion for probably thousands of monks and hermits.

The lower storeys of the monastery are stone; the upper are mud brick and it is these that have most fallen into decay or vanished altogether. You enter the *portal*, and before you, on a height, it the three-storey *keep*, open to the sky, cells on either side of the long corridors. Stucco seems to have been applied throughout the monastery, and on it, in the apses of the *basilica* to your left, are badly damaged paintings. There is a Christ Pantokrator in the central apse; on the sides, the faces of saints have been cut out. Names are carved right into the paintings by Arabs and tourists alike – it is not only time that has taken its toll. The monastery has never been systematically excavated, nor has there been any reconstruction: it is largely a confusion of vaults, staircases, walls, workshops and quarters. From the tops of the *walls* there is a glimpse of Aswan, of green, but around 350 of the other degrees there is only the desert sea, luridly red at sundown. Yet there is an evening breeze, and amidst the gardens and within the shadow of the towering walls it must have been cool. It is strange to wander round these arches, vaults and apses of familiar shape and significance; and even before the Arabs came it must have been like that, this comforting bastion against the fierce landscape.

On the way back, my camel was grunting and snorting and emitting high-pitched complaints, and with the Nubian chiding and crying at her, it was like a dialogue, a dialogue of those inarticulations of a man and woman in bed. I would guess that there is an extensive woman-as-camel (or vice versa) folklore in the East.

Sailing to Sehel

By now you have become addicted to sailing in a felucca on the Nile, and the only cure is to have more of it. The longer journey upstream to the island of Sehel is recommended. The current is against you but the prevailing wind is in your favour and the gaff is extended upwards giving great height and grace to the sail. Sehel is just below the First Cataract, and even at the north end the boat is shoved about by turbulent whirlpools. Hawks hovering above the cliffs wheel and dive for fish. You land on the east side and walk southwards over the sands to a granite outcrop streaked with bird droppings and covered with inscriptions from the IV Dynasty to the Ptolemaic period. Up top and towards the south is one of the most interesting (No. 81), Ptolemaic in date but depicting Zoser and the god Khnum. The inscription relates to a famine lasting seven years through Zoser's reign. Zoser asks the governor of Aswan why the Nile has not flooded and is told that is in the power of Khnum to whom Zoser then erects a temple. From here there is a view of the rocks and swirling waters of the cataract, but the pounding Nile and foam passed into history with the construction of the British dam. It is cool as you sail upon the river, though the sun can be dangerous; on the island there is no mistaking its ferocity. You need to be well shod, for the sand and piles of rock are blisteringly hot. A Nubian village lies off to the west and here you can enter a house and enjoy a refreshing cup of mint tea. The walls are thick and insulating, and the barrelled or domed roof reflects the heat at every angle; it is very cool inside.

The felucca tacks back down the Nile, taking advantage of the current. The round trip to Sehel is about 3 hours. The boatmen drink directly from the Nile, pointing out that there is no bilharzia above Esna and certainly not in the middle of the river where the current flows swiftly. It is said that to drink from the Nile is to ensure your return, so I drank: a fresh and slightly organic taste. Nor, with bilharzia no nearer than Esna and the crocodiles held at bay by the High Dam, could I resist plunging into the river altogether and opening my eyes on the almost impenetrably green water. Afterwards, you smell like the Nile, but a shower admits you once again onto the terrace of the Old Cataract. Just as they are designed to catch the slightest breeze, so in the last faint blue of sunset the felucca sails catch that glimmer of light off the horizon, and like crescent moons glide among the rocks in the Nile below.

Outlying sights

Early another morning you are collected by your hired car and are driven round the outlying sights. A road leading off the roundabout by the public gardens turns south towards the Fatimid cemetery with its domed mausolea of holy figures,

Fatimid cemetery and the unfinished obelisk

some local, others–such as Sayyida Zeinab, Ali's daughter and granddaughter of the Prophet – more widely revered. A turning to the left brings you to the ancient granite quarries and the unfinished obelisk. Roughly dressed and cut nearly free from the surrounding bedrock, in its finished state it would have weighed over one million kilograms (2.3 million pounds) and would have been the largest piece of stone handled in history. But work stopped after a flaw was discovered in the stone.

Back on the road south and 5 kms from town you come to the Aswan Dam, built by the British between 1898 and 1902. The road passes over it and across the cataract; the water swirls round the jagged stones, plays white, but has lost its boil. The height of the dam was twice raised to increase irrigation and its hydroelectric capacity was multiplied, but Egypt's fast growing population and the need both to further increase her cultivable land area and to provide vast new supplies of power for a necessary industrialisation programme led to work beginning in the mid-1960s on the High Dam 6 kms upriver. The road linking the two runs through disturbed desert on the west bank, a giant disused sand pit it seems; you can't imagine that this is the shore of an uncharted sand ocean going on forever. Numerous electricity pylons add to the impression of it being a manmade litter ground. At the west approach to the dam there is a giant lotus-shaped monument commemorating Russian-Egyptian co-operation, with Nasser's profile in outline and Sadat's superimposed. The police here take the opportunity to check your papers and impose a charge.

The High Dam

The High Dam has commanded world attention. Its construction became a political issue between East and West. Its sheer size, its effect on the economic potential of the country, and the sudden attention it forced on the Nubian antiquities threatened by the rising waters of Lake Nasser, have all been extraordinary. The dam was completed in 1971 and since then the water contained by it has reached a height of 182 metres and has backed up 500 kms, deep into the Sudan. Evaporation from the artificial lake amounts to 5000 million cubic metres annually (about seven percent of the lake's volume) and is causing unusual clouds and haze in the surrounding area. But the lake also retains the silt that once renewed Egypt's fields. Chemical fertiliser plants running off the dam's hydroelectric power are filling that gap, while it is estimated that in 500 years' time the silt will have filled the lake. By then, however, some other means of water conservation may have become available, or the wasteland to the south may have reverted to the lushness of long distant millenia. The water table beneath the Sahara has already risen noticeably as far away as Algeria. Downstream, Egypt's cultivable land area has increased by 30 percent, while the High Dam's dynamos have doubled the country's supply of electricity. The British dam regulated the flow of the Nile during the course of the year; the High Dam can store surplus water over a number of years, balancing low floods against high and ensuring up to three harvests a year. The god Khnum has answered Zoser's prayer.

The structure that achieves this contains the equivalent in material of 17 pyramids the size of the Great Pyramid of Cheops, and enough metal has been used in its gates, sluices and power plant to build 15 Eiffel Towers. The road runs across the top back to the east bank. In merely driving along, somehow the hugeness of the enterprise is lost upon you, and because it is not ancient, and because it is functional and it works, it is easy not to be impressed. It is even possible for some to complain that it was not worth the drowning of so many Nubian monuments. The same was said when the British built their dam, to which Churchill replied: "This offering of 1500 millions of cubic feet of water to Hathor by the Wise Men of the West is the most cruel, the most wicked and the most senseless sacrifice over offered on the altar of a false religion. The state must struggle and the people starve, in order that the professors may exult and the tourists find some place to scratch their names". Some feeling for the controlled energy of the place is realised at the viewing platform over to the eastern end of the dam. The green water rises in eddies, like large bursting bubbles from somewhere below the visible tops of the sluices. The generators hum as the river is put through its paces. Scores of lesser pylons flick currents of electricity towards the larger pylons striding across the desert, and bound by thick cables this energy is delivered into Egypt. Downstream, the Nile slips its harness and runs free beneath a glassy surface.

Kalabsha temple On an island immediately upriver from the High Dam and towards the west bank, you can see the Temple of Kalabsha, built during the reign of Augustus to the familiar blueprint of his Ptolemaic predecessors. Considering the effort that went into saving the temple from drowning at its original site 50 kms further into Nubia, little encouragement is given to visiting this stone-by-stone reconstruction. Three permissions and a hydrofoil full of passengers are required before a local travel agency will contemplate the undertaking. A German team removed the temple here, and as a reward the west pylon was presented to the Berlin Museum. As the temple was being dismantled, evidence of earlier structures dating from the time of Amenophis II (XVII Dyn) and Ptolemy IX was found. Considered to rank second only to Abu Simbel as the finest monument south of Philae and enjoying a harmony of proportion, nevertheless the temple was never completely adorned with reliefs and inscriptions, and the reliefs are generally of poor workmanship. Dedicated to Mandulis, a Nubian god associated with Isis, the Kalabsha temple later became a Christian church. Its greatest delight for the visitor is the spectacular view from its roof across the vast blue of Lake Nasser.

Philae The redoubtable Amelia Edwards described Philae in 1877: "It is one of the world's famous landscapes, and it deserves its fame. Every sketcher sketches it; every traveller describes it. Yet it is just one of those places of which the objective and subjective features are so equally balanced that it bears putting neither into words nor colours. The sketcher must perforce leave out the atmosphere of association which informs his subject; and the writer's description is at best no better than a *catalogue raisonnée*". That was before construction of the British dam, when you could winter at Aswan and visit the Temple of Isis standing proud on its sacred island. But the dam all but submerged the temple for half the year, during the winter at that, and Philae became a name only, hardly a place to visit. Yet there was romance in that visit, and perverse though it might seem to say it, a romance, once established, far greater than any satisfaction gained from seeing Philae raised again on new and profane ground. In *Daniel Martin,* John Fowles records the experience many travellers have enjoyed this century: "Then they drove to see the temple of Philae; a long row out into the lake, followed by the slow gondola-like tour round the submerged columns, shadowy shafts in the translucent green water. An exquisite light shimmered and danced on the parts that rose into the air. They and the guide were rowed by two old men, with scrawny wrists and mummified bare feet. Every so often, on the long haul, the pair would break into a strange question-and-answer boating-chant, half sung, half spoken. Work on transporting the temple to its new site, the guide proudly told them, would begin within the next few months; very soon sunken Philae would be abusimbelized. They didn't argue with him, but voted it a vulgarity, the whole project, over lunch".

Saving the temple The annual rise and fall of the Nile, elevated behind the British dam, slowly wore on the inscriptions and reliefs of the temple and eventually, though perhaps after only hundreds of years, would have brought the whole thing down. But then the High Dam was built and Philae, between the two, was permanently almost completely submerged, and worse, where it rose just clear of the river, suffered swift daily tide-like movements that would have destroyed the temple far sooner. With Hathor doubly gratified, it has now been the turn of professors and tourists to avenge Churchill's words. Whether Isis would have preferred drowning to the new *son et lumiere* is unknown.

I have not padded about the new Philae. The nearby island, Algikia, on which it has been resurrected was opened only shortly before this edition was published. My description of it as it appears for the first time on dry land for more than three-quarters of a century must necessarily be a *catalogue raisonnée* based entirely on old accounts, principally ancient Baedekers. I have circled round the island after temple reconstruction but before the landscaping was complete. If the boatmen sang, they could not be heard over the noise of the outboard motor. The island was a dust heap, littered with Italian earth-moving equipment. It was anything but romantic, and for some years there must remain a strong feeling of artificiality about the new site. Whether the old magic will return, I do not know, but nature certainly will impress herself, mimosa and lantana quickly growing, palms and acacias taking firm root with the years, birds settling and the stones themselves fired from grey dampness to tawny warmth by the sun.

Touring the new island

Algikia has been carved and sliced to replicate the original island, so that it is 450 metres long and 150 metres across, with the blunt nose and truncated tail of a primitive fish. The Temple of Isis has been arranged along the dorsal position, the lesser temples placed elsewhere, all corresponding as nearly as possible to their previous relationships. The logical starting point for a tour is the *Vestibule of Nectanebos I* (XXX Dyn) at the southwest corner of the island. The temple it once led to was washed away by the Nile, but this vestibule was rebuilt by Ptolemy II Philedelphos. Nearly every other monument on the island dates from the Ptolemaic and Roman periods, and Herodotus, who visited Elephantine c.450 BC, seems to have found no reason to make any mention of Philae, though it is probable that older temples stood on the island then. Northwards extends the *outer temple court*, the first pylon of the Temple of Isis at its far end, colonnades on either side. The East Colonnade is unfinished, with many of the columns only rough-hewn; the West Colonnade follows the shoreline, its columns bearing reliefs of Tiberius offering gifts to the gods, the capitals of varying plant motifs, no two alike.

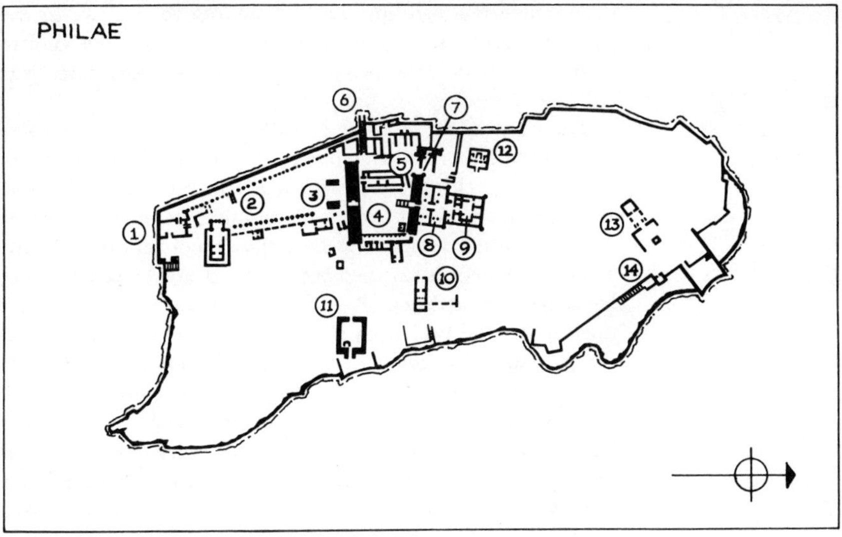

1. Vestibule of Nectanebos I
2. Outer temple court
3. Fir Pylon
4. Central court of the Temple of Isis
5. Birth House
6. Nilometer
7. Second Pylon
8. Pronaos
9. Noas and Sanctuary
10. Temple of Hathor
11. Kiosk of Trajan
12. Temple of Harendotes
13. Temple of Augustus
14. Roman Gate

The *First Pylon,* 18 metres high, 45 metres wide, consists of two massive towers with a gateway between them. The towers were begun by Ptolemy II Philadelphos and completed by Euergetes I, though the decorations were carried out over a longer period. On the front of the right or eastern tower, Ptolemy XII Neos Dionysos is shown in the traditional pharaonic pose of seizing his enemies by the hair, about to bash their brains out with a club; Isis, Hathor and the falcon-headed Horus of Edfu look on placidly. Above and to the right, Neos Dionysos offers the crowns of Upper and Lower Egypt to Horus the child. On the left or western tower, Neos Dionysos is again sacrificially braining his foes while above he appears before Unnefer (the name given to Osiris after his resurrection) and Isis, and before Isis and Harsiesis, a form of Horus. The reliefs have been severely damaged by the Copts. The vertical grooves on the towers were for holding flagstaffs. The *main gateway* was built earlier by Nectanebos and bears reliefs of him as well as Coptic crosses and, as you pass through, a French inscription on the right commemorating the victory of General Desaix over the Mamelukes in 1799 ("an VII de la République"). Round to the rear of the right tower there is a winding *stairway* leading to the top; in the past, its ascent was recommended for a comprehensive view of the island. Visitors should trouble to discover if the stairway is still open.

The gateway through the First Pylon admits to the *forecourt* of the temple, with the colonnaded quarters of the priests to the right, the *Birth House* to the left. The birth house became an essential feature of Ptolemaic temples, its purpose similar to Hatshepsut's depiction at Deir el Bahri of her divine birth.

The cult of Osiris

There, Hatshepsut justified her temporal rule by proclaiming her descent from Amun-Re; with the spread of the Osiris cult until under the Ptolemies it became the universal religion of Egypt, each Pharaoh legitimised his accession by demonstrating his descent from Horus, first Pharaoh and prime law-giver in the land. There are many strands to the Osiris legend, and many accretions to the story and levels of meaning. Osiris, son of Re, was a king who ruled and was greatly loved in distant times. Isis was his sister and wife, Seth his brother. When Seth killed Osiris and dismembered his body, Isis searched out the pieces and put them together again, wondrously restoring Osiris to life in the underworld where he reigned as judge and king. Isis' son Horus was secretly raised to manhood in Lower Egypt and after a long and desperate struggle overcame Seth and established order over all Egypt. Historically, this may recall the subjection of the south by the north in pre-dynastic times. Mystically, Horus is the incarnation of his father, while Isis is the agent of both resurrection and reincarnation. Celebration of the rites relating to the legend, and in particular to the birth of Horus, took place at these birth houses, the Pharaoh proclaiming his legitimacy through his involvement in them. The Birth House at Philae is surrounded on four sides by colonnades and round their walls and columns are reliefs and inscriptions dating from Euergetes II, Neos Dionysos, Augustus and Tiberius. In the last (northernmost) chamber within are reliefs of Horus as a falcon in the marshes, and Isis suckling Horus in the marshes of the Delta. On the west shore of the island, beyond the Birth House, is a nilometer.

The *Second Pylon* is at an angle to the first and not quite so large. Again, Neos Dionysos is shown before the deities, this time offering animal sacrifices and incense; the reliefs on the eastern tower are better preserved than those on the western. Shallow steps lead to the *gateway* between the two. Figures here of Euergetes II and deities are greatly defaced; on the right there is an inscription to Bishop Theodoros, in whose name, most likely, much of the defacement occurred. It is testimony to the sheer quantity of antiquities in Egypt that through 4000 or more years, with one pharaoh defacing the work of another, Christians defacing the work of pagans, Moslems defacing the work of Christians and tourists defacing the work of everybody, there still remains so much to be defaced by those who can find the time and excuse for doing so.

It is through the Second Pylon that you enter the *pronaos* of the Temple of Isis proper. Pharaohs might have justified themselves at the Birth House, but this would have been the all-important goal of select pilgrims not only from Egypt but from all over the Mediterranean right through to the mid-6th C.AD. For Isis was the hinge upon which the Osiris legend hung, and through her suffering and her joy the goddess offered an emotive identification so powerful and satisfying that she became identified too with all other goddesses of the Mediterranean, whom she finally absorbed. Isis was the Goddess of Ten Thousand Names, Shelter and Heaven to All Mankind, the House of Life, the Great Mother of All Gods and Nature, Victorious over Fate, the Promise of Immortality, Sexuality and Purity, the Glory of Women – when all else failed, she still could save. She was passionately worshipped by men and women alike. Cleopatra deliberately identified herself with Isis, and called herself the New Isis, casting Antony as Dionysos, the Greek equivalent of Osiris, so that on earth they effected the already existing cosmological bond. Christianity, with its male-oriented antecedents in the Judaic and Greek religions, may never have given the prominence it did to the Virgin Mary had not a figure been needed to absorb in turn the great popularity and success of the rival Isis cult. It was a rivalry that continued late into the Christian era. In spite of the edicts of the Roman Emperor Theodosius I, which succeeded in terminating the Olympic Games after a thousand years in the 4th C. AD, pagan Philae continued as a centre of Isis worship till the reign of Justinian in the 6th C., while further into Nubia the worship of Isis probably persisted until the Arab Islamic conquest.

The cult of Isis

For Flaubert, the pronaos and the small court preceding it held "a thousand charming details", while Amelia Edwards gushed: "Here is a place in which time seems to have stood as still as in that immortal palace where everything went to sleep for a hundred years. The bas-reliefs on the walls, the intricate paintings on the ceilings, the colours upon the capitals are incredibly fresh and perfect...Above all, it is with the colour – colour conceived in the tender and pathetic minor of Watteau and Lancret and Greuze – that one is most fascinated...Every tint is softened, intermixed, degraded. The pinks are coralline; the greens are tempered with verditer; the blues are of a greenish turquoise, like the western half of an autumnal evening sky". Whether the Watteaus have survived their long immersion is doubtful; in any case, even before full flood Baediker was colourless: "The walls are covered both outside and inside with reliefs of Ptolemies (Philadelphus, Euergetes II, etc.) and Roman emperors (Augustus, Tiberius, Antoninus) performing the customary ceremonies in the guise of Pharaohs...The Court had a small colonnade on each side, the roof of which rested on a single column. The uncovered portion could be shaded from the sun by means of a velarium [awning]...The Vestibule [pronaos], with eight columns, was originally separated from the preceding court by stone screens...Christian services were celebrated in the court and vestibule, of which the numerous Coptic crosses chiselled in the walls are memorials". In the doorway of a room to the right is another Greek inscription to Bishop Theodoros, claiming credit for "this good work".

Three antechambers lead through the naos to the *Sanctuary* with two small windows and a pedestal on which stood the sacred boat with the image of Isis. To the west of the first antechamber entered, a staircase runs up to the roof and to the *Osiris chambers* with fine reliefs of mourning for Osiris. Flaubert again is brief: "In one of the upper rooms, scenes of embalming: in the corner to the right a woman on her knees lamenting, her arms raised in despair; here the artist's observation cuts through the ritual of the conventional form".

Back at the bottom of the stairway, a door in the west wall of the naos opens onto *Hadrian's Gateway*. The most interesting relief is on the north wall of the vestibule and depicts the source of the Nile: the Nile god, entwined by a serpent, pours water from two jars. This relates to the ancient belief that the source of the Nile was at the First Cataract. The waters so swirled and seemed to flow in different directions that it was thought the river rose here from underground, flowing north to the Mediterranean and south into Africa. The belief hinged, as most beliefs do, on laziness and the desire not to spoil a good story: the most cursory examination of the river's flow at any point south of the First Cataract would have revealed, as no doubt it did reveal a thousand times, that the Nile always flowed north. Herodotus, who always enjoyed a good story himself, nevertheless dismissed the notion expressed in this relief, traced the northerly flow of the Nile back deep into Africa, and even reported a theory, based almost certainly on lost knowledge, that the source of the Nile, and the cause of its floods, lay in distant snowfalls, – a theory he rejected (though 2000 or so years later it was proved right) because he could not imagine high snow mountains somewhere in the hot interior of Africa.

Off to the east of the Second Pylon is the *Temple of Hathor,* comparable to the Greek Aphrodite despite the usual convention of cow's ears, built by Ptolemy VI Philometor and Euergetes II. The colonnade was decorated during the reign of Augustus with amusing carvings of music and drinking – apes dancing and one playing a lute, dwarfish Bes beating a tambourine, while Augustus offers a festal crown to Isis. To the south stands the unfinished *Kiosk of Trajan,* a rectangular building of 14 columns with beautifully carved floral capitals. On the only two screen walls between the columns to have been completed are scenes of the Emperor Trajan offering incense and wine to Isis, Osiris and Horus. The elegance of the kiosk has made it the characteristic symbol of the island.

Abu Simbel

Originally, the rock-temples of Abu Simbel stared from sandstone cliffs which rose like gigantic pylons over the narrow Nile. In 1812, John Lewis Burkhardt, the first educated man in modern times to visit Abu Simbel, was not immediately impressed; he had come upon the cliffs from above, and only as he gained the river and turned upstream was he struck by the four colossal statues of Ramses II. "Could the sand be cleared away," he said, "a vast temple would be discovered." The sand was repeatedly cleared away during the 19th C. There is a remarkable photograph taken in 1850 by Maxime du Camp, Flaubert's travelling companion, of the sand rising over the faces of the two right-hand colossi. On Holy Thursday, Flaubert noted, "We begin clearing operations, to disengage the chin of one of the exterior colossi". It was only later in the century, with the coming of the British, that Abu Simbel and so many other monuments were properly cleared. Then, usually by Cook's steamer, tourists came. Laid bare in all their glory, and enhanced by the unique and striking beauty of the setting, the temples at Abu Simbel excited the enthusiasm of early visitors. Baedeker allowed himself a large adjective: they "are among the most stupendous monuments of ancient Egyptian architecture"; and he went on to say: "the temples produce a very grand effect by moonlight or at sunrise. The interior of the great temple is illuminated at night by electricity provided from the steamer". Those were the days.

Getting there

There is no road or railroad to Abu Simbel, tourist steamers no longer make the voyage, and even the hydrofoil service has been discontinued. You must fly. Admittedly, the pilot swoops back and forth before the temples so that first, unlike Burkhardt, you see the facades. But the colossi are small from the air, and further lose all advantage of proportion by having to outstare the vastness of Lake Nasser. Once the plane lands, you bumble along a desert road by bus, disembark behind the artifical mounds, tread round to the front, gaze upon Ramses in quadruplicate, and say, "So what". That's what I said, anyway, though the journey itself, and the phoniness of the climax, were in their way worthwhile.

The flight is a mixture of sensations: orbiting round the Moon; going on a school outing. The latter because you know everyone else on board is going exactly where you are going, will stay as long as you are staying, will look at what you are looking at, and that you will appear in a thousand of their photographs and they on a roll of yours. The former because the landscape enroute is spectacularly alien, a rippling sand plateau interrupted by sharpened buttes, perhaps the cores of eroded ancient volcanoes which later from ground level will occasionally look like pyramids; and Lake Nasser, peculiar and varying in its colours, a giant drifting oil slick upon the desert sea.

Saving Abu Simbel

As the waters of Lake Nasser rose during the mid-1960s, the original site of the temples was protected momentarily behind a coffer dam while the friable sandstone was injected with synthetic resin and then hand-sawn into 1050 blocks. The first block was cut in spring 1965; by autumn 1967, block had been replaced upon block at the new site 210 metres from the old one and 61 metres higher up. The $42 million operation was organised and funded by UNESCO. The temples were saved, the dam was breached, and the sacred site, which had known human activity since prehistoric times, was swallowed by the lake.

There is such a thing as spirit of place. That place lies behind you and below you somewhere beneath the waters as you stand facing the colossi of Ramses. The reconstruction has been impeccable; you knock your knuckles against Ramses' foot and are assured it is stone, not plaster; you look for the filled-in joins in the torsos but can't detect them; and if you are there at dawn you will see that the sun's rays fall flat upon the pharaonic faces and, if the temple door is open, penetrate to the innermost sanctuary. Everything is as it was before, except that it is here and not where it used to be, and that greatly weakens the force of the new Abu Simbel. The genius of the place lay in working with the living rock, the temple facades set into cliff faces seemingly prepared by nature for the purpose, the colossi of Ramses at the south temple, those of Nefertari at the north temple, seeming to step out from the mountain, liberated from the imprisoning rock by the divine force of the rising sun. But when the cliffs are themselves reconstructions, that dramatic relationship between architecture and topography, and that mystical emergence of man from nature, is lost. To have left those ancient and powerful links intact would have meant surrendering the temples to the waters. Instead, it was decided to save the body and lose the soul. We now examine the carcass.

Touring the temples

The temples stand on the west bank of the lake, the more southerly Temple of Re-Harakhte, with its colossi of Ramses II, facing east, the smaller and more northerly Temple of Hathor, with its colossi of Nefertari, Ramses' wife, angled slightly towards the south. Before the lake, the temples overlooked a bend in the Nile and must have dominated the landscape. This in part explains their purpose. Travellers into Africa would first have seen the imposing colossi of Ramses, a proud spur to Egyptians, a warning of Egypt's might to any fractious Nubians. On the return, Hathor, in the guise of Nefertari, would welcome Egyptians and Nubians alike to the embrace of a great civilisation. Also, the temples would have served as a convenient store for the gold and other riches exacted from Nubia as tribute, just as nearly a thousand years later the Parthenon served as the Athenian treasury. But the political and strongbox functions of Abu Simbel would have relied greatly on the religious character of the temples, and that the architects addressed themselves to religious symbolism of magnificent scale and quality there can be no doubt.

Temple of Re-Harakhte

You come first upon the *Temple of Re-Harakhte,* its trapezoidal *facade* crowned by a corvetto cornice surmounted by dog-headed creatures worshipping the rising sun. The falcon-headed sun god stands within the niche above the entrance door. Arranged in pairs on either side of the entrance are the four enthroned *colossi of Ramses* wearing the double crown. Each figure is 20 metres high, taller than the Colossi of Memnon at Thebes, and hewn from the cliff face. Between and beside the massive legs are smaller figures of members of the royal family. The feet and legs of the colossi are crudely carved, as though deliberatly inchoate, but the work grows finer up through the torsos (the head and torso of the second colossus from the left fell sometime in the past and has been left that way), and the heads are excellently executed. This is most true of the first head on the left, of which Burkhardt remarked, "a most expressive, youthful countenance, approaching nearer to the Grecian model of beauty than that of any ancient Egyptian figure I have seen". The sides of the thrones on either side of the entrance are decorated with Nile gods symbolically uniting Egypt, while below are fettered prisoners: those to the left, black Africans; those to the right, Syrians.

Entering the temple, the first room is the *Hypostyle Hall,* corresponding to an open court with covered colonnades. There are four pillars on either side, against which and facing the central aisle are 10-metre high Osiris-type figures of Ramses, though this is Ramses alive, not dead, in an athletic near-nudity showing a process of heroisation at work. The best is the fourth figure in the north row. Heroic martial deeds are depicted in *sunk relief around the walls.* If you face the entrance you will see on the left (north) entrance wall a vigorous account of the battle of Kadesh in the fifth year of Ramses' reign. It was a battle Ramses endlessly boasted about, and boast he needed to do as it was no more than a Pyrrhic victory. Ramses cut himself out of a Hittite trap, but he failed to take Kadesh. Above Ramses is a vulture, and behind him his ka, who acted as guardian angel in the struggle. On the right (north) entrance wall a corresponding scene shows Ramses in the presence of Amun-Re, to whom the king appealed at his most desperate moment: "What ails thee, my father Amun? [Amun was absorbed in Amun-Re.] Is it a father's part to ignore his son? Have I done anything without thee, do I not walk and halt at thy bidding? I have not disobeyed any course commanded by thee...What careth thy heart, O Amun, for these Asiatics so vile and ignorant of God?...What will men say if even a little thing befall him who bends himself to thy counsel?"

Poem of Pentaur

Facing again the interior, the left (south) wall of the hall bears an epic masterpiece depicting (below the top five reliefs showing the king making offerings to the gods) the king in his chariot storming a Syrian fortress, at centre the king piercing a Libyan with his lance, and to the right the king's triumphal return from battle with black captives. On the opposite (north) wall are further scenes from the Hittite campaign, while on the rear wall Ramses is shown leading Hittite and black captives. *Lateral chambers* leading off from this top end of the Hypostyle Hall were probably used for storing the Nubian tribute.

In the next *hall of four pillars,* reliefs on the left (south) wall show Ramses and Nefertari before the sacred boat of Amun, and on the opposite (north) wall a similar scene before the boat of Re-Herakhte. Three doors lead from here into a transverse chamber from which in turn three doors lead off, the central one into the *Sanctuary*. Four seated mutilated figures are carved out of the rear wall: Ptah, god of Memphis, Amun, god of Thebes, the divinised Ramses, and Re-Harakhte, god of Heliopolis. Before them is a stone block on which would have rested the sacred boat. The symbolism is one of unity, the Pharaoh and gods of Egypt's three greatest cities at one; but there is also Ramses as the living and visible god, perhaps again to awe the Nubians. The entire temple leads to this central message: Ramses as conqueror, hero and then god, the awesome progression enhanced by the heightened perspective of ever-smaller chambers, ever-smaller doorways, and at the dawns when the sun rose exactly opposite the temple, a brilliant shaft of light pointing to the sacred boat and Ramses with his fellow gods in the Sanctuary. Leaving the temple you should stand before the facade again, before the entrance with its falcon-headed sun god, and imagine that effect.

Temple of Hathor

You now walk on to the Temple of Hathor. On the edge of the forecourt there are some trees and welcome shade. While I was here, and perhaps now too, there was a low rectangle beneath these trees, hardly more than an outline on the ground with a gap at one end, a niche at the other. It was a mosque, just broad enough for two prostrate figures, so great a contrast to the massive temples, so great a witness to the immanence and power of Allah.

The *Temple of Hathor* is secondary and complementary to the larger Temple of Re-Harakhte, and in some ways more symbolically satisfying. Hathor was wife to the sun god during his day's passage and mother to his rebirth. As Ramses is identified with the god of the first temple, so his wife Nefertari is identified with the goddes of this, and so god, goddess, Pharaoh and wife are each mated with one another at Abu Simbel. The *facade* is again a pylon, though the cavetto cornice has fallen. A series of buttresses rise into the cliff, and between them six *colossal statues* of Ramses and Nefertari. You should get up close to them. There is here the uncanny impression that they are emerging from the rock, that they are forming and will at any moment stride out towards the sunrise. The royal children stand knee-high in the shadows.

Inside the *Hypostyle Hall* with its crudely carved heads of Hathor on the six pillars, turn to examine the entrance wall. Ramses is smiting his enemies; Nefertari's hands are raised, perhaps as part of the ritual, though she seems to be seeking to moderate the fury of Pharaoh. In any case, she cuts a delightful figure, a slender form in flowing dress, appealing, graceful, dignified. The side walls show Ramses before various gods, while the rear wall shows Nefertari before Hathor (left) and before Mut (right). Three doors lead to a *transverse chamber*. On either side is a further chamber above the entrances to which are Hathor's cow in her boat. In the *Sanctuary* there is the startling sight of the divine cow emerging from the rear rock wall, a suggestion of the world beyond where her milk brings life to the souls of the dead.

By now you are parched and you discover a small door leading into the rock face to the right of Re-Harakhti's temple. The atmosphere is suddenly air-conditioned and there is a man selling cold drinks and post cards. You climb some stairs at the back and with even more surprise than seeing a cow coming at you from a stone wall you enter a vast echoic dome. It is the bubble that surmounts the major temple and over which fill has been dumped and shaped to recreate the contour of the original bluff. A walkway runs right round the inside where there are abandoned displays and sheets of data explaining how it was all done. There is much to be said for this bubble. It is the one thing at Abu Simbel that is real.

PRACTICAL INFORMATION

ACCOMMODATION

Aswan's winter high season extends from November through April and reservations are important. Summer is slack, however, though the heat should not deter you – it's a dry heat, there's air conditioning if you want it, and the older hotels, with their voluminous rooms, remain tolerably cool even without air conditioning. Prices given here are for double rooms during high season. Half board, where compulsory, will add to your bill, while service and taxes will account for a further 18%. A discount of at least 10% applies to summer rates and to single occupancy at any time.

The Cataract Hotel, Sharia Abtal el Tahrir, at the south end of the corniche. Tel: 3222 and 3434. Telex: 92720 ASCAT UN. Like Luxor's Winter Palace, this is now 2 hotels, the New Cataract (5-star) and the Old (4-star). The New is a dead ringer for the New Winter Palace and equally lacking in style. The Old stands apart, on higher ground, with the most magnificent view in Aswan, and for my money is the finest place to stay in Egypt. Also like the Winter Palace, however, guests at the Old Cataract must dine at the New (half board is compulsory year-round) in a dull restaurant with poor service and lousy food. Whether you stay at the Old or the New, insist on a Nile-side room (rear-facing rooms are a bit cheaper). The Old Cataract's outstanding amenity is its terrace; the New has shops, bank, a hairdresser, etc., and there is an Olympic-size pool for all Cataract guests. Doubles are LE24 at the New Cataract, LE14 at the Old (not all rooms are air conditioned here, but it doesn't matter). Expect to cough up about LE6 for dinner.

The Aswan Oberoi Hotel (5-star), on Elephantine Island. Tel: 3455. Telex: 93455 ASOBRO UN. Owned by the same company as the Mena House Oberoi at the Pyramids, this modern hotel looks like an airport control tower rising absurdly from the north end of the island. It is reached by regular ferries designed like ancient Egyptian royal barges (free for guests and the curious alike). Deplorable though its concreté monumentality is, the Oberoi offers fine views, particularly westwards at sundown from the rear terrace across to Kitchener's Island. There's a bank, bookshop, hairdresser, boutiques, café, nightclub, pool and other luxury trappings. Egyptair also has a branch here. Doubles are LE34, singles about 15% less.

The Kalabsha Hotel (4-star), Sharia Abtal el Tahrir. Tel: 2999. A further couple of hundred metres or so south of the Cataract hotels, the extra distance from town is not compensated for by the inferior river views and the prosaic mood of the place. With better hotels to stay at in all price ranges, the Kalabsha is to be avoided if possible. All rooms are air-conditioned; there's a bank, some shops, a bar and a restaurant which serves as a nightclub (open to Cataract guests by voucher) with Western and Nubian entertainment. Boxlike doubles are LE13. Half board is compulsory year-roound, the food uninteresting.

The Amun Hotel (4-star), Amun Island. Tel: 2555. The island is beautifully and peacefully situated just south of Elephantine and is reached by launches by the public gardens near the Egyptair office. Half board is compulsory year-round, though here the food is better than at most members of the Egyptian Hotel Company chain; there's also a bar. The verandah and rooms overlook the gardens and Nile. All rooms have bathrooms and air conditioning, prices identical to the Kalabsha.

The Abu Simbel Hotel (3-star), Corniche el Nil. Tel: 2888. You come to this hotel soon after reaching the corniche from the train station; it's surrounded by tree-shaded gardens. The bar and restaurant are over the lobby and have a view of the Nile – only Continental breakfast is compulsory. Most of the rooms have only curtained-off bathrooms, though for a bit more you get a wall. All rooms are simple, some are air-conditioned. Doubles start at LE8, singles are 25% less.

The Philae Hotel (2-star), Corniche el Nil. Tel: 2117. This is further south along the corniche from the Abu Simbel Hotel. There's a bar and better than average restaurant – only Continental breakfast is compulsory. All rooms have bathrooms, a few have air conditioning. The place is simple and clean. Doubles start at LE7, singles are 30% less.

The Grand Hotel (1-star), Corniche el Nil. Tel: 2707. Still further south along the corniche and directly opposite Elephantine, the Grand has the cachet of faded glory. Its dignified exterior and cavernous rooms (none of them air-conditioned) testify to the days when Baedeker singled it out, along with the Cataract, for star rating. Indeed, after the Old Cataract, the Grand is my favourite Aswan hotel. Admittedly it's gone to seed, but it's Nile-side rooms have superb views; it has style, it's clean, its high ceilings keep it fairly cool in summer, and it's cheap (indeed in summer you can get at least one-third off). Doubles with bathroom are LE6.50; without, they're LE5.50; and singles are 40% less in each case. Prices include breakfast. There's a pleasant garden round the side for afternoon and evening drinks and snacks.

Aswan's **youth hostel** (70PT) is on Sharia Abtal el Tahrir (Tel: 2313) at its station end – in a hot and crummy part of town away from the corniche. Walk 1 block from the station, turn left and then proceed half a block: it's on your right. My advice is to splurge and stay at the Grand.

There's also a hotel at **Abu Simbel,** the **Nefertiti** (3-star). It's half way between the airport and the temples, in other words in the middle of nowhere. The only excuse for staying here is if you want more time to see Abu Simbel. All rooms are air-conditioned; half board is compulsory; reservations a necessity. Doubles are LE14, singles LE13.

The alternative is to bring a sleeping bag and without making yourself too obvious to **sack out right at the temples.** It can get very windy, but the dawn is magnificent.

EATING PLACES AND ENTERTAINMENT

Apart from the **Philae** and **Oberoi** hotels, both of which have good food for their price range, there are several Egyptian restaurants along the corniche, tables outside. Better than these, however, is **El Masri,** tucked away in the centre of town just off the main market street, Sharia Abtal el Tahrir. Ask and you will be directed. A good kebab, salad and taheena will cost you about LE1.25.

Both the **Kalabsha** and **Oberoi** hotels have nightclubs with Western and Nubian music, the Oberoi usually having a belly dancer too. In winter, the **Aswan Cultural Centre**, between the Abu Simbel and Philae hotels, presents exciting Nubian dancing.

SHOPPING

The **Aswan Cultural Centre,** on the corniche between the Philae and Abu Simbel hotels, sells Nubian handicrafts. A block of two back from the river, however, Sharia Abtal el Tahrir is Aswan's sinuous market street, the best **bazaar** outside of Cairo, with an atmosphere still and an array of goods suggesting trade with Africa deeper south. Woven blankets and rugs are particularly good here and cheaper than elsewhere in Egypt; also there's ivory, ebony, spices, galabiyyas and everything else conceivable. As you wander along, have a glass of pressed cane juice. At the northern end there are several shops selling delightfully kitsch post cards.

OF INTEREST

On **Elephantine Island** is the museum, admission 25PT, open winter from 9am to 2pm daily, 10am to 2pm Sundays; in summer (1 May-31 October) from 8.30am to 1pm daily, 8.30am to 11am Fridays, and 10am to 1pm Sundays. There is also the nilometer, the site of the ancient town of Yebu, and the pleasant walk through Nubian villages. Small ferries cross to the island from the Grand Hotel and from the public gardens opposite the Egyptair office. You should pay about 10PT for the return trip. You cannot get to the rest of Elephantine from the Oberoi compound at the north end of the island.

To reach the **west bank** of the Nile for the Mausoleum of the Aga Khan, St Simeon's Monastery and the tombs of the nobles, and to reach Kitchener's Island, you must hire a felucca by the public gardens across from the Egyptair office, or below the bluff at the Old Cataract Hotel. Expect to pay LE2 for the first hour; for longer use (including keeping the felucca waiting) you can negotiate a flat price, working out less per hour. Your bargaining position will be stronger if you don't seek a felucca by the Old Cataract and if it's summer.

Once at the west bank you can proceed by foot, donkey or camel. Camel is best and will cost, for example, no more than LE2 for the jaunt to St Simeon's and back. Donkeys are less. There is a camel and donkey corral as you land below the mausoleum.

Groups, including a few of you together, may benefit by making all your felucca and camel hire arrangements through an agent. I recommend Wagons-lits at the Grand Hotel.

A visit to the granite **quarry,** the **old Aswan Dam** and the **new High Dam,** as well as a trip out to **Philae,** can be done in a morning, starting early. The day before, you should go to Wagons-lits and arrange for a car. If they know of other people interested, they will put together a small group which can share the cost. Car, boat and fees will add up to about LE5 per person among. 3-4 people. The **Kalabsha temple** is difficult to visit: a group of a least 20 is necessary to justify revving up the hydrofoil which departs from the High Dam; also 3 permissions are required. The whole thing is a headache to agents and they don't bother except with ready-made groups. The cost is about LE4.50 per person.

Other expeditions, like a morning's or afternoon's **sail along the Nile to Sehel** in a felucca, or a **drive to Kom Ombo and Edfu**, are best arranged through an agent like Wagons-lits. They can assure you of a good price and reliability. The 3-4 hour sail to Sehel should cost no more than LE6; a car with driver to Kom Ombo and Edfu and back, no more than LE12. Those amounts are of course to be divided amongst the number of persons going, so 4 people can take either trip at very reasonable cost.

Some boatmen will offer to sail you downriver to Kom Ombo or beyond, and some agents have refurbished old steamers for journeys to Luxor at far less the price of the Hilton and Sheraton behemoths (see *Travel* below).

The only way to reach **Abu Simbel** is to fly from Cairo, Luxor or Aswan. You should reserve a seat at the earliest opportunity, but it's always worthwhile trying even at the last moment. I was told in Cairo that all seats for Abu Simbel were booked up a week in advance; I asked again at the Egyptair office in Aswan and was given a seat for the following day. I've heard, though can't confirm it, that Egyptair always holds back 10% of its seats for counter sales on the last day or so – on all flights, not just those to Abu Simbel. It's marginally better to sit on the right-hand side of the plane for a good view of the temples on approach, though the pilot sweeps round to let passengers on the left-hand side get a view and take some pictures too. And it's certainly better to go in the morning when the sun is full on the temple facades. Unless you can show that you have made a booking at the Nefertiti Hotel at Abu Simbel, Egyptair will often insist that you fly back from Abu Simbel on the same day – an obstacle that anyone wanting to sack out at the temples in their sleeping bag should be on the look out for. A 2-hour stay at Abu Simbel is sufficient; the flight takes 25 minutes, though check-in at Aswan is anywhere from 1 to 1½ hours before the flight, which is usually late anyway. In short, allow 5 hours for the trip. Admission to the temples is LE1.50 and includes the return bus journey from Abu Simbel airport. 50PT is payable for the tour which is superficial and wastes a lot of time. Cold drinks are for sale through a door to the right of the Temple of Re-Harakhte, ie inside the dome.

TRAVEL

The best source of **information** and advice on travel and much else is **Wagon-lits** at the front of the Grand Hotel on the corniche. It acts as agent for Thomas Cook, and also operates its own Nile cruises. In the same arcade is **Eastmar**, a Nile cruise specialist.

The **train station** is at the north end of town, several blocks back from the corniche (see *Background* chapter for timetable). A taxi from the station to, say, one of the Cataract hotels should cost around 50PT on the meter, though in an unmetered taxi or carriage you're likely to be asked for LE1.

Egyptair is at the south end of the corniche, past the Grand Hotel. The airline runs a bus service between here and the airport, 50PT each way.

For a **car with driver** to **Kom Ombo** and **Edfu**, also onwards to **Esna** and **Luxor**, make arrangements through Wagons-lits. To Kom Ombo and Edfu and back should cost no more than LE12, to be divided amongst the passengers. Or go by **service (shared) taxi**: their depot is by the Abu Simbel Hotel on the corniche and the day's ride to Kom Ombo, Edfu, Esna and Luxor, requiring a change of taxis each time, should cost around 50-60PT a leg, or LE2.50 in all, per person. (See *Practical Information* at the end of the *Luxor* chapter.)

The most enjoyable way of visiting places between Aswan and Luxor is by **felucca**. You can get to Kom Ombo for about LE20, or LE30 return; to Edfu for about LE50, or LE75 return; and to Luxor, one way, for about LE75. Among 4 people or so, it can work out quite reasonably. Hire through or at least consult with Wagons-lits.

To reach the **Sudan**, either you can **fly from Cairo** (Egypt's only international airport) or **sail from Aswan** (in fact from Sadd el Ali, the High Dam). The voyage lasts for 2 nights up the length of Lake Nasser to Wadi Halfa on the border. Departure from Sadd el Ali is at 4pm on Mondays and Thursdays, arrival at Wadi Halfa is on the third day at 8am. A connecting train to Khartoum departs at 4.40pm. In fact, these schedules are for the amusement of those enchanted by such things: the boat may not leave on time; it will almost certainly arrive at Wadi Halfa late; the train will wait, however, but instead of taking the scheduled 24 hours to Khartoum is more likely to take 36 hours.

Before you will be sold a boat ticket, you must have a visa for the Sudan and must offer proof that you are paying in Egyptian pounds bought officially (ie must show a bank receipt). First and second class tickets should (some say *must*) be bought in Cairo, at the **Nile Navigation Company**, 8 Sharia Qasr el Nil (Tel: 48883). Third class tickets can be bought at the **Nile Company for River Transport** (Tel: 2300) – it's on a street off the corniche; ask for directions – or on the quayside at Sadd el Ali. First class to Wadi Halfa is about LE12, second class about LE8.50, third class about LE5.

If the boat makes good time, you'll pass Abu Simbel just as the sun goes down on the second night out; more likely you won't even get that glimpse. There are no stops between Sadd el Ali and Wadi Halfa, and food availability on board is erratic: bring your own. The boat is a paddle steamer with a barge tied alongside. Deck (third) class means sleeping in the lower metal deck of the barge; it can get very cold at night and a sleeping bag is essential. Deck class also gets crowded, so get to the boat as early as possible.

There's a train from Aswan to Sadd el Ali; take one leaving around noon to allow plenty of time for customs and passport formalities. Also, you can take a taxi for several Egyptian pounds.

Once at Wadi Halfa, you continue to **Khartoum** by first, second or third class train. Air conditioning is in first class only. Second class is bearable; third is uncomfortable and usually extremely crowded, passengers often riding on the roof (which, incidentally, is very cold at night). Sleepers cost LE28, first class LE21, second class LE11, third class LE6.

THE DESERT AND THE SEA

Egypt is a land of pairs – arranged as opposites, as complementaries, as identities. There is this life and the afterlife; the river and the sky; the cultivated land and the desert; and there is the desert and the sea. It is the desert and the sea that bound Egypt, protect it, preserve it, sometimes suddenly change it, and with the Nile determine its fortunes.

The deserts and the sea have always provided Egypt with her security, but have provided her conquerors with avenues of attack. It has generally been the forces of the West that have come by sea or at least secured themselves by Mediterranean routes of supply. Alexander marched into Egypt from Gaza, but founded his city by the sea, his Ptolemaic successors governing from Alexandria. The Crusaders landed repeatedly at Damietta. The French and British came by sea and prized Egypt less for herself than for her strategic position on the route to India. They underlined this by building and operating the Suez Canal, and as recently as 1956 fought in vain along with Israel to keep it under their control. The Germans attacked across the desert and met defeat at El Alamein, one of the most important battles of the Second World War; they had come in tanks to break British naval power in the Mediterranean, and that naval power broke them in turn.

In its effects, the greatest desert attack on Egypt came in AD 640-1 when Amr swept across the sands under the banner of Islam. He had with him only 3500 men.

Oases

There is the strange story of Alexander's visit in 331 BC to Siwa, an oasis in the Western Desert, 550 kms from Cairo as the crow flies, 300 kms from the sea. After founding Alexandria, he made the long and dangerous journey, attended only by a small number of men, to consult the Oracle of Ammon, a ram-headed Libyan god associated with Egyptian Amun and Greek Zeus. Only twice in Alexander's career did his route diverge from strategic dictates; the first time he went to Troy, the site of his hero Achilles' glory; the second he went to Siwa.

Alexander's journey to Siwa

Writers ancient and modern have adduced a variety of reasons why Alexander should have made the journey, but there is the recurring theme that he went to seek confirmation that he was the son of Zeus. Alexander himself never explained his motive, nor did he ever reveal what he had asked the oracle, nor what he had been told, though from that time on he was shown on coins with the horns of a ram.

Before entering Egypt, Alexander had defeated Darius at the battle of Issus, appropriating the fleeing King's 365 concubines. After Egypt, Alexander would strike at the heart of the Persian Empire, march to the Indus, and appropriate the world. In doing so, he would combine East and West, and the journey to Siwa may have been an early example of this policy of amalgam. Alexander the son of Ammon; the son of Amun; the son of Zeus. It is a usefully embracing pedigree for a young man on the threshold of universal domination.

Even today on an asphalt road the journey to Siwa takes eight hours or more from Mersa Matruh on the coast. Enough petrol must be taken for the return journey and an ample supply of water too, for the wells along the way may have dried up and in any case are reserved for emergencies. At least two cars should travel together so that one can go for assistance in the event of a breakdown. (As this is a sensitive military area near the Libyan border, prior permission is required from Cairo or the frontier police at Mersa Matruh. It can also be possible, with permission, to hire a private plane for the journey.)

Alexander and his guides and companions took eight days to cover the distance from the coast, getting lost in a sandstorm and after four days exhausting their water; then clouds gathered and a sudden storm broke, "not without the help of the gods", and they were able to refill their leather water-bottles. They travelled by night along a chain of hills, their way rising and falling through valley after valley and into a final pass which wound down a ravine to the sandy plains beyond. In this pass, beneath the light of the moon and desert stars, the ground was covered with shells which reflected the moonbeams till the whole road sparkled. Bayle St John, a 19th C. traveller, followed Alexander's route and described it at this point: "A gorge black as Erebus lies across the path, and on the right stands a huge pile of rocks, looking like the fortifications of some vast fabulous city...There were yawning gateways flanked by bastions of tremendous altitude; there were towers and pyramids and crescents and domes and dizzy pinnacles and majestic crenellated heights, all invested with unearthly grandeur by the magic beams of the moon but exhibiting, in wide breaches and indescribable ruin, that they had been battered and undermined by the hurricane, the thunderbolt, the winter torrent and all the mighty artillery of time".

Here Alexander lost his way again, but was rescued by a pair of crows, some writers say also by a pair of talking snakes, who set him on the proper track. Bayle St John also saw crows here, and the valley is still known to the Berbers of the region as the Pass of the Crow.

Arrival at Siwa

Gazelles are seen along the way, until the last blinding 15 kms of whitened sand and land hardened with natural salt; and then suddenly there is the oasis, palms and fruit trees, streams and meadow grasses, quail and falcons, and the remains of the Temple of Ammon. For both Alexander and the people of the oasis, the sudden arrival must have been momentous. Alexander had survived the phantasms and perils of the desert and was lucky to be alive; the natives had never seen a pharaoh, but here was a Macedonian conqueror. Desert caravans and the occasional pilgrim were its only link with the outside world, and after the oasis was visited by Pausanias in AD 160, it was not visited by a European again until 1792. Its local customs, including homosexuality to the point of all-male marriage, survived into this century, and the language spoken by its population of 5000 is as often Berber as Arabic. There is a feeling of the Sahara, of the African land mass; Egypt is distant, though Siwa's dates and olives find their way around the country and have the reputation for being the finest. Women still live secluded lives, kept often indoors, emerging wearing the veil and long robes. But their heads, their necks, their arms and legs are decorated in enormous amounts of silver jewellery, some sold at Khan el Khalili in Cairo. Amidst these unusual and gradually vanishing scenes, and innovations and new building, the old village of Siwa, its mosques and houses built of mud brick with blank and windowless facades, contributes still to the mood of isolation.

Temple of Ammon

The scant remains of the Temple of Ammon are on the hill of Aghurmi to the east. Alexander entered into the innermost shrine, a small room about 3 metres wide and 6 metres long, and put his questions directly to the god. As at Kom Ombo in Upper Egypt you can still see here – can see more than Alexander knew – the means by which the god replied: a narrow passage ran behind the right-hand wall and was linked to the shrine by a series of small holes. Through these the priest could speak as though the god were answering in person. But it was on the temple steps, as Alexander entered or departed, that the words which came to establish Alexander's divinity were spoken. Accounts and interpretations differ. Alexander had come to Siwa via Alexandria and Memphis, and the priest in welcoming him may simply have called him "son of Amun", that is "Pharaoh", and this translated into Greek would have been "son of Zeus". Another story is that the priest, who would not have known much Greek, addressed Alexander as "my boy", but saying *"o paidios"* for *"o paidion"*.

To Alexander and his Macedonians this would have sounded like the two words *"pai dios"*, "son of Zeus". In any case, Greeks attached great significance to slips of the tongue, so even if they realised the error it would happily have been taken as a truth. What is historically important is not what was said that day, but what was believed in the four years between Siwa and the Indus, and it is true that Alexander did come as close as any mortal might to being the son of Zeus.

Ninety-three percent of Egypt lies on either side of the Valley and the Delta and overwhelmingly this is desert wasteland. No more than one percent of Egypt's total population inhabits these regions, most of these in oases. These oases are all in the Western Desert, Siwa the furthest west, Bahariya and Farafra 300 and 450 kms southwest of Cairo, Kharga and Dakhla 200 and 375 kms due west of Luxor. Egypt needs to develop her deserts, and this she has begun to do with the New Valley project, centred round the Kharga oasis.

Kharga oasis and the New Valley

The series of oases scattered across the Western Desert mark the line of an ancient channel of a branch of the Nile. In 1958 it was decided to try to bring this area to life again, to create a New Valley in parallel with the present valley of the Nile. Kharga is the easiest of the oases to get to, there are no restrictions, and though not the most romantic it is in some ways the most interesting. There is a good road running 230 kms from Assiut and less modern roads from Abydos and opposite Luxor. You should take the precaution of having sufficient petrol for the return journey and ample water. There is a rest house serving refreshments along the road from Assiut.

The Kharga oasis was fertile in Greek and Roman times. Attempts are being made to raise the water level, and wells, some of them 1.5 kms deep, have been drilled. The water is estimated to have been in the ground 25,000 years, the time it has taken to percolate through from Lake Chad. Understandably, the project has proved more difficult and costly than anticipated, and the intended mass transfer of population, mostly landless fellahin from the Delta and the 'old' Valley, too ambitious. Nevertheless, at the Kharga oasis there is a population of around 20,000, model villages have been built, new roads laid, electricity (which often blacks out) installed. Accommodation is at the government rest house, oppressively hot in summer.

Persian, Roman and Christian remnants

About 4 kms to the north of the rest house is the Temple of Hibis, dedicated to Amun by Darius I, he whose soldiers met defeat at Marathon and whose namesake Alexander would thrash 150 years later. It has been restored and makes a picturesque scene amidst groves of date palm, in contrast to the edge of desert situation of so many temples along the Nile. Extending to the north are ruins of the Roman town of Hibis and on a ridge beyond this a Christian cemetery of pre-Coptic decoration, mud brick mausolea, some surmounted by domes, with interior paintings on Biblical themes.

The Mediterranean coast

West from Alexandria at 106 kms is El Alamein, scene of that series of battles which from July to November 1942 halted Rommel's thrust to the Delta and reversed the tide of war in northern Africa. On 1 July as the Afrika Korps arrived at Alamein, the British fleet left Alexandria and withdrew through the Suez Canal into the Red Sea; clouds of smoke rose from the chimneys of the British military headquarters in Cairo as their files were hastily burned; Cairenes, certain that the British were fleeing Egypt, besieged the railway station in a rush to get away; and the outside world took it to mean that Britain had lost the Middle East. But Rommel was over-extended, his men exhausted, and the majority of his supplies consigned by the British Navy to the bottom of the sea.

El Alamein

General Auchinleck coolly gauged the situation. "On 17 July 1942, Auchinleck had won a historic battle. It had been as desperate, difficult and gallant as Wellington's repulse of Napoleon at Waterloo...He saved the Middle East, with all that this implied for the general course of the war. It was the turning point" (General J.F.C. Fuller). Later, Montgomery took command of the Eighth Army: "a man of dynamic personality and of supreme self-confidence...a past-master in showmanship and publicity; audacious in his utterances and cautious in his actions...He was the right man in the right place at the right moment" (Fuller), and during 23 October-5 November decisively defeated the Germans and put Rommel on the run. Within little more than six months the Germans and Italians were cleared from Africa altogether.

Museum and cemeteries

There is a museum at Alamein, with tanks, heavy artillery and other debris left behind after the battle, while to the east of the town is the starkly beautiful British Cemetery, and to the west the German and Italian cemeteries, each of them haunting. There are also unexploded mines still buried in the sand, and you should be careful about wandering off the beaten path.

Mediterranean beaches

The drive along the coastline is astonishing, the desert on the left, broad scallops of fine white sand beaches on the right and the brilliant turquoise of the Mediterranean beyond. There is no transition, just sharp jumps in colour and texture. The road is good all the way to Mersa Matruh (291 kms from Alexandria), the beaches beautiful, cooled by sea breezes and still only occasionally developed – though the Egyptian government is aware of their tourist potential and has drawn up plans. At present there are modest resort facilities at Sidi Abdel Rahman (20 kms past El Alamein), where there are a hotel, villas and camping, and at Mersa Matruh, with a number of hotels along the corniche.

Christendom's first monasteries

The early Christian churches in Old Cairo have already been mentioned, but the soul of Christian Egypt is in the desert. In *Desert Pilgrimage,* James Wellard makes the extraordinary assertion that "beyond the green belt of the river, both on the west towards Libya and on the east towards Arabia and north towards Palestine, lies an Egypt which has influenced the course of history far more than the Pharaohs". Egypt was one of the earliest strongholds of Christianity, its believers persecuted terribly by the Romans, especially under Diocletian in 303, so that thousands of Christians retreated into the desert where they lived in caves or founded the first monasteries. "O Desert, bright with the flowers of Christ! O Solitude, whence come the stones of which the Apocalypse, the city of the Great King, is built! O Wilderness, gladdened with God's special presence! What keeps you in the world? How long shall gloomy roofs oppress you? Oh, that I could behold the desert, lovelier to me than any city" (St Jerome).

The Wadi Natrun

Wellard's assertion seems extraordinary to us only because mysticism is no longer in fashion and monasticism outdated, its achievements in defining Christian thought and in harbouring and extending learning overlooked or devalued in our secular age. St Jerome was in fact a visitor, in 385, to the monasteries of the Wadi Natrun, over 100 at one time, now only four, but among the oldest and holiest shrines of Christendom. You can visit these monasteries today – they lie just west of the Desert Road about halfway between Cairo and Alexandria.

The Wadi Natrun is a valley, in part cultivated, extending southeast to northwest for 40 kms, with a width of 8 to 10 kms. It lies below sea level and takes its name from its salt lakes which dry up in summer, leaving a deposit of sodium carbonate (natron), once used in mummification and glass-making. The monasteries look like fortresses, as they were intended to be, in defence against Bedouin attacks. Until recently inhabited by a declining population of preponderantly old men, Coptic monasticism is experiencing something of a revival and there are now many young monks, dressed head to ankle in black robes, their hoods embroidered with white stars, sometimes a pair of tennis shoes incongruously completing the costume. Full beards and dark eyes, soft footfalls and quiet certainty, impress powerfully as they show you round their fortified man-made oases. From among the monks of the Wadi Natrun is chosen the Coptic Pope, who at present is Shenouda III, 117th Successor to St Mark the Apostle.

Getting to the monasteries

From Cairo, the Desert Road is gained by turning off the Pyramid Road just before the Mena House Hotel. A rest house (95 kms) about halfway to Alexandria marks the point where you turn left into the wadi. By car, the journey can be made in half a day, or the visit can be made enroute to Alexandria. Of course before the building of the road in 1917 the monasteries were in the middle of nowhere.

You drive into the valley, passing through a village, and come to a sign indicating the Monasteries of St Bishoi (Deir Amba Bishoi) and the Syrians (Deir el Suriani). The road is paved all the way to Bishoi, and Suriani is only a short distance over the sands. From Bishoi the road continues to the Monastery of St Makarios (Deir Abu Makar) at the southern extremity of the wadi (though the easiest way to reach Makar is to turn off the Desert Road 14 kms before the rest house, a paved road leading 5 kms into the desert). The northernmost Monastery of Baramous (Deir el Baramus) still keeps its distance from the world across a long trek of sand.

All Egypt's monasteries are coenobitic, that is food and possessions are shared and the monks submit absolutely to the authority of the 'householder', as the Copts call their abbot. The monasteries of the Wadi Natrun were all founded during the 4th C., though to varying degrees their structures date from the 8th C., being restorations and fortifications following Bedouin attacks.

Deir Amba Bishoi

St Bishoi founded two of these monasteries, the one bearing his name and the Suriani. The shrine and body of Bishoi are in the first, indeed the body lies uncorrupted and unwithered beneath a dusty red cloth, though unless the saint reaches out his arm to shake your hand (apparently a not uncommon courtesy extended to true believers), you will not be allowed to check for yourself. This was one of the rewards bestowed upon Bishoi for having washed Christ's feet when the Saviour appeared before him. He was also permitted to drink the water afterwards. Next to him lies the body of Paul of Tamweh, who achieved a reputation for sanctity after committing suicide seven times. Otherwise the monastery is unremarkable, with much new building and an air of administrative bustle – at least when I was there, which corresponded with a visit from Shenoudi III.

Deir el Suriani Though lacking in illustrious corpses, the Monastery of the Syrians is altogether a better place. It is in fact the most interesting of the four. Once inside its high forbidding walls, there is an atmosphere of serenity which you regret having to leave. There are several small domed churches, courtyards and gardens, and also tall bell towers with comforting bongs. Here Iphlogios with merry eyes showed me around: entering the Chapel of the Virgin, he opened a casket full of relics – Mary Magdalene's hair, somebody else's teeth, I could not remember them all as he went on and on. Then in a cave, now abutting the chapel, I saw the very place where Bishoi chained himself upright by the hair and did not sleep for four days until he saw Christ and washed His feet. You can imagine my delight – but I am being serious, as serious as Iphlogios, for these monasteries are strange and wonderful places, holding out against time, against the desert, against Islam; they are themselves miracles, and the least surprising (but most confirming) thing about them is that they should be storehouses for the fantastic.

Deir Abu Makar The Monastery of St Makarios has suffered most from Bedouin pillaging and destruction and consequently is the poorest of the four. Apart from portions of the saint's church, little remains of its earliest past, architecturally or decoratively, though it does possess what the monks would regard as far greater treasures. A disproportionate number of Coptic popes came from Makar and many are interred in the monastery, while beneath the floor of the saint's church are the remains of the Forty-Nine Martyrs, monks slain by Bedouins in 444. Recently, and perhaps still, the monastery has been closed (you should enquire beforehand), for during renovations a crypt was found containing what some claim to be the remains of John the Baptist. Against this, Mary Magdalene's hair or even the uncorrupted body of the man who drank from Christ's foot bath pale, and one can understand the monastery's desire to keep away the curious while it satisfies itself as to the authenticity of its find.

Deir el Baramus The Monastery of Baramous to the north across the sands is difficult to get to. Its isolation has had a paradoxical effect. On the one hand, its small number of monks have allowed themselves a greater degree of comfort than elsewhere and live in rooms instead of cells. Yet its remoteness attracts hermits to its environs where they live in self-dug caves. Indeed, Shenoudi's immediate predecessor, Kyrillos VI, spent ten years in a cave nearby as an 'athlete of Christ'. For those wishing to stay overnight at Wadi Natrun, Baramous could be the best choice for a feeling of both the wilderness and the fold. Out here in the desert what had seemed absurd in Old Cairo, those macabre relics as vessels for a putrefying mysticism and a faith in retreat, comes close to comprehension. As all life-giving as the Nile seems to be, one cannot understand Egypt without taking account of the void.

The city of St Menes

Closer to Alexandria there is another Christian site, the city of St Menes. Either you can turn off the Cairo-Alexandria Desert Road at Bir Abu Hush, or, if travelling along the Alexandria-Mersa Matruh road you turn off at Borg el Arab for Bahig and then travel southwards 15 kms. St Menes' city is in the vicinity of Bir Mishlat. The company of a local villager as guide is advisable once you leave either of the main roads. In Arabic the site is known as *Karm Abum* or *Karm Abu Mena,* the Vineyard of St Menas.

Menas was a young Egyptian officer who was martyred in 296 during his service in Asia Minor because he would not abandon Christ. When the army moved back into Egypt his friends brought his ashes with them, but at this spot the camel carrying the burden refused to go further. Menes was buried and forgotten, but later a shepherd noticed that a sick lamb that crossed the spot became well. Then a sick princess was healed. The remains were exhumed and a church built (350) over the grave. The great Basilica of the Emperor Arcadius was added at the beginning of the 5th C., and soon houses, walls and cemeteries were built, a city in the desert. The secret of this rapid growth was water; there were springs in the limestone that have since dried up. But in its heyday the cult was carried by caravans across the deserts (Menas is always shown between two camels) and extended throughout the Mediterranean, pilgrims coming from as far as Italy and France for "the beautiful water of St Menas that drives away pain". Souvenirs of these pilgrims' visits, little earthenware flasks with the saint depicted between the camels, have been found all over Europe and Africa.

As the water gave out, the city declined, though in the 11th C. the Arab geographer El Mekri could still describe "superb and beautifully constructed palaces" and "the Cathedral of St Menes, an enormous building ornamented with statues and the most beautiful mosaics...Over the church is a dome covered with paintings which, they say, represent the angels...The whole countryside round about is planted with fruit trees which produce excellent fruit and there are also many vines which are cultivated for wine" – this when water was already scarce. A century later, when the wells finally did dry up, the city and its vineyards simply disappeared beneath the sands. For nearly a thousand years El Mekri's description was regarded as the fantasy of an oriental geographer, until, in 1905, the site was excavated almost single-handedly by Monsignor Kaufmann.

Menes, however, has not been resurrected, the Western Church abandoning him as part of its rejection of monophysite Christianity, while only the most zealous Copts still revere him – though in 1943, the Coptic Pope Christopher II issued an encyclical letter ascribing the saving of Egypt from invasion at the Battle of El Alamein to "the prayers to God of the holy and glorious martyr Menas, the wonderworker of Egypt" – which was something else Rommel never counted on. Menes has been, in fact, a very practical saint. A paralytic man and a dumb woman both happened to implore his help at the same time. During the night, the saint came to the man in a vision and said, "Don't be afraid, but fasten your lips to the dumb woman's. Then get into bed with her and you will be cured". Although astonished, the paralytic followed instructions: the dumb woman awoke and screamed; the paralytic, alarmed at being caught, fled – and both were cured.

The Basilica of Arcadius stands at what was the centre of the city. Its dome has fallen, damaging the altar, but otherwise it is largely intact. The crypt in which St Menes was buried is down a marble staircase in the original church, incorporated into the portico of Arcadius' addition. A baptistry, octagonal within a square, is immediately to the west of the church. To the north of these buildings are the monastery, the sacred baths and the major cemetery. Most of the artefacts and decorations found during the excavations can now be seen at the Graeco-Roman Museum in Alexandria.

Other monasteries

There are other Christian sites and active monasteries in the Egyptian deserts; the Red and White Monasteries along the Valley and the Monastery of St Simeon across the Nile from Aswan are mentioned elsewhere. But that leaves two famous monasteries unvisited, until recently inaccessible because both were in military zones: St Antony's in the Eastern Desert and St Catherine's in Sinai. Neither requires a government permit, but St Antony's requires permission from the Coptic Patriarchate in Cairo. See the practical information section at the end of this chapter, and as with any other remote place in

Egypt, always check beforehand with the tourist office or other authorities.

Monastery of St Antony

A good road runs along the Red Sea from Suez and can also be joined across the Eastern Desert from Qena, north of Luxor. St Antony's is 130 kms south from Suez along this road and then 45 kms west into the Eastern Desert. It is the largest of the Coptic monasteries, more like a village with streets but surrounded by high walls and strikingly positioned beneath the cliffs of Mt Kalalah. There are several churches, decorated with frescoes; the oldest structure in the monastery is the Church of St Antony built over the saint's tomb by his disciples. Up the cliff face at an elevation of 680 metres, and 276 metres above the monastery, is St Antony's cave where he kept himself apart from his pursuing disciples. The climb is worth it for the superb view, but a monk should be taken as guide.

St Antony came here is 294, accompanying a caravan bound for the Red Sea, to escape the growing number of disciples who had joined him at his hermit's tomb along the Nile. He was born the son of a village merchant, but at 20 took literally a sermon heard in church: "If though wilt be perfect, go and sell all thou hast". In his cave on Mt Kalalah, high above the world, his only companions the wild animals he treated as God's creatures, he lived out the remainder of his 105 years, dying in 356. (Perhaps we should not be surprised that these men who endured the extremes of the desert and lived only on beans did generally live to be very old. Comforts kill.) He did not escape fame, however, and apart from the foretaste of St Francis 800 years later, became spiritual father of such great figures of the early Church as Jerome and Augustine of Hippo.

St Catherine's Monastery

St Catherine's is 250 kms southeast of Suez towards the tip of Sinai and is surrounded by a dramatic array of bare stone mountains. The site is traditionally that where God manifested himself to Moses in the burning bush; that and a supply of holy oil from Catherine's corpse (see Old Cairo) have had pilgrims, or tourists, coming here ever since 400. The monastery, however, is Greek Orthodox and not Coptic. A chapel erected by St Helena, mother of the Emperor Constantine, already stood on the site when Justinian, urged on by his formidable harlot-actress wife Theodora (Procopius said she had made love through every orifice of her body), built a fortified monastery here in 527. Apart from its fortifications, it has survived marauding Bedouins because Moslems revere Moses as one of their prophets, and because of its close connections in the Middle Ages with Europe, particularly France where the cult of St Catherine was especially strong. With sometimes hundreds of visitors on any one day of the year, it grew wealthy and was never lost to the Western world in the way that the desert monasteries of the Copts were. It has continued a success, at least as a tourist attraction, but for that reason, its dwindling number of monks and its electric lighting and thrumming generator (gifts of the British army before pulling out of the Canal Zone), it lacks the unworldly atmosphere of Egypt's other monasteries.

The principal attractions are the *Basilica of Justinian* with its 6th C. Byzantine mosaic in the apse and its Chapel of the Burning Bush, the most sacred spot in the monastery; the *Old Refectory,* used by Western pilgrims and covered with their graffiti from the 14th to 16th C.; the *Library* with one of the richest monastic collections in the world and a museum of Byzantine ikons; and in the garden the *Charnel House,* the skulls of monks piled high on one side, their limbs on the other. The monks are first buried and after ten years exhumed. But unburied was St Stephen, who died in 580 while sitting in a chair, his head in his hands – he is still there, at the entrance, looking rather dry.

The Suez Canal

In days gone by, many visitors to Egypt were no more than passers-though the Suez Canal, disembarking from their ship at one end, racing to Cairo to see the Pyramids, then racing back to board ship as it reached the other end of the canal. Today, the process is reversed and visitors who have flown into Cairo will sometimes take a day-trip to the canal to watch the ships sail through. The spectacle of a tanker seemingly ploughing across the desert is remarkable; but that and a swim are just about the only reasons for making the journey.

Earlier schemes

The idea of a Suez Canal is by no means a modern conception. The earliest authenticated attempt to connect the Red Sea with the Nile, and thereby with the Mediterranean, was made by Necho (XXVI Dyn). Heredotus says that 120,000 Egyptians perished while engaged in the work which was abandoned when an oracle warned that only the Persians would profit by it. And indeed it was Darius I (he of Marathon) who completed it a century later, c.500 BC. Tradition, however, reports a canal as early as the reign of Tuthmosis III (XVIII Dyn). Darius' canal (which ran from the Red Sea to the Great Bitter Lakes and then westwards to Bubastis, modern Zagazig) was maintained by the Ptolemies and improved by Trajan. It was later restored by Amr, the Arab conqueror of Egypt, in order to supply Arabia with corn, but was abandoned 100 years later to starve out Medina which had risen in revolt against the Caliph. The Venetians, the

Ottomans and the French under Louis XIV all contemplated its renewal. It was during Napoleon's sojourn that for the first time a canal was porposed direct from the Red Sea to the Mediterranean, but his engineer wrongly calculated a difference of 10 metres between their two levels and the plan was dropped.

Construction of the modern canal

At its narrowest, the Isthmus of Suez is 144 kms long and apart from dividing the two seas is also the divide between Africa and Asia. The present canal, at 167 kms, is the third longest in the world. Its construction is owed to Ferdinand de Lesseps, formerly French consul in Cairo, who obtained a *firman* from the Khedive Said (whence Port Said) granting a concession to run 99 years after the canal's completion. Work began in 1859, two-thirds of the finance coming from private investors, one-third from the new Khedive, Ismail (after whom Ismailia was named). The official opening took place on 17 November 1869 amidst much fanfare, the Empress Eugénie the principal attraction after the ditch itself. The expense of the canal contributed largely to Ismail's bankruptcy, his shares purchased by the British government in 1875, and Egypt falling under the authority, in effect, of British and French bankers. It was this event which led Ismail to speak the words which serve as an ironic commentary on the significance of the canal: "My country is no longer in Africa; we are now part of Europe. It is therefore natural for us to abandon our former ways and to adopt a new system adapted to our social conditions".

The Suez Canal crisis

Nasser's nationalisation of the Suez Canal Company in July 1956 was a reaction to the continued manipulation of Egypt by the West. Nasser wanted to build a new dam at Aswan which would increase farming land by one-third, and went to Britain, France and the United States for loans. These were refused because of Nasser's willingness to deal with both East and West. Nationalisation was intended to prevent canal revenue from draining to the West; instead it would help finance the High Dam. In response, Israel, France and Britain invaded Egypt in October, Sir Anthony Eden for one deluding himself that Egypt's legitimate rejection of imperialism was no more than a replay of Hitler's reoccupation of the Rhineland. World opinion was outraged and the invaders were forced to withdraw. Nasser was left with both the canal and a considerable moral victory.

The Six Day War in 1967 closed the canal for eight years. This time the British, French and American governments proved more cooperative and aided in its dredging. But meanwhile the canal towns were impoverished by the closure and devastated by Israeli shelling, Suez even being entirely evacuated. In 1975, however, President Sadat officially re-opened the canal – it is now operating at full capacity and there are plans to enlarge it, while the Egyptian-Israeli peace has permitted its cities to get back on their feet.

Port Said and Ismailia

Port Said at the north end of the canal is the most flourishing, owing to its status as a free port. Anything can be imported here, though duty must be paid on most items taken elsewhere in Egypt. It is very much a canal city and with a plain grid pattern, a touch of the picturesque only along Sharia el Gumhuria where there are many beautiful old wooden buildings with balconies dating from the last century and reminiscent of the French Quarter in New Orleans. There is also swimming along its Mediterranean beaches, less crowded than at Alexandria. But it is the furthest from Cairo and not really worth the trek. Ismailia, which is actually on Lake Timsa, the smallest of the Bitter Lakes, has pleasant parks and gardens and an attractive expanse of water with swimming, but otherwise there is absolutely nothing to do. De Lesseps lived in a chalet here during construction of the canal; it is on Sharia Mohammed Ali which runs parallel to the waterfront and Sharia Ahmed Orabi running down from the train station. It is open to visitors.

Suez and swimming

Suez is at the southern end of the canal and like Ismailia is easily reached from Cairo. It was the worst affected by the 1967 and 1973 wars and the sporadic shelling in between and is a city in the throes of reconstruction. It does offer the best views of ships passing through the canal and also more distant views of Sinai stretching away to the south. Also it offers superior swimming off the beaches running down the Red Sea coast. The best of these begin about 25 kms along the road to Ain el Sokhna and are entirely deserted. Ain el Sokhna itself (55 kms south of Suez) is being developed as a resort, the nearest to Cairo.

Hurghada: Red Sea resort

The fishing village of Hurghada (395 kms from Suez or 214 kms from Qena on the Nile near Luxor and across the Eastern Desert) is the modest centre of the Red Sea region, with oil derricks nearby, a marine biology station and a new Sheraton hotel emphasising its development as a beach, skin diving and sport fishing resort. It is served by three flights a week from Cairo and two from Luxor. This might suggest bustle, but it is still a quiet, unfrequented place of lovely white sand beaches scattered with delicate shells, of crystalline waters, coral islands, hot sun and relieving breezes. There is a wide variety of aquatic sports, with lessons available for the uninitiated; some entertainment; and attached to the marine station a marine museum (5 kms north of town) with a huge collection of brilliantly coloured fish, Red Sea sharks and rare manatees. Also, you can take an excursion 50 kms to the north to the porphyry quarries where the Romans hewed so much of that magnificent red stone (at terrible human cost) for the adornment of their basilicas, baths and private houses.

PRACTICAL INFORMATION

OASES:

The poor relations between Egypt and Libya finds **Siwa** within a restricted area, off-limits to foreigners. It's worth enquiring, though, whether the situation has changed.

The easiest way to reach **Kharga** in the New Valley is to **fly**. There are twice-weekly flights from Cairo, on Wednesdays and Saturdays, departing at 6am. **Accommodation** is at the Rest House at the north end of town, doubles with bathrooms costing LE8.

THE MEDITERRANEAN COAST:

There is a good **road** and also a **railway** from Alexandria to Alamein and Mersa Matruh, and also a train service to Mersa Matruh from Cairo, bypassing Alexandria (see *background* chapter for timetables).

Accommodation at Mersa Matruh includes:

The Beau Site (2-star), on the Lido beach. Tel: 2066. Doubles are LE7, breakfast included.

The Lido (2-star), also on the Lido beach. Tel: 2133. This is an older place, rather worn, room rates varying with their position. Doubles are from LE3 to LE6.

The Riviera Hotel (1-star), in the market area. Tel: 2051. For the less fussy; doubles are under LE3.

At **Alamein** there's a hotel and a camping site.

For **information** on the Mediterranean coast, call on **Misr Travel** in Alexandria, or in Mersa Matruh contact the **Matruh Agency** (Tel: 2384).

CHRISTIAN MONASTERIES AND SITES:

Permission is no longer required from the Coptic Patriarchate to visit the monasteries of the Wadi Natrun. St Antony's does still require permission, however, though none is required for a visit to the city of St Menes. St Catherine's in Sinai is Greek Orthodox. The **Coptic Patriarchate** is now at the new Cathedral of St Mark at 222 Sharia Ramses in the Abbasia district, a 15-minute walk or short taxi ride northeast of the Cairo railway station at Midan Ramses.

There are no organised tours to either **Wadi Natrun** or the **city of St Menes**, though arrangements for a car can be made through Thomas Cook. The St Menes site is most conveniently reached from Alexandria. Wadi Natrun is nearly equidistant from either Cairo or Alexandria along the Desert Road. A taxi from Cairo to the Desert Road Rest House will cost around LE15 return; a service (shared) taxi will cost about LE1 or so each way; or you can take the Cairo-Alexandria desert bus and get off at the Rest House. (See the *Practical Information* sections at the end of the *Cairo 1* and *Alexandria* chapters.) At the Rest House you can hire a car for the monasteries.

Also there are no tours to **St Antony's**, and no public transport. You'll have to hire a car. A visit could be included in a drive along the Red Sea coast between Suez and Hurghada.

St Catherine's in Sinai has until recently been in Israeli-occupied territory, tours coming down through the Negev. You'll have to check with the Tourist Information Offices in Egypt for the latest information on accessibility. When Sinai has normally been visitable from the rest of Egypt, tours have left from Suez.

THE CANAL TOWNS:

Port Said, Ismailia and Suez have never been much of a tourist attraction; their *raison d'etre* has been the canal and their facilities have matched this purpose. The closing of the canal and the damage inflicted by fighting have hurt the canal towns economically and physically. Now they are developing again, Port Said in particular, but the visitor should not expect too much in the way of accommodation, restaurants, etc.

All 3 towns can be reached by **car, bus** and **train** from Cairo, and Port Said by car and bus from Alexandria. Buses depart from Midan el Tahrir in Cairo, trains from Midan Ramses station; services are frequent and fairly cheap, eg LE2 by express bus from Cairo to Port Said.

Accommodation in Port Said includes:

The Etap Motel (4-star), on the corniche. Tel: 8823 and 8920. Telex: 54175 and 54174 PDS UN. The motel overlooks both the sea and the canal. All rooms have a refrigerator, TV and bathroom. Doubles are about LE15.

The Abu Simbel Hotel (2-star), 15 Sharia Gumhuriya. Tel: 3371. A clean and quiet family hotel, the double rooms face the street and have balconies, TVs and refrigerators, while the singles face a back alley and are without TVs and fridges. Doubles are LE8.

The Regent Hotel (1-star), 27 Sharia Gumhuriya. Tel: 4582. Like the Abu Simbel, the Regent is situated on Sharia Gumhuriya which runs parallel to the canal, though a couple of blocks back from it. Doubles without bath are LE7.50, with bath LE10.60, breakfast included.

There's also the **Nasr Youth Hostel**, Sharia el Amin. Tel: 3202.

Accommodation in Ismailia boils down to:

The Nefertari Hotel (1-star), Sharia Sultan Hussein. Tel: 422. Rooms are clean and cool, all have balconies. Doubles are LE5.50 without bath, LE6.50 with.

El Salam (1-star), Sharia el Geish, near Midan el Gumhuriya. Tel: 401. A new, very clean hotel on a pleasant tree-lined street, and with a fairly good restaurant. Doubles are LE9 with bath, singles the same.

Accommodation in Suez boils down to:

The Misr Palace Hotel (1-star), 2 Sharia Saad Zaghloul. Tel: 3531. The rooms have balconies and some have bathrooms, but it's not much of a place. Doubles start at LE7.

The Bel-Air Hotel, Sharia Saad Zaghloul. Tel: 3711. This is a no-star place across the street from the Misr Palace, no worse than its neighbour and much cheaper. A few rooms have baths, and those along the front have balconies. Doubles are LE3.50 without bath, LE4.50 with. The place does have a decent restaurant.

Also, there's a **youth hostel** on Sharia Tarik el Horreya. Tel: 3245.

THE RED SEA:

Known as *Ghardaka* in Arabic, the one-time fishing village of **Hurghada** is being developed as the main resort along the Red Sea coast. You can drive along the wild, undeveloped coastline from Suez or across the Eastern Desert from Qena, but the usual approach is on one of Egyptair's daily flights from Cairo, departing 7am.

The resort is centred on the new **Sheraton Hotel** (4-star) which will set you back about LE30 for a double, LE21 for a single, and half board is compulsory. Nearby is a new **tourist village** owned by Misr Travel and run by Club Mediterrannee, with doubles at LE50, singles at LE 38 – though prices include 3 meals a day plus use of recreational facilities including beach, pool, tennis, archery, boating and scuba diving.

ALEXANDRIA AND THE DELTA

The Delta

Politically, economically and culturally, the Delta has played no less an important role from the earliest times to the present than has Upper Egypt, yet it almost entirely lacks the historical survivals of the deserts and the Valley. Where the aridity and limited cultivation of the south has preserved the past, the fanning Nile and its irrigation channels, some Mediterranean rainfall and the consequent rich earth of the north have all but obliterated it. This imposes some distortion on our apprehension of Egyptian history, for it was the Delta that was cosmopolitan, influenced and often settled by peoples beyond Egypt's borders, while it was and still is Upper Egypt that has been provincial. Provincialism and orthodoxy, however, go hand in hand, and when reaching the pitch of zealotry they can become a moulding force – from Upper Egypt came the impetus for the unification of Egypt, as came also the expression in stone, as pyramids and titanic temples, of the nomad's confrontation with the cosmos. We see one and forget the other.

Reasons for the lack of concrete history

Where the Delta did build in limestone and granite, these blocks had to be brought great distances from the deserts and the Valley. It was common already in pharaonic times for the stone of earlier structures to be re-used in later ones rather than to go to the far-off quarries for more. The disassembling of the past was even more intense during the Middle Ages when the Delta people would plunder ancient buildings, burning the limestone in their kilns and using the granite for foundations or grinding stones. Right up until recent decades the sebakhin (mentioned at Medinet el Fayyum) would work the tells (or *koms*, to use the particularly Egyptian word for those great mounds of debris marking the sites of ancient settlements) for fertiliser, so that some that were 10 metres high in Napoleon's time are near-level today. In any case, mud brick was more often used, and where these remains have been excavated, they have immediately begun to suffer weathering. Finds from the famous sites of the Delta have been taken away to the museums of Cairo, Alexandria or abroad, and what remains *in situ* does no justice to their historical renown.

Nevertheless, the Delta knew greatness, and during the first millenium BC it dominated the affairs of Egypt. The XXI Dynasty came from Tanis; the XXII Dynasty was founded at Bubastis; the XXIII Dynasty came also from Tanis; the XXIV, XXVI and XXVIII Dynasties all came from Sais.

Visiting the Delta

These sites and a few others will be mentioned briefly below, as well as places of later significance like Damietta and Rosetta. The Wadi Natrun and the city of St Menas in the sands to the west of the Delta have already been covered in *The Deserts and the Sea* chapter. These and other places both within the Delta and nearby can be visited enroute to Alexandria from Cairo, or in some cases most conveniently by using Alexandria as your base for excursions. There is a good railway service linking Cairo with Zagazig (for Ismailia) and Cairo with Alexandria, with stops along the way, while there are numerous good paved roads. The alternative to the Cairo-Alexandria Desert Road is the shorter though more heavily trafficked main road through the Delta via Benha, Tanta and Damanhur, paralleling the railway.

Whatever one's interest in the ancient sites, there is the fascination of a drive or train ride through the Delta landscape – its extraordinary flatness and vast fields of cotton, rice and maize; buffalo with sleek oily coats and down-turned horns like large floppy ears, grazing or ploughing or turning wheels for grinding or pumping; also sheep, donkeys, camels; and huge dovecotes like Cambodian temples. High clouds blow in from the Mediterranean, a reminder that here in the north during the winter months it is advisable to have a raincoat, and along the coast a warm sweater for evening breezes throughout the year. And spectacle though it is to see a tanker seemingly plough through the desert at Suez, it is enchanting to see the sails of feluccas billow across fields furrowed with canals – the effect of Norman church towers at stages across the water flatness of the Suffolk landscape.

An excursion from Cairo around the eastern Delta, which could be combined with the Suez Canal, or which otherwise could be a roundabout way of reaching Alexandria, would take in Zagazig (85 kms from Cairo) for ancient Bubastis and San el Hagar (159 kms from Cairo) for ancient Tanis. Though Zagazig was founded only in the 1820s, off to the right as you approach you can see the site of Bubastis, one of the most ancient cities in Egypt. The name means House of the goddess Bastet, represented as a lioness, later as a graceful domestic cat, and the most impressive feature of the site is the remains of her temple, begun by Cheops and Chephren (IV Dyn), altered by Ramses II (IXX Dyn) and given its final form by the Pharaohs of the XXII Dynasty, who resided here. Of all the temples of Egypt, Herodotus said this gave the greatest pleasure to look at, both for its own merits but also because the city all round it had been raised to a higher level, so you could

Bubastis

look down upon it where it stood amidst shade trees on almost an island formed by two embracing canals which stopped short without meeting. A licentious festival was held here: "They come in barges, men and women together, a great number in each boat; on the way, some of the women keep up a continual clatter with castinets and some of the men play flutes, while the rest, both men and women, sing and clap their hands. Whenever they pass a town on the riverbank, they bring the barge close inshore, some of the women continuing to act as I have said, while others shout abuse at the women of the place, or start dancing, or stand up and hitch up their skirts. When they reach Bubastis they celebrate the festival with elaborate sacrifices, and more wine is consumed than during all the rest of the year. The numbers that meet there, are, according to a native report, as many as 700,000 men and women". Nearby are underground galleries for the burial of cats, where many fine bronzes of cats or of Bastet have been found.

Tanis The site of Tanis at San el Hagar is a huge kom, 3.5 kms from north to south, 1.5 kms broad and rising to 35 metres above sea level. A number of excavations since 1825 have still only turned up a small portion of the whole, revealing structural remains from the XXI Dynasty through Ptolemaic times. But also a great quantity of stone, originally statues, stelae, carvings and blocks from the time of Ramses II and frequently bearing his cartouche, have been found incorporated into later buildings or littered about. It is argued by Pierre Montet, who excavated here from 1927 to 1956, that this was Ramses, named after the great Pharaoh, where the Hebrews suffered their afflictions as recorded in the Bible, and where later in the XX Dynasty a conflict between the people of the south who worshipped Amun and those of the east who worshipped Seth, led to the destruction and then rebuilding of the city. The site is a walled compound enclosing a sacred lake, several temples, a royal necropolis and much Ramessid statuary and carving; you should climb the hill to the east for an overall view of the mostly still buried city.

Damietta Damietta (Dumyat in Arabic) is at the mouth of the eastern branch of the Nile, 68 kms beyond El Mansura (which is 126 kms from Cairo and where St Louis was captured and held for ransom) and 70 kms along the coast from Port Said. It has some interesting old town houses like those at Rosetta, but is not worth a diversion. Its history during the Crusades, however, deserves mention.

Its position as a port was undercut by the construction of the Mahmudiya Canal in the 19th C. which fostered the rise of modern Alexandria and it suffered final eclipse with the opening of the Suez Canal. But it had been a prosperous Arab trading city and achieved fame for its struggle against the Crusaders, those vandalising European mercenaries who sacked the Christian city of Constantinople and slaughtered the inhabitants of Jerusalem. Damietta was taken in 1218, principally by Germans, and abandoned again in 1221, but not before its townspeople were sold into slavery. Its inhabitants fled when in 1249 St Louis landed nearby, but Damietta was returned to Egypt a year later as part of St Louis' ransom. It was these experiences which helped turn a religiously tolerant Egypt, with a still substantial Christian population, against Christianity both without and within. Even so, it says something for Egypt's underlying moderation, and the tenacity of its Coptic population, that it is the only country in northern Africa where Christianity has survived.

The Crusades

St Francis

One of those amongst the besiegers of Damietta in 1218 was St Francis, and his story here illustrates the abysmal ignorance of European Christianity in its medieval encounters with the country that had been, after all, one of the most important nurturers of that religion. Seeing that the attack was at first going badly, despite the fact that the Christians had God on their side, not to mention a papal legate at the head of their ranks, St Francis courageously crossed the enemy lines to confront the Sultan Kamil in person. He informed the Sultan that he had come to convert him and his people to the religion of Jesus, apparently unaware that Kamil was surrounded with Coptic advisors and fully familiar with the Christian faith. St Francis offered to enter a fiery furnace on the condition that should he come out alive, Kamil and his people would embrace Christianity. The Sultan replied to the saint with a lesson in humanity and common sense, saying that gambling with one's life was not a valid proof of one's god, and saw St Francis on his way with oriental courtesy and lavish gifts.

As a footnote on the loyalty of Copts to their homeland, I record a conversation I had in Cairo in August 1973 (that is two months before the Ramadan/Yom Kippur War – take your pick) with a family of Copts. Three had been students at UCLA and were returning to Egypt for the first time in five years. I asked their mother about Israel. "No animosity. But they are the enemy." I asked what would happen. "We will fight. They have occupied our country." I turned to her daughter who had spent five years in California. "Egyptians are not aggressive," she said. "There is less aggression here than in America. But this is our land and we will fight for it."

And if you lose again? They smiled. "Egypt has been here forever. It will be here forever. We will fight forever for our land." A Coptic general was in command of the Second Army in the brief, successful and hopefully final war that followed.

Ancient sites in the western Delta

The ancient sites in the western Delta are not worth visiting at all. Sais is to the northwest of Tanta; once a royal capital, it was sacred to the goddess Neith who protected the embalmed bodies and entrails of the dead and is often depicted on sarcophagi and at the entrances to tombs. Buto lies to the east of Desuk and is most conveniently reached via Damanhur; its deity was the cobra goddess Wadjet, represented as the uraeus on the pharaonic crown. Hellenistic Naukratis is a level and desolate patch of ground to the left of the Tanta-Damanhur road. Damanhur stands on the site of the Roman Hermopolis Parva, no remains of its past surviving.

Rosetta (Rashid in Arabic) and Abu Qir (ancient Canopus) are covered later as excursions from Alexandria.

To Alexandria

Cairo is still only minutes behind as the train drives into the widening Delta, into a land hardly changed over thousands of years. Canals and irrigation channels molten gold in the setting sun thread through a patchwork of flat green fields. Lines of windbreak trees bend southwards with the incessant Mediterranean breeze. These, and the occasional palm, mud brick house, a string of electricity pylons, the only exceptions to an unending flatness.

Camels on their haunches by the track, ignoring the passing train. Saw-toothed waterwheels, each tooth a cup drawing water from a pool and splashing it into a long straight channel disappearing into the cotton fields.

At night there is nothing to be seen. Perhaps a path of water faintly reflecting the starlight and moonlight or the lemon headlamps of a car strobing through a line of trees on the horizon. Otherwise no lights, no house lights, a small fire by a mud house at most. The Delta cedes to darkness and the train tunnels through the desert-black night, the Alexandrian cocoon, and slowly writhes through the lights of the city.

The city

When I first came to Alexandria, I used Lawrence Durrell's *Justine* as a guide. I am a nightwalker and paused when I read his account of the Swedish vice-consul whose car having broken down one night went off to phone the consulate, leaving his wife in the back seat. When he returned his wife was still sitting there – without a head. That was then, in the 1930s, when Alexandria was divided into European and 'native' quarters. Now it is all 'native', which I presumed would mean crimes had changed.

So at two o'clock in the morning I set out to Midan el Tahrir and along Sharia Faransa towards the slums of El Anfushy where Darley and Nessim had followed Justine in her search for her kidnapped daughter amongst the bordellos and "smashed and unlimbered houses" behind Sharia Tatwig. The streets were dark and only a few people were about, but a light shone from a little *souk el tabachin* where I stopped for some cigarettes. Instead, a chair was produced and I was invited to join four or five men sitting out in the street drinking tea. I was given tea, given cigarettes and a hubbly-bubbly was filled with dark moist *masil salom* and conversation began in English, French, Italian, Greek, Arabic and sign language in the earnest Egyptian attempt to welcome and talk with visitors.

One fellow who painted ships' hulls but had never been out of Alexandria: his dream was to go to Italy, Spain, France or England. A smacking of his lips after mention of each. In Arabic he had read Agatha Christie and some English history as well. He reeled off a list of English monarchs: "Charlie, Charlie, George, George, George, Victoria, Edward, Elizabeth". Then he asked me what I thought of Nasser and Sadat. I said "okay". He showed me his shoe and put Nasser and Sadat under it, squashing them into the street and emitting a snort.

I asked him, "Why don't you like Sadat?" (This was before the 1973 war.)

"I work and work" (he mopped his brow), "I get little money" (he rubbed his fingers and thumb together), and then he said "Anwar Sadat", and let out a loud, long, ugly snort till he was out of breath.

But the others were content. A student translated the Arabic of a grease-covered mechanic: "Tomorrow in the sun you will see the Mediterranean round Alexandria and you will go back home and tell your friends how beautiful it is".

Alexandria stands on the edge of two worlds, and there is yearning in her balance. It is right that you should come here *after* Cairo, *after* Upper Egypt, to understand this.

Alexandrian facades have the same dull brown colour as those of Cairo. Possibly a little lighter, especially the rooftops, almost white and gleaming in the morning sun. Instead of brushed by desert sand, frosted perhaps by the salt air of the Mediterranean. When open to the sea, playing a role in the broader life of the Mediterranean, receiving into her the Greeks, the Jews, the French and others, the milieu has been intoxicating and Alexandria has thrived. But like the desert, the Arabs encroached upon the sea, they stood with their backs to it, and Alexandria withered. The meteorological fact of the prevailing northern breeze driving the sea against the rocks along the corniche reminds you of the city's past and possibilities.

The founding of Alexandria

When Alexander the Great entered into Egypt in November 332 BC he marched straight to Memphis. But early in the year 331 he sailed northwards down the Nile, as though one last time to gaze upon the uncertain Hellenic sea, and on the site of a small fishing village made his most lasting contribution to civilisation. He did not stay long enough to see a single building erected, and instead made his mysterious visit to Siwa and then back across the desert to Memphis before committing his life to the conquest of Asia. Eight years later, at the age of 33, he was dead. His body was brought to Memphis but the priests refused it, saying, "Do not settle him here, but at the city he built at Rhakotis, for wherever this body must lie the city will be uneasy, disturbed with wars and battles". So he descended the Nile again, wrapped in gold and enclosed in a coffin of glass, and he was buried at the centre of Alexandria, by her great crossroads, to be her civic hero and tutelary god. Memphis has slipped into the mud; Alexandria after many battles survives.

Arrian wrote: "It seemed to him that the place was most beautiful for founding a city and that the city would be greatly favoured; he was seized by enthusiasm for the work and marked out the plan in person, showing where the gathering-place should be built and which gods should have temples where, Greek gods being chosen along with the Egyptian Isis; he arranged where the perimeter wall should be built".

Perhaps the motive for founding the city was as simple as that; a Greek gesture, a seed planted in time. There would have been some strategic value: the Persian fleet, though enfeebled, could still disturb Alexander's lines of communication; another Greek harbour could be useful. Trade could not have been important in itself, the Aegean was infested with pirates, and even in its maturity more trade was thought to pass into Alexandria from inland Egypt than from the entire Mediterranean. Yet its unique geography survives, has power, has mastery; it required Alexander to put it in motion, but once he did its growth was irresistable.

Alexandria is an abstract place – *here* (some spot) is where Alexander lay entombed; *here* Cleopatra committed suicide; *here* the Library, the Serapeum, etc...and there is nothing physically there. It is all idea, sensation, memory, emotion, poetry. But it has form. Once flying to Egypt it was nighttime

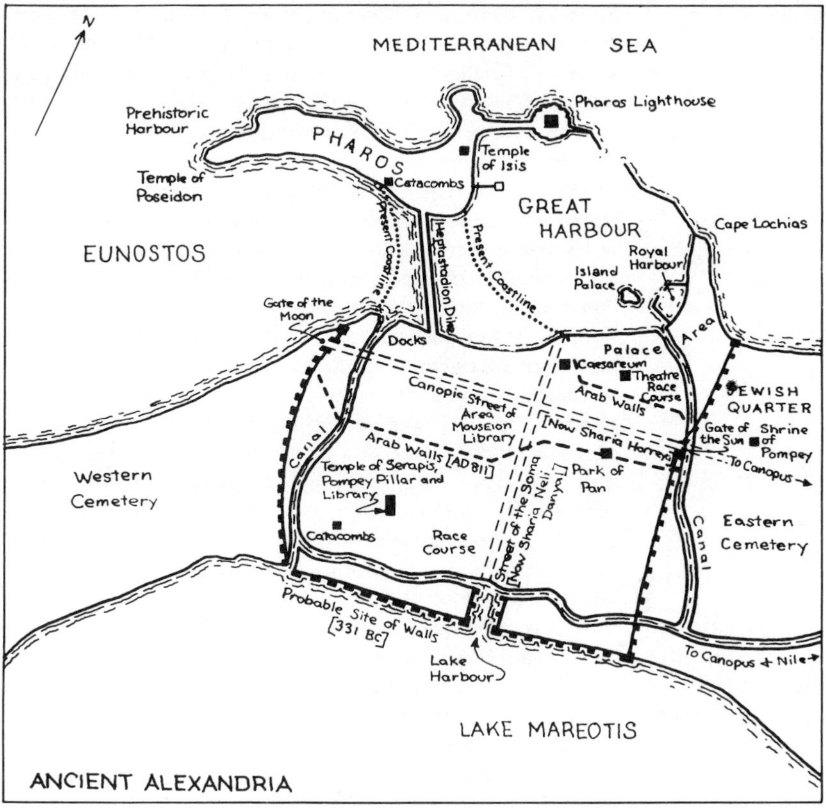

and all below was black. I did not know if it was the Mediterranean or the desert. And then the captain said that we had crossed the coast, were approaching Cairo over the Western Desert, and that to the left you could see Alexandria. And there it was, far away, bright with lights – and unmistakable. No other city in the world has such an unmistakable and enduring form. Amr or Cleopatra could have recognised it, and perhaps even Alexander himself: the island of Pharos attached to Rhakotis by the causeway that has silted up so that the city looks like an anvil reaching out to sea. The sea defines one side, the desert and Lake Mareotis ensure that the bottom of the anvil remains permanently flat. There is no sprawl, except to the east along the low limestone ridge of Ramleh, a string of beaches and often wealthy homes.

History of the city

When Alexander died, one of his Macedonian generals made Egypt his portion of the divided empire and Alexandria his capital, ruling as Ptolemy I Soter, and founding a dynasty that was to end with the suicide of Cleopatra VI – "It is well done and fitting for a princess/Descended of so many royal kings." Under Cleopatra and Antony, the city very nearly supplanted Rome which both strategically and culturally was Alexandria's inferior.

During the reign of the Ptolemies Alexandria became a resort of artists and scholars, and was outstanding particularly in its mathematicians and scientists, Euclid and Eratosthenes most notable amongst them. Claudius Ptolemy, the astronomer, lived during the Roman period when philosophy also flourished. Eratosthenes (see Aswan) determined the circumference and diameter of the Earth, while Claudius Ptolemy less accurately proclaimed the revolution of the universe round the Earth. The first was forgotten; the second received the blessing of the medieval Church which threatened Galileo with the stake for presuming to correct the error. Here between desert and sea philosophers struggled with the problems of the universe in a way that the earlier Egyptians never admitted, though unlike some of their predecessors in Greece never doubting the existence of God.

Christianity and the persecutions of Diocletian

It was Alexandria which raised Christianity, until then addressed to the poor and unlearned in Palestine, to the level of philosophy, and Egypt which provided it with many of its images: the resurrection of Osiris; Isis with Horus her child – we can recognise these in Christ and the Virgin, while the pharaonic *ankh* appears unaltered on some early Christian tombstones as a looped cross and slightly altered on others as a cross with a handle. These early Christians suffered heavily for their faith: Diocletian (early 4th C.) demolished all churches, demoted all Christian officials and enslaved the rest, also killing 60 a day over five years, according to the Coptic Church. It was this persecution which caused the great flight into the desert, the founding of the first monasteries. "The desert so swarmed with monks that their chaunts and hymns by day and by night made the whole country one church of God", wrote a contemporary.

It was Diocletian who divided the Roman Empire into four administrative regions, an emperor each for East and West, each emperor assisted by a caesar; and it was Diocletian who began the Caesaropapism, albeit in pagan form, that later marked the rule of the Christian Emperors of Byzantium. His persecutions made such an impression on the Egyptian Church that it dates its calendar from the Era of the Martyrs. It is understandable that in Egypt this struggle between Christianity and paganism should have given rise to a kind of nationalism – indeed Copt means Egyptian – and that it should have continued even after the Emperors at Constantinople were Christians themselves, for whatever the religion of the Empire, it was still a foreign (now Greek) oppressor.

The monophysite controversy

It was this undercurrent of nationalism that fuelled an otherwise seemingly abstruse debate on the nature of Christ. The Alexandrian theologians had decided that though born of Mary, the man in Christ had been entirely absorbed into the divine. Christ had one nature, the divine, and the adherents of this view were monophysites. However at Chalcedon (conveniently across the Bosphorus from Constantinople) it was decided in 451 that Christ had two natures, unmixed and unchangeable but at the same time indistinguishable and inseparable – this is the view of the Western Church to this day, just as the Copts are monophysites and so heretics in the Western view. The issue may not seem terribly important, or even comprehensible, and really it was more a slogan by which two political groupings denounced one another, but it was the device by which Christian Egypt was lost to the world.

The Arabs welcomed

The hatred between Constantinople and Alexandria was so intense that when in 641 the Arab general Amr rode into Egypt with his 3500 Bedouin horsemen, the Alexandrians signed an armistice and in the following year admitted him into their city as a lesser evil than the evacuating Greeks. The city was still recognisably that of its glorious past; colonnades of marble lined Amr's triumph along the Canopic Way; the Tomb of Alexander rose to his left, the Pharos to his right. Amr reported back to the Caliph in Arabia: "I have taken a city of which I can only say that it contains 4000 palaces, 4000 baths, 400 theatres, 1200 greengrocers and 40,000 Jews". E.M. Forster writes: "There was nothing studied in this indifference. The Arabs could not realise the value of their prize. They knew that Allah had given them a large and strong city. They could not know that there was no other like it in the world, that the science of Greece had planned it, that it had been the intellectual birthplace of Christianity. Legends of a dim Alexander, a dimmer Cleopatra, might move in their minds, but they had not the historical sense, they could never realise what had happened on this spot nor how inevitably the city of the double harbour should have arisen between the lake and the sea. And so though they had no intention of destroying her, they destroyed her, as a child might a watch. She never functioned again for over 1000 years".

In fact, and it must be held to their eternal credit, the Arabs did absorb much of what Alexandria offered, creating with its help a civilisation for many centuries incomparably more beautiful, more intelligent, more humane than existed in Europe, storehousing, adding to and then passing on to the world the learning of the ancients. But Alexandria herself did suffer, and eventually Egypt too relapsed. By the time Napoleon landed Alexandria was no more than a fishing village once again. What brought her back to life was the construction of the Mahmudiya Canal by Mohammed Ali, giving her access to the vital Egyptian hinterland, and bringing Egypt again face to face with the Mediterranean. During the 19th C. the Greeks returned and the Jews, and also came the French, the English, the Italians, leading to that era evocatively described by Durrell in his *Alexandria Quartet,* though the allure was as much dependent on colonialism as on cosmopolitanism. Post-war and post-Suez nationalism meant the ejection of the Jews, Greeks and other foreigners and for some years the Arabs were again in possession of no more than a skeleton.

The modern city

In the last few years, however, Alexandria has begun showing something of her former sparkle. I was walking one evening back along the corniche from Silsileh where Cleopatra had her palace to Midan Saad Zaghloul where she built the Caesareum for Antony, and Sadat drove past preceded by a motorcyclist and two police cars, flanked by four more motorcyclists. I wondered, does he think of Alexander, of Cleopatra, of the Pharaohs; or of Arabi or Zaghloul; or only of Carter and Begin, Schmidt and Guiscard? But Alexandria, except in the post-mortem literature of the West, has not needed romance (though for romantics it has plenty); it has needed a good harbour, a canal, a railway line, and it has needed before any of these things a political will to link Egypt with the broader world. The man who drove by in the limousine had that will.

Alexandrian women are attractive and often smartly dressed. They are of a wide range of colour and beauty, reflecting a cosmopolitan ancestry. At restaurants, cafés, patisseries – Alexandria has a reputation for the best food in Egypt – you are often served by women (almost unheard of in Upper Egypt and not all that common in Cairo), and they are pleasant, self-assured, chatty, even flirtatious. (There is much to be said for judging a place by the rapport you can have with the opposite sex.) Alexandria is cleaner, less congested than Cairo, not desperate. There are slums, but on the whole the city does not have Cairo's problems. There is a sense of well-being; Alexandrians stream about the streets late into the night, shopping or simply walking, sitting at cafés talking. Only children ask for baksheesh as a rule, and adults shoo them away. With the relaxation of import controls there is now a mass of shops and stalls in central Alexandria selling minor luxuries from English toothpaste to American cigarettes to French perfumes to Japanese watches – the activity and the prices are reminiscent of Naples. Indeed that is the impression, of a truly Mediterranean city, living at a standard difficult to distinguish from that of Naples, no more than a decade behind Athens and Piraeus. This may be a materialistic way of evaluating a city. There is another sign, on the tall white illuminated mosque near Ramleh station. In Polish, Italian, Greek, English, French and German it reads: "Welcome. To have a fair idea about Islam, please take your free pamphlet from this mosque. Thank you."

Orientation

I have said that modern Alexandria has the shape of an anvil. Its head, which juts out into the Mediterranean, is the old, rundown and interesting area called El Anfushi. But this was once the island of Pharos, and prophetically it was a Greek who gave a first account of it: "There is an island in the surging sea, which they call Pharos, lying off Egypt" (The *Odyssey*); it was here that Menelaus was becalmed on his way home from Troy. Towards the western tip of the headland is the Ras el Tin Palace; at the eastern tip Fort Qaytbay, which stands on the foundations, indeed is part built, of Alexandria's ancient lighthouse which gave its name, Pharos, to lighthouses everywhere and was one of the Seven Wonders of the World.

El Anfushy (Pharos)

Sharia Faransa and Midan el Tahrir (the Heptastadion and Rhakotis)

The island was connected to the mainland by a causeway 7 stades long, the Heptastadion. Silting has made it the permanent broad neck of the anvil. Along this neck runs Sharia Faransa, the former Rue de France (street signs are still often lettered in French, the second language of upper class 19th and early 20th C. Alexandrian Greeks). This runs south into Midan el Tahrir, the former Place Mohammed Ali; at the southern end of the midan was, approximately, the former mainland coastline and the fishing village of Rhakotis.

The harbours

To either side of the Heptastadion were the two ancient harbours, the Eunostos or Harbour of Safe Return to the west, the Great Harbour to the east. Their roles have been reversed in modern times; Mohammed Ali developed the Western Harbour for commerce and it can be difficult to get to for all its docks and warehouses, but under the Ptolemies it was the less important of the two. The Eastern Harbour makes a graceful sweep and with its long corniche, Sharia 26 July, is the most pleasing attraction of the city. Fort Qaytbay marks the tip of its northern arm; the lesser promontory of Silsileh, hardly developed but for a military compound, forms its eastern arm.

From Silsileh westwards ran the palace of the Ptolemies where Cleopatra killed herself.

Midan Saad Zaghloul (the Caesareum)

Whereas the main square of the city was, until the Second World War or even after, the Place Mohammed Ali (now Midan el Tahrir), the centre has shifted to Midan Saad Zaghloul which is between the Ramleh tram station and the corniche. Here Cleopatra began the Caesareum in honour of Antony and Octavian finished it in honour of himself. Two obelisks here, the famous 'Cleopatra's Needles', are now on London's Embankment and in New York's Central Park. In the midan is a statue of Saad Zaghloul, a nationalist leader who after the First World War negotiated the British withdrawal from Egypt, though they maintained a military presence in the Canal Zone. Another nationalist leader was the fellah officer Arabi who in 1882 led an uprising against the British. British warships retaliated by devastating Alexandria. Where Arabi failed, Nasser later triumphed. He is remembered by a square in downtown Cairo and in Alexandria by Midan Orabi which extends from Midan el Tahrir to the corniche.

Shopping and tourist facilities

The Hotel Cecil stands on the west side of Midan Saad Zaghloul, and the streets to the south of the midan and between it and Midan el Tahrir form the central shopping district of Alexandria. The most fashionable street is Sharia Salah-Salem, formerly Rue Sherif Pasha, running southeast out of Midan el Tahrir. Also in this area, and around Ramleh Station, as well as along Sharia Horreya, are many airline offices and travel agencies.

The train station

Sharia Nebi Danyal runs nearly north to south through this area, at its southern end running into Midan el Gumhuriya with the train station for Cairo. About halfway along its length, Nebi Danyal intersects a street called Sharia el Mitwalli to the west, Sharia Horreya to the east. Nebi Danyal was anciently the Street of the Soma and the east-west street was the famous Canopic Way. Their intersection was once the crossroads of the world, and here was Alexander's tomb. To the west the Canopic Way left the city through the Gate of the Moon, to the east through the Gate of the Sun – by which Amr entered in triumph, Antony in final defeat after his last resistance against Octavian outside the walls. A poem by Constantine Cavafy (1863-1933), translated by George Valassopoulos, describes this moment as the god Hercules, whom Antony loved and who loved him, was heard passing away from Alexandria in mysterious music and song. It is called 'The God Abandons Antony'.

Alexander's tomb

The god abandons Antony

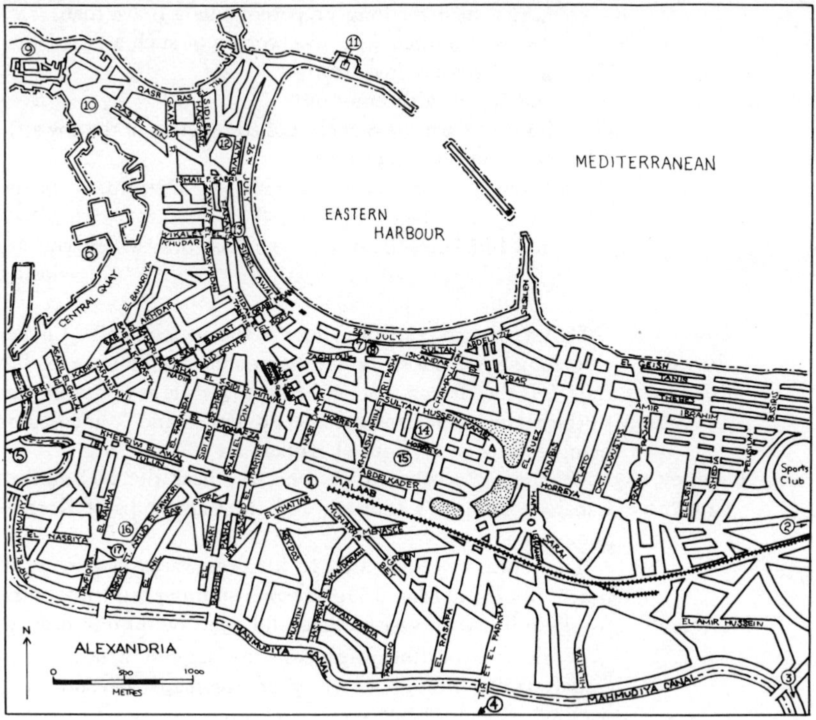

1. Midan el Gumhuriya and Misr Station (for Cairo)
2. Sidi Gaber Station (for Cairo and Abu Qir)
3. Delta Road to Cairo
4. Desert Road to Cairo
5. Road to Alamein and Mersa Matruh
6. Passenger ships (Venice, Piraeus, Beirut, etc.)
7. Midan Saad Zaghloul
8. Ramleh Tram Station
9. Ras el Tin Palace
10. Anfushi Tombs
11. Fort Qaytbay (site of Pharos)
12. Ebu el Abbas Mosque
13. Terbana Mosque
14. Graeco-Roman Museum
15. Kom el Dikka
16. Pompey's Pillar
17. Catacombs of Kom el Shogafa

When at the hour of midnight
an invisible choir is suddenly heard passing
with exquisite music, with voices –
Do not lament your fortune that at last subsides,
your life's work that has failed, your schemes that have proved illusions.
But like a man prepared, like a brave man,
bid farewell to her, to Alexandria who is departing.
Above all, do not delude yourself, do not say that it is a dream,
that your ear was mistaken.
Do not condescend to such empty hopes.

Like a man for long prepared, like a brave man,
like to the man who was worthy of such a city,
go to the window firmly,
and listen with emotion,
but not with the prayers and complaints of the coward
(Ah! supreme rapture!)
listen to the notes, to the exquisite instruments of the mystic choir,
and bid farewell to her, to Alexandria whom you are losing.

The Graeco-Roman Museum

Still within the vanished lines of the ancient walls, further east along Sharia Horreya and then a short way down a road to the left is the Graeco-Roman Museum, while at this point but to the right of Horreya are the Ptolemaic and Roman ruins being excavated at Kom el Dikka.

Pompey's Column

To the far southwest of the city, near the Mahmudiya Canal, is Pompey's Column and the Catacombs of Kom el Shogafa.

Montazah

The modern city extends 16 kms eastwards in a string of beach suburbs to Montazah, a former summer residence of the royal family, with vast gardens and good swimming nearby.

While this outline might already suggest a number of casual strolls through the city or excursions beyond, four detailed itineraries follow.

1. From Midan Saad Zaghloul to Kom el Dikka

South along Sharia Nebi Danyal and over the intersection with Sharia Horreya you come, on the right, to a building set back from the street and with four antique columns serving as gate posts. This is the typical way you encounter the past, if you encounter it tangibly at all, in Alexandria – a dwindling number of remnants used in building after successive building, their original purpose only to be guessed at. It is possible that the Mouseion once stood here and that these columns once adorned its facade. Founded by Ptolemy Soter, the Mouseion was the great intellectual accomplishment of his dynasty, a vast complex of lecture halls, laboratories, observatories, a library, a dining hall, a park and a zoo. It was like a university, except that the scholars, scientists and literary men it supported were under no obligation to teach. It would have been here that Euclid and Eratosthenes worked.

Possible site of the Mouseion

Mosque of Nebi Danyal and site of Alexander's tomb

Directly opposite is the Mosque of Nebi Danyal (the Prophet Daniel) on the site of Alexander's tomb, the Soma where he and some of the Ptolemies lay. If you go in you can gaze down upon a crypt where Daniel and an uncertain figure called Lukman the Wise lie. It is easy to imagine a still deeper crypt where Alexander himself still lies, for the cellars and foundations of the mosque have never been properly examined. The body is thought to have been destroyed in city riots of the late 3rd C. AD, but in the absence of any certain knowledge rumour has flourished. In 1850 a dragoman from the Russian Consulate said that down in the cellars through a hole in a wooden door he saw "a human body in a sort of glass cage with a diadem on its head and half bowed on a sort of elevation or throne. A quantity of books or papyrus were scattered around". Suetonius tells a good story of Octavian's (later Augustus) visit here: "When Alexander's sarcophagus was brought from its shrine, Augustus gazed at the body, then laid a crown of gold on its case and scattered some flowers to pay his respects. When they asked if he would like to see Ptolemy too, 'I wished to see a king,' he replied, 'I did not wish to see corpses'".

The Canopic Way

Going back (north) now to Sharia Horreya and standing on this rather ordinary-looking corner, the great crossroads of the Street of the Soma (Nebi Danyal) and the Canopic Way (Horreya), you might need this description by Achilles Tatius, a 5th C. bishop, to assist your imagination: "The first thing one noticed in entering Alexandria by the Gate of the Sun was the beauty of the city. A range of columns went from one end of it to the other. Advancing down them, I came in time to the place that bears the name of Alexander, and there could see the other half of the town, which was equally beautiful. For just as the colonnades stretched ahead of me, so did other colonnades now appear at right angles to them".

The Graeco-Roman Museum

Turning right (east) into Sharia Horreya as though to walk towards the Gate of the Sun, the third street on your left runs along the entrance to the Graeco-Roman Museum which fills the historical gap between the Egyptian Museum in Cairo and the Coptic Museum in Old Cairo. The rooms are numbered but the exhibits are not always numbered, or their numbers are hard to find. Nor is everything labelled, though usually the most important exhibits are, but not always. Furthermore, there is some rearrangement going on. In short, take what follows with a sense of adventure. The guide books on sale are useless. The museum could be greatly improved by maps, plans, models, etc., showing the development of the city. Nevertheless, it is fascinating as it is, and pleasant.

You enter a *vestibule* with a statue of Nike (26019) carved from several marble blocks. It is probably Roman, 2nd C. AD, based on a Hellenistic model. Until 1950 it was part of the flotsam of the city, lying on a site just off Sharia Horreya.

Modern Alexandria troubles little about its past. There is also a cast of the Rosetta Stone. The original is in the British Museum.

For the sake of a very approximate chronology, you should now turn left into *Room 6.* What you will find here I do not know for the room is undergoing alterations and was largely empty during my last visit. However, there was at that time, and for many decades before a fine black granite statue of the Apis bull here. Also, and perhaps only temporarily, masks which were placed over the faces of the Roman dead before burial and afterwards hung about the house as mementoes.

Room 7 has a statue of a Hyksos pharaoh (Second Intermediate Period) at the centre. It was appropriated by Ramses II and on its shoulder appears Ramses' daughter Hout-Ma-Ra, traditionally the princess who found Moses in the bullrushes. On the left between Room 7 and 8 is a Hathoric capital (476) of black basalt dating from the Ptolemaic period.

Room 8 contains five mummy cases and includes two Roman mummies with painted portraits, elaborate diamond-pattern wrapping and, in one instance, a glimpse of Roman toes. There is also a Heliopolitan bas-relief (380) from over the door of a tomb, the deceased on the left amidst delicately carved scenes of rejoicing: an old harpist singing and accompanied by a girl on a drum and by two others who clap their hands. To the right, a man prepares a drink; then two dancing girls.

Crocodile cult

At the centre of *Room 9* is a wooden stretcher bearing a mummified crocodile. The room illustrates the Ptolemies in their Egyptian aspect, and here it is crocodile worship in the Fayyum. There are the remains of the chapel (19678-81) of a crocodile god with the wooden door of the first pylon and the coffin and beir of the sacred animal (2nd C. BC). On the rear wall of the room are photographs taken at the time of the discovery and excavation of the chapel. The entire chapel has been reconstructed in the north garden of the museum.

Room 10 is a collection of small objects of the pharaonic period. Most strange is the mummy of a baby. Apart from its smallness, no concession is made to its babyness, eg the face mask is the usual stereotype.

Room 11 has objects in which the Greek and Egyptian influences mingle – never very well. There are some curious blocks with footprints, votive offerings to Isis and Serapis. The finest object is the headless woman, on the left as you enter, Egyptian in style but Greek in feeling.

At the centre of *Room 12* is a dull colossal statue of Marcus Aurelius; a sea-worn head of Alexander is on the right-hand shelf. Both of these were found in Alexandria, the Aurelius

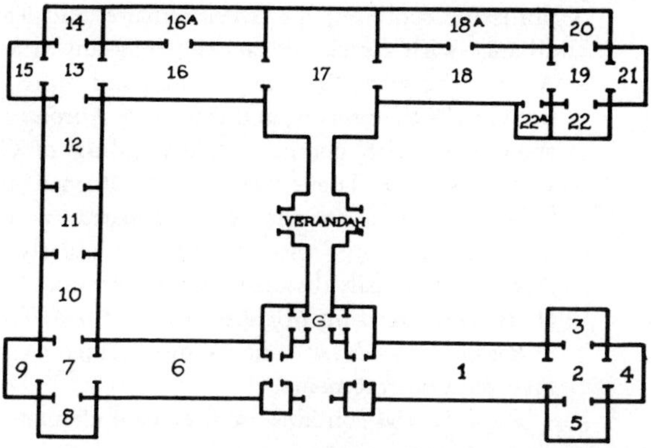

along the Canopic Way. In a case on the left is a bronze head of Hadrian with inlaid eyes. He looks a bit surprised and vulnerable, as though at that moment his trousers had fallen down. Also, he looks like Freddy Laker. On the left, too, is a magnificent statue of Serapis (22158), a great jolly fellow like Dickens' Ghost of Christmas Past.

The cult of Serapis

Serapis was the only god every successfully made by a modern man. Egyptians at Memphis had worshipped Osiris in his Apis form as Osorapis; Ptolemy I combined this deity with Dionysos and made what was in effect a new god. The intention, probably, was to unite Greeks and Egyptians in a common worship, but the Egyptians would not accept him and he became the Greek god of Alexandria. His cult statue (this is a contemporary copy) of white marble was painted blue, its gilt head and jewelled eyes gleaming from the darkened recess of its shrine, the Alexandrian Serapeum, which stood near Pompey's Pillar. His worship spread throughout the Aegean, his cult established at Athens and particularly at Delos, though he was venerated as far away as India. His importance can be gauged by the fact that when Bishop Theophilos destroyed the Serapeum and its statue in 391, it was taken by the world as the definitive triumph of Christianity.

Cleopatra identified herself with Isis, that still greater deity, and so naturally, and with useful effect, Antony was identified with her consort Serapis, or at least with Dionysos.

This may have assisted Roman propagandists (from whom Shakespeare took his cue) in depicting Antony as a debauched Bacchic figure – more a measure of Roman methods and philistine contempt for Greek culture (and fear of Antony's alliance with Greek Alexandria) than any true reflection on Antony the man. Romans admired and copied *things* Greek, but Greeks themselves, and those like Antony who immersed themselves with genuine understanding in Greek culture, were despised. There was a ready Roman audience for a 'scheming' and 'treacherous' Cleopatra, a 'cowardly' and 'besotted' Antony, and history, particularly the Battle of Actium, was easily distorted to provide proof for the slanders. (It is worth reading Michael Grant's *Cleopatra* on this.)

Rooms 13 and 14 contain miscellaneous sculptures and architectural fragments.

Room 15 too contains architectural elements, and decorations; at the centre is a portion of wall with a painted scene (27029) of oxen turning a *sakiyeh* or waterwheel, a Greek work from a tomb and with good perspective.

Room 16 is devoted to sculpture. There is a limestone head of another Serapis (3917) on a shelf to the left. Against the wall at the far end is the repulsive Mithras (24407), sun god of the Persians, his worship introduced into the Roman Empire during the 1st C. BC. This statue comes from Minya. He is lion-headed, cloven-hoofed and winged, with hairy legs, and is draped with snakes.

Hellenistic sculpture

In *Room 16A* are the finest pieces of Hellenistic sculpture in the museum. In a case on the left is a small white marble head of Alexander (3402); the nose and torso are restorations. The larger torsos at the left end of the room are particularly impressive: a seated woman with a standing girl (14942)); two unclothed male torsos (3923 and 3925); and a female torso (3924) wearing a light tunic.

In *Room 17* is the largest known statue (5934) carved from a monolithic block of porphyry; some authorities say he is Diocletian, others that he is Christ Pantokrator – about as wide a split as you could hope for. Among the six marble sarcophagi is one (17927) showing the sleeping Ariadne surprised by Dionysos on Naxos.

Funerary objects

Room 18 has pottery, terracotta and funerary urns. In the far left corner is an urn (16152) from the Chatby necropolis which still retains its wreath of artificial flowers, bright green and gold (4th C. BC). The terracottas on the right wall, from Fayyum, are stupid and vulgar.

But in *Room 18A* are perhaps the finest objects in the museum: miniature terracotta figures of great delicacy and charm. These come from Alexandrian cemeteries, late 4th to early 2nd C., and occur only in tombs of children, adolescents or young women. In Case K, note the child on a man's shoulder (9205); but the best are the figurines of women in Case L, full of detail and dignity. These works were prompted by the sadness of death in youth; they are entirely sincere and noble, and they live.

Rooms 19, 20 and 21 contain terracottas and pottery; in *Room 20* there is a caseload of bronze wreaths, their flowers gilded. These are ugly and were probably more ugly at the time, but they are impressive for being so old.

Room 22 displays tenth-rate Hellenistic material from excavations at Canopus.

The Treasure Room

Finally in this gallery, there is the *Treasure Room.* There is a collection of Ptolemaic coins. The most beautiful items are the torso of Aphrodite (24042) in silver and the silver gilt goblet (24201) decorated with cupids gathering grapes. The most important, however, are the foundation plaques (8357-66 and 9431-40) in gold, silver, bronze, Nile mud, green faience and opaque glass, carved with Greek and hieroglyphic inscriptions, each recording Ptolemy III's dedication of the Temple of Serapis. Only when these were found in 1943-5 was it established with certainty that the Serapeum had stood on the plateau where Pompey's Pillar stands.

Tomb and chapel reconstructions

You can now walk back towards the entrance, visiting the gardens via the verandah. The *South Garden* has reconstructions of two rock-cut tombs. One (21004) of the 3rd C. BC contains a sarcophagus in the form of a bed. The other (20986) of the 1st C. AD has an arched entrance with shell decoration in relief. In the *North Garden* is the reconstruction of the three pylons and chapel of the crocodile god whose furnishings have already been seen in Room 9.

Re-entering the building, you pass through *Room G* with a number of white marble statues from a private sanctuary of the 2nd C. AD dedicated to Isis.

Christian antiquities

Room 1 contains Christian antiquities. There is the surprising sight of a Christian mummy. Note the cross painted at the neck. There are also many objects from the city of St Menas. On the left wall, in Cases G and G1, are the little souvenir flasks once filled with spring water and taken by departing pilgrims all over the Christian world. Note the motif of St Menas between two camels. There is a bas-relief of the saint which is a crude copy of the one that stood in his desert shrine. And near Case N are two absurd reliefs from the Christian era of Leda and the swan – in one of them she holds an egg.

Rooms 4 and 5 have Christian tapesty fragments on their walls.

In *Room 3,* in painted stucco, are Christian designs and saints from the Alexandria vicinity.

At the centre of *Room 3* is a Christian capital.

Kom el Dikka: Moslem, Roman and Ptolemaic remains

Returning again to Sharia Horreya, the excavations at Kom el Dikka lie immediately to the south. It is likely that a great deal of Alexandria's past could be uncovered, and the work here, begun by the Polish Centre of Mediterranean Archaeology, in 1959, marks a start. Layers of *Moslem tombs* were found, dating from the 9th to 11th C., and a large complex of 3rd C. *Roman baths.* The spur to further and intensive excavation came in 1964 with the unearthing of a small *Roman odeon,* a covered theatre for musical performances, with seating for 700 to 800. Inscriptions suggest it was used also for wrestling contests. It is pretty, the area around it landscaped, which is all very well, but it possesses none of the excitement of an excavation in progress.

That is provided by the deep broad trenches still being dug to the northeast of the Odeon. The dusty walls of the trenches are layered with extraordinary amounts of potsherds, and as you peer down several metres from the surface of the kom you can see substantial stone walls and the remains of brick houses. Best of all is to climb down. You walk along a *Ptolemaic street* lined with shopfronts. If Cleopatra ever went shopping, then here you can say to yourself is where Cleopatra walked. It is a sensation of immediacy rare to Alexandria.

Pastroudis

You can now slip into the city of Durrell's *Quartet*. Near Kom el Dikka, on a triangular block on the south side of Sharia Horreya (the former Rue Rosette) and one block east of Sharia Nebi Danyal is Pastroudis. This is one of the old Greek tea rooms, and Darley and Nessim, and Balthazar for an arak, would gather here. It is pleasant still to sit here, indoors or out, with a drink, a coffee, a rich pastry – there is also a restaurant – and let time pass.

2. From Midan Saad Zaghloul to the Pharos via Sharia Faransa

You should walk south again along Nebi Danyal and turn right on Horreya (west of Nebi Danyal it is called Sharia el Mitwalli) and then almost immediately right again into Sharia Salah-Salem, formerly Sherif Pasha, once Alexandria's most exclusive shopping street "bristling with flag staffs" (Forster), though not as smart as it was. It says little for the merchant citizenry of 19th and earlier 20th C. Alexandria that in Forster's opinion the finest building in the city was the Banco di Roma, now the National Bank of Egypt, on the right side of the street. It is handsome enough, but how much better the descriptions of the ancient city. On the left, as you enter into Midan el Tahrir, is (or was – I can imagine it being pulled down) the Bourse, once housing the Cotton Exchange. "The howls and cries that may be heard here of a morning proceed not from a menagerie but from the wealthy merchants of Alexandria as they buy and sell" (Forster). It is derelict now, boarded over with political posters, its arcaded facade used as a public latrine.

Midan el Tahrir

Midan el Tahrir (Liberation Square as in Cairo) was formerly Place Mohammed Ali and laid out by him in 1830 as the centre of his new city. In Ptolemaic times this was the coastline and site of Rhakotis. Once attractively planted with trees and gardens (now destroyed for bus and trolley depots) and flanked by government buildings, this was until the Second World War the European centre of the city. An equestrian statue of Mohammed Ali is at the centre; on the right (entering from Sharia Salah-Salem) is the Anglican Church of St Mark. Inside it commemmorates British regiments which saw action against Arabi.

Along Sharia Faransa

Sharia Faransa, the former Rue de France, starts at the opposite (north) end of the midan. Here you are walking along the Heptastadion through what is very much an Egyptian quarter of the city, often picturesque. There are several mosques along the way; the most interesting is the Terbana Mosque, dating from 1684. Its exterior is white except for its high doorway of brick, painted red and black in Delta Style (there is much more of this at Rosetta), with occasional courses of wood and a Kufic inscription: "There is no God but God" and "Mohammed is the Prophet of God".

Terbana Mosque

Before going in, have a look at the entrance to the cellars round the left-hand side of the building. The columns are ancient. Now go up the steps of the main entrance, arriving at an open air terrace with two great Corinthian columns of granite. The entire building seems to have been made out of Alexandria's antique past; there are more ancient columns propping up the interior and painted gloss white. You will probably be shown round, the gloss paint and similar refurbishments pointed out with pride. Tiles decorate this upstairs entrance to the mosque, but they are in a bad state, the enamel dropping off, but fine where they survive. There are excellent tiles too in the mihrab inside, predominantly blue, though some green; the larger tiles with white daisies are inferior modern work.

The Turkish town As you continue north along Sharia Faransa from the Terbana and cross a main intersection, the street becomes narrower and winding with several overhanging balconies in the Turkish style. This is landfall for the island of Pharos. Continue north along Sharia Tatwig; it runs into a square and the scene all around is 18th C. oriental. Dominating the square is the large Mosque of Abou el Abbas Moursi, built in 1767 by Algerians over the tomb of the 13th C. saint. At the end of the square where two tall palm trees rise is the little Mosque of Sidi Daoud with his tomb. This was the main square of the Turkish town, the reduced settlement, its population 4000, to which Alexandria had shrunk when Napoleon landed in 1798. Between the Abu el Abbas Mosque and the harbour is a modern mosque called the Bouseiri, its own square illuminated with white lights visible from anywhere along the corniche at night. From this mosque there is a view of Fort Qaytbay and fishing boats, their nets stretched along the harbour wall.

The Anfushi Tombs But first follow Sharia Ras el Tin towards the western tip of the anvil's head, to the Tombs of Anfushi near the end of the tram line. These are Ptolemaic, their decorations principally Greek but with Egyptian elements. They have been cut into the limestone ridge that was the island of Pharos; there are four of them, arranged in pairs, each pair sharing an atrium. Their walls are painted to simulate marble, or alabaster blocks, or tiles; archaeologists call this the First Pompeian Style, with all the shoddiness that suggests. In the tomb furthest to the right are scenes of a felucca and a warship of the sort Cleopatra may have sailed in to Actium. The keeper rubs the felucca with his moistened thumb to show that it will not come off – it does not, but is covered with smudgy thumb prints. Also in this tomb are Greek scribblings left by a workman of the period named Diodoros, who immortalises his friend Antiphiles. How innocent these ancients were in their graffiti; we know by what signs our present period would instantly be recognised by archaeologists of the future. The attempt in all these tombs of simulated materials is poor. They are very much bourgeois tombs; their inhabitants paid the going rate for an eternity of tastelessness.

Ras el Tin Palace Further towards the western tip is the Palace of Ras el Tin, built by Mohammed Ali, though altered this century. Here on 26 July 1952 King Farouk abdicated and sailed away to Italy aboard his yacht. You cannot get in.

Fort Qaytbay and the Pharos

Now walk eastwards along the seafront towards Fort Qaytbay. There is a poor beach and a fish market enroute. The fort is at the end of a breakwater and has been restored since the British shelling in 1882. It was built in 1480 by Sultan Qaytbay on the site and partly from fragments of the Pharos lighthouse, the wonder of the ancient world.

The Pharos was built during the reign of Ptolemy Philadelphus, its architect Sostratus, an asiatic Greek. "The sensation it caused was tremendous. It appealed both to the sense of beauty and to the taste for science – an appeal typical of the age. Poets and engineers combined to praise it. Just as the Parthenon had been identified with Athens and St Peter's was to be identified with Rome, so, to the imagination of contemporaries, the Pharos became Alexandria and Alexandria became the Pharos. Never, in the history of architecture, has a secular building been thus worshipped and taken on a spiritual life of its own. It beaconed to the imagination, not only to ships at sea, and long after its light was extinguished memories of it glowed in the minds of men" (Forster).

The Pharos exceeded 125 metres in height and might possibly have touched 150 metres. Its square bottom storey was pierced with many windows and contained perhaps 300 rooms where the mechanics and attendants were housed. A double spiral ascent ran through the centre and perhaps hydraulic machinery for raising fuel to the top. At its cornice was an inscription by which Sostratos dedicated the Pharos "to the Saviour Gods; for sailors", the gods being Castor and Pollux who protect mariners, but an allusion to Ptolemy Soter and Berenice, whose worship their son Philadelphos was promoting. Above this was an octagonal second storey, then a circular third storey, and finally the lantern. Its workings were mysterious. Visitors spoke of a mirror, perhaps of polished steel for reflecting the sun by day, the fire by night; though others described it as made of glass or transparent stone, and declared that a man sitting under it could see ships at sea that were invisible to the naked eye. It might have been a lens, and it is not at all impossible that Alexandrian mathematicians did discover the lens and that their discovery was lost and forgotten when Pharos fell.

The Pharos retained its form and functions up to the Arab conquest in 641. About 700 the lantern fell, and perhaps at the same time but certainly soon after the two top storeys fell too–the tale is that the Byzantine Emperor, frustrated in his ambitions against Egypt because of the early detection of his ships, put it about that the Pharos stood upon Alexander's treasure, whereupon the Caliph commenced demolition. The first storey survived intact and Ibn Tulun restored the octagonal storey around 880, but an earthquake around 1100 destroyed his work and its place was taken by a mosque. Finally the bottom storey was ruined by a final earthquake in the 14th C. Interestingly, the four stages of the Pharos – square, octagon, round and summit – are exactly reproduced in the minaret of Qaytbay's Mausoleum in Cairo's City of the Dead.

Here on this promontory, Qaytbay built in part at least from the debris of the Pharos and you can see where bits of it have been incorporated into the fort. As the fort has anti-aircraft emplacements and barracks, you are not encouraged to be too curious; nevertheless, along the right (east) side of the fort you can see fragments of granite columns and traces of the original foundations. Forster reports seeing as many as 30 broken columns of pink Aswan granite and blocks of speckled granite and one of marble either built into the left (west) wall or lying on the beach; some pieces in the wall are evident, but those on the beach have been cleared away. Also, as the fort was built to contain a mosque, its orientation diverged slightly from the Pharos foundations. This you can make out on the west side: the Pharos was a bit counterclockwise from the fort in its alignment; where the fort meets the sea, the sea must first lap against a just barely submerged 'reef'.

The Naval Museum

Within the compound is a Naval Museum with a model of the Pharos, while as you approach the fort along the causeway there is an Oceanographic Museum and an Aquarium, though these last are not worth visiting.

3. To Pompey's Pillar, Kom el Shogafa and Lake Mareotis

You must now make your way to the southwest quarter of the city, perhaps by following Sharias Salah al-Din and Amud el Sawari. Walking along Salah al-Din towards Pompey's Pillar, the side streets are lined with fine old French-style houses, a touch of lightness not found in Cairo. Along the pavement, strange brown sheep, long curled tails, udders bulging. The sheep are tied by the feet to rings hammered into the walls. Sleeping, lying, smelling each other, occasionally a jig when tormented by some unseen insect. Amud el Sawari: a dead dog rotting on the pavement, covered by flies so intent on their meal that they pick away undisturbed as I step over the carcass. Elsewhere: a small cat with a rat nearly as big as himself in his mouth. A boy crouches in front of me, staring at me blankly, taking a shit. Impressions, in paint, in mud, of children's hands against the walls of squalid streets: to avert the evil eye. A shop sign: 'MAURICE FEINBERG... MATERIEL ARTISTIQUE'.

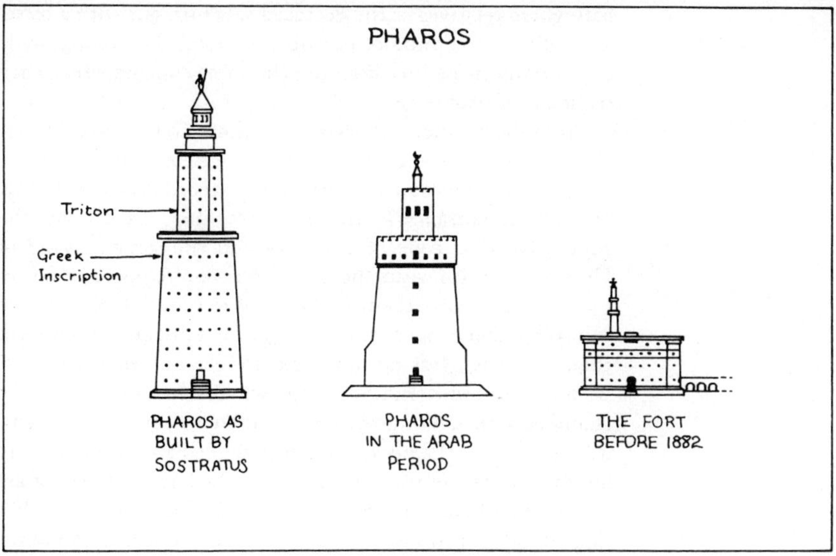

Pompey's Pillar

Pompey's Pillar (wrongly named such by the Crusaders; it was raised in honour of Diocletian) stands solitary like a needle without a haystack by the site of the Serapeum and the Library which replaced the earlier one burnt when Julius Caesar fought to maintain himself in the city. Both Serapeum and Library were destroyed when the Patriarch Theophilos led a mob against them in the final triumph of Christianity. Paganism was overthrown, as was learning. The column is 30 metres high and has a circumference of 9 metres; it is of pink Aswan granite and is entirely uninteresting. I have preferred watching Egyptians catching pigeons here. An orange beetle is used to bait a small wire trap hidden in the dry powdery soil. Pigeons are frequently on Egyptian menus; only chickens taste worse. This hill was already built upon when Alexander came; it served as the citadel of Rhakotis; for the Ptolemies it was their acropolis.

Catacombs of Kom el Shogafa

A short distance south are the Catacombs of Kom el Shogafa, the largest Roman funerary complex in Egypt and run by a syndicate for the benefit of non-Christians. The catacombs date from the 2nd C. AD and are decorated in a curious blend of classical and Egyptian styles. They are a sort of underground Forest Lawn.

The catacombs are on three levels, the lowest usually flooded and inaccessible. A winding staircase leads up to a rotunda encircled by chambers with sarcophagi and niches for funerary urns. The large room to the left was the banqueting hall where relatives of the deceased saw him out with a feast. The table in the middle, probably of wood, has disappeared, but cut out of the limestone are the three couches where they reclined on mattresses.

From the rotunda a stairway goes down to the second level. You are now at the central tomb. The decorations are composite, not to say weird. Bearded serpents adorn the vestibule wall at the entrance to the inner chamber. Each holds the suggestive pine cone of Dionysos and the serpent wand of Hermes, and also wears the double crown of Upper and Lower Egypt, while above them are Medusas in round shields. In the tomb chamber proper are three large sarcophagi, cut out from the rock. Their lids do not open, for the bodies would have been introduced from the passage which runs right round the chamber with accommodation for 300 mummies. In the niche over each sarcophagus is a relief in Egyptian style. Turning around and facing the entrance, on either side of the door are two extraordinary figures. On the right is Anubis, with a dog's head, but dressed up as a Roman soldier, with sword, lance and shield; on the left is Sobek who, despite being a crocodile, is also shoved into a military costume, with cloak and spear. "Perhaps the queer couple were meant to guard the tomb, but one must not read too much into them or into anything here – the workmen employed were only concerned to turn out a room that should look suitable for death, and judged by this standard they have succeeded" (Forster).

To Lake Mareotis

One of the enjoyments of using Forster's guide (see *Selected Reading*) is in seeing how the city and its environs have changed since it was first published here in 1922, and in following up leads. He writes about the railway line running along the edge of Lake Mareotis: "Just before Gabbari Garden Station is a fishing village built on a tiny creek and quite Japanese in appearance. It is worth going down here when there has been a catch: the lake fish are uncanny monsters. The neighbourhood is very fertile – palms, bananas and vegetable gardens. But it does not make pleasant walking owing to the smells". So I went, and if you want a strange excursion, you can follow me.

The Mahmudiya Canal

From Pompey's Pillar or the catacombs, you return to Sharia Amud el Sawari and walk south. It becomes Sharia Qarmus and leads to a bridge over the Mahmudiya Canal. The canal was the artery by which Mohammed Ali brought Alexandria back to life; today it is stagnant, stinking and blocked by islands of vegetation and hulks of rusting barges. A donkey lay in the water beneath me, bloated and white. The canal's function has now been taken over by roads and the railway to Cairo.

Cross this small steel bridge and immediately turn right, following the bank of the canal perhaps 200 metres until, on your right, you notice a cable ferry (you can return to town this way: on the other side catch the yellow No.2 tram to Midan el Tahrir). At the point where you see the ferry, but on your left, is a low narrow tunnel through which you must stoop to cross under the railway line. Emerging, turn left, then right past the cotton factory. This is a place where old clothes are reduced to cotton fibre and baled. All around is a wasteland of dirt and mud and industrial refuse and stench. Off to your left you will see the raised road leading from Alexandria's Western Harbour to Cairo. Cross this road – and Lake Mareotis (Mariyut) lies before you, blue and vast against the flat horizon, broken by islands of reeds. And running off to the right, squeezed now between the lake and the road, a long line of huts, and flat-bottomed boats pulled up along the shore, and it does look perfectly Japanese.

Village on the lake

I sat on the edge of a boat for a long while and looked out across the lake. The sun was setting. Behind me were the slums and factories of Alexandria, the backside of the city – though these days, I suppose, really its heart – with smoke belching black from high chimneys. But I could just turn my back on it and watch the ducks waddling up from the lake, the flat-bottomed boats laden with nets being punted back to the village, fishermen standing astern wielding long poles.

A woman came out from a shack and gave me a glass of mint tea. Children gathered round, the girls quite beautiful, wearing baggy white trousers rolled up to their knees, bright, almost luminescent shirts and blouses and headscarves of green and red. I tried taking their pictures and they ran away, but then curiosity returned and I took several. And I sat some more, talking and laughing with them, and gazing out upon the lake until it was nearly dark, unbelieving that Alexandria was a stone's throw behind me waiting to receive me back from this tranquillity.

"If a man make a pilgrimage round Alexandria in the morning, God will make for him a golden crown, set with pearls, perfumed with musk and camphor, and shining from the East to the West" (Ibn Duqmaq).

4. Beaches and excursions from Alexandria

To the west of Alexandria, the city of St Menas and El Alamein have already been mentioned in *The Desert and the Sea* chapter. In this direction but within an easy taxi or bus ride of the city are two good beaches, Agami and Hanoville. There are numerous public beaches along the city's seafront between the Eastern Harbour and Montazah – Chatby, Sporting, Ibrahimiya, Cleopatra, Stanley, Glym, San Stefano (also a private beach, small fee, belonging to the hotel of that name), Sidi Bishir, Miami, Asfara and Mandara; the public beaches are free but usually crowded and often dirty. There are better beaches at Montazah and nearby.

Montazah

At Montazah is the former summer residence of the royal family. Farouk was here when the 1952 coup occurred in Cairo – he fled to Ras el Tin. Until recently the palace was open as a museum but it has been renovated – rumour has it as a presidential residence – and is not open to the public. You can enjoy this gaudy fantasy from the outside, however, and the extensive grounds (admission fee), planted with pines imported from Europe and palms. Within the grounds also are two hotels, the Palestine, modern and vulgar, overlooking the sea, and the Salamlek, built as a royal reception pavillion by Khedive Abbas II (who also built the palace) in the style of a chalet to please his Austrian mistress. Though set back from the sea, it has commanding views.

Adjacent to the Palestine and a short walk down from the Salamlek is a beautiful cove for gentle swimming. A small part is reserved for the Palestine, the central part is for those who want to rent cabanas and has umbrellas, paddle boats and all the paraphernalia of a beach available. To the right, against the arm of the cove on which Farouk built a tea house (now reserved for government officials), is the public beach. The next bay east is Maamoura with a long fine beach (small fee) and full services. In the distance you can see the long limestone spur running out to Abu Qir.

Abu Qir and the Battle of the Nile

Abu Qir (or Aboukir), 24 kms east of Alexandria, is most famous for the two battles fought here in 1798 and 1799. The first was the Battle of the Nile at which Nelson surprised Napoleon's anchored fleet and over the course of two days (1 and 2 August) annihilated it. Though still in control of the country, Napoleon was cut off from France by sea and eventually had to abandon his army and his dreams of Eastern dominion. The circumstances were similar to Antony's at Actium, except that Napoleon's tide was still rising. A year later, in July, he personally commanded a battle here against a Turkish force of 15,000, landed by British ships. Napoleon had raced down from Cairo with Kleber and Murat, and with 10,000 men, mostly cavalry, drove the Turks back into the sea, drowning a third of them. That same year he returned to France and overthrew the Directory.

Nearby is the site of ancient Canopus, once one of the most important cities in Egypt owing to its position on the Canopic mouth of the Nile, since dried up. There is little to see. Hadrian like to stay here, and tried to recreate its pleasures in the garden of the Villa Hadriana at Tivoli, near Rome.

There is a good beach at Abu Qir, and its shrimps are renowned throughout Egypt.

Rosetta The excursion to Abu Qir and on to Rosetta will take about half a day, either by car or by train. Rosetta (Rashid) is 63 kms from Alexandria and stands on the western branch of the Nile near the sea. Its name is associated most famously in the West with the discovery here of the Rosetta Stone, inscribed in ancient hieroglyphs, demotic Egyptian and Greek, enabling the eventual decipherment of the pharaonic language by Champollion. It is testimony to Napoleon's expedition, which included numerous savants and a well-informed soldiery, that when a Captain Bourchard was shown the stone, turned up by one his men while restoring Fort Rashid, he immediately recognised its significance.

The town is visited, however, for other reasons. Founded in the 9th C., it flourished while Alexandria faded and declined again as modern Alexandria prospered. It reached its apogee in the 17th and 18th C., when it was the most important port in Egypt, and there are still some fine houses dating from this period, built in red and black brick, their facades decorated in the Delta Style illustrated, though not nearly so well, by the Terbana Mosque in Alexandria. Many, too, incorporate ancient stones and columns, and have delicately carved mushrabiyyas. The oldest and finest of these is the House of Ali el Fatairi, 17th C., just off the main street which runs south, parallel with the Nile, from the train station. Others are the Arab Keli, 18th C., now a museum; and El Amaciali, early 19th C. At the bottom of the main street is the most important building in town, the Mosque of Zaghloul, really two mosques, the western one founded in 1600. It is of imposing size, with fine perspectives. To the east, close to the river, is the Mosque of Mohammed el Abbas, built in 1809 in a similar courtyard style, though unlike the other mosques of Rosetta it has a dome over the tomb of its saint.

Rosetta makes an interesting footnote to Alexandria's history. Its fortunes were built on the default of the greater city, on the default of the kind of civilisation Alexandria represents. The coast of Egypt here is delta, the shifting sediment of a senseless river. Rosetta can have no sea harbour;

the limestone ridges that created the two harbours of Alexandria do not continue eastward of Abu Qir. Alexandria required organising by human science. Its potential has always been; its realisation the measure of creative intelligence.

PRACTICAL INFORMATION

There is no tourist class accommodation in the **Delta**, and so you should base yourself in Cairo, along the canal, or in Alexandria for excursions. The following listings apply to **Alexandria**.

ACCOMMODATION

The *Background* chapter can be referred to for general information on Egyptian hotels. In Alexandria, the high season is opposite to that in Upper Egypt and runs from mid-June to mid-September. At this time, rooms will be more difficult to come by and rates may be higher, though the most common way of imposing a high season surcharge is to make half board compulsory. (Summer rates are shown below, exclusive of meals.) Category for category, however, Alexandrian hotels are less expensive than those in Cairo. Also, single occupancy is commonly 20% less than double, as much as 40% less at cheaper hotels. Apart from the cost of meals, where compulsory, expect to pay an additional 15% in service charges and taxes.

The Palestine Hotel (5-star), Montazah. Tel: 861687. Telex: 94027 PTOLTL UN. This is the most luxurious hotel in Alexandria and the most vulgar in Egypt. Its beautiful situation on the shore at Montazah and in the grounds of the former royal palace may compensate for its great distance (16 kms) from downtown and most sights of interest, but the bathing facilities do not: its 'beach' at one side of a small bay is only a ledge of sand behind a retaining wall, and the water itself is scummy. The rooms are of course comfortable, air-conditioned and have TV, radio and their own baths. There's a bar, night-club and casino. Half board is compulsory Doubles are LE12.

El Salamlek Hotel (4-star), Montazah. Tel: 860233. Also in the grounds of the royal palace, and indeed itself once a royal pavillion, the Salamlek is set back from the shore but has commanding views. It's a very much more pleasant place than the Palestine. Rooms are not air-conditioned, but that is not necessary in Alexandria; all have private baths. Half board is compulsory in summer. Doubles are LE11.

The Cecil Hotel (4-star), Midan Saad Zaghloul. Tel: 807055. This is my favourite hotel in Alexandria and something of an institution. It was here in Durrell's *Alexandria Quartet* that Darley first met Justine as she fixed her hair in the long mirrors by the splintered palms. The mirrors are still here, the hotel a refuge of period elegance. The hotel is right in the centre of town, many of its spacious and well-furnished rooms overlooking the sweep of the Eastern Harbour. Private baths, TV and refrigerators are standard; the rooms on the corniche have balconies. Also there's bar, tea lounge and casino, a bank and an Avis desk. Doubles are from LE11.

The Windsor Palace (4-star), 17 Sharia el Shohada. Tel: 808700. Two blocks west of the Cecil along the corniche, though the entrance is on a side street, the Windsor is comparable in atmosphere. There's an agreeable pavement cafe out front. Doubles with bath start at LE12.50; you pay more for a harbour view, less for a room without a bath.

The Metropole (3-star), 52 Sharia Saad Zaghloul. Tel: 21467. Telex: 54350 METROUN UN. This is another of Alexandria's fine old hotels, owned by a Greek who has remained in the city. Refurbishment is underway, almost certainly at some cost to style, though the entirely modern bathrooms are welcome. Half board is compulsory in summer. Doubles are LE12.

Hotel Leroy (2-star), 25 Sharia Talaat Harb. Tel: 809099. The hotel occupies the top 3 floors of a 7-storey building; the rooms are large and high, solidly furnished, with views over the city's rooftops. From the top floor restaurant there are superb views over Alexandria. Doubles are around LE4 with bath.

The Hyde Park Hotel (1-star), 21 Sharia Amin Fikri. Tel: 35666. This is a very simple, clean place on the top floor of a building overlooking the Ramleh tram station, some rooms having views of the harbour. Doubles with bath are LE5, without bath LE4.

The **youth hostel** is on Sharia Port Said, at Chatby. Tel: 75459.

EATING PLACES AND ENTERTAINMENT

Alexandria has a reputation for good food, particularly seafood. One of the most agreeable places to eat is at the **Mustafa Darwish Restaurant** along the corniche, a few blocks east of Midan Saad Zaghloul. You can sit indoors, protected from the breeze, but if it's warm you should sit out at a pavement table. There's fish, chicken and a number of Egyptian meat dishes, plus an unsolicited variety of taheena, salad, pickles and onions. For dessert you should not miss the Mohallabiya Darwish: fruit in thick fluffy cream with cherry sauce. A full meal with beer will set you back about LE5.

For a Greek meal, try the **Taverna Diamantakis**, across from the Ramleh tram station. Here there's fried and grilled fish, squid or shellfish, all ordered by weight, and Greek salads. A meal should cost from LE3.

Pastroudis, best known as a tea room, also has a good restaurant. It's at 39 Sharia Horreya, at Kom el Dikka.

In the vicinity of Sharia Saad Zaghloul are a number of places serving simple Egyptian food, eg taheena, fool, tamaa, etc., where a meal can be had for piastres rather than pounds.

You would expect Alexandria to have quite a **nightlife.** It doesn't. Belly dancing is not so common here as in Cairo, almost a Hellenic rejection of the oriental. There are small **casinos** at the **Cecil** and in the grounds of **Montazah Palace** by the Palestine Hotel. There are several **discos**, or stereos as they are called, where the music is recorded and loud and you can dine and dance. One of the best known is **Calvados** on the ninth floor of the Admiral Hotel, Midan Ramleh. The principal **nightclub** is the **Crazy Horse**, along the corniche, a few blocks east of Midan Saad Zaghloul. There's a band, a show, a belly dancer. Next door on Midan Ramleh is **Athineos,** a Greek nightclub, and this is the one really funky place in Alexandria. The city's remaining Greeks gather here, listening to rough, wailing, loud rembetika music and smashing plates with abandon.

During summer, the **Reda Folklore Dance Troupe** base themselves in Alexandria, performing at an open-air theatre along the corniche several blocks east of Midan Saad Zaghloul. The dances are from the regions of Egypt, often having a narrative content which is plain even without an understanding of Arabic; also there's some belly dancing. Performances start at 9.45pm and continue exhuberantly through the night. Tickets range from about 70PT to LE3 for a front seat.

Dining along the corniche one night, a woman positions herself before my table, juggles two flaming torches and extinguishes them both in her mouth. Now she puts a can of benzine to her lips, applies the torch and breaths a ferocious blast of flame. I am astounded and laugh, but looking round see all the Arabs poker-faced. None of them gives so much as a piastre. In Egypt you can toil in the hot wet fields of the Delta for a lifetime, or breathe fire along the Alexandrian corniche: it makes no difference, you are not noticed. The woman's assistant is her tawny-skinned, blonde-haired daughter, 4 years old at the most, who refuels and relights the torches — and now accidentally knocks over the benzine and shrinks like a child who has opened the wrong sluice and flooded the year's crop with water and mud.

A baboon with slim waist, red arse, a lead around his full mane, walks along the corniche, his owner clutching a tambourine. Broad hot daylight.

The *Egyptian Gazette* and Saturday's *Egyptian Mail* carry entertainment listings for Alexandria. Advertisements for clubs, etc., will be found in the free booklet *Alexandria Night and Day*, available at hotels and the Tourist Information Office.

OF INTEREST

Much of what there is to see in Alexandria can be reached on foot, and visiting mosques or standing at a street corner imagining that it was once the crossroads of the world is free and depends little, if at all, on hours of opening.

The Graeco-Roman Museum, off Sharia Horreya, costs 50PT to enter. It's open year-round from 9am to 4pm daily except Fridays when it closes at 1pm. The guide books on sale are useless.

Nearby is **Kom el Dikka,** the site of excavations into Alexandria's Ptolemaic and Roman, and indeed Moslem, past. Entrance is from Sharia Nebi Danyal and costs 25PT; hours are from 9am to 5pm daily. You are free to wander about the Roman amphitheatre and to glimpse down into the Ptolemaic excavations. To get down to Cleopatra's street-level, however, requires an invitation from the Polish archaeologists on the site, or a sense of illicit adventure.

To get to Anfushi, the head of the anvil, to see the tombs there and Fort Qaytbay, take tram 4 or 5 from Midan Orabi or bus 6 or 83 from Midan Ramleh. The **Anfushi Tombs** have no strict hours of opening, though the keeper is usually there from 10am and the fee is a few piastres of baksheesh. **Fort Qaytbay** can be entered at any time of day, but its inner keep, where the museum is, opens only from 9am to 2pm daily except Fridays when it closes at noon. Admission to the museum is 10PT.

Pompey's Pillar and the site of the **Serapeum** is reached by tram 2 from Misr Station (the main railway station), tram 5 from Midan Orabi, or buses 9 or 14 from Midan Ramleh. The area is open from 9am to 5pm, admission 25PT. Nearby are the **Catacombs of Kom el Shogafa,** same hours, same fee as Pompey's Pillar.

To reach **Montazah,** you can take the 20 bus from either Midan Orabi or Midan Ramleh, also the 28 bus from Midan Orabi or Misr Station. There is an entry fee of about 26PT to the grounds, the beaches additional. The area is open from 7am to sunset – unless of course your hotel is here.

The easiest way of getting to **Abu Qir** and **Rosetta** would be by car. However, you can take a bus to Abu Qir: the No. 28 from Midan Orabi or the 29 from Misr Station or Sidi Gabir. The cost will be about 75PT each way. Or for Abu Qir and Rosetta (ask for it in Arabic, *Rashid*), you can take a train from Sidi Gabir Station to Maamoura Station (just past Montazah), changing and continuing from there.

INFORMATION

The principal **Tourist Information Office** is in Midan Saad Zaghloul (Tel: 807985), on the same side as the Cecil Hotel. There are branches at Misr Station (Tel: 25985) and at the port (Tel: 800100). Information can also be obtained at travel agencies and hotels.

You should pick up a copy of the free booklet *Alexandria Night and Day* at any of these places. As with the Cairo version, it contains hotel listings, addresses and phone numbers of various ministries and consulates, advertisements for restaurants, entertainments and travel agencies, and some travel information (city trams and buses, trains to Cairo, etc.). It includes, too, an inadequate map of the city.

TRAVEL

Alexandria is a compact city and much of it can be covered **on foot.** There's a good system of **trams** and **buses,** their principal termini being Midan Orabi, Midan Ramleh and Misr Station. Fares are first and second class, most journeys costing 2PT and 3PT depending on class and distance. From downtown to Montazah you'll pay about 5PT to 7PT.

Taxis, which are orange and black, are inexpensive – especially as you are more likely to pay the metered fare than in Cairo. A car, with or without driver, can be hired from **Avis,** at the Hotel Cecil in Midan Saad Zaghloul (Tel: 807532 and 807055). Rates are as those for Cairo.

Tours can be arranged through Thomas Cook, Menatours and others.

Travel Agents in Alexandria are located in or not far from Midan Saad Zaghloul and include:

De Castro and Co., 33 Sharia Salah Salem (Tel: 35770). Agents for Adriatica shipping lines (to Piraeus and Venice).

Eastmar, 16 Sharia Salah Salem (Tel: 802960). All tourist services, plus operators of their own Nile cruises.

Menatours, Midan Saad Zaghloul, next to the Cecil Hotel (Tel: 809676). For sightseeing tours around Alexandria and vicinity. Also agents for DFDS Seaways (to Heraklion, Patras and Ancona).

Misr Travel, 33 Sharia Salah Salem. (Tel: 29617). The Egyptian state travel agency, helpful with all accommodation and travel arrangements.

Thomas Cook, 15 Midan Saad Zaghloul (Tel: 27830). All travel arrangements, tours, travellers cheques.

Alexandria is not served by **air internationally,** except by charter (see Nile Valley Aviation under Cairo). But Egyptair and other airlines have offices in the city.

There are **sailings,** however, for Greece and Italy by **DFDS Seaways** and **Adriatica** (see travel agents above); also for Greece and Italy by the **Egyptian Navigation Co.**, 2 Sharia El Nasr (Tel: 800050), and the **Federal Arab Maritime Co.**, 5 Sharia Gabarti (Tel: 21209); and to Syria and Lebanon by the **Alexandria Shipping and Navigation Co.**, 557 Sharia Horreya (Tel: 62923). All but the Egyptian Navigation Co. carry cars.

Egyptair, 19 Midan Saad Zaghloul (Tel: 20778), flies to Cairo. A good **bus service to Cairo** via the Desert Road departs from Midan Saad Zaghloul; its booking office near the Cecil Hotel. The main **railway station,** Mahattat Misr, is at Midan el Gumhuriya, at the south end of Sharia Nebi Danyal. This is where you get the train to Cairo (see *Background* chapter for timetables). There is a secondary station, Sidi Gabir, in the eastern part of the city which serves Abu Qir and Rosetta, though Cairo trains stop here too. Another way of covering long distances is by **service (or shared) taxi**; try for these at Midan Saad Zaghloul and Midan Orabi.

OTHER THINGS

The chief attraction of Alexandria for some is its **beaches**; the No.20 bus runs from Midan Orabi and Midan Ramleh all the way along the corniche to Montazah and Maamura, as do convoys of service taxis. Also the **breeze** off the Mediterranean makes Alexandria a desirable place to be during summer. But as soon as the sun goes down, it can get chilly, and in winter it can be both chilly and rainy during the day. So when going about Alexandria, dress accordingly.

There's a **post office** at Midan Ramleh.

To **exchange money,** go to the banks at the Cecil, San Stefano or Palestine hotels, or to Thomas Cook.

For **medical care,** ask at your hotel. Also the Tourist Police or your consulate can advise. Recommended is the **University Hospital** in Chatby (Tel: 25952).

The **Tourist Police** can be reached through the Tourist Information Office, or direct by dialling 60000, 25977 or 807611. For **urgent help** of any sort, telephone 123.

The best **bookshop** in town is the **Al-Ahram,** 10 Sharia Horreya, on the corner of Sharia Nebi Danyal. It has French- and English-language paperbacks, guides and newspapers.

PLACE INDEX

The following Index is in two parts, the first covering Cairo, the second covering the rest of Egypt.

But the Index is not exhaustive, and it should be used in combination with the side-headings in the margins of the text. For example, the Index shows *Karnak* at page 209. Turning to page 209, you can then look down the margins to find the *History of Karnak,* the *Temple of Amun,* the *Hypostyle Hall,* the *Temple of Ptah and the Precinct of Mont,* etc. – all of these aspects of the Karnak complex.

You should also refer to the *Practical Information* section at the end of each chapter for further information on places of interest. At the end of the *Cairo 5* chapter, for example, you will find mention of the *Ethnological Museum* and *President Nasser's Mausoleum* which were not mentioned in the main text, while the *Papyrus Institute,* which was mentioned in the main text but only in passing, is treated in greater detail here.

MAP AND PLAN INDEX

The following Index is arranged alphabetically by place, ie sites at *Abydos* first, at *Thebes* last.

NOTES

NOTES

NOTES

NOTES

NOTES